Grid Computing: Software Environments and Tools

José C. Cunha and Omer F. Rana (Eds)

Grid Computing: Software Environments and Tools

With 121 Figures

 Springer

José C. Cunha
CITI Centre
Department of Computer Science
Faculty of Science and Technology
New University of Lisbon
Portugal

Omer F. Rana
School of Computer Science
Cardiff University
UK

A catalogue record for this book is available from the British Library

Library of Congress Control Number: 2005928488

ISBN-10: 1-85233-998-5
ISBN-13: 978-1-85233-998-2

Printed on acid-free paper

Printed in the United States of America   (SPI/MVY)

9 8 7 6 5 4 3 2 1

Springer Science+Business Media
springeronline.com

Preface

Grid computing combines aspects from parallel computing, distributed computing and data management, and has been playing an important role in pushing forward the state-of-the-art in computer science and information technologies. There is considerable interest in Grid computing at present, with a significant number of Grid projects being launched across the world. Many countries have started to implement their own Grid computing programmes – such as in the Asia Pacific region (including Japan, Australia, South Korea and Thailand), the European Union (as part of the Framework 5 and 6 programmes, and national activities such as the UK eScience programme), and the US (as part of the NSF CyberInfrastructure and the DDDAS programmes). The rising interest in Grid computing can be seen by the increase in the number of participants at the Global Grid Forum (http://www.gridforum.org/), as well as through regular sessions on this theme at several conferences.

Many existing Grid projects focus on deploying common infrastructure (such as Globus, UNICORE, and Legion/AVAKI). Such efforts are primarily aimed at implementing specialist middleware infrastructure that can be utilized by application developers, without providing any details about *how* such infrastructure can best be utilized. As Grid computing infrastructure matures, however, the next phase will require support for deploying and developing applications and associated tools and environments which can utilize this core infrastructure effectively. It is therefore important to explore software engineering themes which will enable computer scientists to address the concerns arising from the use of this middleware.

However, approaches to software construction for Grid computing are ad hoc at the present time. There is either deployment of existing tools not really meant for Grid environments, or tools that are not robust – and therefore not likely to be re-used in communities other than those within which they have been developed (examples include specialized libraries for BioInformatics and Physics, for instance). On the other hand, a number of projects are exploring the development of applications using specialist tools and approaches that have been explored within a particular research project, without considering the wider implications of using and deploying these tools. As a consequence, there is little shared understanding of the common needs of software construction, development, deployment and re-use. The main motivation for this book is to help identify what these common themes are, and to provide a series of chapters offering a more detailed perspective on these themes.

Recent developments in parallel and distributed computing: In the past two decades, advances in parallel and distributed computing allowed the development of many applications in Science and Engineering with computational and data intensive requirements. Soon it was realized that there was a need for developing generic software layers and integrated environments which could facilitate the problem solving process, generally in the context of a particular functionality. For example, such efforts have enabled applications involving complex simulations with visualization and steering, design optimization and application behavior studies, rapid prototyping, decision support, and process control (both from industry and academia). A significant number of projects in Grid computing build upon this earlier work.

Recent efforts in Grid computing infrastructure have increased the need for high-level abstractions for software development, due to the increased complexity of Grid systems and applications. Grid applications are addressing several challenges which had not been faced previously by parallel and distributed computing: large scale systems allowing transparent access to remote resources; long running experiments and more accurate models; increased levels of interaction e.g. multi-site collaboration for increased productivity in application development.

Distributed computing: The capability to physically distribute computation and data has been explored for a long time. One of its main goals has been to be able to adapt to the geographical distribution of an application (in terms of users, processing or archiving ability). Increased availability and reliability of the systems architectures has also been successfully achieved through distribution of data and control. A fundamental challenge in the design of a distributed system has been to determine how a convenient trade-off can be achieved between transparency and awareness at each layer of its software architecture. The levels of transparency, as provided by distributed computing systems, has been (and will continue) to change over time, depending on the application requirements and on the evolution of the supporting technologies. The latter aspect is confirmed when we analyze Grid computing systems. Advances in processing and communication technologies have enabled the provision of cost-effective computational and storage nodes, and higher bandwidths in message transmission. This has allowed more efficient access to remote resources, supercomputing power, or large scale data storage, and opened the way to more complex distributed applications. Such technology advances have also enabled the exploitation of more tightly coupled forms of interactions between users (and programs), and pushed forward novel paradigms based on Web computing, Peer-2-Peer computing, mobile computing and multi-agent systems.

Parallel computing: The goal of reducing application execution time through parallelism has pushed forward many significant developments in computer system architectures, and also in parallel programming models, methods, and languages. A successful design for task decomposition and cooperation, when developing a parallel application, depends critically on the internal layers of the architecture of a parallel computing system, which include algorithms, programming languages, compilers and runtime systems, operating systems and computer system architectures. Two decades of research and experimentation have contributed to significant speedup improvements in many application domains, by supporting the development of parallel codes for simulation of complex models and for interpretation of large volumes of data. Such developments have been supported by advanced tools and environments, supporting processing and visualization, computational steering, and access through distinct user interfaces and standardized application programming interfaces.

Developments in parallel application development have also contributed to improvement in methods and techniques supporting the software life cycle, such as improved support for formal specification and structured program development, in addition to performance engineering issues. Component-based models have enabled various degrees of complexity, granularity, and heterogeneity to be managed for parallel and distributed applications – generally by reducing dependencies between different software libraries. For example, simulators and mathematical packages, data processing or visualization tools were wrapped as software components in order to be more effectively integrated into a distributed environment. Such developments have also allowed a clear identification of distinct levels of functionalities for application development and deployment: from problem specification, to resource management and execution support services. Developments in portable and standard programming platforms (such as those based on the Java programming language), have also helped in the handling of heterogeneity and interoperability issues.

In order to ease the computational support for scientific and engineering activities, integrated environments, usually called *Problem-Solving Environments (PSEs)* have been developed for solving classes of related problems in specific application domains. They provide the user interfaces and the underlying support to manage an increasingly complex life cycle of activities for application development and execution. This starts with the problem specification steps, followed by successive refinements towards component development and selection (for computation, control, and visualization). This is followed by the configuration of experiments, through component activation and mapping onto specific parallel and distributed computing platforms (including the set up of application parameters), followed by execution monitoring and control, possibly supported through visualization facilities.

As applications exhibit more complex requirements (intensive computation, massive data processing, higher degrees of interaction), many efforts have been focusing on easing the integration of heterogeneous components, and providing more transparent access to distributed resources available in wide-area networks, through (Web-enabled) portal interfaces.

Grid computing: When looking at the layers of a Grid architecture, they are similar to those of a distributed computing system:

1. User interfaces, applications and PSEs.
2. Programming and development models, tools and environments.
3. Middleware, services and resource management.
4. Heterogeneous resources and infrastructure.

However, researchers in Grid computing are pursuing higher levels of transparency, aiming to provide unifying abstractions to the end-user, with single access points to pools of virtual resources. Virtual resources provide support for launching distributed jobs involving computation, data access and manipulation of scientific instruments, with virtual access to remote databases, catalogues and archives, as well as cooperation based on virtual collaboration spaces. In this view, the main distinctive characteristic of Grid computing, when compared to previous generations of distributed computing systems, is this (more) ambitious goal of providing increased transparency and "virtualization" of resources, over a large scale distributed infrastructure.

Indeed, ongoing developments within Grid computing are addressing the deployment of large scale application and user profiles, supported by computational Grids for high-performance computing, intelligent data Grids for accessing large datasets and distributed data repositories – all based on the general concept of "virtual organizations" which enable resource sharing across organizational boundaries. Recent interest in a "Grid Ecosystem" also places emphasis on the need to integrate tools at different software layers from a variety of different vendors, enabling a range of different solutions to co-exist for solving the same problem. This view also allows a developer to combine tools and services, and enables the use of different services which exist at the same software layer at different times. The availability of suitable abstractions to facility such a Grid Ecosystem still do not exist however.

Due to the above aspects, Grids are very complex systems, whose design and implementation involves multiple dimensions, such as large scale, distribution, heterogeneity, openness, multiple administration domains, security and access control, and dynamic and unpredictable behavior. Although there have been significant developments in Grid infrastructures and middleware, support is still lacking for effective Grid applications development, and to assist software developers in managing the complexity of Grid applications and systems. Such applications generally involve large numbers of distributed, and possibly mobile and intelligent, computational components, agents or devices. This requires appropriate structuring, interaction and coordination methods and mechanisms, and new concepts for their organization and management. Workflow tools to enable application composition, common ways to encode interfaces between software components, and mechanisms to connect sets of components to a range of different resource management systems are also required. Grid applications will access large volumes of data, hopefully relying upon efficient and possibly knowledge-based data mining approaches. New problem-solving strategies with adaptive behavior will be required in order to react to changes at the application level, and changes in the system configuration or in the availability of resources, due to their varying characteristics and behavior. Intelligent expert and assistance tools, possibly integrated in PSEs, will also play an increasingly important role in enabling the user-friendly interfacing to such systems.

As computational infrastructure becomes more powerful and complex, there is a greater need to provide tools to support the scientific computing community to make better use of such infrastructure. The last decade has also seen an unprecedented focus on making computational resources sharable (parallel machines and clusters, and data repositories) across national boundaries. Significantly, the emergence of Computational Grids in the last few years, and the tools to support scientific users on such Grids (sometimes referred to as "eScience") provides new opportunities for the scientific community to undertake collaborative, and multi-disciplinary research. Often tools for supporting application scientists have been developed to support a particular community (Astrophysics, Biosciences, etc), a common perspective on the use of these tools and making them more generic is often missing.

Further research and developments are therefore needed in several aspects of the software development process, including software architecture, specification languages and coordination models, organization models for large scale distributed applications, and interfaces to distributed resource management and execution services. The specification, composition, development, deployment, and control of the execution of Grid applications require suitable flexibility in the software life cycle, along its multiple stages, including application specification and design, program transformation and refinement, simulation and code generation, configuration and deployment, and the coordination and control of distributed execution. New abstractions, models and tools are required to support the above stages in order to provide a diversity of functionalities, such as:

- Specification and modelling of the application structure and behavior, with incremental refinement and composition, and allowing reasoning about global functional and non-functional properties.
- Abstractions for the organization of dynamic large scale systems.
- Representation and management of interaction patterns among components and services.
- Enabling of alternative mappings between the layers of the software architecture, supported by pattern or template repositories, that can be manipulated during the software development and execution stages.

– Flexible interaction with resource management, scheduling and discovery services for flexible application configuration and deployment, and awareness to Quality of Service.
– Coordination of distributed execution, with adaptability and dynamic reconfiguration.

Such types of functionalities will provide the foundations for building environments and frameworks, developed on top of the basic service layers that are provided by Grid middleware and infrastructures.

Outline of the book: The aim of this book is to identify software engineering techniques for Grid environments, along with specialist tools that encapsulate such techniques, and case studies that illustrate the use of these tools. With the emergence of regional, national and global programmes to establish Grid computing infrastructure, it is important to be able to utilize this infrastructure effectively. Specialist software is therefore necessary to both enable the deployment of applications over such infrastructure, and to facilitate software developers in constructing software components for such infrastructure. We feel the second of these is a particularly important concern, as the uptake of Grid computing technologies will be restricted by the availability of suitable abstractions, methodologies, and tools.

This book will be useful for:

– *Software developers* who are primarily responsible for developing and integrating components for Grid environments.
– It will also be of interest to *application scientists and domain experts*, who are primarily users of the Grid software and need to interact with the tools.
– The book will also be useful for *deployment specialists*, who are primarily responsible for managing and configuring Grid environments.

We hope the book will contribute to increase the reader's appreciation for:

– Software engineering and modelling tools which will enable better conceptual understanding of the software to be deployed across Grid infrastructure.
– Software engineering issues that must be supported to compose software components for Grid environments.
– Software engineering support for managing Grid applications.
– Software engineering lifecycle to support application development for Grid Environments (along with associated tools).
– How novel concepts, methods and tools within Grid computing can be put at work in the context of existing experiments and application case studies.

As many universities are now also in the process of establishing courses in Grid Computing, we hope this book will serve as a reference to this emerging area, and will help promote further developments both at university and industry. The chapters presented in this book are divided into four sections:

– Abstractions: chapters included in this section represent key modelling approaches that are necessary to enable better software development for deployment over Grid computing infrastructure. Without such abstractions, one is likely to see the continuing use of ad-hoc approaches.
– Programming and Process: chapters included in this section focus on the overall software engineering process necessary for application construction. Such a process is essential to channel the activity of a team of programmers working on a Grid application.

– User Environments and Tools: chapters in this section discuss existing application environments that may be used to implement Grid applications, or provide a discussion of how applications may be effectively deployed across existing Grid computing infrastructure.
– Applications: the final section provides sample applications in Engineering, Science and Education, and demonstrate some of the ideas discussed in other section with reference to specific application domains.

José Cunha, Universidade Nova de Lisboa, Portugal
Omer F. Rana, Cardiff University, UK

Contents

List of Contributors

Marco Aldinucci[1,2], Massimo Coppola[1,2], Marco Danelutto[2], Marco Vanneschi[2], Corrado Zoccolo[2]
[1] Dipartimento di Informatica, Universit' di Pisa, Italy
[2] Istituto di Scienza e Tecnologie della Informazione, CNR, Pisa, Italy

Giovanni Aloisio, Massimo Cafaro, and Italo Epicoco
Center for Adavanced Computational Technologies, University of Lecce, Italy

Laurent Baduel, Françoise Baude, Denis Caromel, Arnaud Contes, Fabrice Huet, Matthieu Morel, and Romain Quilici
OASIS - Joint Project CNRS / INRIA / University of Nice Sophia - Antipolis, INRIA 2004, route des Lucioles - B.P. 93 - 06902 Valbonne Cedex, France

Xin Bai[1], Han Yu[1], Guoqiang Wang[1], Yongchang Ji[1], Gabriela M. Marinescu[1], Dan C. Marinescu[1], and Ladislau Bölöni[2]
[1] School of Computer Science, University of Central Florida, P.O.Box 162362, Orlando, Florida 32816-2362, USA
[2] Department of Electrical and Computer Engineering University of Central Florida, P.O.Box 162450, Orlando, Florida 32816-2450, USA

Antonio Congiusta[1,2], Domenico Talia[1,2], and Paolo Trunfio[2]
[1] ICAR-CNR, Institute of the Italian National Research Council, Via P. Bucci, 41c, 87036 Rende, Italy
[2] DEIS - University of Calabria, Via P. Bucci, 41c, 87036 Rende, Italy

Anthony Finkelstein, Joe Lewis-Bowen, and Giacomo Piccinelli
Department of Computer Science, University College London, Gower Street, London, WC1E 6BT, UK

Christopher E. Goodyer[1] and Martin Berzins[1,2]
[1] Computational PDEs Unit, School of Computing, University of Leeds, Leeds, UK
[2] SCI Institute, University of Utah, Salt Lake City, Utah, USA

Sergei Gorlatch and Martin Alt
Westfälische Wilhelms-Universität Münster, Germany

Andreas Hoheisel, Thilo Ernst, and Uwe Der
Fraunhofer Institute for Computer Architecture and Software Technology (FIRST), Kekulestr. 7, D-12489 Berlin, Germany

Maozhen Li[1] and Mark Baker[2]
[1] Department of Electronic and Computer Engineering, Brunel University Uxbridge, UB8 3PH, UK
[2] The Distributed Systems Group, University of Portsmouth Portsmouth, PO1 2EG, UK

Zsolt Németh[1] and Vaidy Sunderam[2]
[1] MTA SZTAKI Computer and Automation Research Institute H-1518 Budapest, P.O. Box 63, Hungary
[2] Math & Computer Science, Emory University, Atlanta, GA 30322, USA

Victor Pankratius[1] and Gottfried Vossen[2]
[1] AIFB Institute, University of Karlsruhe, D-76128 Karlsruhe, Germany
[2] ERCIS, University of Münster, D-48149 Münster, Germany

Graeme Pound and Simon Cox
School of Engineering Sciences, University of Southampton, Southampton, SO17 1BJ, UK

Diego Puppin[1], Fabrizio Silvestri[1], Salvatore Orlando[2], Domenico Laforenza[1]
[1] Institute for Information Science and Technologies, ISTI - CNR, Pisa, Italy
[2] Università di Venezia, Ca' Foscari, Venezia, Italy

1.3   Use Scenarios

The assumptions made for conventional distributed versus grid computing are best summarized by use scenarios. These scenarios reveal all relevant features that would be hard to list otherwise.

Distributed applications are comprised of a number of cooperating processes that exploit resources of loosely coupled computer systems. Distributed computing, in the high performance computing domain, for example, may be accomplished via traditional environments (e.g., PVM, MPICH) or with emerging software frameworks termed computational grids. Both are aimed at presenting a virtual machine layer by unifying distributed resources (Fig. 1.2).

Conventional-distributed environments differ from grids on the basis of resources the user owns. Sharing and owning in this context are not necessarily related to the ownership in the usual sense. *Sharing* refers to *temporarily* utilizing resources where the user has no direct (login) access otherwise. Similarly, *owning* means having *permanent* and unrestricted access to the resource.

An application in a conventional-distributed environment assumes a pool of computational nodes from (a subset of) which a *virtual concurrent machine* is formed. The pool consists of PCs, workstations, and possibly supercomputers, provided that the user has access (valid login name and password) to all of them. The most typical appearance of such a pool is a cluster that aggregates a few tens of mostly (but not necessarily) homogeneous computers. Login to the virtual machine is realized by login (authentication) to each node, although it is technically possible to avoid per-node authentication if at least one node accepts the user as authentic. Since the user has his or her own accounts on these nodes, he or she is aware of their features: architecture type, computational power and capacities, operating system, security concerns, usual load, etc.

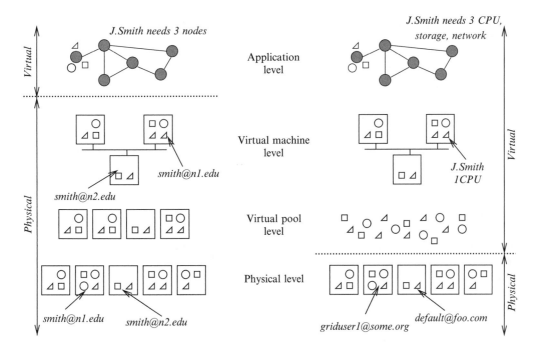

FIGURE 1.2. The concept of conventional distributed environments (left) and grids (right). Geometric shapes represent different resources, squares represent nodes.

Furthermore, the virtual pool of nodes can be considered static, since the set of nodes to which the user has login access changes very rarely.

In contrast, computational grids are based on large-scale resource sharing [9]. Grids assume a virtual pool of resources rather than computational nodes (Fig. 1.2). Although current systems mostly focus on computational resources (CPU cycles + memory) [11] that basically coincide with the notion of nodes, grid systems are expected to operate on a wider range of resources like storage, network, data, software, [17] and atypical resources like graphical and audio input/output devices, manipulators, sensors, and so on [18]. All these resources typically exist within nodes that are geographically distributed, and span multiple administrative domains. The virtual machine is constituted of a set of resources taken from the pool.

In grids, the virtual pool of resources is dynamic and diverse, since resources can be added and withdrawn at any time according to their owner's discretion, and their performance or load can change frequently over time. For all these reasons, the user has very little or no a priori knowledge about the actual type, state, and features of the resources constituting the pool.

Due to the large number of resources and the diversity of local security policies it is technically impossible—and is in contradiction with the motivations for grids—that a user has a valid login access to all the nodes that provide the resources. Access to the virtual machine means that the user has some sort of credential that is accepted by the owners of resources in the pool. A user may have the right to use a given resource; however, it does not mean that he or she has login access to the node hosting the resource.

As it can be seen in Fig. 1.2, there are no principal differences in the applications or at the physical level. Nevertheless, the way in which resources are utilized and the manner in which the virtual layer is built up are entirely different. Note that none of the commonly accepted and referred attributes are listed here: the main difference is not in performance, in geographical extent, in heterogeneity, or in the size of applications. The essential difference, the notion of virtualization, is revealed in the following sections.

1.4   Universes and the Signature

The definition of the universes and the signature places the real system to be modeled into a formal framework. Certain objects of the physical reality are modeled as elements of universes, and relationships between real objects are represented as functions and relations. These definitions also highlight what is *not* modeled by circumscribing the limits of the formal model and keeping it reasonably simple.

When using the modeling scheme in the realm of distributed computing, we consider an application (universe $APPLICATION$) as consisting of several processes (universe $PROCESS$) that cooperate in some way. Their relationship is represented by the function $app : PROCESS \rightarrow APPLICATION$ that identifies the specific application a given process belongs to. Processes are owned by a user (universe $USER$). Function $user : PROCESS \rightarrow USER$ gives the owner of a process. Processes need resources (universe $RESOURCE$) to work. A distinguished element of this universe is $resource_0$ that represents the computational resource (CPU cycles, memory) that is essential to run a process. $request : PROCESS \times RESOURCE \rightarrow \{true, false\}$ yields true if the process needs a given resource, whereas $uses : PROCESS \times RESOURCE \rightarrow \{true, false\}$ is true if the process is currently using the resource. Note that the *uses* function does not imply either exclusive or shared access, but only that the process can access and use it during its activity. Processes are mapped to a certain node of computation (universe $NODE$). This relationship is represented by the function $mapped : PROCESS \rightarrow NODE$ which gives the node the process is mapped on. On the other hand, resources cannot exist on their own; they belong to nodes, as characterized by relation $BelongsTo : RESOURCE \times NODE \rightarrow \{true, false\}$. Processes execute a specified task represented by universe $TASK$. The physical realization of a task is the static representation of a running process, therefore it must be present on (or accessible from) the same node ($installed : TASK \times NODE \rightarrow \{true, false\}$) where the process is.

Resources, nodes, and tasks have certain attributes (universe $ATTR$) that can be retrieved by function $attr : \{RESOURCE, NODE, TASK\} \rightarrow ATTR$. (Also, *user*, *request*, and *uses* can be viewed as special cases of $ATTR$ for processes.) A subset of ATTR is the architecture type represented by $ARCH$ ($arch : RESOURCE \rightarrow ARCH$) and location (universe $LOCATION$, $location : RESOURCE \rightarrow LOCATION$). Relation *compatible* : $ATTR \times ATTR \rightarrow \{true, false\}$ is true if the two attributes are compatible according to a reasonable definition. To keep the model simple, this high level notion of attributes and compatibility is used instead of more precise processor type, speed, memory capacity, operating system, endian-ness, software versions, and so on, and the appropriate different definitions for compatibility.

Users may login to certain nodes. If $CanLogin : USER \times NODE \rightarrow \{true, false\}$ evaluates to true it means that user has a credential that is accepted by the security mechanism of the node. It is assumed that initiating a process at a given node is possible if the user can log in to the node. $CanUse : USER \times RESOURCE \rightarrow \{true, false\}$ is a similar logic function. If it is true, the user is authentic and authorized to use a given resource. While $CanLogin$ directly corresponds to the login procedure of an operating system, $CanUse$ remains abstract at the moment.

Processes are at the center of the model. In modern operating systems processes have many possible states, but there are three inevitable ones: *running*, *ready to run*, and *waiting*. In our model the operating system level details are entirely omitted. States *ready to run* and *running* are treated evenly assuming that processes in the *ready to run* state will proceed to *running* state in finite time. Therefore, in this model processes have essentially two states, that can be retrieved by function $state : PROCESS \rightarrow \{running, waiting\}$.

During the execution of a task, different events may occur represented by the external function *event*. Events are defined here as a point where the state of one or more processes is changed. They may be prescribed in the task itself or may be external, independent from the task—at this level of abstraction there is no difference. To maintain simplicity here, processes are modeled involving a minimal set of states and a single event $\{req\_res\}$. It further states that communication procedures and events can be modeled to cover the entire process lifecycle [30].

1.5   Rules for a Conventional Distributed System

The model presented here is a distributed multiagent ASM where agents are processes, i.e., elements from the $PROCESS$ universe. The nullary $Self$ function represented here as p ("a process") allows an agent to identify itself among other agents. It is interpreted differently by different agents. The following rules constitute a module, i.e., a single-agent program that is executed by each agent. Agents have the same initial state as described below.

1.5.1 Initial State

Let us assume k processes belonging to an application and a user: $\exists p_1, p_2, ...p_k \in PROCESS$, $\forall p_i, 1 \leq i \leq k : app(p_i) \neq undef; \forall p_i, 1 \leq i \leq k : user(p_i) = u \in USER$. Initially they require certain resources ($\forall p_i, 1 \leq i \leq k : \exists r \in RESOURCE : request(p_i, r) = true$) but do not possess any of them ($\forall p_i, 1 \leq i \leq k : \forall r \in RESOURCE : uses(p_i, r) = false$). All processes have their assigned tasks ($\forall p_i, 1 \leq i \leq k : task(p_i) \neq undef$) but no processes are mapped to a node ($\forall p_i, 1 \leq i \leq k : mapped(p_i) = undef$).

Specifically, the following holds for conventional systems (but not for grids) in the initial state:

- There is a virtual pool of l nodes for each user. The user has a valid login credential for each node in her pool: $\forall u \in USER, \exists n_1, n_2, ...n_l \in NODE : CanLogin(u, n_i) = true, 1 \leq i \leq l$.
- The tasks of the processes have been preinstalled on some of the nodes (or accessible from some nodes via NFS or other means): $\forall p_i, 1 \leq i \leq k : \exists n \in NODE : installed(task(p_i), n) = true$ in such a way that the format of the task corresponds to the architecture of the node: $compatible(arch(task(p_i)), arch(n))$.

Rule 1: Mapping

The working cycle of an application in a conventional-distributed system is based on the notion of a pool of computational nodes. Therefore, first all processes must be mapped to a node chosen from the pool. Other rules cannot fire until the process is mapped. **Rule** 1 will fire exactly once.

```
if mapped(p) = undef then
    choose n in NODE satisfying CanLogin(user(p), n)
                              & installed(task(p), n)
            mapped(p) := n
    endchoose
```

Note the declarative style of the description: it does not specify how the appropriate node is selected; any of the nodes where the conditions are true can be chosen. The selection may be done by the user, prescribed in the program text, or may be left to a scheduler or a load balancer layer, but at this level of abstraction it is irrelevant. It is possible because the user (application) has information about the state of the pool (see Section 1.3). Actually, the conditions listed here (login access and the presence of the binary code) are the absolute minimal conditions and in a real application there may be others with respect to the performance of the node, the actual load, user's priority, and so on.

Rule 2: Resource Grant

Once a process has been mapped, and there are pending requests for resources, they can be satisfied if the requested resource is on the same node as the process. If a specific type of resource is required by the process, it is the responsibility of the programmer or user to find a mapping where the resource is local with respect to the process. Furthermore, if a user can login to a node, he or she is authorized to use all resources belonging to or attached to the node: $\forall u \in USER, \forall r \in RESOURCE : CanLogin(u, n) \rightarrow CanUse(u, r)$ where $BelongsTo(r, n) = true$. Therefore, at this level of abstraction it is assumed realistically that resources are available or will be available within a limited time period. The model does not incorporate information as to whether the resource is shared or exclusive.

```
if  (∃r ∈ RESOURCE) : request(p, r) = true
    &  BelongsTo(r, mapped(p))
    then
        uses(p, r) := true
        request(p, r) := false
```

Rule 3: State Transition

If all the resource requests have been satisfied and there is no pending communication, the process can enter the *running* state.

```
if  (∀r ∈ RESOURCE) : request(p, r) = false
    then
        state(p) := running
```

The running state means that the process is performing activities prescribed by the *task*. This model is aimed at formalizing the mode of distributed execution and not the semantics of a given application.

Rule 4: Resource Request

During execution of the *task*, events can occur represented by the external *event* function. The event in this rule represents the case when the process needs additional resources during its work. In this case process enters the *waiting* state and the *request* relation is raised for every resource in the *reslist*.

```
if  state(p) = running & event(task(p)) = req_res(reslist) then
    state(p) := waiting
    do forall  r ∈ RESOURCE : r ∈ reslist
        request(p, r) := true
    enddo
```

Other rules may be added easily to this model describing the complete process lifecycle, process interaction, communication, etc. see [30]. They have less importance at highlighting the essential grid characteristics, yet with no limitations, any aspects of a distributed system can be modeled in this framework.

1.6   Rules for a Grid

1.6.1   Initial State

The initial state is exactly the same as in the case of conventional-distributed systems except for the specific items (see Section 1.5.1) that is

- There exist a virtual pool of resources and the user has a credential that is accepted by the owners of resources in the pool: $\forall u \in USER, \exists r_1, r_2, ...r_m : CanUse(u, r_i) = true$, $1 \le i \le m$.

As is evident, the initial state is very similar to that of the conventional-distributed systems, and once applications start execution there are few differences in the runtime model of conventional and grid systems. The principal differences that do exist pertain mainly to the acquisition of resources and nodes. Conventional systems try to find an appropriate node to map processes onto, and then satisfy resource needs locally. In contrast, grid systems assume an abundant pool of resources; thus, first the necessary resources are found, and then they designate the node onto which the process must be mapped.

Rule 5: Resource Selection

To clarify the above, we superimpose the model for conventional systems from Section 1.5 onto an environment representing a grid according to the assumptions in Section 1.3. We then try to achieve grid-like behavior by minimal changes in the rules. The intention here is to swap the order of resource and node allocation while the rest of the rules remain intact. If an authenticated and authorized user requests a resource, it may be granted to the process. If the requested resource is computational in nature (resource type $resource_0$), then the process must be placed onto the node where the resource is located. Let us replace Rules 1 and 2 by Rule 5 while keeping the remaining rules constant.

```
if  (∃r ∈ RESOURCE) : request(p, r) = true
     &  CanUse(user(p), r)
   then
        if  type(r) = resource₀  then
             mapped(p) := location(r)
             installed(task(p), location(r)) := true
        endif
        request(p, r) := false
        uses(p, r) := true
```

For obvious reasons, this first model will not work due to the slight but fundamental differences in working conditions of conventional-distributed and grid systems. The formal description enables precise reasoning about the causes of malfunction and their elimination. In the following, new constructs are systematically added to this simple model in order to realize the inevitable functionalities of a grid system.

1.6.2   Resource Abstraction

The system described by Rules 3, 4, and 5 would not work under assumptions made for grid environments. To see why, consider what r means in these models. r in $request(p, r)$ is abstract in that it expresses the process' needs in terms of resource types and attributes in general, e.g., 64MB of memory or a processor of a given architecture or 200MB of storage, etc. These needs are satisfied by certain physical resources, e.g., 64MB memory on machine foo.somewhere.edu, an Intel PIII processor and a file system mounted on the machine. In the case of conventional-distributed systems there is an *implicit* mapping of abstract resources onto physical ones. This is possible because the process has been (already) assigned to a node and its resource needs are satisfied by local resources present on the node. *BelongsTo* checks the validity of the implicit mapping in Rule 2.

This is not the case in grid environments. A process' resource needs can be satisfied from various nodes in various ways, therefore $uses(p, r)$ cannot be interpreted for an abstract r. There must be an *explicit* mapping between abstract resource needs and physical resource objects that selects one of the thousands of possible candidate resources that conforms to abstract resource needs. Let us split the universe $RESOURCE$ into abstract resources $ARESOURCE$ and physical resources $PRESOURCE$. Resource needs are described by abstract resources, whereas physical resources are those granted to the process. Since the user (and the application) has no information about the exact state of the pool, a new agent executing module $\Pi_{resource\_mapping}$ must be introduced that can manage the appropriate mapping between them by asserting the $mappedresource : PROCESS \times ARESOURCE \rightarrow PRESOURCE$ function as described by the following rule:

$\Pi_{resource\_mapping}$

```
if (∃ar ∈ ARESOURCE, proc ∈ PROCESS) : mappedresource(proc, ar) = undef
   & request(proc, ar) = true
   then
        choose r in PRESOURCE
          satisfying compatible(attr(ar), attr(r))
              mappedresource(proc, ar) := r
        endchoose
```

This rule does not specify how resources are chosen; such details are left to lower level implementation oriented descriptions. Just as in the case of node selection (Rule 1), this is a minimal condition, and in an actual implementation there will be additional conditions with respect to performance, throughput, load balancing, priority, and other issues. However, the selection must yield relation $compatible : ATTR \times ATTR \rightarrow \{true, false\}$ as true, i.e., the attributes of the physical resource must satisfy the prescribed abstract attributes. Based on this, Rule 5 is modified as:

```
let r = mappedresource(p, ar)
if (∃ar ∈ ARESOURCE) : request(p, ar) = true
   & r ≠ undef
   & CanUse(user(p), r)
   then
        if type(r) = resource₀ then
            mapped(p) := location(r)
            installed(task(p), location(r)) := true
        endif
        request(p, ar) := false
        uses(p, r) := true
```

This rule could be modified so that if $CanUse(user(p), r))$ is false; it retracts $mappedresource(p, ar)$ to $undef$ allowing $\Pi_{resource\_mapping}$ to find another possible mapping.

Accordingly, the signature, and subsequently **Rules** 3 and 4 must be modified to differentiate between abstract and physical resources. This change is purely syntactical and does not affect their semantics; therefore, their new form is omitted here.

1.6.3   Access Control Mechanism (User Abstraction)

Rule 5 is still missing some details: accessing a resource needs further elaboration. $uses(p, r) := true$ is a correct and trivial step in case of conventional-distributed systems, because resources are granted to a local process and the owner of the process is an authenticated and authorized user. In grids however, the fact that the user can access shared resources in the virtual pool (i.e., can login to the virtual machine) does not imply that he or she can login to the nodes to which the resources belong: $\forall u \in USER, \forall r \in PRESOURCE, \forall n \in NODE : CanUse(u, r) \not\rightarrow CanLogin(u, n)$ where $BelongsTo(r, n) = true$.

At a high level of abstraction $uses(p, r) := true$ assigns any resource to any process. However, at lower levels, resources are granted by operating systems to local processes. Thus, a process of the application must be on the node to which the resource belongs, or an auxiliary, handler process ($handler : PRESOURCE \rightarrow PROCESS$) must be present. In the latter case the handler might be already running or might be installed by the user when necessary. (For instance, the notion of handler processes appear in Legion as object methods [18] or as services [12].)

Thus by adding more low level details (refinements, from a modeling point of view) **Rule 5** becomes:

```
let  r = mappedresource(p, ar)
if  (∃ar ∈ ARESOURCE) : request(p, ar) = true
      &  r ≠ undef
      &  CanUse(user(p), r)
      then
            if  type(r) = resource₀ then
                mapped(p) := location(r)
                installed(task(p), location(r)) := true
            else  if(¬∃p' ∈ PROCESS) : handler(r) = p'
                      extend PROCESS by p' with
                          mapped(p') := location(r)
                          installed(task(p'), location(r)) := true
                          handler(r) := p'
                          do forall  ar ∈ ARESOURCE
                              request(p', ar) := false
                          enddo
                      endextend
                  endif
            endif
            request(p, ar) := false
            uses(p, r) := true
```

This refined rule indicates that granting a resource involves starting or having a local process on behalf of the user. Obviously, running a process is possible for local account holders. In the initial state there exists a user who has valid access rights to a given resource. However, users are not authorized to log in and start processes on the node to which the resource belongs. To resolve this contradiction let user be split into global user and local user as $globaluser, localuser :$ $PROCESS \rightarrow USER$. Global user identifies the user (a real person) who has access credentials to the resources, and for whom the processes work. A local user is one (not necessarily a real person) who has a valid account and login rights on a node. A grid system must provide some functionality that finds a proper mapping between global users and local users $usermapping :$ $USER \times PRESOURCE \rightarrow USER$, so that a global user temporarily has the rights of a local user for placing and running processes on the node. Therefore, another agent is added to the model that performs module $\Pi_{user\_mapping}$.

$\Pi_{user\_mapping}$

```
let  r = mappedresource(proc, ar)
if  (∃ar ∈ ARESOURCE, proc ∈ PROCESS) : request(proc, ar) = true
      &  r ≠ undef
      &  CanUse(user(proc), r)
      then
            if  type(r) = resource₀
```

```
or  (¬∃p′ ∈ PROCESS) : handler(r) = p′
then
   choose u  in  USER
                 satisfying  CanLogin(u, location(r))
      usermapping(globaluser(proc), r) := u
   endchoose
else
   if  (∃p′ ∈ PROCESS) : handler(r) = p′  then
       usermapping  (globaluser(proc), r) :=
                   localuser(handler(r))
   endif
endif
```

If the process is going to be placed onto the node (directly or via a handler process), then a valid local login name is chosen to be mapped. The choice mechanism is undefined at this level. If the resource is used by an existing handler process, the chosen local user name is the owner of the handler process. In other words, the handler process owned by a local account holder will temporarily work on behalf of another user. (This, again, corresponds to the Legion security mechanism [26].) To include this aspect into **Rule 5**, a valid mapping is required instead of a check for authenticity and authorization.

```
if  (∃ar ∈ ARESOURCE) : request(p, r) = true
    & usermapping(globaluser(p), mappedresource(ar)) ≠ undef
   then
       request(p, ar) := false
       uses(p, mappedresource(ar)) := true
```

1.6.4   Semantical definition for Grid

Rules 3, 4, and 5 together with $\Pi_{resource\_mapping}$ and $\Pi_{user\_mapping}$ constitute a reference model for distributed applications under assumptions made for grid systems in Section 1.3. A grid must minimally provide *user* and *resource* abstractions. A system is said to be a grid if it can provide a service equivalent to $\Pi_{resource\_mapping}$ and $\Pi_{user\_mapping}$ according to some reasonable definition of equivalence (the issue of equivalence is explained in [24]). The functionality described by modules $\Pi_{resource\_mapping}$ and $\Pi_{user\_mapping}$ are often referred as virtualization and their vitality is shown here.

1.7   Discussion

1.7.1   Refinement: From Abstract Functionalities to Real Services

The rules in Section 1.6 describe a grid-like behavior of a distributed system. The most elementary functionalities, i.e., resource and user abstraction revealed by the model answer the question of *what* a grid must provide minimally to be semantically different from conventional environments. The obvious question of *how* they can be realized can be answered within the framework of the same formal model. One approach is to follow the well established procedure called model refinement (see Section 1.2.2), i.e., hidden details at a higher level of abstraction can be elaborated and specified at a lower level. In such a way, by successive refinement the components of a system can be separated, specified, and the functional equivalence between two refinement steps can be ensured (Fig. 1.3). An exact refinement step is beyond the scope of this paper, but an informal example is presented here to show how the framework can serve system design.

By asking the *how* question, the following services can be separated at the next level of abstraction. The key in resource abstraction is the selection of available physical resources. According to general principles in Section 1.6.2, the actual selection method is not specified, but should yield relation $compatible(attr(ar), attr(r))$ true. In the model, at the current level of details, this relation is external and acts like an oracle: it can tell if the selection is acceptable or not. In practice however, a mechanism must be provided that implements the functionality expressed by the relation. Resource abstraction in a real implementation must be supported at least by two components: a *local information provider* that is aware of the features of local resources, their current availability, load, etc.—in general, a module Π_{ip} that can update $attr(r)$ functions either on its own or by a request, and an *information system* Π_{is} that can provide the information represented by $attr(r)$ upon a query (Fig. 1.3).

User abstraction, defined in Section 1.6.3, is a mapping of valid credential holders to local accounts. A fundamental, highly abstract relation of this functionality is $CanUse$ $(globaluser(p), r)$. It expresses the following: the user $globaluser(p)$ has a valid credential, it is accepted through an authentication procedure, and the authenticated user is authorized to use resource r. Just as in case of resource abstraction, this oracle-like statement assumes other assisting services: a *security mechanism* (module Π_s) that accepts global users' certificates and authenticates users, and a *local resource management* (module Π_{rm}) that authorizes authentic users to use certain resources (Fig. 1.3).

This example is not the only way to decompose the system, but it is a very straightforward one since, for example, these modules exist in both Globus [6], [8] and Legion [5], [26] albeit in different forms. If the highest level, model presented in this paper is represented by an abstract state machine ASM1 and the decomposed system by ASM2; then it can be formally checked if ASM2 is operationally equivalent to ASM1 despite their obviously different

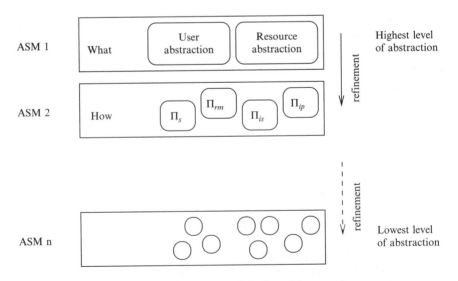

FIGURE 1.3. The concept of the formal framework.

appearance. By asking further *"how"* questions, the realization of the four modules of ASM2 can be defined in ASM3, then that can be refined to ASM4, etc. They are closer and closer to a technical realization (and thus, would differ significantly from system to system), yet they must be operationally equivalent to ASM1; i.e., provide the grid functionalities defined at the highest level.

1.7.2   System Analysis

Currently, a number of projects and software frameworks are termed "grid" or "grid-enabled"— although the meaning of such terms is rather blurry. The model presented in this paper allows a formal or informal analysis of these systems.

The presence of the functionalities defined by $\Pi_{resource\_mapping}$ and $\Pi_{user\_mapping}$ can be checked as follows. An initial state is defined within this framework (together with conditions in Sections 1.5.1, 1.6.1, respectively) as:

1. $\forall u \in USER, \exists r_1, r_2, \ldots r_m \in PRESOURCE : CanUse(u, r_i) = true, 1 \leq i \leq m$ (every user has access to some resources)
2. $\exists r \in PRESOURCE : u \in USER : CanLogin(u, location(r)) = false$ (there are some nodes where the user cannot login—this ensures the real need for grid environment otherwise, there is no resource sharing but resource scheduling)

Similarly, a final state is defined as:

1. $\forall ar \in ARESOURCE, \forall p \in PROCESS : request(p, ar) = true, mappedresource$ $(p, ar) \neq undef$ (all resource needs can be satisfied by appropriate resources)
2. $\forall ar \in ARESOURCE, \forall p \in PROCESS : request(p, ar) = true, usermapping$ $(globaluser(p), mappedresource(ar)) \neq undef$ (all resources can be accessed by finding authorized users)

It must be shown either formally or informally that if a system (an ASM) is started from the defined initial state, it can reach the defined final state in finite steps no matter how this state transition is realized technically. This state transition implies the presence of grid functionalities as defined in Section 1.6.4.

According to our definition, there are some systems that qualify as grids even though they are not classified as such, and others that do not meet the criteria for qualification despite their use of the term in their descriptions.

The SETI@home effort is aimed at harnessing the computing power of millions of (otherwise idle) CPUs for analyzing radio signals [28]. Although it has no specially constructed infrastructure, and was not deliberately designed as such, the SETI@home project demonstrated a new computing paradigm that is semantically equivalent to grids. By providing the functionalities of resource and user abstraction, it realizes a grid.

Condor is a workload management mechanism aimed at supporting high-throughput computing [4]. Its primary goal is effective resource management within a so-called Condor pool which, in most cases coincides with a cluster or network of workstations. By a matchmaking mechanism, based on classads expressing the features of the offered resources and the requirements of jobs [31], it clearly realizes resource abstraction. However, the owners of different pools may have an agreement that under certain circumstances jobs may be transferred form one cluster to another. This mechanism is called flocking [7] and it means that a job submitted to a cluster by a local user may end up in another cluster where the user has no login access at all. Although, technically this solution is far from the security required by grids, semantically it realizes the user abstraction.

The main feature of grids is resource sharing. Nevertheless, attainment of sharing alone does not make a system a grid. For example, by deploying frameworks like the Sun Grid Engine [33], any organization may use its PC intranet for distributed computing by allocating jobs to idling or underloaded processors. While resource abstraction is present in limited form, user abstraction is either not necessary or not realized (e.g., "all Sun Grid Engine, Enterprise Edition users have the same user names on all submit and execution hosts" [33]). As a consequence, such systems satisfy other definitions cited in Section 1.1; yet, in our view, they are semantically not equivalent to grids, according to our definition developed above.

1.8   Conclusion

We conclude that a grid is not defined by its hardware, software, or infrastructure; rather, it is a semantically different way of resource usage across ownership domains. The intent of this paper is to reveal the semantics of virtualization and evolve a definition for clearly distinguishing between systems, to determine whether or not they provide grid functionalities.

Although applications executed in these environments are structurally similar, it is shown in this chapter that a conventional-distributed system cannot provide the necessary functionalities that enable the applications to work under assumptions made for grids. While in conventional-distributed systems the virtual layer is just a *different view* of the physical reality, in grid systems both *users and resources* appear differently at the virtual and physical levels, and an appropriate mapping must be established between them (see Fig. 1.2). Semantically, the inevitable function-alities that must be present in a grid system are resource and user abstraction. Technically, these two functionalities are realized by various services like resource management, information system, security, staging, and so on. Based on the central notions of resource and user abstraction, this paper has attempted to provide a high level semantical model for grid systems formalized by the ASM method.

References

[1] E. Börger, *High Level System Design and Analysis using Abstract State Machines*, in Current Trends in Applied Formal Methods ed. by D. Hutter et al. (FM-Trends 98), LNCS 1641, (Springer, 1999), pp. 1–43

[2] E. Börger and R. Stärk, Abstract State Machines, in *A method for High-level System Design and Analysis* (Springer, 2003)

[3] E. Börger (ed.), *Architecture Design and Validation Methods* (Springer, 2000)

[4] J. Basney and M. Livny, Deploying a High Throughput Computing Cluster, in *High Performance Cluster Computing*, chap. 5, vol. 1, ed. by R. Buyya (Prentice Hall, 1999)

[5] S.J. Chapin, D. Karmatos, J. Karpovich, and A. Grimshaw, *The Legion Resource Management System*, in Proc. of the 5th Workshop on Job Scheduling Strategies for Parallel Processing (JSSPP '99), in conjunction with the International Parallel and Distributed Processing Symposium (IPDPS '99), April 1999

[6] K. Czajkowski, S. Fitzgerald, I. Foster, and C. Kesselman, *Grid Information Services for Distributed Resource Sharing*, in Proc. 10th IEEE International Symposium on High-Performance Distributed Computing (HPDC-10), (IEEE Press, San Francisco, 2001)

[7] D.H.J. Epema, M. Livny, R. van Dantzig, X. Evers, and J. Pruyne, A Worldwide Flock of Condors : Load Sharing Among Workstation Clusters. *Journal on Future Generations of Computer Systems* 12 (1996)

[8] I. Foster, C. Kesselman, G. Tsudik, and S. Tuecke, *A Security Architecture for Computational Grids*, in Proc. of the 5th ACM Conference on Computer and Communication Security, November 1998

[9] I. Foster, C. Kesselman, and S. Tuecke, The Anatomy of the Grid. *International Journal of Supercomputer Applications* 15(3) (2001)

[10] I. Foster and C. Kesselman, *The Grid: Blueprint for a New Computing Infrastructure*, (Morgan Kaufmann, San Francisco, 1999)

[11] I. Foster and C. Kesselman: The Globus Toolkit. In [10] pp. 259–278.

[12] I. Foster, C. Kesselman, J.M. Nick, and S. Tuecke, Grid Services for Distributed System Integration, *IEEE Computer* (6), 37–46 (2002)

[13] I. Foster, C. Kesselman, J.M. Nick, and S. Tuecke, *Physiology of the Grid: An Open Grid Services Architecture for Distributed Systems Integration*, in Open Grid Service Infrastructure WG, Global Grid Forum, June 22, 2002 http://www.globus.org/research/papers/ogsa.pdf

[14] I. Foster, What is the Grid? A Three Point Checklist, *Grid Today* 1(6) (2002) http://www.gridtoday.com/02/0722/100136.html

[15] A. Geist, A. Beguelin, J. Dongarra, W. Jiang, B. Manchek, and V. Sunderam, *PVM: Parallel Virtual Machine—A User's Guide and Tutorial for Network Parallel Computing* (MIT, Cambridge, MA, 1994)

[16] W. Gentzsch, Response to Ian Foster's "What is the Grid?" *Grid Today* 1(8) (2002) http://www.gridtoday.com/02/0805/100191.html

[17] A.S. Grimshaw, W.A. Wulf, J.C. French, A.C. Weaver, and P.F. Reynolds, *Legion: The Next Logical Step Toward a Nationwide Virtual Computer*, Technical report No. CS-94-21. June, 1994

[18] A.S. Grimshaw and W.A. Wulf, *Legion—A View From 50,000 Feet*, in Proceedings of the Fifth IEEE International Symposium on High Performance Distributed Computing, Los Alamitos, CA, August 1996 (IEEE Press, 1996)

[19] Grid Computing—Today and Tomorrow: Another View, *Grid Today* 1(9) (2002) http://www.gridtoday.com/02/0812/100221.html

[20] W. Gropp, E. Lusk, N. Doss, and A. Skjellum, A High-performance, Portable Implementation of the MPI Message Passing Interface Standard. *Parallel Computing* 22(6), 789–828 (1996)

[21] Y. Gurevich, Evolving Algebras 1993: Lipari Guide, in *Specification and Valdation Methods*, ed. by E. Börger (Oxford University Press, 1995) pp. 9–36

[22] Y. Gurevich, Evolving Algebras: An Attempt to Discover Semantics, in *Current Trends in Theoretical Computer Science*, ed. by G. Rozenberg and A. Salomaa (World Scientific, 1993) pp. 266–292

[23] Y. Gurevich, *May 1997 Draft of the ASM Guide* http://www.eecs.umich.edu/gasm/papers/guide97.html

[24] Y. Gurevich and J.K. Huggins, Equivalence is in the Eye of Beholder. *Theoretical Computer Science* (1–2), 353–380 (1997)

[25] Y. Gurevich, Sequential Abstract State Machines Capture Sequential Algorithms, *ACM Transactions on Computational Logic* 1(1), 77–111 (2000)

[26] M. Humprey, F. Knabbe, A. Ferrari, and A. Grimshaw, *Accountability and Control of Process Creation in the Legion Metasystem*, Proc. of the 2000 Network and Distributed System Security Symposium NDSS2000, San Diego, CA, February 2000

[27] W.E. Johnston, A Different Perspective on the Question of What is a Grid? *Grid Today* 1(9) (2002) http://www.gridtoday.com/02/0812/100217.html

[28] E. Korpela, D. Werthimer, D. Anderson, J. Cobb, and M. Lebofsky, SETI@home: Massively Distributed Computing for SETI. *Computing in Science and Engineering* (1) (2001)

[29] G. Lindahl, A. Grimshaw, A. Ferrari, and K. Holcomb, *Metacomputing—What's in it for Me. White Paper.* http://legion.virginia.edu/papers.html

[30] Zs. Németh and V. Sunderam, Characterizing Grids: Attributes, Definitions, and Formalisms, *Journal of Grid Computing* 1(1), 9–23 (2003)

[31] R. Raman and M. Livny, *High Throughput Resource Management*, chap 13 in [10].

[32] R. Stärk, J. Schmid, and E. Börger, *Java and the Java Virtual Machine. Definition, Verification, Validation* (Springer, 2001)

[33] Sun Grid Engine, *Enterprise Edition 5.3 Administration and User's Guide* (2002)

Chapter 2

Using Event Models in Grid Design

2.1 Introduction

A method for evaluating grid system designs with event models is presented in this chapter. Grid projects must satisfy demanding requirements by combining the functionality of distributed components (see Subsection 2.1.1). In the AstroGrid and European Grid of Solar Observation (EGSO) projects, innovative architectural designs have been proposed to achieve this (see Subsection 2.1.2). We have assessed these before implementation by developing formal models.

The modelling language, Finite State Process (FSP), and its analysis tool, Labelled Transition System Analysis (LTSA), are well established [30]. Enough detail of the dynamic modelling language is presented here for readers to apply this method themselves. We also report on our experience of modelling astronomy grid systems; models proved valuable throughout the early project lifecycle.

AstroGrid and EGSO followed iterative development (after [7]), best in novel domains. The models therefore evolved as the system became concrete; they accurately complemented initial concepts, formal design, and Java GUI prototypes (also used to validate designs). Both projects settled on Web services (whilst reusing other standards and libraries), though such technology choice is not demanded by the abstract FSP models. The models to capture design patterns (as defined in [19]), yet to be proven in deployment.

Our models of astronomy data–grids bridge requirements and design to validate the planned systems. They do not bridge design and implementation (a lower level "soft" management process challenge). Before discussing the modelling method and experience, we introduce our projects' requirements and design solutions to demonstrate the relevance of data–grid architecture models.

2.1.1 Data–Grid Requirements

The European Grid of Solar Observations (EGSO [12]) for solar physicists and AstroGrid [3] for night-side astronomers both provide an initial framework for "virtual observatories." Their similar requirements are typical of data–grid projects—which enable access to and analysis of widely distributed complex data—that help scientific progress.

Astronomers need online data and analysis tools to effectively address their scientific problems. However, it is often difficult to locate and match these [10]. Existing online archives of observations (for example NASA SDAC [35] and Strasbourg, Centre de Données astronomiques de Strasbourg (CDS) [9]) have diverse, labor intensive access methods. Data organization standards are not generally followed as different instrument teams work within different physical parameters. There is also a variety of specialist software available (for example, SolarSoft [5] and Starlink [37]). Also, much larger datasets are planned.

A virtual observatory should provide a common infrastructure to federate resources, as well as enabling transparent access to diverse datasets and automated analysis so that collaborative investigations should be possible. It should also maximize the benefit derived from collected data and accelerate the growth of knowledge, in line with the e-science vision [25].

At an abstract level, these requirements are also shared by grids in which diverse distributed computational resources are the critical resource. Both must share resource in a transparent infrastructure across traditional domain boundaries to support flexible, efficient services— enabling virtual organizations essential to the grid vision [16].

The description of EGSO's requirements, phrased in a general way below, are therefore exemplars for the domain. They may be used as a checklist for other data–grid projects' requirements. Requirements also validate the earliest models of the proposed system, as shown in Section 2.3. A general review of data–grid requirements are given elsewhere [23]. The techniques used to elicit requirements are also presented to demonstrate that they accurately capture user needs.

EGSO requirements.   The classified essential system requirements follow. They emphasize operational and maintenance aspects (as classified by [4], also called nonfunctional or quality of service requirements). As such, overall quality of service and maintainability cannot be implemented by an isolated component; they must be considered when planning the general system architecture.

Data and metadata.   The system should enable users to gain access (subject to a security policy) to data and nondata resources. Cache space, computation resources, and data processing applications are examples of nondata resources.

To achieve this, the system should support a framework of metadata structures that incorporate all resource attributes in the current solar physics archives. It should include administrative, structural, and descriptive information. The framework should be capable of supporting semi-structured and incomplete data and metadata.

The system should be able to translate between metadata structures and correlate multiple data resources as required. Metadata structures should not be dependent upon references to other information resources for their use, wherever possible.

When accessing data, the user should also be able to view the corresponding metadata.

Data processing.   The system should enable users to access computing facilities to prepare and analyze data, and execute user processing tasks.

The system should support the migration of existing and user uploaded software and data to these facilities, binding user parameters to tasks interactively. Interfaces should be provided to promote increased uniformity of access to computing resources independent of underlying mechanisms.

Monitoring and management.   The system should include components to monitor the state of resources, infrastructure, and submitted user tasks. Tasks should be managed so that users may be notified of their state changes.

Security.   The infrastructure should enable both authorization and authentication to uphold security. These mechanisms should support policy for different types of request at different granularity (from the whole system to parts of a dataset).

The security infrastructure should protect the resources available via the system. At the same time, scientific users and the providers of resources should find the security mechanisms easy to use.

Interoperability.   The system should be interoperable with other grid projects (in solar physics and related domains); it should make use of their standards for metadata and protocols.

Within EGSO, uniform standards for data management, access, and analysis should be used by all system entities. Common interfaces support the incorporation of multiple, heterogeneous, and distributed resources.

Requirements analysis.   The technical EGSO requirements were derived from a wider user requirements investigation conducted during the first step in the project. The European Grid of Solar Observation's (EGSO's) vision was illustrated with informal system diagrams and usage scenarios, which formed the basis of the models described in Section 2.3.1.

The methodology adopted for eliciting firm requirements involved established techniques [21], [24], and [26]. Direct sources of information included interviews, group discussions, small workshops, questionnaires, and scenario-based feedback. Indirect sources of information included domain-specific documents, analysis of similar projects, and analysis of existing systems (as described in [17, 39]).

The requirements, including domain knowledge of existing working practice and future goals, were presented as tree-like relations (Fig. 2.1). This representation aided requirements reviews in feedback sessions. Separate branches of the tree covered different areas of concern for the system. The depth of a node within the tree (its distance from the root) captured the scope of the concern addressed. Node color was used to categorize requirements. The tree was encoded in XML and a tool was developed for its automated management (which generated Fig. 2.1).

This representation greatly helped various stakeholders gain an immediate perception of the relations between different requirements (related to "viewpoints" [14]). In particular, the tree-based format played a crucial role in requirement prioritization. Situations in which a narrow requirement, believed to be important, was within the scope of a wider requirement area, accepted as less important, were immediately exposed.

Also, the tree format enabled a clear view of areas of concern for which an adequate level of detail had not been achieved. Such situation was highlighted by shallow branches including nodes of high priority. Areas such as security and user interface were expanded based on this technique.

The requirement engineering activity generated EGSO's Negotiated Statement of Requirements (NSR) [24]. Detailed scenarios were also derived, which provided evaluation criteria for the models described in Section 2.3.1.

2.1.2   Astronomy Data–grid Designs

As the EGSO requirements were refined, the envisioned system was captured in a formal architecture. Following Model-Driven Architecture (MDA) [18] principles, different levels of refinement were used for multiple layers; the infrastructure middleware components were specified between user interfaces and local resource applications. Unambiguous architecture diagrams were defined with Unified Modelling Language (UML) [8] profiles, exploiting the language's flexible notation. For example, Fig. 2.2 shows the architecture of one subsystem.

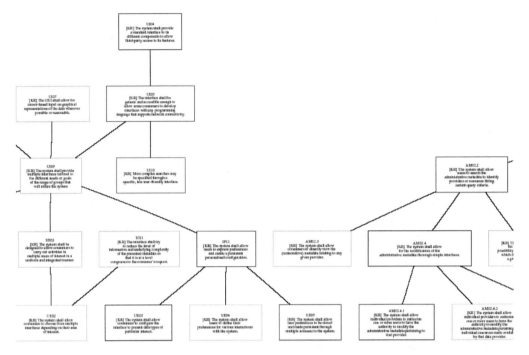

FIGURE 2.1. A view of the EGSO requirement tree as produced by the requirement management tool.

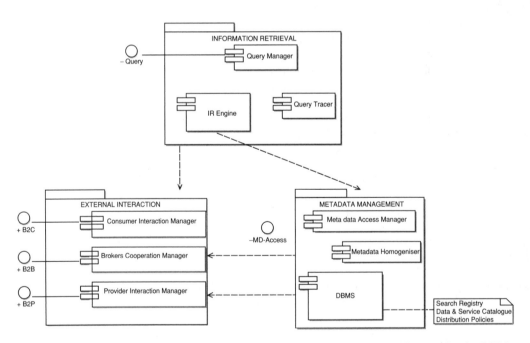

FIGURE 2.2. An example UML component diagram capturing the high-level architecture for the EGSO broker subsystem.

The components of the EGSO architecture are described below, with notable features of the whole system. The architecture of AstroGrid and other data–grids are presented too; their solutions to similar problem domains are compared with EGSO's.

EGSO.   The European Grid of Solar Observation (EGSO) resolves the heterogeneous data and metadata of scattered archives into a "virtual" single resource with a unified catalogue. This broad catalogue provides a standardized view of other catalogues and allows richer searches with information on solar events and features.

Resources are accessed via connectors for diverse protocols, and information is exchanged using adaptors that homogenize different formats. The EGSO framework for creating connectors and adaptors enables access to a wide range of software system.

The EGSO system architecture distinguishes three roles: data consumers, data providers, and brokers. Note that an organization which hosts an EGSO node can play multiple roles, and that all broker instances behave consistently. The roles are best understood by their interaction, apparent in design walk-throughs, so several usage stories follow.

A consumer submits its initial requests to a broker to find which providers hold the data or services specified. The broker provides the consumer with references to providers and information to help selection. The consumer then refines its request with one or more providers to receive the data or service directly.

A provider publishes information on its available data and services by contacting a broker. They agree what information is provided (for example: data format, resource ontology, update frequency, and access policy). A provider may also use a broker when contacted by a consumer (for example: to get information on the consumer).

Brokers monitor the interaction of consumers and providers, and manage information about resource availability. They interact with each other (in a decentral peer-to-peer relationship), sharing this information to present consistent behavior. Brokers can therefore manage the state of user tasks and resource availability, and ensure security policies are upheld.

Supporting functionality (for example: caching, logging, auditing, format transformation, and workflow management) are modelled as provider services. For example, if a broker saves queries or results, it is presented as a caching service provider.

The roles are reminiscent of the tiered architectural style with client, back-end, and middle tiers. However, each acts as a server in a middleware layer that cuts across the system. Diverse user interfaces are served by the consumer, and there are clients for the broker and provider administrators. The provider wraps the primary back-end resources, but the broker and consumer roles also have back-end interfaces to databases and other local operating system resources.

The EGSO system architecture therefore meets the requirements. Rich metadata (in the catalogues) is provided to facilitate data and data processing resource discovery (via brokers) and access (via provider connectors). Interoperability is enabled (using adaptors to homogenize information) in a secure, monitored framework (maintained by the brokers).

AstroGrid.   The AstroGrid architecture has different components to EGSO, but their essential interaction is strikingly similar. The users initially contact a registry of available services to locate their required data and data processing capabilities. A job control agent acts on behalf of users to submit requests directly to resource providers. Also, a special class of registry accepts updates to service availability and distributes the update. Requests (and their results) are represented in a homogenous format wherever necessary via a provider adaptor.

However, unlike EGSO, results are not returned directly to the user—instead the user is notified that they are available in a shared data area. This behavior fits well with the AstroGrid philosophy for asynchronous stateless communication and collaborative working practices.

This architecture does not have an analogue to the EGSO broker, though the registry and job control components partially fulfill its function. Without a component that coordinates resource access and user tasks, the AstroGrid system has less emphasis on infrastructure management. This architecture may prove more scalable, but may be unable to provide a consistent service.

Other projects.   The European Grid of Solar Observation (EGSO) and AstroGrid alone illustrate grid scale adaptations of general architectural styles; EGSO's broker is a tiered solution, whilst AstroGrid's decentralized functionality has an asynchronous service model.

The following paragraphs survey other data–grid projects' key architectural components. It is apparent that their architectures provide some of same functionality as EGSO, without clearly abstracting responsibility. Note that quality and quantity of information about these projects in the public domain varied significantly, so their review may be misrepresentative.

In the European Data Grid (EDG [13]), early project architecture documents describe organizations playing more than one role. A "Consumer" interacts with a "Registry" to locate "Producers." The Consumer then contacts a Producer directly to obtain data. A "Metadata Catalogue" is present to store attributes of logical file names.

In the Grid Physics Network (GriPhyN [22]), the focus is on a "Virtual Data Toolkit" (VDT). The VDT provides a data tracking and generation system to manage the automatic, on-demand derivation of data products. A "Metadata Catalog Servicel" (MCS) contains information about logical files. "User Applications" submit queries to the MCS based on attributes of the data. The MCS returns the names of logical files that satisfy the query. The User Application then queries a Replica Location Service (RLS), to get handles for physical files before contacting the physical storage systems where the files reside.

In the Biomedical Informatics Research Network (BIRN [6]), a "Data Mediator" component provides a semantic mapping, creating the illusion of a single domain from a user perspective. The BIRN uses the Metadata Catalogue (MCAT) and associated Storage Resource Broker (SRB) to perform basic data retrieval functions. The Data Mediator liaises with associated "Domain Knowledge Bases" in response to queries. "Handles" for data resources that satisfy the query are returned to the User Application. The MCAT then enables refinement of the query based on attributes of these data resources.

These projects have defined their available architectural models in terms of physical components or tools, rather than functional roles. Where comparisons can be drawn with the roles of the EGSO model, it appears that queries and requests for information are typically refined between the entities playing the part of the "Consumer" and the "Broker." Two projects provide an inference to the "Provider" for refining requests. In nearly all projects, the "two-step" nature of information retrieval is made explicit, with the discovery of logical file names being a process distinct from the discovery of physical file names and locations.

2.1.3   Overview

This introduction to EGSO demonstrates a well engineered design to fulfill rigorously gathered requirements that exemplify data–grid projects. In the remainder of the chapter we discuss how to verify designs for this class of system requirements.

```
TASK =
    ( submit.usr[ u:1..2 ] -> queued ->
      work.usr[ u ] -> done -> TASK ).
USER =
    ( submit.tsk[ new_t:1..3 ] -> request.tsk[ new_t ] -> USER
    | result -> done.tsk[ old_t:1..3 ] -> USER ).
SVC =
    ( usr[ new_u:1..2 ].request.tsk[ new_t:1..3 ] ->
      tsk[ new_t ].queued -> SVC
    | tsk[ do_t:1..3 ].work.usr[ do_u:1..2 ] ->
      usr[ do_u ].result -> SVC ).
||SYS =
    ( tsk[ t:1..3 ]:TASK || usr[ u:1..2 ]:USER || SVC ) /{
        usr[ u:1..2 ].submit.tsk[ t:1..3 ] /tsk[ t ].submit.usr[ u ],
        usr[ u:1..2 ].done.tsk[ t:1..3 ] /tsk[ t ].done }.
```

FIGURE 2.4. Service model with concurrent users and tasks.

Debugging. Errors when matching event prefixes are common, and cause unexpected events. These should be checked for in LTSA by noting inappropriate possible events when manually tracing state transition sequences. For example, if a typographic error made the first service process event prefix `user[ new_u:1..2 ].request.tsk[ new_t ].1..3`, "request" would be possible before the user process had made the "submit" event.

Event matching errors can also be easily introduced in the synonyms. This risk is mitigated by the naming convention used here, where suffix and prefix values are symmetrically swapped. Note that this is not a hard rule; here it was decided that though the "done" event needs to indicate the task index for the user processes, the equivalent event in the task process does not need the user suffix.

Named constants and ranges may be substituted for the integers given (using the "const" and "range" keywords in declarations, as in Fig. 2.6). This can make the code easier to understand and enable the number of entities to be changed easily, notably when the combined state space is too large for LTSA to compose.

Errors in ranges are also common (though this model is not especially at risk). For example, a variable may represent a range of states for events, whilst some process sharing the event may only operate on a subset of possible states. If the full range is used in the process definition, inappropriate progress may be made when the process transforms states with incorrect indexes; an example applied to this tutorial's model would be the service process doing the submit event.

Design patterns. The distributed state model is more advanced in this version; the task process instances carry information about the user that submitted them. In this way task metadata is represented independently of a specific component. Therefore the service functionality is kept simple, pending tasks may be actioned in an arbitrary sequence, and completed tasks are returned to the correct user.

The asynchronous session state that the information represented here is an essential feature of grid services (in contrast with web services [17]). This pattern scales well when several functions are required to complete a task, and service points action several task types. It therefore models a grid system's flexible workflow management with dynamic resources supporting heterogeneous applications.

Step 4 – Refinement with a Semaphore

Model goal.   Analyzing the model shown in Fig. 2.4 in LTSA demonstrates that the system deadlocks. This is because a user acts as both a client and a server by generating requests and consuming results. If both are attempted simultaneously, neither the user nor the service can make progress.

Deadlock in the concurrent implementation of Fig. 2.4, is avoided by adding a semaphore as in Fig. 2.5. The semaphore ensures safe operation as it must be claimed by the competing components before they exchange a message. A progress check is also added to ensure the system will not reach a livelock and tasks are guaranteed to eventually complete.

At least three other methods could avoid the deadlock. Each user request could block until the result is returned, or connectionless communication could be simulated by allowing messages to be lost between in transmission. Alternatively, existing tasks could be shared by multiple user and server processes, dividing responsibility for message generation and consumption—this may

```
SEMA = SEMA[ 0 ], SEMA[ b:0..1 ] =
    ( [ x:{ usr[ u:1..2 ], svc } ].claim ->
        ( when ( b ) [ x ].fail -> SEMA[ b ]
        | when ( !b ) [ x ].raise -> SEMA[ 1 ] )
    | when ( b ) [ x:{ usr[ u:1..2 ], svc } ].drop -> SEMA[ 0 ] ).
TASK =
    ( submit.usr[ u:1..2 ] -> queued ->
      work.usr[ u ] -> done -> TASK ).
USER = USER[ 0 ], USER[ t:0..3 ] =
    ( when ( ! t ) submit.tsk[ new_t:1..3 ] -> USER[ new_t ]
    | when ( t ) claim ->
        ( raise -> request.tsk[ t ] -> drop -> USER[ 0 ]
        | fail -> USER[ t ] )
    | result -> done.tsk[ old_t:1..3 ] -> USER[ t ] ).
SVC = SVC[ 0 ], SVC[ u:0..2 ] =
    ( usr[ new_u:1..2 ].request.tsk[ new_t:1..3 ] ->
      tsk[ new_t ].queued -> SVC[ u ]
    | when ( ! u ) tsk[ do_t:1..3 ].work.usr[ do_u:1..2 ] ->
      SVC[ do_u ]
    | when ( u ) svc.claim ->
        ( svc.raise -> usr[ u ].result -> svc.drop -> SVC[ 0 ]
        | svc.fail -> SVC[ u ] ) ).
||SYS =
    ( tsk[ t:1..3 ]:TASK || usr[ u:1..2 ]:USER || SVC || SEMA ) /{
        usr[ u:1..2 ].submit.tsk[ t:1..3 ] /tsk[ t ].submit.usr[ u ],
        usr[ u:1..2 ].done.tsk[ t:1..3 ] /tsk[ t ].done }.
progress PROG = { usr[ u:1..2 ].done.tsk[ t:1..3 ] }
```

FIGURE 2.5. Refined FSP service model.

be implemented as concurrent threads within a subsystem. These solutions are unacceptable as the hypothetical requirements demanded that multiple asynchronous tasks for each user should be possible with just two reliable components.

Language features. Process state suffixes (for example, SEMA[b:0..1]) and conditional event paths (using the keyword "when") are introduced in this model with the new semaphore process. Process state suffixes allow a process to hold different states between state transition sequences. The initial semaphore state is false—the first claim will be successful and change the process state; the next claim would fail.

In a similar way, user and service process states are used to hold information on the task to be submitted and the user to return the completed task to, respectively. These parameters ensure that events are repeated for the correct task when a semaphore claim fails.

The progress check is indicated by the named set of target events (declared with the "progress" keyword). The LTSA proves that there must be a path to these events from anywhere in the combined state space; the tool gives equal priority to possible event paths, unless otherwise indicated, to determine whether the events can be reached.

Debugging. When introducing the semaphore process, it is easy to overlook the necessary event prefix (for example, [x:{ usr[u:1..2], svc }].claim). This is necessary to make the event names unique, though the semaphore itself has one state model for all processes using it. The variable "x" can take values over the user process instance prefix range or the value "svc"—the prefix used when the service uses the semaphore. Without this, the system quickly reaches deadlock (as each semaphore event is synchronized to every processes that uses it).

State parameters were added to the user and service processes that use the semaphore. Without them, the processes would have to repeat the "submit" or "work" events when a semaphore claim failed. This would represent a poorly designed system that has to repeat application functions when communication fails. By adding them, the user and service processes are guaranteed to complete their action on one task before starting another. However, this solution makes the processes more complex and less flexible. These faults would be aggravated if the components performed more than one function. By having to refine the model in this way, we may have exposed possible problems in the two component design; adding additional staging components may simplify the model and, ultimately, the system.

Design patterns. The semaphore is a generally used pattern in concurrent distributed systems. To be used effectively, it must guard the critical resource; for this model (and decentral grid systems in general), the service communication channel. As there is a single service, a single semaphore instance is sufficient. For protected communication between components in an N to M relation, an $N \times M$ semaphore combination may be necessary—requiring complex synonyms to model.

Process state tests, like the semaphore's, can represent the distributed state transitions of a data–grid task. The range of values can be enumerated with named constants to help debugging. This method is applied to our task process in Fig. 2.6. As well as determining when to do the transitions that represent application functions, other processes can use test events that do not update the task state. Monitoring services and other components that are essential to support data–grid infrastructure can be modelled in this way. Flexible services that support complex task workflows, dependent on shared system state, can also be built using this pattern element.

```
const TS_INI = 1
const TS_QUE = 2
range TS_R = TS_INI..TS_QUE
TASK = TASK[ TS_INI ], TASK[ ts:TS_R ] =
    ( when ( ts == TS_INI )
       submit -> queued -> TASK[ TS_QUE ]
    | when ( ts == TS_QUE )
       work -> done -> TASK[ TS_INI ]
    | test[ ts ] -> TASK[ ts ] ).
```

FIGURE 2.6. Task process with integer state parameter.

Step 5 – Hypothetical Demonstration

If presenting the worked example to the stakeholder who required asynchronous response or the designer who specified the components and interface, the modeler may demonstrate features of the listing in Fig. 2.5. Communication with the shared service point has been guarded to make it safe, and the components have been modified to prevent progress with other tasks until an actioned task is communicated. These features can be demonstrated by stepping through scenarios, illustrated with LTSA's animation and state transition graphs. The stakeholders may then decide to implement further models to evaluate alternative designs in which the user acts as a blocking client, or that have task staging components.

Commonly, by making a model concurrent at step 3, or by resolving errors at step 4, it becomes too complex for LTSA compose and analyze. The simple composed system listed in Fig. 2.5 has 2^{27} states. (LTSA could not compose the 2^{41} states for three users and four tasks on our small development machine; the Java 1.4.1 run-time environment runs out of memory at 133MB.) In this case, the modeler must demonstrate a partial model and identify parts at risk to faulty interaction, before repeating the cycle of model development for a reduced system specification. The worked example in this section could be seen as such a simplified system; a single service point for multiple users and tasks would be the risky part of a larger system in which actions behind the "submit" and "work" events has been ignored.

2.3   Evidence

This section discusses models developed at four different design stages—three within the lifecycle of the EGSO project, the last in AstroGrid. It shows that dynamic models have been understood by the authors' colleagues and have improved their grid projects' designs. Those who are interested in software engineering methods can read this discussion to evaluate the technique.

The narrative presentation of this concrete evidence reflects the previous section's abstract introductory material. For each stage we describe: the project state, the model implementation, language limitations noted, other observations, and details of how the model was communicated to colleagues. Model validity is demonstrated if it faithfully represents the conceptual system and is successful if it informs design refinements. These indicate the model development method being applied—from the system specification input to presentation, via iterative model development.

Limitations.   The FSP does not precisely represent the message sequence charts; synchronous events can indicate a message exchange, but not its direction (from the source process to the sink). Some of the hidden events, implemented for the process acting as a client, were therefore necessary to represent the message's origin. Correspondingly, the other events in the model that were not synchronized between processes, representing the hidden work of a process acting as a server, were necessary to enable concurrent asynchronous progress.

Observations.   The direct association between the designed messages and model events ensures the models' validity. When models were refined, diverging from the message sequence charts, it remained clear which messages were excluded, which decomposed, and which should be added to the design.

Models were tested by animating the message sequence charts, as done for the scenarios in the previous stage. Asynchronous concurrent progress was demonstrated, and events for errors were introduced when paths could lead to undocumented, unexpected states.

The LTSA safety checks for the second model proved that the design implemented a reliable service that could not block due to process instance conflict or circular dependencies. The FSP progress criteria were used to show that repeating cyclic paths must eventually resolve consumer queries.

The third model showed that a safe solution to reliable query resolution against distributed metadata was more complex than the design had described. Even with a simple ring topology and query parameterization with the forwarding node, extra query history was required–this could not be easily represented in FSP.

The modelling completed at this stage therefore validated the interfaces and evaluated alternative designs. These designs are also domain independent, and demonstrate behavior common to many data–grids—so they indicate design patterns. The second model represents a generic resource metadata management solution, and the third model a peer-to-peer service discovery network.

Communication.   We successfully used the model to argue for some modifications to the EGSO design. Eight undocumented messages had been added to the model. These included a necessary indication that a message sequence was complete and alternative responses for error cases. The model also demonstrated the importance of guarding communication between entities that act both as client and server, at risk of deadlock or requests loss. The second model from this stage may be maintained in parallel with interface development, so that future design changes can also be validated against the design original goals.

2.3.3   *Stage 4 –* AstroGrid *Detailed Design*

Project state.   The AstroGrid project had begun detailed design whilst EGSO was at the interface design stage described above. Their object models included descriptions and message sequence charts for classes interacting via public methods that were complex and subject to change. However, by discussing the distributed interaction and exploring design risks with the project's software engineers, we extracted a message sequence chart that spanned the system elements for the essential data–grid task of query resolution and delivery of an analyzed data product.

Implementation.   Just two working days were spent developing two models based directly on the message sequence chart. As at the previous stage, we created process synchronization events for documented messages and added hidden events for other activity. The first model implemented the complete message set in 39 events, but only represented a single instance of each of the nine interacting entities (with an additional process for the job state shared by three of the objects). The second model introduced concurrency to explore a risky circular dependency, representing the three classes involved as well as a job state process and a job factory. These five entities shared 12 types of events.

Observations.   As at stage three, the direct translation of messages to events ensures model validity. The first model animated the essential message sequence chart, demonstrating that the message set was complete (no more messages were needed to invoke or censure required process activity). The second model did reveal a possible deadlock in the circular dependency of three job control processes when there are as many active jobs as entities.

Communication.   Discussion with the engineers distinguished stateful from asynchronous communication interfaces. Therefore, the demonstrated deadlock should not be a risk, as the job control objects in question do not establish reliable connections; their "fire and forget" interfaces should be able to ignore messages that would block progress. This behavior is actually demonstrated in the first model with simpler logic that represents a nondeterministic choice to avoid deadlock.

The refined AstroGrid design includes a daemon that detects inconsistent state and repeats lost messages; this has yet to be modelled to demonstrate the logical reliability of the design. The cycle of design, modelling and design review will therefore need at least one more iteration in this project.

In fact, the engineers are keen to know the expected job recovery time based on factors including the probability of failure and the recovery daemon's schedule. As poor performance is seen as a greater risk than component interaction failure, we plan to use stochastic FSP instead of the basic language described in this chapter.

General Limitations.   An advanced EGSO model safeguarded communication with semaphores, whilst the last AstroGrid model fails to synchronize the distributed state of tasks across components. AstroGrid's design side-steps synchronization failure by accommodating lost messages, whilst EGSO must implement blocking communication with its critical brokers. It is therefore clear that reliable progress in a decentralized, scalable data–grid architecture is sensitive to connector design. However, FSP has only represented connection oriented communication with synchronized event in our models.

Some other formal modelling languages (notable ADLs, see Section 2.4.2) have rich semantics for connector typing, which may capture different data–grid component connection strategies. However, despite FSP's simplicity and the experience given here, it may be used to represent connector logic directly. Reference processes that represent different connection types have been developed and used between arbitrary components in system models. This method does add further complexity, restricting the representation of complex systems.

2.4 Conclusion

The experience (presented in Section 2.3) of applying the modelling technique (demonstrated in Section 2.2) shows how our method for assessing data–grid architecture is applied within the early software lifecycle. The process and our findings are summarized below in Section 2.4.1; we conclude that our method helps the reliable application of LTSA. Section 2.4.2 contrasts our method with other modelling techniques, and Section 2.5 discusses the direction of our work.

2.4.1 Summary

The formal representation of designed events allows the proposed system to be verified. The basic analysis operation of LTSA detects deadlocks, and may therefore demonstrate overall progress. The state transition models generated also indicate processes that can incorrectly make independent progress when interaction events are missing. It is possible to demonstrate that the system satisfies its behavioral requirements by stepping through event sequences. Scenarios and stories derived from the specific user information and general system requirements were used to determine the test sequences.

It is apparent that data–grids are a challenging domain that need front-loaded development to reduce risk, and that initial designs did not represent nonfunctional system properties. We have shown how dynamic models of two data–grid projects have been developed in FSP and analyzed by LTSA at four stages of the software lifecycle to tackle this problem. Initially informal diagrams were animated to gain confidence in conceptual design. Later scenarios were used to construct a dynamic model that complemented the component architecture; this model allowed system design testing and bridged the gap between concrete requirements and an abstract static design. Once message sequence charts had been specified, models could evaluate both interface and detailed design, exposing gaps and risks. Specific properties exposed at each stage are summarized in the list below.

1. The four conceptual models demonstrated that: service providers can be protected against infrastructure faults and insecure access, a broker enables fair scheduling, users can reliably access hidden distributed resources, and there is no logical constraint to these entities scalability.
2. The architectural scenario model also demonstrated how users could simply use a decentralized network; metadata management (for both the persistent association of providers to data sets and their volatile availability) enabled dynamic growth and robust service.
3. The three interface design models demonstrated that the design reliably made progress; they also uncovered hidden complexity of one design option, found missing messages in interactions and highlighted the protection required for symmetric dependencies.
4. The two models of the object interaction for data–grid query resolution demonstrated the risk of stateful connection deadlock (where there was a circular dependency)—avoided by nondeterministic asynchronous messaging.

Grid systems are characterized by complex, concurrent transactions where user progress and resource management depends on the system's dynamic distributed status. The resulting nondeterministic interaction is hard to capture, making grid design error prone. The FSP can express the simple component processes and states that make up the system, and LTSA can compose the complex combined state space, prove safe concurrent progress, and demonstrate the model's emergent behavior. The language and tool are therefore well suited to represent and evaluate designs for grid systems.

2.4.2 Related work

Models are widely used in software engineering; five common ways of applying models are listed below.

1. Informal box and line diagrams are easy to generate and understand, and are common early in project's life. Their components may be generated for the major envisioned tasks of the conceptual system. Several different sketches may be used to guide imagination and discussions between customer and engineering representatives (applied in object modelling by [31]). Their ambiguity means that they cannot strongly support analysis of system properties or guide implementation.
2. Architecture description languages support formal analysis of a high level design's components and connectors. An ADL may be chosen because it expresses a high-risk area well, for example by supporting heterogeneous connector protocols or domain-specific performance properties. Models generated may be analyzed by tools that employ formal methods to prove constraints or goal satisfaction, but they are typically hard to generate and understand. ([32] reviews many ADLs, and [36] introduces architectural modelling.)
3. Object modelling may be employed from the initial system conceptualization and architectural design (where MDA is applied), but most widely used at detailed design (where UML is widely used [8]). The abstract and concrete properties and relationships of objects in the system can be captured unambiguously and intelligibly. Basic analysis (for example for design consistency) and quality guidance (for example for decoupled encapsulation) is ensured, and extra mechanisms (for example OCL formal methods) may be applied.
4. Prototypes may be implemented to demonstrate a subset of the system's behavior or as a stepping-stone toward full implementation (in evolutionary development [7]). They may tackle high-risk system components and interfaces, or be generated automatically by development tools. The prototype's accuracy may therefore converge on the actual system representation, so it can be analyzed by increasingly realistic system tests.
5. Simulation typically focuses on one view of system behavior, such as performance. Its implementation may include a model of the system's domain, but shouldn't be reused in the real system—in contrast with a prototype. The statistical analysis of a valid simulation's operation unambiguously demonstrates the real system's properties.

All of these methods may represent both static and dynamic views of the system; object modelling and prototyping capture dynamic behavior better than typical informal diagrams and ADL specifications, but only simulation is targeted at exposing the emergent properties of live operation.

The FSP/LTSA modelling technique that we have used for data–grids is strictly dynamic, being guided at combinatorial state space analysis. It is designed to work with a traditional ADL, Darwin [29], that represents static components with diverse connectors hierarchically. As it is also a teaching aid, it is easy to understand.

All of the five modelling techniques introduced above have been applied in grid projects, and all but simulation have been used specifically in AstroGrid and EGSO. This section will review this effort, making reference to our projects where possible. Other artifacts of the astronomy data–grids' early software lifecycle will be mentioned, as these give the background against which our modelling effort is judged. This overview also demonstrates that our models represent a unique investigation.

Chapter 3

Intelligent Grids

3.1 Introduction and Motivation

Data, service, and computational grids, collectively known as information grids, are collections of autonomous computers connected to the Internet and giving to individual users the appearance of a single virtual machine [4, 12, 23]. The interaction of individual users with such a complex environment is greatly simplified when the supporting infrastructure includes intelligent components, able to infer new facts given a set of existing facts and a set of inference rules, and capable to plan and eventually learn. In this case we talk about an intelligent grid.

A *data grid* allows a community of users to share content. An example of a specialized data grid supporting a relatively small user community is the one used to share data from high energy physics experiments. The World Wide Web can be viewed as a data grid populated with HTTP servers providing the content, data, audio, and video.

A *service grid* will support applications such as electronic commerce, sensor monitoring, telemedicine, distance learning, and Business-to-Business. Such applications require a wide spectrum of end services such as monitoring and tracking, remote control, maintenance and repair, online data analysis and business support, as well as services involving some form of human intervention such as legal, accounting, and financial services. An application of a monitoring service in health care could be monitoring outpatients to ensure that they take the prescribed medication. Controlling the heating and cooling system in a home to minimize energy costs, periodically checking the critical parameters of the system, ordering parts such as air filters, and scheduling repairs is an example of control, maintenance, and repair services respectively. Data analysis services could be used when arrays of sensors monitor traffic patterns or document visitor's interest at an exhibition. There are qualitative differences between service and data grids. The requirements for a service grid are more stringent; the end result is often the product of a cooperative effort of a number of service providers, it involves a large number of sensors, and it is tailored to specific user needs. Individual users may wish to compose dynamically a subset of services. Dynamic service composition has no counterpart in the current Web where portals support static service coordination.

A *computational grid* is expected to provide transparent access to computing resources for applications requiring a substantial Central Processing Unit (CPU) cycle rate, very large memories, and secondary storage that cannot be provided by a single system. The `seti@home` project, set up to detect extraterrestrial intelligence, is an example of a distributed application designed to take advantage of unused cycles of PCs and workstations. Once a system joins the project, this application is activated by mechanisms similar to the ones for screen savers. The participating systems form a primitive computational grid structure; once a system is willing to accept work it contacts a load distribution service, it is assigned a specific task and starts computing. When interrupted by a local user, this task is checkpointed and migrated to the load distribution service. The requirements placed on the user access layer and societal services are even more stringent for a computational grid than for a service grid. The user access layer must support various programming models and the societal services of a computational grid must be able to handle low-level resource management.

The contribution of this paper is an in-depth discussion of intelligent computational grids, an analysis of some core services, the presentation of the basic architecture of the middleware we are currently constructing, and applications of the system to a complex computation. This paper is organized as follows: first, we discuss some of the most important requirements for the development of intelligent grids and present in some depths the coordination and planning services; then we present an overview of event, simulation, ontology, persistent storage, and security services and finally, we present the BondGrid, our approach for building a platform for grid services.

3.1.1 Resource Management, Exception Handling, and Coordination

Whenever there is a contention for limited set of resources among a group of entities or individuals, we need control mechanisms to mitigate access to system resources. These control mechanisms enable a number of desirable properties of the system, e.g., fairness, provide guarantees that tasks are eventually completed, and ensure timeliness when timing constraints are involved. Security is a major concern in such an environment. We want to ensure confidentiality of information and prevent denial of service attacks, while allowing controlled information sharing for cooperative activities. Considerably simpler versions of some of the problems mentioned above are encountered at the level of a single system, or in the case of small-scale distributed systems (systems with a relatively small number of nodes in a single administrative domain). In case of a single system such questions are addressed by the operating system which transforms the "bare hardware" into a user machine and controls access to system resources. The question of how to address these problems in the context of a grid has been the main focus of research in grid environments, and, at the same time, the main stumbling block in the actual development of computational grids.

Some research in this area proposes to transfer to grid computing some concepts, services, and mechanisms from traditional operating systems, or from parallel and distributed systems without taking into account their impact on system reliability and dependability. For example, there is a proposal to extend the Message Passing Interface (MPI) to a grid environment. But, in its current implementation, the MPI does not have any mechanism to deal with a node failure during a barrier synchronization operation. In such a case, all the nodes involved, other than the defective one, wait indefinitely and it is the responsibility of the user to detect the failure and take corrective actions. It may be acceptable to expect the programmer to monitor a cluster with a few hundred nodes housed in the next room, but it is not reasonable to expect someone to monitor tens of thousands of nodes scattered over a large geographic area. Thus, we cannot allow MPI to work across system boundaries without some fault detection mechanism and the ability to take corrective actions.

Coordination allows individual components of a system to work together and create an ensemble exhibiting a new behavior without introducing a new state at the level of individual components. Scripting languages provide a "glue" to support composition of existing applications. The problem of coordinating concurrent tasks was generally left to the developers of the parallel scientific and engineering applications. Coordination models such as the coordinator–worker, or the widely used Single Program Multiple Data (SPMD) were developed in that context.

The problem of coordination of complex tasks has new twists in the context of grid computing. First, it is more complex and it involves additional activities such as resource discovery and planning. Second, it has a much broader scope due to the scale of the system. Third, the complexity of the computational tasks and the fact that the end user may only be intermittently connected to the network force us to delegate this function to a proxy capable of creating the conditions for the completion of the task with or without user intervention. It is abundantly clear that such a proxy is faced with very delicate decisions regarding resource allocation or exception handling. For example, should we use a more expensive resource and pay more to have guarantees that a task completes in time, or should we take our chances with a less expensive resource; in the case of the MPI example, should we kill all the processes in all the nodes and restart the entire computation; should we roll back the computation to a previous checkpoint if one exists, or should we simply restart the process at the failing node on a different node.

There is little doubt that the development of computational grids poses formidable problems. In this paper we concentrate on problems related to resource management, exception handling, and coordination of complex tasks. We argue that only an intelligent environment could reliably and seamlessly support such functions.

3.1.2   Intelligent Grid Environments

Most of the research in grid computing is focused on relatively small grids (hundreds of nodes) dedicated to a rather restricted community (e.g., high energy physics), of well-trained users (e.g., individuals working in computational sciences and engineering), with a rather narrow range of problems (e.g., computer-aided design for the aerospace industry).

The question we address is whether a considerably larger grid could respond to the needs of a more diverse user community than in the case of existing grids without having some level of intelligence built into the core services. The reasons we consider for such systems are precisely the reasons computational grids were introduced for in the first place: economy of scale and the ability to share expensive resources among larger groups of users. It is not uncommon that several groups of users (e.g., researchers, product developers, individuals involved in marketing, educators, and students) need a seamless and controlled access to existing data or to the programs capable of producing data of interest. For example, the structural biology community working on the atomic structure determination of viruses, the pharmaceutic industry, and educational institutions ranging from high schools to universities need to share information. One could easily imagine that a high school student would be more motivated to study biology if s(he) is able to replay in the virtual space successful experiments done at the top research laboratories that lead to the discovery of the structure of a virus (e.g., the common cold virus) and understand how a vaccine to prevent the common cold is engineered.

An intelligent environment is in a better position than a traditional one to match the user profile (leader of a research group, member of a research group with a well defined task, drug designer, individual involved in marketing, high school student, doctoral student) with the actions the user is allowed to perform and with the level of resources (s)he is allowed to consume. At the same time, an intelligent environment is in a better position to hide the complexity of the grid infrastructure and allow unsophisticated users, such as a high school student without any training in computational science, to carry out a rather complex set of transformations of an input data set.

Even in the simple example discussed above we see that the *coordination service* acting as a proxy on behalf of the end user has to deal with unexpected circumstances or with error conditions, e.g., the failure of a node. The response to such an abnormal condition can be very diverse, ranging from terminating the task, to restarting the entire computation from the very beginning, or from a checkpoint. Such decisions depend upon a fair number of parameters, e.g., the priority of the task, the cost of each option, the presence of a soft deadline, and so on. Even in this relatively simple case, it is non trivial to hardcode the decision making process into a procedure written in a standard programming language. Moreover, we may have in place different policies to deal with rare events, policies which take into account factors such as legal considerations, the identity of the parties involved, the time of the day, and so on [3]. At the same time, hardcoding the decision-making will strip us of the option to change our actions depending upon considerations we did not originally take into account, such as the availability of a new system just connected to the grid.

Very often the computations carried out on a grid involve multiple iterations and in such a case the duration of an activity is data-dependent and very difficult to predict. Scheduling a complex task whose activities have unpredictable execution times requires the ability to discover suitable resources available at the time when activities are ready to proceed [8]. It also requires market-based scheduling algorithms which in turn require metainformation about the computational tasks and the resources necessary to carry out such tasks.

The more complex the environment, the more elaborate the decision-making process becomes, because we need to take into account more factors and circumstances. It seems obvious to us that under such circumstances a set of inference rules based upon facts reflecting the current status of various grid components are preferable to hardcoding. Oftentimes, we also need to construct an elaborate plan to achieve our objective or to build learning algorithms into our systems.

Reluctant as we may be to introduce a complex system such as a grid, we simply cannot ignore the benefits the Artificial Intelligence (AI) components could bring along. Inference, planning, and learning algorithms are notoriously slow and we should approach their use with caution. We cannot use AI approaches when faced with fast-approaching deadlines. The two main ingredients of an intelligent grid are software agents [1, 2, 11, 15] and ontologies.

The need for an intelligent infrastructure is amply justified by the complexity of both the problems we wish to solve and the characteristics of the environment. Now we take a closer look at the architecture of an intelligent grid and distinguish between several classes of services. System-wide services supporting coordinated and transparent access to resources of an information grid are called *societal* or *core* services. Specialized services accessed directly by end users are called *end-user services*. The core services, provided by the computing infrastructure, are persistent and reliable, while end-user services could be transient in nature. The providers of end-user services may temporarily or permanently, suspend their support. The reliability of end-user services cannot be guaranteed. The basic architecture of an intelligent grid is illustrated in Fig. 3.1.

A nonexhaustive list of core services includes: authentication, brokerage, coordination, information, ontology, matchmaking, monitoring, planning, persistent storage, scheduling, event, and simulation. *Authentication* services contribute to the security of the environment. *Brokerage* services maintain information about classes of services offered by the environment, as well as past performance databases. Though the brokerage services make the best effort

original virus particle projections, which introduce too much noise in the reconstruction process. It would be very difficult to automate such a decision which requires the expertise of a highly trained individual. In such a case the coordination service should checkpoint the entire computation, release most resources, and attempt to contact an individual capable of making a decision. If the domain expert is connected to the Internet with a palmtop computer with a small display and a wireless channel with low bandwidth, the coordination service should send low resolution images and summary data enabling the expert to make a decision.

In summary, the coordination service acts as a proxy for the end user and interacts with core and other services on user's behalf. It hides the complexity of the grid from the end user and allows user interfaces running on the network access devices to be very simple [13]. The coordination service should be reliable and able to match user policies and constraints (e.g., cost, security, deadlines, quality of solution) with the corresponding grid policies and constraints.

A coordination service relies heavily on shared ontologies. It implements an abstract machine which understands a description of the complex task called a *process description*, and a description of a particular instance of the task, a *case description*.

3.2.2 Process and Case Description

A *process description* is a formal description of the complex problem a user wishes to solve. For the process description, we use a formalism similar to the one provided by Augmented Transition Networks (ATNs) [20]. The coordination service implements an abstract ATN machine. A *case description* provides additional information for a particular instance of the process the user wishes to perform, e.g., it provides the location of the actual data for the computation, additional constraints related to security, cost, or the quality of the solution, a soft deadline, and/or user preferences [12].

The BNF grammar for the process description used by our implementation of the planning service follows.

```
S ::= <ProcessDescription>
<ProcessDescription> ::= BEGIN <Activities> END
<Activities> ::= <SequentialActivities> | <ConcurrentActivities>
                | <IterativeActivities> | <SelectiveActivities>
                | <Activity>
<SequentialActivities> ::= <Activities> ; <Activities>
<ConcurrentActivities> ::= FORK <Activities> ; <Activities> JOIN
<IterativeActivities> ::= ITERATIVE <ConditionalActivity>
<SelectiveActivities> ::= CHOICE <ConditionalActivity> ;
                          <ConditionalActivitySet> MERGE
<ConditionalActivitySet> ::= <ConditionalActivity>
                | <ConditionalActivity> ; <ConditionalActivitySet>
<ConditionalActivity> ::= { COND <Conditions> } { <Activities> }
<Activity> ::= <String>
<Conditions> ::= ( <Conditions> AND <Conditions> )
                | ( <Conditions> OR <Conditions> )
                | NOT <Conditions>
                | <Condition>
<Condition> ::= <DataName>.<Attribute> <Operator> <Value>
<DataName> ::= <String>
<Attribute> ::= <String>
```

```
<Operator> ::= < | > | = | <= | >=
<Value> ::= <String>
<String> ::= <Character> <String> | <Character>
<Character> ::= <Letter> | <Digit>
<Letter> ::= a | b | ... | z | A | B | ... | Z
<Digit> ::= 0 | 1 | ... | 9
```

3.3   Planning and Planning Services

The original process description is either created manually by an end user, or automatically by the *planning* service. Process descriptions can be archived using the system knowledge base. The *planning service* is responsible for creating original process descriptions (also called plans) and, more often, for replanning, i.e., for adapting an existing process description to new conditions.

Planning is an AI problem with a wide range of real-world applications. Given a system in an initial state, a set of actions that change the state of the system, and a set of goal specifications, we aim to construct a sequence of activities, that can take the system from a given initial state to a state that meets the goal specifications of a planning problem [21].

A planning problem, P, in an intelligent grid environment is formally defined as a three tuple: $P = \{S_{init}, G, T\}$, where

1. S_{init} is the initial state of the system, which includes all the initial data provided by an end user and their specifications;
2. G is the goal specification of the problem, which includes the specifications of all data expected from the execution of a computing task;
3. T is a complete set of end-user activities available to the grid computing system.

A *plan* consists of two types of activities, end-user activities and flow-control activities. Every *end-user activity* corresponds to a computing service available in the grid. Such activities run under the control of *Application Containers* (ACs). Every end-user activity has preconditions and postconditions. The *preconditions* of an activity specify the set of input data, as well as specific conditions necessary for the execution of the activity. An activity is *valid* only if all preconditions are met before execution. The *postconditions* of an activity specify the set of conditions on the data that must hold after the execution of the activity.

Flow control activities do not have associated computing services. They are used to control the execution of activities in a plan. We define six flow control activities: Begin, End, Choice, Fork, Join, and Merge. Every plan should start with a Begin activity and conclude with an End activity. These Begin and the End activities can only occur once in a plan.

The *direct precedence* relation reflects the causality among activities. If activity B can only be executed directly after the completion of activity A, we say that A is a *direct predecessor* activity of B and that B is a *direct successor* activity of A. An activity may have a *direct predecessor set* of activities and a *direct successor set* of activities. We use the term "direct" rather than "immediate" to emphasize the fact that there may be a gap in time from the instance an activity terminates, and the instance its direct successor activity is triggered. For the sake of brevity we drop the word "direct" and refer to predecessor activity set, or predecessor activity and successor activity set, or successor activity.

A Choice flow control activity has one predecessor activity and multiple successor activities. Choice can be executed only after its predecessor activity has been executed. Following the execution of a `Choice` activity, only *one* of its successor activities may be executed. There is a one-to-one mapping between the transitions connecting a `Choice` activity with its successor set and a *condition set* that selects the unique activity from the successor set that will actually gain control. Several semantics for this decision process are possible.

A `Fork` flow control activity has one predecessor activity and multiple successor activities. The difference between `Fork` and `Choice` is that after the execution of a `Fork` activity, all the activities in its successor set are triggered.

A `Merge` flow control activity is paired with a `Choice` activity to support the conditional and iterative execution of activities in a plan. `Merge` has a predecessor set consisting of two or more activities and only one successor activity. A `Merge` activity is triggered after the completion of *any* activity in its predecessor set.

A `Join` flow control activity is paired with a `Fork` activity to support concurrent activities in a plan. Like a `Merge` activity, a `Join` activity has multiple predecessor activities and only one successor activity. The difference is that a `Join` activity can be triggered only after all of its predecessor activities are completed.

3.4   Other Core Services

3.4.1   Asynchronous Communication and Event Services

In the following discussion an *event* is caused by the change of the state of a system. The system where the change of state occurs is called the *producer* of the event and all systems which react to this event are *consumers* of the event. An *event service* connects a producer of events with the consumer(s) of the event. Most reactive systems are based upon the *event-action model* with an action associated with every type of event. For example, the First Level Interrupt Handler (FLIH) of an operating system is driven by an event-action table; in this case each event has a distinct priority, the actions are nonpreemptive (concurrent events are typically queued by the hardware), and short-lived.

Let us now dissect the handling of an error condition in the context of MPI-based communication. In case of a node failure we expect MPI to generate an event signaling the node failure and to deliver this event to the event service. A coordination service, acting on behalf of the user, should subscribe to the event service at the time the computation is started and specify the type of events it wishes to be notified about. When a node failure occurs, the event service would notify this entity acting as a proxy for the end user. Then the proxy could: (i) force the termination of the computation in all functioning nodes, (ii) attempt to reassign the computation originally assigned to the faulty node to a functioning one, (iii) attempt to restart the faulty node and resume the computation assigned it from a checkpoint, or take any number of other actions. This example shows that an action may be rather complex.

Most distributed systems such as CORBA or JINI support event services. The need for an event service is motivated by several considerations. First, the desire to support asynchronous communication between producers and the consumers of events intermittently connected to the network. For example, when a complex task terminates, the coordination service is informed and, in turn, it generates an event for the end user. Whenever the end user connects to the Internet, the event service will deliver the event to the user interface. Second, in many instances there are multiple consumers of an event and it would be cumbersome for the producer to maintain state (a record of all subscribers to an event) and it would distract the producer from its own actions.

Third, it is rather difficult to implement preemptive actions, yet multiple events of interest to a consumer may occur concurrently. An event service may serialize these events and allow the consumer to process them one after the other. Last, but not the least, the event service may create composite events from atomic events generated by independent producers. For example, the event service may generate a composite event after receiving an event signaling the failure of `resource` A followed by an event signaling the failure of `resource` B.

An event is characterized by a name, producer, time of occurrence, priority, and types. A *type* relation partitions the events into several classes:

1. *Action* type index informs the consumers whether the event needs to take some actions or not.
2. *Error*. Computation and communication errors are two major classes of errors in a computational grid.
3. *Temporal*. Events of type *Time* are expected to happen multiple times during a producer's life span, while events of type *Once* occur only once.
4. *Atomic/Composite*.

Table 3.1. lists the event types and possible values of each type.

3.4.2   Grid Simulation and Simulation Services

Not unexpectedly, a major problem in grid research is related to the scalability of various architectural choices. Solutions optimized to work well for a system with hundreds of nodes may be totally inadequate for a system one or two orders of magnitude larger. For example, we understand well that in the Internet, the implementation of virtual circuits is unfeasible when routers have to maintain state information about 10^6 or more circuits. In spite of the ability to facilitate the implementation of rigorous quality of service (QoS) constraints, the virtual circuit paradigm is rarely implemented at the network layer.

Ideally, we wish to understand the behavior of a system before actually building it. This is possible through simulation, provided that we have a relatively accurate model of the system and some ideas regarding the range of the parameters of the model. So it seems obvious to us that a two-pronged approach to build a complex system has a better chance of success:

1. Construct a testbed to study basic algorithms and policies and use it to develop a model of the system. Gather data useful to characterize this model.
2. Use the model and the parameters of the model obtained from experimental studies for simulation studies.

We should be prepared to face the fact that a model based upon the study of a testbed may be incomplete. Also, solving global optimization problems, often using incomplete or inaccurate model parameters is a nontrivial task.

TABLE 3.1. A list of event types and possible values of each type.

Type	Value
Action	Informative, Imperative, N/A
Error	ComputationError, CommunicationError, InputError, N/A
Temporal	Time, Once, N/A
Structure	Atomic, Composite, N/A

Creating a simulation system for a grid environment is extremely challenging due to the entanglement of computing with communication and to the diversity of factors we have to consider. Most simulation systems are either dedicated to the study of communication systems and protocols, or to the study of various scheduling algorithms for computational tasks.

Once we have a system capable of simulating the behavior of a grid, we wish to exploit it further as a grid service. Indeed, a user may be interested to see how his task would be carried out on the grid before actually submitting the task. Such a simulation would give the user (or the coordination service which is the user's proxy) a more precise idea of:

1. When each resource is needed, and allow the user to reserve resources if this is possible,
2. What are the costs associated with the entire task,
3. Which is the best alternative, when multiple process and case description pairs are possible.

In turn, various core services could improve their performance by posing various types of queries to the simulation service. For example, we know that reliability and performance considerations require that core services be replicated throughout the grid. Once a node performing a core service is overloaded, a request to replicate it is generated, and the grid monitoring and coordination center could request the simulation service to suggest an optimal placement of the server.

3.4.3   Ontologies and Ontology Services

Transferring *data* between two computers on the grid is a well-understood problem. The transfer of *information* is much more difficult, while the transfer of *knowledge* is almost impossible without some form of explicit human intervention. For example, it is easy to transfer the number 42 from a client to a server—using an integer representation. If we want to specify that this data represents the temperature in Fahrenheit, we need the appropriate syntactic representation. For example, using an Extended Markup Language (XML), the representation of this fact is

```
<temperature value="42" unit="Fahrenheit">
```

This representation is still meaningless for someone who is familiar with the Celsius, but not the Fahrenheit temperature scale, or does not understand the concept of temperature at all. Such information becomes knowledge only if we possess an *ontology* which defines the background knowledge necessary to understand these terms. Even from this trivial example it is abundantly clear that primitive concepts, such as temperature, time, or energy are most difficult to understand.

Even the purely syntactic XML representation described above provides more than the number 42 in itself, it allows us to determine whether we understand the information or not. Establishing that we cannot interpret some information is preferable to a misinterpretation of that information. This often-ignored truth is illustrated by the well-known case of the *Mars Climate Orbiter* which crashed onto the surface of Mars due to an error involving the translation of English units of rocket thrusts to the metric system.

Ontologies are explicit formal specifications of the terms of a domain and the relationships between them [7]. An ontology has the same relationship to a knowledgebase as a database schema to a relational database, or the class hierarchy to an object-oriented program. We note that:

- Database schemas, object–relationship diagrams describe the syntax of the data, but they are not concerned about its semantics. The format of the representation is the relational database model.
- Object hierarchies and Unified Modelling Language (UML) class diagrams describe the structure of the classes in an object-oriented language. Although data can be represented in class diagrams, the main focus of the class diagram is the active code (methods, functions, etc.,). The relationship of inheritance has a special significance in these hierarchies (which is not true for database systems).
- Ontologies describe the structure of the knowledge in a knowledgebase. Ontologies focus exclusively on knowledge (structured data) and are not concerned with programming constructs. In contrast to relational databases, the representational model of most ontology languages is based on variants of description logics of different expressivity.

Despite their different terminologies, there is a significant overlap between these fields and ideas, therefore their methodologies are frequently cross-pollinated. An important point of view is that any database schema and object hierarchy defines an ontology, even if these are not explicit in an ontology language such as DAML–OIL or OWL. An object-oriented program is its own interpretation; if the same programs would be running on the client and the server, there would be no need for explicit ontologies. The ontologies are needed to specify the common knowledge behind heterogeneous entities, and thus enable the operation of the computing grid.

Ontologies in the context of the grid.   The computational grid is a heterogeneous collection of resources. This heterogeneity is a source of many potential benefits, but it also creates problems in the communication between the different entities. For example, when submitting tasks to a scheduling or a planning service, it is important that the client and the server have a common understanding of terms such as host, memory, storage, or execution. There are large numbers of ontologies for various aspects of grid computing, developed by different research groups and commercial entities; these ontologies are largely incompatible with one another. The Grid Scheduling Ontology Working Group (GSO–WG) is developing a standard for scheduling on the grid, currently expected to be completed by late 2005. Even in the presence of a standard, we can expect that multiple ontologies remain in use for a long time. Ontologies for specific subdomains are developed continuously.

The role of the ontology service in a computational grid is to provide the necessary ontology resources for the service providers and clients of the computational grid. Thus, the ontology service:

- Provides a repository for high level standard ontologies such as the Dublin Core Ontology, vCard, vCalendar, Suggested Upper Merged Ontology (SUMO), etc.
- Allows the components of the grid to register their own custom ontologies and guarantees the unique naming of every ontology.
- Allows grid entities to download the custom ontologies.
- Provides services for translation, merging, and alignment of knowledge represented in different ontologies.

If a grid entity receives a piece of information (for example, a request) which cannot be interpreted in the context of existing ontologies, the entity will contact the ontology service for further information. In the best case, by simply downloading the required ontology, the server can interpret the message. For example, the server can learn that the class Task in ontology A is equivalent to the class `Job` in the ontology B, previously known to the server. This can be achieved using the `owl:equivalentClass` relation in the OWL ontology language.

The information can be translated from one ontology to the other, for instance, from the metric system into the English system. It is desirable that the translation be done by a centralized ontology service, instead of local translators which might give different interpretations to the various concepts. This scenario is illustrated in Fig. 3.2.

Finally, if the translation between ontologies is not possible, the request is rejected. The host can then indicate which are the ontologies that it could not interpret correctly and suggest potential ontologies in terms of which the request needs to be reformulated.

3.4.4 Security and Authentication Services

Grid environments pose security problems of unprecedented complexity for the users and the service providers. The users are transparently using services of remote computers, utilizing hardware and software resources over which they do not have immediate control. The data are uploaded to remote computers, over public links.

The service providers should allow foreign data and/or code to be uploaded to their computers. The code might require access to resources on the local computer (e.g., reading and writing files) and communicate with remote computers.

The fact that many grid applications take a long time, and autonomous agents need to act on behalf of the user prevents us from using many of the safest security technologies, such as biometry. The rights of the user need to be delegated to the services which act on his behalf, developing complex networks of trust relationships.

The security problems of the grid are not only complex, but they also involve relatively high stakes. The computers involved in the grid can be expensive supercomputers. The data processed on the grid is valuable and potentially confidential. The correct execution of the required

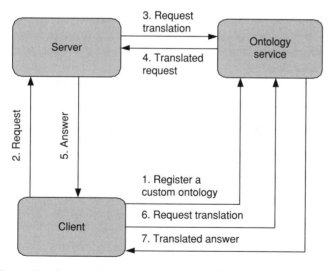

FIGURE 3.2. The interactions between the client, server, and ontology service in a scenario involving ontology translation.

computation can make or break the development of a new life-saving drug or the early warning of a terrorist action.

The participants in the grid environment have different interests, which might make them bend the rules of interaction to their favor. End users might want to have access to more computational power than they are entitled to. Service providers might want to fake the execution of a computation, execute it at a lower precision or claim failure. Service providers might want to overstate their resources in the hope of attracting more business. Malicious entities might perform a variety of actions to disturb the regular functioning of the grid, such as denial of service attacks against various services, or eavesdropping on the communication channels.

Authentication.   One of the assumptions behind every security approach to grid computing is the need of the users, hosts, and services to authenticate themselves to the Grid environment. One of the basic requirements of the authentication is that the entities have a grid-wide identity, which can be verified by the other grid entities. The local identities (for instance, Unix accounts) are not appropriate for this scope. In fact, it is possible and even likely that some user is identified with different accounts in different domains. Due to the heterogeneity of the grid architecture, different machines might use different authentication services.

The goal of the authentication process is to enable the two parties to establish a level of trust in the identity of the communication partner. Frequently, the authentication step also leads to the establishment of a secure communication channel (such as `ssh`, `https`, or `tls`) between the two entities, such that the authentication need not be repeated after the channel has been established. In some systems every message must be authenticated.

Authentication establishes only the identity of a user, not its rights, which is the subject of authorization and/or capabilities management. It is a good principle to separate the grid-wide authentication service from the authorization of the user to execute specific tasks, which is a mostly local decision of the service provider.

One of the additional problems is the requirement of unattended user authentication. In the classical, interactive authentication, the user enters an account name and a password manually. On the grid however, long running jobs might need to authenticate themselves to the remote machines. Storing the password of the user in the program in plaintext is not a safe option. The unattended authentication solutions are done through the use of *certificates*, either permanent, or temporary proxy certificates.

The established method for grid wide authentication is based on public-key cryptography, usually on the use of different variations of the X.509 public-key certificates. These certificates contain the public key of the user, a multicomponent distinguished name (DN) and an expiration date. This data is then rendered unenforgeable by the signing with the private key of a trusted third party, called a Certification Authority (CA). The use of the CA presents a number of practical problems such as:

- Who certifies the CA. The identity of the CA (or multiple CAs) should be part of the original setup of the grid. The private key of the CA should be very closely guarded. If compromised, the complete security of the grid can collapse, as the intruder can certify itself to have an arbitrary identity.
- How does the CA identify the individuals requiring certificates (the problem of "identity vetting"). The operator of the CA can not possibly know all the individuals requesting certificates, thus it will need to rely on trusted Registration Agents (RA), who will identify the users based on personal knowledge, biometrics, verification based on identity cards, and so on. For

example, the European UNICORE grid framework [5] uses videoconferencing for the initial authentication of the user. Despite these drawbacks, the use of certificates has a number of advantages.

Security considerations for typical grid scenarios.   A computational grid can provide a variety of services to the client, each of them with its own security challenges [9]. We consider here the most typical usage scenarios, where the users run large applications which utilize resources collected from multiple machines and have an execution time of the order of magnitude of hours or more.

To run applications on the grid, the client first creates a public-key and private-key pair. Then he authenticates himself to a *registration agent* (RA) through physical or remote means and presents his public key. The registration agent will then obtain from the `Certificate Authority` of the grid a certificate for the client. Because these certificates are usually issued for a timeframe of several months, the load on the `Certificate Authority` is very light. In some cases, the grid might have multiple `Certificate Authorities`, with cross-signed certificates [5].

Once the user has acquired a certificate, he can use it to authenticate himself when submitting jobs to the coordination service. The user and the authentication service authenticate each other based on their respective certificates, typically through a challenge–response session, which assumes that the entities possess the private keys associated with the public keys contained in the certificate.

If the user submits a relatively short job, the communication channel to the coordination service remains open. If the user needs to authenticate himself to remote services, he can do it online. The continuous maintenance of a secure connection is the key to this process.

However, every authentication session requires the user to use his private key, and the repetitive use of the private key represents a potential security threat. In order to minimize the use of the credentials, the client can generate a *proxy certificate* to represent the user in interactions with the grid. This second certificate is generated by the client, signed by the long-lived keypair, stating that for a certain amount of time (typically 12 h) the public key of the user is the public key of the short-lived pair.

A relatively similar situation happens when the user is running a long-lasting application in an unsupervised mode. The coordination service needs to start remote jobs or access files on behalf of the original user. The coordination service will receive a *delegated credential* [17] from the user. It is in general desirable, if the delegated credential is applicable only in certain well-specified circumstances and for a limited amount of time. This, however, presents a series of difficulties. First, the user does not know in advance which resources would be used to satisfy the request. The current lack of a unifying ontology, which would describe resources in the heterogeneous grid makes the specification difficult. Similar problems apply to the specification of the expiration time, which ideally should be just sufficient for the grid to terminate the task. If the specified expiration time is too optimistic, the certificate might expire before the job is completed; but if the expiration time is too long, it would constitute a security threat.

3.5   A Case Study: The BondGrid

Figure 3.1 summarizes the architecture of the system we are currently building. In the following Sections we describe the BondGrid agents, the ontologies used in BondGrid, the coordination service, the event service, the simulation service, and the monitoring and control center. We have not made sufficient progress in the implementation of other core services in BondGrid to warrant their presentation.

3.5.1 BondGrid Agents

Grid services are provided by BondGrid agents based on the Java Agent DEvelopment Framework (JADE) [24] and Protégé [6, 25], two free software packages distributed by Telecom Italy and Stanford Medical Institute, respectively. The inference engine is based on Jess [10] from Sandia National Laboratory and the persistent storage services on T Spaces [18].

Java Agent DEvelopment Framework (JADE) is a FIPA-compliant agent system fully implemented in Java and using FIPA–ACL as an agent communication language. The JADE agent platform can be distributed across machines which may not run under the same OS. Each agent has a unique identifier obtained by the concatenation (+) of several strings

$$AID \longleftarrow agentname + @ + IPaddress/domainname + portnumber + /JAD$$

Protégé is an open-source, Java based tool that provides an extensible architecture for the creation of customized knowledge-based applications. Protégé uses classes to define the structure of entities. Each class consists of a number of slots that describe the attributes of an entity. The cardinality of a slot can be customized. A class may have one or multiple instances. Protégé can support complex structure: a class may inherit from other classes; the content of a slot can refer to other instances.

BondGrid uses a multiplane state machine agent model similar to the Bond agent system [2]. Each plane represents an individual running thread and consists of a finite state machine. Each state of one of the finite state machines is associated with a strategy that defines a behavior. The agent structure is described with a Python-based agent description language (called blueprint). A BondGrid agent is able to recognize a blueprint, create planes and finite state machines accordingly, and control the execution of planes automatically. For example, the blueprint for a coordination service is

```
openKnowledgeBase("bondgrid/kb/BondGrid.pprj","CS")
addPlane("Service Manager")
  s = bondgrid.cs.ServiceManagerStrategy(agent)
addState(s,"Service Manager");
addPlane("Message Handler")
  s = bondgrid.cs.MessageHandlerStrategy(agent)
addState(s,"Message Handler");
addPlane("Coordination Engine")
  s = bondgrid.cs.CoordinationEngineStrategy(agent)
addState(s,"Coordination Engine");
```

Knowledge bases are shared by multiple planes of an agent. The BondGrid agents provide a standard API to support concurrent access to the knowledge bases. Messages are constructed using ACL. A message has several fields: sender, receivers, keyword, and message content. The keyword enables the receiver of a message to understand the intention of the sender. A message may have one or more user-defined parameter with the specified key. To exchange an instance or the structure of a class we use XML-formatted messages to describe the instance or the structure.

3.5.2   BondGrid Ontologies

Ontologies are the cornerstone of interoperability, they represent the "glue" that allows different applications to use various grid resources. Recall that the term *ontology* means the study of what exists or what can be known; an ontology is a catalog of and reveals the relationships among a set of concepts assumed to exist in a well-defined area. For example, a resource ontology may consist of several types: software, hardware, services, data, and possibly other resources. Hardware resources may consist of computational and networking resources; computational resources consist of processors, primary, secondary, and tertiary storage, network interfaces, graphics facilities, and so on. In turn, the processor will reveal the architecture, the speed of the integer unit, the speed of the floating point unit, the type of bus, and so on.

The task of creating ontologies in the context of grid computing is monumental. Figure 3.3 shows the logic view of the main ontologies used in BondGrid and their relations [22]. A nonexhaustive list of classes in this ontology includes: Task, Process Description, Case Description, Activity, Data, Service, Resource, Hardware, and Software. Task is the description of a computation problem that a user wants to solve. It contains a process description and a case description. The instances of all classes in the knowledge base may be exchanged in XML format.

Activity is the basic element for the coordination of task and can be characterized by:

(i)   Name – a string of characters uniquely identifying the activity.
(ii) Description – a natural language description of the activity.
(iii) Actions – an action is a modification of the environment caused by the execution of the activity.
(iv) Preconditions – boolean expressions that must be true before the action(s) of the activity can take place.
(v)   Postconditions – boolean expressions that must be true after the action(s) of the activity do take place.
(vi) Attributes – provide indications of the type and quantity of resources necessary for the execution of the activity, the actors in charge of the activity, the security requirements, whether the activity is reversible or not, and other characteristics of the activity.
(vii) Exceptions – provide information on how to handle abnormal events. The exceptions supported by an activity consist of a list of pairs: (event, action). The exceptions included in the activity exception list are called *anticipated exceptions*, as opposed to unanticipated exceptions. In our model, events not included in the exception list trigger replanning. *Replanning* means restructuring of a process description, redefinition of the relationship among various activities.

We can use XML to describe instances for exchange. Below is an informal description of instances in XML format. Each instance has a unique ID in order to be referred.

```
<?xml version="1.0" encoding="UTF-8"?>

<project project-name="projectname">
  <instances>
    <instance class-name="classname" ID="id">
      <slot slot-name="slotname">
        <value>
          a value or Instance(an ID)
```

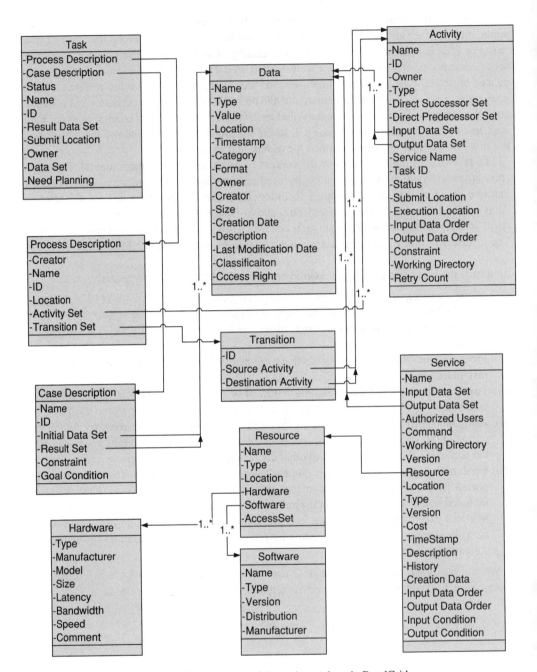

FIGURE 3.3. Logic view of the main ontology in BondGrid.

(ii) **Subscription/Unsubscription.** The consumer of an event subscribes/unsubscribes to an event handled by the Event Service. Each subscription is time-limited.

(iii) **Notification.** The Event Service notifies all the subscribers of an event when the event occurs. A special form of notification occurs when the subscription interval expires.

An event service connects the producer of an event with its consumers. Every core service in BondGrid may be a producer, or a consumer, or both. In the role of *Producer*, a core service registers itself to a set of event services and publishes them as it starts up. In the role of *Consumer*, a core service subscribes events to its producers through event services whenever necessary. When the event service receives an event notification from a producer, it will scan *EST* and send an event notification to all consumers that have subscribed to this event. Table 3.2. shows a nonexhaustive list of defined events in BondGrid. Figure 3.4 illustrates the communication among the producers, the consumers of events, and the Event Service.

Table 3.3. describes the format of all messages exchanged among producers of events, consumers of events, and the Event Service in BondGrid.

3.5.5 *BondGrid Simulation Service*

The simulation service in the authors' system is based on an augmented NS2 [19] with a JADE [24] agent as its front end. The NS2 is a popular network simulation environment developed by the VINT project, a collaboration among USC/ISI, Xerox PARC, LBNL, and UC Berkeley. The NS2 is an object-oriented, event-driven, scalable network simulation framework; it allows simulation of the OSI layers, of network protocols, and of multicast protocols over wireless and wired

TABLE 3.2. A nonexhaustive list of events in BondGrid. Shown are the following services: Coordination Service (CS), Information Service (IS), Planning Service (PS), Application Container (AC), and User Interface (UI).

Producer	Cause	Type
	TaskExecFailure	Imperative, ComputationError, Once, Atomic
	ActivityExecFailure	Imperative, ComputationError, Once, Atomic
	PlanExecFailure	Imperative, ComputationError, Once, Atomic
CS	InvalidPD	Imperative, InputError, Once, Atomic
	InvalidCD	Imperative, InputError, Once, Atomic
	TaskResultNotReady	Informative, N/A, Once, Atomic
	TaskResultReady	Informative, N/A, Once, Atomic
	Status	Informative, N/A, Time, Atomic
IS	ServiceNotFound	Informative, N/A, Once, Atomic
	Status	Informative, N/A, Time, Atomic
	InvalidPD	Imperative, InputError, Once, Atomic
	InvalidCD	Imperative, InputError, Once, Atomic
PS	PlanReady	Informative, N/A, Once, Atomic
	PlanNotFound	Informative, ComputationError, Once, Atomic
	Status	Informative, N/A, Time, Atomic
	DataNotReady	Imperative, InputError, Once, Atomic
	DataReady	Informative, N/A, Once, Atomic
AC	ServiceNotAvailable	Informative, CommunicationError, Once, Atomic
	ServiceReady	Informative, N/A, Once, Atomic
	ServiceExecFailure	Imperative, ComputationError, Once, Atomic
	Status	Informative, N/A, Time, Atomic
UI	Leave	Informative, N/A, Once, Atomic
	Return	Informative, N/A, Once, Atomic

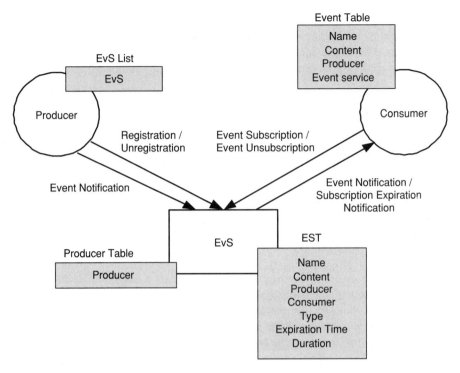

FIGURE 3.4. Communication model among producers of events, consumers of events, and the Event Service.

TABLE 3.3. The format of all messages exchanged among producers of events, consumers of events, and the Event Service in BondGrid.

Keyword	Contents
Register to Event Service	producer AID + authentication information
Unregister from Event Service	producer AID
Event Subscription	name + content + producer AID + duration
Event Unsubscription	name + content + producer AID + priority
Expired Subscription Notification	name + content + producer AID
Event Notification From Producer	name + content + type + priority
Event Notification From EvS	name + content + producer AID + type + priority

networks. The output generated by NS2 can be visualized using the Network Animator (NAM).

The NS2 offers significant advantages over other simulation systems. For example, OPNET Modeler, is a commercial product designed to diagnose and reconfigure communication systems. The source code of OPNET Modeler is not in the public domain, thus one cannot augment the functionality of the simulation package and adapt it to grid simulation.

It is necessary to augment the NS2 simulator to adapt to the specific requirements, e.g., develop application layer protocols that NS2 does not support yet. We have extended the simulation kernel, the application-level data unit (ADU) type, application agents, and other components. The NS2 objects were extended to comply with the complex structure of the objects in a computational grid environment. For instance, an NS2 node was extended to contain resource information, an important feature required by a matchmaking service in order to make optimal decisions.

To transmit our own application-level data over grid nodes, we import an ADU that defines our own data members. In the simulation kernel, the *GridPacket* class of the simulation kernel is extended from the standard NS2 ADU and its instances are transmitted among grid nodes exchanging messages. Every message in the BondGrid corresponds to a GridPacket in the simulation kernel. Every node has one or more *application agents* to handle application-level data. Our extended application agent class GridAgent provides the common attributes and helper functions.

The simulation service uses existing information regarding the network topology, and has access to cumulative history data, and to the current state of other related core services.

3.5.6   *BondGrid Monitoring and Control Center*

A monitoring and control center is used to startup, terminate, and monitor core services provided by different machines in a domain.

A JADE agent platform contains one or more *agent containers* and one of them is the *main agent container*. When a JADE platform is created on a machine, the *main agent container* is built on that machine. Local agent containers can be built on machines that are different from the machine hosting the main container. In this case, the IP address and port number of the machine hosting the main container should be referred to as the address of the main container. An agent can be created in any agent container. Agents in the same agent platform can communicate with each other.

The machine hosting the monitoring and control center starts up the monitoring and control center through its startup script. This machine hosts the main container and should start up before other machines that provide core services. The system startup scripts of other machines include the creation of a local agent container. The IP address and the port number of the monitoring and control center is specified as the address of the main container. So the system hosting the monitoring and control center and the one providing core services belong to the same agent platform. The monitoring and control center maintains a list of agent containers. It provides a GUI to start, terminate, and monitor certain agent(s) providing core service within agent containers.

3.6   Applications to Computational Biology

The 3-D atomic structure determination of macromolecules based upon electron microscopy [14] is an important application of biology computation. The procedure for structure determination consists of the following steps.

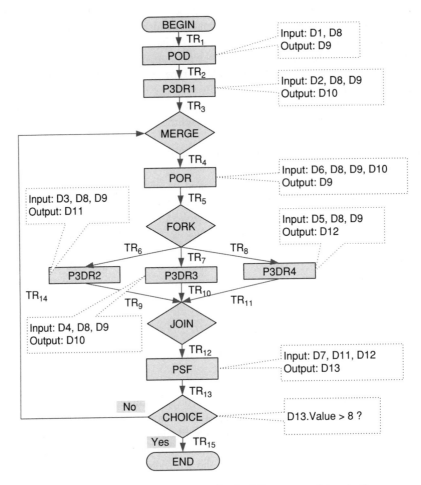

FIGURE 3.5. A process description for the 3-D structure determination.

1. Extract individual particle projections from micrographs and identify the center of each projection.
2. Determine the orientation of each projection.
3. Carry out the 3-D reconstruction of the electron density of the macromolecule.
4. Dock an atomic model into the 3-D density map.

Steps 2 and 3 are executed iteratively until the 3-D electron density map cannot be further improved at a given resolution; then, the resolution is increased gradually. The number of iterations for these steps is in the range of hundreds and one cycle of iteration for a medium size virus

Chapter 4

A Grid Software Process

4.1 Introduction

The term *metacomputing* [1] refers to computation on a virtual supercomputer assembled connecting together different resources like parallel supercomputers, data archives, storage systems, advanced visualization devices, and scientific instruments using high-speed networks that link together these geographically distributed resources. We may want to do so because it enables new classes of applications [2–4] previously impossible and because it is a cost-effective approach to high-performance computing. Recently, metacomputing evolved towards a more general paradigm, *grid computing* [5]. This new field is distinguished from traditional distributed computing and metacomputing because of its focus on large-scale resource sharing. Moreover, the grid infrastructure ties together a number of Virtual Organizations (VOs) [6], that reflect dynamic collections of individuals, institutions, and computational resources. This new paradigm still focuses on traditional high performance scientific applications, however it takes into account innovative classes of applications, that can be classified as follows:

- desktop supercomputing;
- smart instruments;
- collaborative environments;
- distributed supercomputing;
- high throughput.

Desktop supercomputing includes applications that couple high-end graphics capabilities with remote supercomputers and/or databases; smart instruments include scientific instruments like microscopes, telescopes, and satellites that require supercomputing power to process the data produced in near real time. In the class of collaborative environments, we find applications in which users at different locations can interact together working on a supercomputer simulation; distributed supercomputing is the class of application that require multiple supercomputers to solve problems otherwise too large, or whose execution is divided on different components that can benefit from execution on different architectures. Finally, high-throughput applications require an increased completion rate for a stream of jobs and thus are usually exploited for parameter sweep studies.

It is worth recalling here that any of the preceding class of applications may also have the need to access, move, manage, and store data available in distributed wide area network data repositories. The infrastructure to transparently handle storage management and data access is usually called *data grid*.

The grid community focus is now shifted from protocols [6] to Grid Services [7], as envisioned by the Open Grid Services Architecture (OGSA) [8]. Grid Services extend the Web Services framework, and the grid itself becomes an extensible set of Grid Services that may be aggregated to provide new capabilities. However, a Grid Service is "a (potentially transient) stateful service instance supporting reliable and secure invocation (when required), lifetime management, notification, policy management, credential management, and virtualization" [7]. So, Grid Services leverage both WSDL and SOAP but add additional interfaces able to manage service lifetime, policies and credentials, and to provide support for notification that are mandated by the OGSA specification.

However the challenges to be faced before grid computing can be really exploited; they include the following issues:

- scaling and selection;
- heterogeneity;
- unpredictable structure;
- dynamic behavior;
- multiple administrative domains.

Scaling is a concern, because we expect that grid computing environments in the future will become larger, and resources will be selected and acquired on the basis of criteria like connectivity, cost, security, and reliability. Such resources will show different levels of heterogeneity, ranging from physical devices to system software and schedulers policies; moreover traditional high-performance applications are developed for a single supercomputer whose features are known a priori, e.g., the latency, in contrast grid computing applications will run in a wide range of environments thus making impossible to predict the structure of the computation.

Another concern is related to the dynamic behavior of the computation [9], since we cannot be assured that all of the system characteristics stay the same during the course of computation, e.g., the network bandwidth and latency can widely change, and there is the possibility of both network and resources failure. Finally, since the computation will usually span resources at multiple administrative domains, there is not a single authority in charge of the system, so that different scheduling policies and authorization mechanisms must be taken into account.

Grid computing environments are now emerging, bringing the power of High Performance Computing facilities transparently to the user's desktop. Indeed, High Performance Computing is becoming ubiquitous in science, engineering, commerce, medicine, etc., while applications are increasingly complex and multidisciplinary. In order to develop grid-aware applications harnessing computational and data grids, software engineering principles and practices for building distributed software must be adapted to cope with the challenges coming from grids: since grids may be potentially large, dispersed, and usually heterogeneous, designing a grid application can prove to be a difficult task. Traditional distributed applications run in a relatively stable, well-defined, and often dedicated environment, while grid-enabled applications run in a dynamic, sometimes loosely defined, and heavily networked environment.

We show how an agile software life–cycle based on Extreme Programming, properly modified to take into account the intrinsic nature of grid software, and complemented by continuous, dedicated training sessions together with the abstractions and grid design patterns described in later sections, is effective for building industrial quality grid software. Indeed, the abstractions and grid design patterns proposed are actually used within our grid software life–cycle model in the context of designing grid applications, since these provide useful architectural insights; continuous training is also mandatory, since grid applications are built on top of middleware and technologies that undergo many changes due to the rapid evolution in the field.

The chapter is organized as follows. We define our grid software process in Section 4.2, and describe relevant abstractions and grid design patterns that can help software development in Sections 3 and 4 respectively. A number of issues that can arise are analyzed in Section 5. Finally, we conclude the chapter in Section 6.

4.2   Grid Software Process

In this section, we address the problem of choosing a software life–cycle model to develop grid computing applications. The Grid Software Process we present here has been fully evaluated in the context of both small-to-medium-sized academic research and commercial projects. It is worth noting here, before we begin, that to date (July 2004) just two commercial grid applications have been developed (to the best of our knowledge):

* gridMATHEMATICA (Wolfram Research, Inc.); this package extends the well known Mathematica software by allowing the users to transparently take advantage of remote Mathematica kernels installed on grid nodes to perform parallel computations. Mathematica allows complex calculations to be carried out on single-processor machines, while gridMathematica can tackle much larger computations using clusters, multiprocessor machines, and computing grids; it provides a quick way to set up and run large calculations by offering a high-level programming language, a vast collection of fast and reliable mathematical algorithms, and easy-to-use parallel programming constructs.
* Oracle Application server 10g (Oracle Corporation); this latest release of the renowed relational DBMS includes for the first time initial support for database applications running in a grid environment. A single database can run across multiple clustered nodes in a grid and can immediately begin balancing workload across a new node as it gets reprovisioned from one database to another; it can also relinquish a machine no longer needed, thus providing capacity on demand. Multiple databases running on the same cluster automatically load balance based on user's defined policies, and nodes can be added or dropped while the application is running.

Likewise, just a few commercial grid middleware solutions are available:

* Xgrid (Apple Computer, Inc.); this software allows users to exploit an homogeneous, Apple based, computational grid to perform high-throughput computing and/or parallel computations developed using the Message Passing Interface (MPI). Xgrid uses the zero configuration technology Rendezvous to discover available resources to set up a cluster. An easy-to-use System Preference panel allows controlling how a machine gets used by the network, and also tells the cluster which computer can send problems to the group for number crunching. The software can work either in screensaver mode or setting up a dedicated cluster;
* XLR8 (GridIron Software); it is an application development tool to modify code for parallel processing on multiple CPUs. Unlike complex and time-consuming libraries such as MPI, PVM, and shared memory architectures, XLR8 accelerates and simplifies the task of code parallelization, includes a complete runtime infrastructure, and is backed by support, developer training, and ongoing development.
* Avaki Data Grid (Avaki); this software is a complete commercial solution for managing computational/data grids. It is both object and component oriented; and it is worth noting that this

product is the commercial evolution of an academic research project called Legion, developed at the University of Virginia.

- TurboWorx Enterprise (TurboWorx, Inc.); TurboWorx Enterprise is a complete solution to create, manage, and accelerate high performance computing applications and workflows in large, heterogeneous networks, grids, and compute farms. TurboWorx Enterprise, powered by TurboWorx SmartGrid, creates a distributed computing platform, simplifies and eases the creation and execution of large, complex workflows through linked reusable components. The software supports true parallelization for any application or workflow that can be distributed for accelerated throughput. A web portal is also provided for sharing components and data, executing workflows, and monitoring the results.

Thus, professional development of grid software is still in its infancy, and far from mature. This also clearly explains why the grid computing paradigm has not yet seen widespread adoption, even though many valuable academic projects have been started since 1998. However, in this chapter we will focus on industrial development, so that current academic efforts are out of the scope of this work. As always, there is no *silver bullet* [10] for building grid software; even the reuse of objects [11], while valuable, in our opinion is not the desired silver bullet. More than 10 years ago, in [12] the author expressed the view that, as a direct consequence of emerging new technologies, the future will be much brighter with respect to the issue of software complexity. Instead, we firmly believe that new trends and technologies concur to exacerbate the problem of dominating software complexity; grid applications will be a driving factor for new software engineering approaches, since the current trend is towards flexible, evolvable, and decentralized software development processes.

Indeed, software engineering methods evolved from the initial *code and fix* approach that was deemed responsible for the lack of software quality to more disciplined processes built around a fully centralized system architecture. The waterfall lifecycle [13] was the first major evolutionary step. However, it was not able to cope with changing requirements. This led to several *incremental* approaches, including the spiral model [14], rapid prototyping processes [15] [16], the incremental model [17] [18], the synchronize and stabilize model [19] [20], extreme programming (XP) [21] [22], Rational Unified Process (RUP) [23] and object-oriented lifecycle models [24]. The reduction of hardware costs and the consequent high availability of cheap computing resources made possible a major architectural shift, namely the transition from fully centralized systems to distributed multitier architectures, including client-server, peer-to-peer, and service-oriented models. Another reason was the need to integrate legacy applications into the distributed component architecture. Here we faced the evolution of distributed middleware from RPC to CORBA, Java RMI, the Globus Toolkit, Condor and its grid enabled version Condor-G, MPICH-G2, GridRPC, mobile agents, and Web services.

The grid will exacerbate this trend with its need for increased dynamism, decentralization, and decoupling. Even the underlying network infrastructure is now evolving from wired to wireless and future scenarios are certainly based on mobile, nomadic computing [25]. In order to dominate the additional complexity an agile software process is required. Recently a number of agile methodologies have been developed, including SCRUM [26–28], ASD [29], Crystal methodologies [30], DSDM [31] and XP.

Our Grid Software Process derives from XP, however it has been devised in such a way to meet our needs. The XP' focus is on development practices, however we also need, even though minimal, project management. It is true that developers and testers do not like documentation, metrics, and formality. The switch to XP however does not mean that these individuals are aban-

- *Service Migration pattern*; it enables a service to be moved to another computational platform more suitable for its execution; migration may be necessary due to hardware constraints, to support load balancing, or simply to offer a better cost or performance.

The authors of [34] aim to identify an infrastructure that is purely based on the aggregation, decomposition, discovery, and execution of suitable services. They extend the standard component model with specialised components which have time-varying behavior, and which can interact with each other using a standard communication language. Each such component is called an agent, where an agent mediates access to one or more services. The design pattern provided cover a set of fundamental services in a grid environment, since the key assumption of this work is that grid applications will necessarily involve a number of common services.

In this chapter, we show a set of design patterns to complement them. In particular our design patterns focus on authorization mechanisms, data management, and executable handling, since the majority of current grid applications need these services too.

In the next subsections we will describe the following design patterns:

1. Authorization Service;
2. Grid Executable Catalog;
3. Grid Store;
4. Replica Location Service;
5. Grid Credential Repository.

4.4.1 Authorization Service Pattern

Intent   The pattern aims to support the extension of the user's authorization mechanism to a community, considered as a whole (Virtual Organization).

Motivation   The sharing and coordinated use of resources within large, dynamic, multiinstitutional communities is fundamental to an increasing range of computer applications, ranging from scientific collaboratories to healthcare. This sharing may involve not only file exchange but also direct access to computers, software, data, and other resources. This sharing must be, necessarily, highly controlled, with resource providers and consumers defining clearly and carefully just what is shared, who is allowed to share, and the conditions under which sharing occurs.

A key problem associated with the formation and operation of distributed virtual communities is how to specify and enforce community policies. Let us consider, as an example, the situation in which a multi institutional project has received an allocation of time on a shared computational resource. With current technologies, when personnel at participating institutions changes, the project leader is required to contact the resource owner to create an account and allocation for each new team member. Furthermore, as project policies change, the project leader will have to go back to the resource provider to adjust allocations, rights, and priorities for the team members so that these are consistent with the current focus of the collaboration. This interaction places undue burdens on resource providers, who are, indeed, forced to implement the policy decisions of the consortium. Conversely, these interactions also place significant overhead on the administration of the consortium, as every policy alteration can require interactions with every resource provider with which the project has established a relationship.

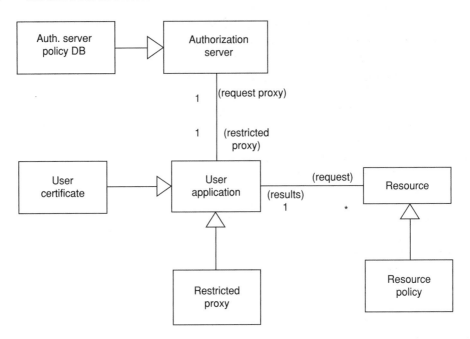

FIGURE 4.1. The structure of the Authorization Service design pattern.

Applicability   Implementations of authorization and authentication of users on the grid have focused exclusively on two levels of rights granularity. These two levels of rights granularity are at the extremes, i.e., rights granted to the individual and rights granted to a community of users as a whole. Authentication typically involves verifying an individual's identity and her/his membership in a Virtual Organization (VO) [35].

These mechanism can be adequate for relatively small VOs that comprise few user communities. But for large VOs comprising up to 2000 individuals, an intermediate granularity of access control is required. The users belonging to a huge VO can be grouped into several user's community in order to define a single access policy for each community and not for each user. On the other hand, this pattern is useful in those cases where a single organization provides its resources to multiple projects. In these cases, the resources will be shared among different project leader and project members, and a mechanism that control the resource accesses and users rights for different group of users (each group belonging to different project) must be adopted. To resume, the pattern can be applied in these cases:

- for a huge Virtual Organization with the need to define subgroups of members and assign them the same access policy;
- for an organization involved in several projects that shares its resources with different organizations belonging to several projects

Structure and Participants   The participants involved in the pattern are (see Fig. 4.1):

User's Certificate: The certificate that identifies the user. This certificate is used to contact the authorization server;

Group's Restricted Proxy: This is the proxy which the user obtains from the authorization service. The restricted proxy contains a policy statement limiting what that proxy can be used for. Relying parties will authorize requests only if the request will have been granted for the proxy issuer, and the request is consistent with the policy embedded in the certificate, and any additional local policy requirements are met;

User Application: The user utilizes her certificate to contact the authorization server; once she gets the proxy certificate for the group with the policy restrictions, she can contact the resource;

Resource: upon receiving a request from the user, the resource will check both the local access policy related to the group and the policy statement included in the restricted proxy provided by the user;

Auth Server Policy DB: it contains all of the rights that must be granted for each member belonging to a given group;

Resource Local Policy: it contains the permission statement for each authorized user; here, a group of users is considered as a whole.

Collaboration   The sequence diagram depicted in Fig. 4.2 shows the interaction between a user, which intend to access a grid resource, and the authorization mechanism, applied to groups of users and not to a single user. Let us consider a user belonging to an organization and more in detail suppose that this user belongs to a subgroup of users, all of which are granted access on the basis of the same access policy. Before accessing a resource, the user must contact the authorization server in order to obtain a proxy certificate. The proxy she will obtain, is a restricted proxy certificate that has the distinguished name of the user's group and contains the policy restrictions defined by the organization for the user. She can then access the grid resource through the obtained proxy. From the resource point of view, the user is identified as a group and the resource checks the authorization related to the group. The user is thus restricted by the policy imposed by the group administrator and also by the access policy defined by the resource administrator for the group.

An organization runs the authorization server to keep track of its membership and fine-grained access control policies. A user wishing to access resources contacts the authorization server, which delegates rights to the user based on the request and the user's role within the organization. These rights are in the form of capabilities, which users can present at a resource to gain access on behalf of the organization. The user effectively gets the intersection of the set of rights granted to the group of users by the resource provider and the set of rights defined by the capabilities granted to the user by the organization.

Consequences   The design pattern helps resource providers to manage a whole group of users in such a way that only a single access policy, common for all of the users belonging to the group, have to be defined, leaving the control for a fine-grained access policy to the group administrator that can, if desired, define different policies for each user belonging to the group.

4.4.2 Grid Executable Catalog Pattern

Intent   The pattern aims to handle the portability of an application that must run in a heterogeneous environment. The portability is realized trough a set of different executable files compiled for all of the computer platforms belonging to the grid environment.

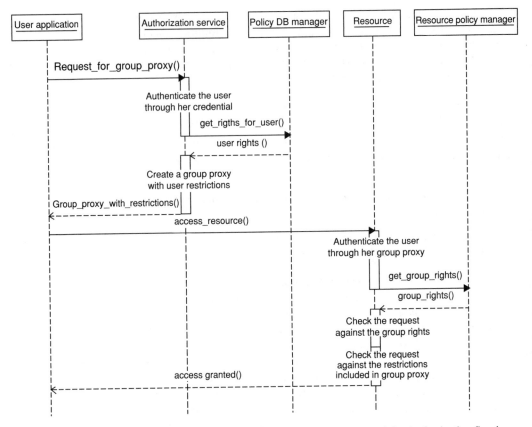

FIGURE 4.2. A sequence diagram showing the interaction between the user and the Authorization Service in order to obtain a user group proxy and access a resource.

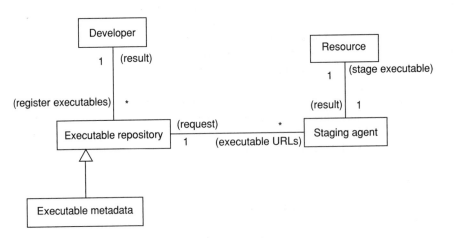

FIGURE 4.3. The structure of the Grid Executable Catalog design pattern.

Motivation   One of the main problem we have to solve when we discuss resource management is the staging of the application executable file from a computational resource, where, for
example, the application has been developed, to all other computational resources involved in
the computation. Staging of the executable file can be an issue when the grid environment spans
heterogeneous resources.

The pattern we propose uses an executable repository that stores the executable files needed
for all of the available platforms. In this scenario, the application developer will cross-compile
and build the application for different platforms and prestage the executable into the repository.
Upon application execution, the appropriate executable file will be selected from the repository
and staged to a remote machine for execution.

Applicability   This pattern should be applied in several cases:

- Job execution: The user starts a grid application delegating a resource broker the choice for
the best resource matching her criteria. In this case the user does not know in advance which
computational resource will be selected, and the selected resource can be an arbitrary computational platform;
- Parameter sweep execution: In a parameter sweep execution, the same application must be
executed many times, each time running with a different set of input data (as an instance, let
us consider a typical simulation for high energy physic). The execution can take advantage of
a grid environment if all of the independent job executions can be automatically submitted to
the available, heterogeneous grid resources;
- Job migration: Let us suppose we have a job running on a given computational resource and
for some reason, the performance decreases. If this happens, it could be better to suspend the
job execution on that resource by checkpointing the application, to ask a broker service to find
on behalf of the user a new resource and migrate the application to the new resource. In order
to migrate an application, the input data files and the executable file must be staged to the new
platform.

Structure and Participants

Executable repository: represents the repository where the executable files are kept (see Fig. 4.3).
Each file is associated with a set of metadata. For each executable we must define a logical name
and the type of platform it can run on;

Staging agent: is the entity responsible for automatic staging the executables. Before staging
an executable, it must select the appropriate executable file from the repository by querying the
available metadata;

Developer: the developer is in charge of populating the repository with all of the required versions of the executable.

Collaboration: the sequence diagram depicted in Fig. 4.4 illustrates the interaction between a
Staging Agent that must stage an executable file to a given platform. The application developer
upon releasing an application targeting several platforms, will put the application executable files
into the repository. For each one, an application logical name and an appropriate description of
the target platform will be provided. On the basis of the application logical name and platform
metadata descriptions, the Staging Agent contacts the executable repository to retrieve the correct
executable file and stages it to the selected computational resource.

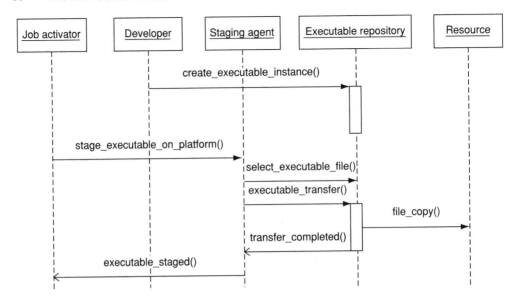

FIGURE 4.4. A sequence diagram showing the interaction between the Staging Agent and the Executable Repository in order to stage an executable file to a given platform.

Consequences: the pattern makes it possible to run applications in heterogeneous grid computing environment transparently. By masking out to the user the presence of different platforms, a service can start remote execution taking automatically into account the platforms. This frees the user from the burden of manually staging executable files before submitting for execution her job. Thus, the pattern promotes a fully automated exploitation of computational resources for job submission.

4.4.3   Grid Store Pattern

Intent   The pattern aims to provide common solutions to typical storage needs of scientific and commercial grid applications

Motivation   The unprecedented growth of the network infrastructure underlying grid computing environments foster the design of an ubiquitous, secure, efficient, and scalable grid file system. The centralized approach adopted by many distributed file system such as NFS and AFS, while allowing a simplified management of distributed applications can not scale as needed with the increasing size of current and future networks.

Applicability   This pattern should be applied in several cases:

- scientific applications that require storing information for high availability and fault tolerance. Many applications synthetize new information from scientific archives such as digital libraries; often, these applications produce a huge quantity of output data that must be stored for later retrieval and further analysis.

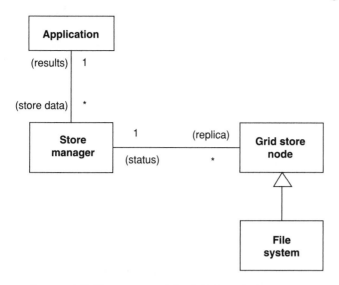

FIGURE 4.5. The structure of the Grid Store design pattern.

- commercial applications that require secure storing of sensitive information (e.g., business transactions).

Structure and Participants

Application: any kind of application with the need to store long-term data with security and/or high availability requirements (see Fig. 4.5);

Storage Manager: an agent, acting on behalf of the application, that coordinates with several Grid Storage Nodes in order to store the data produced by the application

Grid Storage Nodes: one or more distributed servers, cooperating to provide data storage fulfilling the client requirements.

Collaboration   The sequence diagram depicted in Fig. 4.6 illustrates the interaction between an application, a Storage Manager, and some Grid Storage Nodes. Once the application needs to store its output data, it contacts an available Storage Manager delegating its rights and supplying storage requirements. The delegated credentials allows the Storage manager to act on behalf of the client application; it can then parse the supplied storage requirements and proceed to actually storing data to remote servers as follows.

If the client requires high availability and fault tolerance, data are stored on a collection of storage nodes using a replication schema [36] [37], increasing performance by exploiting data locality and keeping access costs low. If data confidentiality is required, the data is encrypted before being stored on each server. If the application requires even tighter security, data are not replicated in encrypted form but transformed according to a secret sharing scheme [38] [39], in pieces called fragments that will be distributed to the available servers.

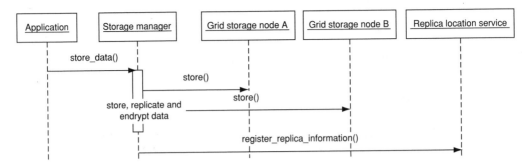

FIGURE 4.6. A sequence diagram showing the interaction between an application, a Storage Manager, and some Grid Storage Nodes.

Once the data has been stored, when a replication scheme has been used, immediately arises the need for an efficient retrieval system in charge of locating replicas of a given file. The Storage Manager thus contacts a Replica Location Server, which will be described in detail in the next design pattern we propose, and registers all of the replicas just handled.

Consequences   The pattern allows grid applications to take advantage of a fully decentralized approach for storing data, which in turn implies a better usage of distributed storage nodes on the grid with respect to fault tolerance, high availability, and security requirements.

4.4.4   Replica Location Service Pattern

Intent   The pattern aims to handle multiple copies of distributed data to improve scalability, reduce access latency, and increase fault tolerance.

Motivation   In wide-area computing systems, it is often desirable to create remote read-only copies (replicas) of data elements (files). Let us consider distributed simulations that produce a huge quantity of data that must be shared among several user community involved or interested in the simulation. Replication can be used to reduce access latency, improve data locality, and increase robustness, scalability, and performance for distributed applications. A system that includes replicas requires a mechanism for locating them.

The design pattern we propose tries to solve the following replica location problem: given a unique logical identifier for desired content, determine the physical locations of one or more copies of this content. A replica location service can be defined as a system that maintains and provides access to information about the physical locations of copies. A Replica Location Service is a distributed registry service that records the locations of data copies and allows discovery of replicas by maintaining mappings between logical identifiers and physical name of the file(s). Mappings can be both one-to-one or one-to-many. In the former case the logical identifier refers to a unique physical file, in the latter it refers to a *collection* of files.

Some assumptions can be done on the replica service pattern: it is possible to assume that files change only infrequently and can be uniquely identified as distinct versions. While these assumptions do not apply universally, they characterize a large class of data-intensive applications. For example, in many scientific collaborations, data are prepared, annotated, and then

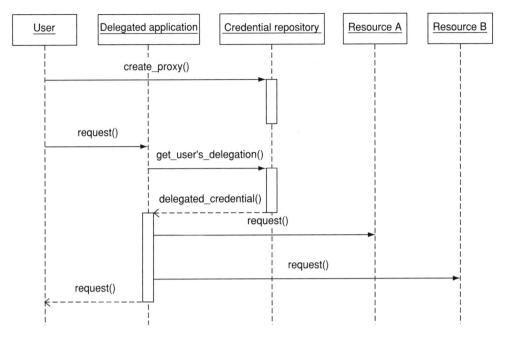

FIGURE 4.11. Interaction between the user, Credential Repository, and a delegated application.

4.5   Issues

A number of risks must be taken into account when undertaking a Grid project. In particular, we need to deal with the following issues:

Grid computing is intrinsically complex. Grids add complexity to traditional distributed computing; the software must be sophisticated enough to manage transparently potentially hundreds or thousands of Grid resources, coordinate job activities, concurrent program execution, the lack of a global clock, and the possibility of computer resources failing independently of each other.

Security. Authentication and authorization are difficult in Grid environments, since we must face the need to support multi institutional, multiple domains Virtual Organizations.

Scheduling. Scheduling must take into account a number of additional parameters, making the process even worse.

Software licenses. When using commercial software on Grid environments, classical licensing schemas *per cpu* are no longer adequate.

Accounting. The Grid and Virtual Organizations make difficult to devise a reliable accounting scheme, since users can belong to multiple VOs at the same time.

Customers. The Grid implies a cultural and social shift. It is difficult for customers to switch to the new computing paradigm.

Developers. Finding developers with previous experience in Grid computing project is difficult. Training them requires time and resources.

Controlled sharing. Customers, in particular industries, are usually against resource sharing; they are totally against sharing of their data.

Evolution of technologies. Technologies evolve fast, and this is true especially for grid computing technologies and middleware. Keeping the pace can be difficult.

Many of these issues are usually solved ad hoc, on a per project basis. We are still in a pioneering, exploratory phase, and consensus about solutions to the problems raised here and others is slowly building. In particular, the Global Grid Forum (GGF) has been established by the Grid community (both industry and academia) and leads the global standardization effort for Grid computing.

4.6   Conclusions

In this chapter, we have addressed the problem of professional Grid software development and presented an agile Grid Software Process based on Extreme Programming. The software life-cycle model has been fully evaluated in the context of both small to medium-sized academic research and commercial projects. We have discussed the XP practices we follow, the ones we have slightly adapted and why, and also the practices we do not recommend. We have also discussed the abstractions and the design patterns on which our Grid software is based.

Finally, we have highlighted a number of risky areas that must be taken into account when developing grid applications and discussed possible solutions. Grid computing is a major new paradigm, and we expect a whole set of theories, middleware, tools, etc., to be developed in the near future. At the same time we will monitor and adjust as needed for our Grid Software Process to make it resilient to the unavoidable changes dictated by the Grid.

References

[1] C. Catlett, L. Smarr, Metacomputing, *Communications of the ACM*, 35, 44–52 (1992)

[2] W. Benger, I. Foster, J. Novotny, E. Seidel, J. Shalf, W. Smith, P. Walker, *Numerical relativity in a distributed environment*, in Ninth SIAM Conference on Parallel Processing for Scientific Computing (1999)

[3] G. Von Laszewski, M. Su, J.A. Insley, I. Foster, J. Bresnahan, C. Kesselman, M. Thiebaux, M.L. Rivers, S. Wang, B. Tieman, I. McNulty, Real-time analysis, visualization, and steering of microtomography experiments at photon sources, in Ninth SIAM Conference on Parallel Processing for Scientific Computing (1999)

[4] S. Brunett, D. Davis, T. Gottshalk, P. Messina, C. Kesselman, *Implementing distributed synthetic forces simulations in metacomputing environments*, in Proceedings of the Heterogeneous Computing Workshop (1998)

[5] I. Foster, C. Kesselman, (eds.), *The Grid: Blueprint for a New Computing Infrastructure* (Morgan Kaufmann, 1998)

[6] I. Foster, C. Kesselmann, S. Tuecke, The anatomy of the grid: enabling scalable virtual organizations, *International Journal of Supercomputer Applications*, 15(3), 200–222 (2001)

[7] I. Foster, C. Kesselmann, J. Nick, S. Tuecke, Grid services for distributed system integration, *Computer*, 35(6), 37–46 (2002)

[8] I. Foster, C. Kesselmann, J. Nick, S. Tuecke, *The physiology of the grid: An open grid services architecture for distributed system integration*, in Technical Report for the Globus project (2002) http://www.globus.org/research/papers/ogsa.pdf

[9] W. Smith, I. Foster, V. Taylor, *Predicting application run times using historical information*, in Proceedings of IPPS/SPDP '98 Workshop on Job Scheduling Strategies for Parallel Processing (1998)

[10] F.P. Brooks, No silver bullet, in Information Processing '86, ed. by Kugler, H.J. (Elsevier, North Holland; reprinted (1987)) *IEEE Computer* 20, 10–19 (1986)

[11] B.J. Cox, There is a silver bullet, *Byte*, (15): 209–218 (1990)

[12] D. Harel, Biting the silver bullet, *IEEE Computer*, 25, 8–24 (1992)

[13] W. Royce, *Managing the development of large software systems: Concepts and techniques*, in 1970 WESCON Technical Papers, Western Electronic Show and Convention, Los Angeles, pp. A/1-1–A/1-9; reprinted (1989) in Proceedings of the 11th International Conference on Software Engineering, Pittsburgh, pp. 328–338 (1970)

[14] B. W. Boehm, A spiral model of software development and enhancement, *IEEE Computer* 21, 61–72 (1988)

[15] J.L, Connel, L. Shafer, *Structured rapid prototyping: an Evolutionary Approach to Software Development* (Yourdon Press, Englewood Cliffs, NJ, 1989)

[16] C. Gane, *Rapid System Development: Using Structured Techniques and Relational Technology* (Prentice Hall, Englewood Cliffs, NJ, 1989)

[17] T. Gilb, *Principles of Software Engineering Management* (Addison-Wesley, Wokingham, UK, 1988)

[18] M. Aoyama, Concurrent-development process model, *IEEE Computer*, 10, 46–55 (1993)

[19] M.A. Cusumano, R.W. Selby, Microsoft Secrets: *How the World's Most Powerful Software Company Creates Technology, Shapes Markets, and Manages People*, (The Free Press/Simon and Schuster, New York, 1995)

[20] M.A. Cusumano, R.W. Selby, How Microsoft builds software, communications of the ACM, 40, 53–61 (1997)

[21] K. Beck, Embracing change with extreme programming, *IEEE Computer*, 32, 70–77 (1999)

[22] K. Beck, *Extreme Programming Explained: Embrace Change* (Addison-Wesley, Longman, Reading, MA, 2002)

[23] P. Kruchten, *The Rational Unified Process: An Introduction*, (Addison-Wesley, Longman, Reading, MA, 2000)

[24] B. Henderson-Sellers, J.M. Edwards, The object-oriented systems life cycle, *Communications of the ACM*, 33, 142–159 (1990)

[25] A. Helal, B. Haskell, J.L. Carter, R. Brice, D. Woelk, M. Rusinkiewicz, *Any Time, Anywhere Computing* (Kluver, Boston, Dordrecht, London, 2002)

[26] H. Takeuchi, I. Nonaka, *The new product development game,* Harvard Business Review, Jan/Feb: pp. 137–146, (1986)

[27] K. Schwaber, *Scrum development process*, in OOPSLA'95 Workshop on Business Object Design and Implementation (Springer-Verlag, 1995)

[28] K. Schwaber, M. Beedle, *Agile Software Development with Scrum* (Prentice Hall, Upper Saddle River, NJ, 2002)

[29] J.A Highsmith, *Adaptive Software Development: A Collaborative Approach to Managing Complex Systems* (Dorset, New York, 2002)

[30] A. Cockburn, *Agile Software Development* (Addison-Wesley, Longman, Reading, MA, 2002)

[31] J. Stapleton, Dynamic Systems Development method—The Method in Practice (Addison-Wesley, Longman, Reading, MA, 1997)

[32] G.S. Blair, R. Lea, The impact of distribution on the object-oriented approach to software development, *IEEE Software Engineering Journal*, 7(2), 130–138 (1992)

[33] E. Gamma, R. Helm, R. Johnson, J. Vlissides, *Design Patterns: Elements of Reusable Object-Oriented Software* (Addison-Wesley, Longman, Reading, MA, 1995)

[34] O.F. Rana, D.W. Walker, Service design patterns for computational grids, in *Patterns and Skeletons for*

Parallel and Distributed Computing, ed. by Rabhi, F.A. and Gorlatch, S. (Springer-Verlag, London, UK, 2003)

[35] S. Cannon, S. Chan, D. Olson, C. Tull, V. Welch, L. Pearlman, *Using CAS to manage role-based VO subgroups,* in Electronic proceedings of CHEP03, (2003) (available as DVD and at http://www.slac.stanford.edu/econf/C0303241/proceedings.html)

[36] F. Schneider, Implementing fault-tolerant services using the state machine approach: A tutorial, *ACM Computing Surveys*, 22(4), 1990

[37] M. Castro, B. Liskov, *Practical byzantine fault tolerance*, in Proceedings of Third Symp, Operating Systems Design and Implementation (1999)

[38] A. Shamir, How to share a secret, *Communications of the ACM*, 22, 612-613 (1979)

[39] A. Herzberg, S. Jarecki, H. Krawczyk, M. Yung, *Proactive secret sharing*, in Proceedings of Advances in Cryptology, Crypto '95 (1995)

[40] A. Chervenak, E. Deelman, I. Foster, L. Guy, W. Hoschek, A. Iamnitchi, C. Kesselman, P. Kunszt, M. Ripenu, B. Schwartzkop, H. Stocking, K. Stockinger, B. Tierney, *Giggle: A framework for constructing scalable replica location services*, in Electronic Proceedings of Super Computing, 2002 Conference (2002)

[41] A. Genoud, D. Caromel, *Non-functional exceptions for distributed and mobile objects*, in Proceedings of EHOOS'03 workshop of ECOOP 2003, Darmstadt, Germany (2003)

Chapter 5

Grid Programming with Java, RMI, and Skeletons

5.1 Introduction

Grid systems aim to combine different kinds of computational resources connected by the Internet and make them easily available to the user community. Initial research on grid computing focused, quite naturally, on developing the enabling infrastructure, systems like Globus, Legion, and Condor being the prominent examples presented in the "Gridbook" [17]. Other efforts have addressed important classes of applications and their support tools, like Netsolve [14] and Cactus, and the prediction of resource availability, e.g., in Network Weather Service (NWS) [36].

Compared to infrastructure and middleware, the topics concerning algorithms and programming methodology appear to have been neglected at this early stage of grid research and are therefore not yet properly understood. Initial experience has shown that entirely new approaches to software development and programming are required for grid systems [23]; the GrADS [10] project was one of the first to address this need. A common approach to developing applications for grid-like environments is to provide libraries on high-performance servers, which can be accessed by clients, using some remote invocation mechanism, e. g. RPC/RMI. Such systems are commonly referred to as Network Enabled Server (NES) environments [26]. There are several systems, such as NetSolve [4] and Ninf [28], that adopt this approach.

An important challenge in application programming for grid systems is the phase of algorithm design and, in particular, performance prediction early on in the design process. Since the type and configuration of the machine on which the program will be executed is not known in advance, it is difficult to choose the right algorithmic structure and perform architecture-tuned optimisations. The resulting suboptimality can hardly be compensated in the implementation phase and can thus dramatically worsen the quality of the whole grid enterprise.

We propose to address grid programming by providing application programmers with a set of reusable algorithmic patterns, called *skeletons*. Compute servers in grid systems may provide different, architecture-tuned implementations of the skeletons. Applications composed of skeletons can thus be targeted for execution on particular servers in the system with the goal of achieving better performance. The idea of the approach is that applications can be expressed using reusable algorithmic skeletons, for which reliable performance estimates on a particular grid server are available. This facilitates systematic rather than ad hoc design decisions on both the algorithmic structure of an application and the assignment of application parts to servers.

99

In this Chapter, we first describe an experimental Java-based programming system with skeletons for a grid environment, with focus on the critical problem of performance prediction in the course of algorithm design. Then we show how skeleton-based applications can be executed efficiently in a grid environment, using an optimised version of the Java Remote Method Invocation (RMI) mechanism. We argue that the traditional RMI mechanism leads to much unnecessary communication flow between clients and servers and show how the communication overhead can be reduced. Finally, we address the challenge of predicting an application's performance in order to make sound scheduling decisions for a grid. We propose to combine different performance models to obtain a performance estimate for the entire application.

The particular contributions and structure of the Chapter are as follows. We present our prototype, proof-of-concept grid environment, and discuss the proposed programming model (Section 5.2). We describe our implementation of the proposed grid architecture using Java RMI (Section 5.3). We propose optimisations of the Java RMI mechanism to reduce the overhead of remote calls in our grid environment and demonstrate the achieved improvement using the FFT example (Section 5.4). We present novel methods for estimating the performance of Java bytecodes that are used as application-specific parameters of algorithmic skeletons and illustrate performance prediction using a case study (Section 5.5). We discuss our results in the context of related work (Section 5.6).

5.2   System Architecture and Programming Model

In our system, application programs are constructed using a set of skeletons. The skeletons are implemented on the server side and invoked remotely from clients. The idea of grid programming with skeletons is to separate two phases of programming—algorithm design and implementation. The user composes his program using predefined algorithmic patterns (skeletons), which appear as function calls with application-specific parameters. The actual organization of parallelism is left to the skeleton implementation, which is provided on the server side and is geared to a particular architecture of a grid server, e. g. distributed- or shared-memory, multithreaded, etc., This provides potential for achieving portable performance across various target machines.

There is a difference between using library functions and skeletons. When a library is used, the programmer supplies the structure of the application, while the library provides application-independent utility routines. When skeletons are used, they supply the parallel structure of the application, while the user provides application-specific customising operators (Java byte codes in our system).

Skeletons have been used with great success in traditional parallel high-performance programming for a variety of different application domains, such as medical image processing [6] or adaptive multigrid methods [33]. A good overview about recent developments in the field of algorithmic skeletons can be found in [31]. Based on the progress made for skeletons in the parallel settings we intend to use skeletons as building blocks for grid applications.

We consider an experimental grid system consisting of three kinds of components: user machines (*clients*), target machines (*servers*), and the central entity, called *lookup service* (see Fig. 5.1). Each server provides a set of skeletons that can be invoked from the clients.
Invoking skeletons remotely involves the following steps, shown in Fig. 5.1:

1. Registration: Each server registers the skeletons it provides with the lookup service to make them accessible to clients. Together with each skeleton, performance information for the server and the skeletons is registered as discussed in Section 5.5.

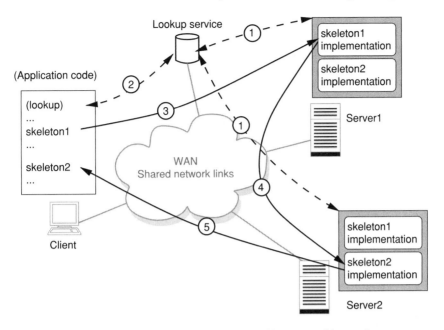

FIGURE 5.1. Experimental grid system: Architecture and interaction.

2. Service request-reply: A client queries the lookup service for a skeleton it needs for an application, and is given a list of servers implementing the skeleton. The skeletons that will actually be used are selected (using heuristics or tool-driven by the user), based on predicted performance.
3. Skeleton invocation: During the program execution, skeletons are invoked remotely with application-specific parameters.
4. Composition: If the application consists of a composition of skeletons, they may all be executed either on the same server or, alternatively, in a pipelined manner across several servers (see Section 5.4).
5. Skeleton completion: When the compute server has completed the invoked skeleton, the result is sent back to the client.

Skeletons address two main challenges that application developers face when programming for grid environments:

• Heterogeneity: Computational grids are usually comprised of servers of different architecture and hardware. In order to make use of the available computing resources, applications should be as portable as possible so they can execute on as many different servers as possible.
• Dynamic environment: Grid environments are highly dynamic and servers join or leave the system frequently. Therefore, an application should not be designed to run on a specific set of nodes in grid systems. Instead it should be able to adapt to the resources it finds available at runtime.

Constructing an application using skeletons provides a solution that is both portable and dynamic:

• Skeletons hide the details about the executing hardware and the server's communication topology from the application. Thus, an application that is expressed as a composition of skeletons is portable across any servers implementing the required skeletons.

- The servers for executing a particular skeleton can be chosen just before the skeleton's execution, thus enabling the application to choose the best available server dynamically.

Additionally, using skeletons has the advantage that the server-sided skeleton implementation can be tuned to the particular server architecture, allowing hardware-specific optimisations without loss of portability. Because skeleton implementations on a particular server can be hand-optimised, single skeletons can provide very good performance. However, applications are usually not composed of single skeletons but of several ones. Although a highly optimised hand-coded implementation for a particular hardware architecture can be expected to outperform the skeleton implementation, it has been reported that programs based on skeletons or similar highly abstract computational patterns often perform similarly well as hand-coded ones (see [8, 20]), so the performance penalty paid for the use of skeletons is usually rather small.

Moreover, in the grid setting, it is often not possible or not advisable to exetensively hand-optimize a particular application, because optimizations usually limit the application's portability. Highly-optimized programs are therefore limited to the execution on particular servers which contradicts the grid idea of using heterogeneous resources. In contrast, skeletons have the potential to achieve very good performance at a level of portability similar to Java's, because any server providing a skeleton implementation can be used to execute a skeleton-based application, in the same way as a Java application can be executed on any computer providing a JVM implementation.

Another advantage is that the implementation of a skeleton on a particular server can be reused by different applications. Furthermore, skeletons provide a reliable model of performance prediction (see Section 5.5), offering a sound basis for selecting servers.

Skeleton programming allows for a clear role distribution between skeleton (or system) programmer and application programmer: the system programmer's task is to implement the generic skeleton in the most suitable way on a particular machine, optimizing the implementation for the particular hardware architecture. In contrast, the application programmer's task is to express the application in terms of the available skeletons, without having to know how they are implemented on the server.

5.2.1 A Repository of Skeletons

In the following, we describe a (by no means exhaustive) collection of skeletons. We have restricted the list of skeletons to a few simple data-parallel skeletons, which we will use for implementing the Fast Fourier Transform (FFT) as a case study in Section 5.2.3. More skeletons for different application domains can be found in the literature (e.g., task-parallel skeletons [15], divide-and-conquer patterns [22], multigrid methods [33], and others). Of course, not all applications can be expressed in terms of existing skeletons, and new skeletons need to be derived for such computational patterns. See [13] for a description of a methodology for introducing new skeletons.

It is also important to note that the skeletons presented here are generic patterns of computation and their use is by no means restricted to the FFT application.

In an application program, skeletons appear as function calls with application-specific parameters. Some of these parameters may in turn be functions, i.e., skeletons can be formally viewed as higher-order functions. In practice, functional parameters are provided as program codes, in our system as Java bytecodes. In the following, functional parameters are denoted by f, $\otimes$, and $\oplus$, where f is an arbitrary unary function, and $\oplus$ and $\otimes$ represent arbitrary binary operators.

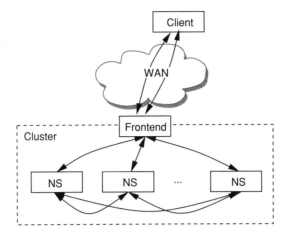

FIGURE 5.6. Structure of the distributed-memory service object implementations.

The node modules for the different service objects are gathered in a single "node server" (*NS* in Fig. 5.6). The node servers are started by the controller before the server is registered with the lookup service. At start up, each node server opens a socket connection to the front-end to register itself with the front-end; thereby the node becomes accessible for computations. The task of the front-end module is to communicate with the clients, distribute the received parameters to the server nodes, and collect the results and send them back to the client.

We will now provide more details of the implementation, using the *reduce* skeleton as an example:

Frontend Module   The front-end provides a remote access to the reduction skeleton by implementing an appropriate Java interface (see Section 5.2.2). The `invoke` methods of the interface are used by the clients to start a reduction on the server side.

When `invoke` is called, it first divides the input list in sublists of equal length, one for each registered node server. The sublists are then sent to the nodes, along with a request to start execution of the reduction on the nodes. The method executed on the front-end then blocks until it receives the result from one of the nodes, which it forwards to the client.

Node Server   After startup and registration with the front-end, the node server waits on the socket for a message from the front end. When the parameters and the request for a specific skeleton are received from the front end, the node server starts a local method corresponding to the called skeleton.

For the reduction example, a `reducelocal` method is started, with the sublist and `BinOp` operator received from the front-end as arguments. The method performs a task very similar to the threads for the shared-memory implementation. The first step is to reduce all local elements. Then the results are again reduced in a tree-like manner, with the node servers communicating results through sockets. When the final result is available in one node, this node contacts the front-end and delivers the result.

5.3.2.1 Class Loading

One problem of the distributed-memory implementation of skeletons is that class loading and code shipping cannot be handled completely by Java's RMI mechanism alone. When the parameters of an RMI call are sent from the caller to the remote server, Java also sends the URL of a so-called codebase. If an argument of the invoked remote method is an object of a class that is unknown on the server, the classloader automatically contacts this codebase URL to retrieve a class definition for the argument.

While this mechanism works well for the shared-memory implementation, it fails for the cluster version of the server for two reasons. First, RMI is only used for invoking methods of the service objects on the front end, while communication between front end and node servers is realised using sockets. Thus, while any unknown classes are loaded automatically for the front end node, that is not the case for the cluster nodes. However, even if RMI was used for communication between front end and node servers, the dynamic class loading would still not work on many clusters, because the cluster nodes usually do not have direct access to network address outside the cluster. Thus an attempt to contact the client's codebase URL from a cluster node would fail.

Therefore, we have implemented a distributed class loader running on both the front end and the nodes (see Fig. 5.7). If a class is not found in the local classpath when a remote method is invoked on the front end, then the class loader contacts the codebase URL provided by the client to retrieve the class files for the unknown classes and stores them locally. In contrast, the standard RMI class loader would not store the class files locally, thus making it impossible to forward the class files to the nodes of the cluster. When a class definition is unknown in one of the node servers, the classloader of the node contacts the front-end to retrieve the classfile and load the class.

5.4   Optimising Java RMI for Grids

In this section, we discuss the specific advantages and disadvantages of the Java RMI mechanism for remote execution in a grid environment and present three optimizations that we have implemented to improve RMI for grid systems.

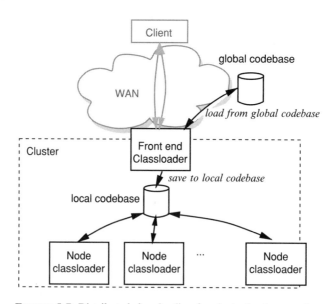

FIGURE 5.7. Distributed class loading for cluster implementation.

Intuitively, distributed execution of an application with remote methods should have the following desirable properties:

- Ease of Programming: From the programmer's point of view, remote invocation and distributed composition of methods should be expressed in a straightforward manner, resembling normal (local) composition of methods as far as possible.
- Flexibility: The assignment of servers should not be hardcoded into the program. Instead, it should be possible for a scheduling entity to change the assignment of servers at runtime to reflect changes in the environment.
- Low Overhead: The overhead incurred by invoking methods remotely from the client should be as low as possible.

Java's standard RMI mechanism satisfies the first two requirements: (1) a remote method call is expressed in exactly the same way as a local one, and (2) the server executing the method can be changed at runtime by changing the corresponding remote reference.

The time overhead of RMI for single remote method invocations can be substantial, but it has been drastically reduced due to recent research efforts like KaRMI [29] and Manta/Ibis (see [25], which also contains a good overview about other approaches using RMI on the grid). An additional problem, not covered by these approaches, arises if remote method calls are composed with each other, which is the case in many applications. Let us consider a simple Java code fragment, where the result of `method1` is used as an argument by `method2`, as shown in Fig. 5.8.

The execution of the code shown in Fig. 5.8 can be distributed: different methods potentially run on different servers, i.e., different RMI references are assigned to `server1` and `server2`. When such a program is executed on the grid system of Fig. 5.1, methods are called remotely on a corresponding server. If a method's result is used as a parameter of other remote methods, the result of the first method should be sent directly to the second server (arrow ④ in Fig. 5.1). However, using RMI, the result of a remote method is always sent back to the client.

We proceed now by first presenting the situation with the standard RMI mechanism (standard RMI) and then describing our optimizations, illustrating them in Fig. 5.9.

5.4.0.1.1 Standard RMI

Using standard RMI for calling methods on the server has the advantage that remote methods are called in exactly the same way as local ones. Thus, the code in Fig. 5.8 would not change at all when using RMI instead of local methods. The only difference would be that `server1` and `server2` are RMI references, i.e., references to RMI stubs instead of "normal" objects.

However, using standard RMI to execute a composition of methods as in Fig. 5.8 is not time efficient because the result of a remote method invocation is always sent back directly to the client. Figure 5.9(a) demonstrates that assigning two different servers to `server1` and `server2` in our example code leads to the result of `method1` being sent back to the client,

```
... //get remote reference for server1/2
result1 = server1.method1();
result2 = server2.method2(result1);
```

FIGURE 5.8. Sample Java code: Composition of two methods.

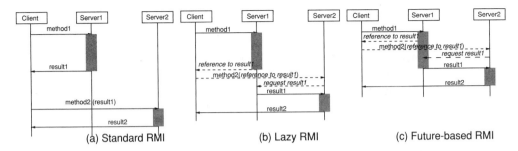

FIGURE 5.9. Timing diagrams for the standard and two improved RMI versions.

and from there to the second server. Furthermore, even if both methods are executed on the same server, the result is still sent first to the client, and from there back to the server again. For typical applications consisting of many composed methods, this feature of RMI results in very high time overhead.

To eliminate this overhead of the standard RMI, we propose three optimizations, called lazy, localized, and future-based RMI.

5.4.0.1.2 Lazy RMI

Our first optimization, called *lazy RMI*, aims to reduce the amount of data sent from the server to the client upon method completion. We propose that instead of the result being sent back to the client, an RMI remote reference to the data be returned. The client can then pass this reference onto the next server, which uses the reference to request the result from the previous server. This is shown in Fig. 5.9(b), with horizontal lines for communication of data, dotted horizontal lines for sending references, and thick vertical lines denoting computations.

This mechanism is implemented by wrapping all return values and parameters in objects of the new class `RemoteReference`, which has two methods: `setValue()` is called to set a reference to the result of a call; `getValue()` is used by the next method (or by the client) to retrieve this result and may be called remotely. If `getValue()` is called remotely via RMI, the result is sent over the network to the next server. Apart from the necessary packing and unpacking of parameters using `getValue` and `setValue`, a distributed composition of methods is expressed in exactly the same way with lazy RMI as with RMI.

5.4.0.1.3 Localised RMI

Our next optimization of RMI deals with accesses to the reference which points to the result of the first method in a composition. While there is no real network communication involved, there is still substantial overhead for serialising and deserialising the data and sending it through the local socket. To avoid this overhead, our implementation checks every access to a remote reference, whether it references a local object or not. In the local case, the object is returned directly without issuing an RMI call, thus reducing the runtime.

This is achieved by splitting the remote referencing mechanism into two classes: a remote class `RemoteValue` and a normal class `RemoteReference`. The local class is returned to the client upon method completion. It contains a remote reference to the result on the server, wrapped in a `RemoteValue` object. In addition, it contains a unique id for the object and the server's IP-address. When `getValue` is called at the `RemoteReference`, it first checks if the object is available locally and, if so, it obtains a local reference from a hashtable.

5.4.0.1.4 Future-based RMI

Since methods in grid applications are invoked from the client, a method cannot be executed until the remote reference has been passed from the previous server to the client, and on to the next server. Returning to our example code in Fig. 5.8, even if both methods are executed on the same server, the second method cannot be executed until the remote reference for the result of the first has been sent to the client and back once, see Fig. 5.9(b).

This unnecessary delay offers an additional chance for optimization, which we call *future-based RMI*. The idea is that all method invocations immediately return a remote reference to the result. This reference is sent to the client and can be passed onto the next method. All attempts to retrieve the data referenced by this reference are blocked until the data becomes available. Thus, computations and communication between client and server overlap, effectively hiding communication costs. This is shown in Fig. 5.9(c), with thick vertical lines denoting computations. Since RMI itself does not provide a mechanism for asynchronous method calls, it is up to the implementation of the methods on the server side to make method invocation asynchronous, e.g., by spawning in the client a new thread to carry out computations and returning immediately.

It is important to note that the optimizations presented here are not limited to a sequence of methods with only one parameter (i.e., pipeline patterns): arbitrary method compositions can be optimized. For example, in the skeleton program for FFT presented in (Eq. 5.4), the computation of Ω can be executed on a different server than the *apply(triple)* skeleton, which in turn may use a different server than the subsequent *dh* skeleton. Using future-based RMI, *dh* is called with two futures pointing to placeholders for the results of *apply* and *scan*. The server of *dh* will request the results from the two different servers and wait until these results are received before executing *dh*.

5.4.1 Experimental Results

To demonstrate the improvements achievable by using future-based RMI, we measured the performance of the FFT program discussed in Section 5.2.3 on a system similar to the testbed of Fig. 5.1. It consists of two university LANs—one at the Technical University of Berlin and the other at the University of Erlangen. They are connected by the German academic internet backbone (WiN), covering a distance of approx. 500 km. We used a SunFire 6800 with 12 US-III+ 900 MHz processors as our server and an UltraSPARC–IIi 360 MHz as client, both using SUN's JDK1.4.1 (HotSpot Client VM in mixed mode). Because there were several other applications running on the server machine during our experiments, a maximum of eight processors was available for measurements.

Figure 5.10 shows the runtimes for different problem sizes (ranging from 2^{15} to 2^{18}) and four different versions of the program: the first running locally on the client ("local FFT"), second using plain RMI, third version using future-based RMI, and the fourth version where the FFT is executed as a single server sided method called from the client ("ideal remote"). We consider the fourth version as ideal, as there is no overhead for remote composition of skeletons for that version; it corresponds to copying the whole program to the server and executing it there. For the plain RMI version, only the *scan* and *dh* skeletons are executed on the server, because all parameters and results are transmitted between client and server for each method call using plain

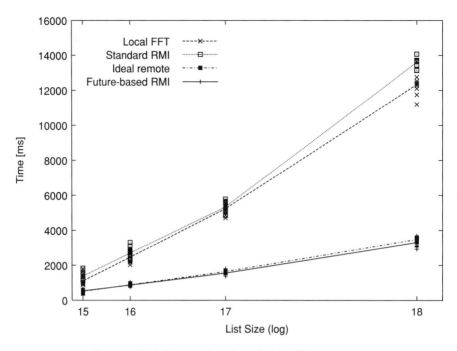

FIGURE 5.10. Measured runtimes for the FFT programs.

RMI, so that executing the *repl*, *apply* and *map* skeleton remotely would slow down the program unnecessarily. For the future-based RMI version, all skeletons are executed on the server.

The figure shows 10 measurements for each program version, with the average runtimes for each parameter size connected by lines. The plain RMI version is much (three to four times) slower than the future-based RMI version and unable to outperform the local, client sided FFT. Thus, the communication overhead outweighs the performance gain for execution on the server.

By contrast, the future-based RMI version eliminates most of the overhead and is three to four times faster than the local version. Compared with the "ideal remote" case the runtimes are almost identical. For large input lists (2^{17} and 2^{18}), the future-based version is even slightly faster than the remote version. This is due to the fact, that the future-based version invokes skeletons asynchronously, so the *apply* skeleton is already called while the *scan* skeleton is still running. Thus, using future-based RMI allows an efficient execution of programs with compositions of remote methods, in particular compositions of skeletons.

5.5   Performance Prediction

To ensure good quality of scheduling and mapping of skeletons to servers, it is very important to be able to estimate the performance of applications accurately. The runtime of grid-based applications is influenced by many different factors (see Fig. 5.11):

- the application specific code provided by the clients,
- the bandwidth and latencies of the network connections,

- the implementation of the skeletons on the servers as well as the architecture of the underlying hardware.

To predict the overall performance for a grid application, accurate models for the different factors influencing performance are necessary. If a library is implemented entirely on a server and not parameterized with application-specific code, benchmarks can be used to obtain a performance estimate. As the runtime of skeletons depends on application-specific code, it is not possible to use benchmarks. In the following, we outline a different performance prediction approach suitable for skeletons. For the prediction of the availability of network and computational resources, a tool such as the NWS ([36]) can be used.

5.5.1 Performance Prediction Functions for Skeletons

To decide whether to compute a skeleton remotely—and, if so, on which server—each server must provide a function to determine the performance of each skeleton provided by the server. A client obtains this function t_{skel} from the lookup service for every server on which the particular skeleton *skel* is available. It can then use the functions for each particular skeleton in an algorithm to compute the overall execution time.

5.5.2 Example: Performance of the dh Skeleton

The performance of the *dh* skeleton naturally depends on how and on what machine it is implemented.

We consider a performance prediction function for the shared-memory implementation. The implementation is obtained from the skeleton definition (Eq. 5.1) in Section 5.5.5 and consists of two nested loops; the outer one iterating over the recursion depth and the inner one iterating over all elements of the list. Figure 5.12 shows the algorithm in Java pseudocode.

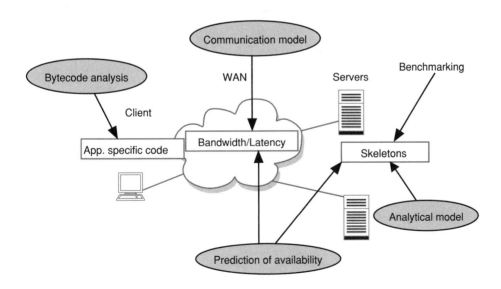

FIGURE 5.11. Performance prediction using multiple performance models.

Because there are no dependencies between the iterations of the inner loop, it can be computed in parallel. The algorithm consists of $\log n$ steps, where n is the length of the input list. In each step, array a represents the input list and `result` the output list. As the result of one iteration is the input for the next iteration, the references to array a and `result` are exchanged at the end of each iteration, which is denoted by a $\leftrightarrow$ `result`. When using threads to compute the inner loop in parallel, we need a synchronization before swapping the two references, which is implemented by `barrier()`.

Our goal is to provide a function $t_{dh}(n, p, t_\oplus, t_\otimes)$ that yields the time to compute the dh on the list of length n, using p threads, where the customizing operators $\oplus$ and $\otimes$ require times $t_\oplus$ and $t_\otimes$, respectively. The outer loop in Fig. 5.12 is executed $\log n$ times, while the inner loop consists of n iterations. When using p threads, every thread computes n/p iterations, the time needed for one iteration being equal to $\max(t_\oplus, t_\otimes)$. Thus, the time needed to compute the dh is:

$$t_{dh}(n, p, t_\oplus, t_\otimes) = n/p \cdot \log n \cdot \max(t_\oplus, t_\otimes) \tag{5.5}$$

The dh implementation for distributed-memory computers exploits a logical hypercube topology. Figure 5.13 presents the implementation in an MPI-like pseudocode notation.

The program is a loop over the hypercube dimensions. Each iteration starts with exchanging data with the neighbour, followed by operations $\oplus$ and $\otimes$ of (Eq. 5.1), which are implemented by functions op1 and op2. The MPI primitive `MPI_Sendrecv` has, according to the standard, 12 parameters, but in our context only four are of interest: the send buffer (`data`), the rank of the source and destination process (`neighbor`), and the receive buffer (`recvbuf`). The rank of the neighbor in dimension d is computed by inverting the d-th bit of the bit representation of the processor's own rank, in Java syntax `rank^(1<<d)`.

5.5.3 Performance Prediction of Java Bytecode

As discussed above, with each skeleton implementation provided by a server we associate a performance prediction function, parameterized by the runtime of the customizing operators.

```
for(int i=1; i<a.length; i=i*2) { // sequential loop
    for(int j=0; j<a.length; j++) { // parallel loop
        if( leftSide(i,j) ) result[j] = a[j]    ⊕ a[j+i];
        else                result[j] = a[j-i] ⊗ a[j]; }
    barrier();
    a ↔ result; }
```

FIGURE 5.12. Java pseudocode of the shared-memory implementation of dh.

```
for(d=0; d<k; d++) {
    neighbour=rank^(1<<d);
    MPI_Sendrecv(data,...,neighbour,...,recvbuf,...,
    neighbour,...);
    if( myrank < neighbour ) data=op1(data, recvbuf);
    else                     data=op2(recvbuf, data);
}
```

FIGURE 5.13. MPI pseudocode of the distributed-memory implementation of the dh skeleton.

For example, the estimate in (Eq. 5.5) refers to $t_\oplus$ and $t_\otimes$, the runtimes of operators $\oplus$ and $\otimes$, respectively. These operators are, in our implementation, Java bytecodes, and our next problem is how to estimate their runtimes.

5.5.3.1 The Challenges and Our Approach

To estimate an operator's runtime, its bytecode can first be analyzed to determine how often each instruction is invoked. This analysis essentially consists in executing the operator with a set of sample parameters and recording how often each instruction is executed. For more insight into the problem, see e.g., [11]. The obtained number and sequence of invocations can then be used to predict the runtime of the operator using a *timing model* for the server machine. At the moment, timing models in our system simply consist of a table with previously measured runtimes for each instruction type, which are multiplied by the number of invocations for each instruction. However, timing models could also take cache and pipelining information into account to increase prediction accuracy [5].

As for our simple timing model, estimating the runtimes for each instruction type is a nontrivial task, as the following considerations show. The straightforward way of measuring runtime for a particular bytecode instruction would be to execute a loop containing only instructions of that kind and divide the measured time by the number of loop iterations. However, Java bytecode instructions are stack-oriented, so every operand for an instruction must be brought to the stack before execution and is then popped from the stack when the instruction is invoked. Within a loop, additional push or pop operations are often required to adjust the stack size. In this case, only the runtime of particular instruction combinations—rather than individual instructions—can be measured.

For example, Fig. 5.14 shows a loop containing the `iadd` instruction, which sums the stack's two topmost elements. Before execution, the operands must be brought to the stack, e.g., by using two `bipush` instructions for pushing a (one-byte integer) constant onto the stack. Then the `iadd` instruction can be invoked, replacing the two operand words with the result. Another call to `iadd` cannot therefore be issued until a second word is placed on the stack using `bipush` again. Thus, each execution of the `iadd` instruction in a loop requires at least one more `bipush` instruction to provide the second operand.

This problem is circumvented in our system as follows. Assuming the execution time of a sequence of instructions to be the sum of the runtimes of each instruction contained, the above example leads to the equation $t_{bipush} + t_{iadd} = T$. Measuring the runtimes for other code sequences containing `iadd` and `bipush` instructions leads to a set of linear equations, which can be used to compute an approximation for t_{iadd} and t_{bipush}.

We generalize this simple idea for m different instruction kinds: each program or code sequence can be represented as an m-dimensional "program vector" $\vec{p} = (p_1, p_2, \ldots, p_m)$ where the i-th entry indicates that instruction i occurs p_i times in the program. Note that the order of instruc-

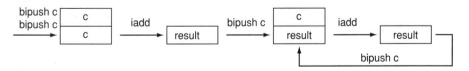

FIGURE 5.14. Different stack sizes for execution of `iadd` in a loop

tions does not matter in this vector representation. The runtime for the program characterised by vector p can then be written as

$$\vec{p} \cdot \vec{t} = \sum_i p_i t_i = T \tag{5.6}$$

with $\cdot$ denoting scalar product and t being the vector $(t_1, \ldots, t_m)$ containing the (unknown) run-times t_i for instructions of type i. Time T is the execution time for the whole program which can be measured.

If the runtime for n different test programs is measured, this leads to the following system of linear equations:

$$\vec{A}\vec{t} = \begin{pmatrix} \vec{p}^T_{(1)} \\ \vec{p}^T_{(2)} \\ \vdots \\ \vec{p}^T_{(m)} \end{pmatrix} \begin{pmatrix} t_1 \\ t_2 \\ \vdots \\ t_m \end{pmatrix} = \begin{pmatrix} p_{11} & p_{12} & \cdots & p_{1m} \\ p_{21} & p_{22} & \cdots & p_{2m} \\ \vdots & \vdots & & \vdots \\ p_{n1} & p_{n2} & \cdots & p_{nm} \end{pmatrix} \begin{pmatrix} t_1 \\ t_2 \\ \vdots \\ t_m \end{pmatrix} = \begin{pmatrix} T_1 \\ T_2 \\ \vdots \\ T_n \end{pmatrix} = \hat{\vec{T}} \tag{5.7}$$

Here, $\vec{A}$ contains the program vectors $\vec{p}_{(i)}$ describing the n different programs, and $\hat{\vec{T}}$ contains the measured time values T_i for each program. As before, $\vec{t}$ is the vector of time values for single instructions. This system of equations is solved to obtain values for $\vec{t}$. This timing vector $\vec{t}$ is computed once for every server in our grid system by measuring the runtime of a number of *test programs*. During server registration, $\vec{t}$ is sent to the lookup server and can be retrieved there by the clients. The clients then use the timing vector to estimate the runtime of a skeleton on a particular server.

5.5.3.2 Requirements to Matrix $\vec{A}$

The next question is how to find a useful matrix $\vec{A}$, i.e., how the test programs whose runtimes are measured should be structured. Several requirements for $\vec{A}$ are presented in the next paragraphs.

Size of Test Programs

Solving linear equations to obtain runtime estimates will only yield correct results if the runtime of a program is linear in terms of the number of instructions. This is not the case, however, for very small and homogeneous programs, because the JVM (in our case, Sun's JDK 1.4.1 Client VM in mixed mode) can optimize code sequences, yielding other than the expected execution times. For example, we measured the times for executing 1,000 integer additions and 1,000 integer multiplications in a loop of 10^5 iterations. The loop is structured as in Fig. 5.14, i.e., for each iadd/imul instruction, one more instruction is necessary to bring the second operand to the stack.

The values obtained are given in the "add" and "mul" columns of the first row of Table 5.1. The time for executing a loop with both addition and multiplication (along with the indispensable stack-adjustment operations) would be expected to be the sum of the loops containing only one of the instructions. In fact, a shorter time could be expected, as the combined loop contains more instructions per loop iteration, resulting in less overhead. However, the measured value ("addmul" in Table 5.1.) of 2106 ms is considerably larger (approx. 23%) than the expected value of 1715 ms. Apparently, the difference in the runtime is due to loop optimizations that the standard JVM performs on loops containing arithmetic instructions of the same type and, which are not possible for loops with instructions of different types.

5.6   Conclusions

We have addressed the challenging problem of software design for heterogeneous grids, using a repository of reusable algorithmic patterns called *skeletons*, that are executed remotely on high-performance grid servers. While the use of skeletons in the parallel setting is an active research area, their application for grid systems is a new, intriguing problem.

We have proposed an exemplary (and by no means exhaustive) repository of skeletons, which includes several elementary data-parallel functions, the divide-and-conquer skeleton *dh*, and two auxiliary skeletons which are helpful in a grid environment. We have demonstrated how a mathematical description of FFT can be expressed using our skeletons, leading to an efficient Java program with remote calls for skeletons.

We have described our prototypical grid system. Java and RMI were chosen to implement our system in order to obtain a highly portable solution. Other promising opportunities include, e.g., the Lithium system [15] for executing mainly task-parallel skeletons in Java.

We have presented three optimizations of the RMI mechanism in the context of grid computing. The proposed solutions facilitate more efficient remote execution of compositions of computation-intensive methods on high-performance servers and broaden the class of applications efficiently implementable on grid systems. This extends the scope of grid systems compared with approaches like NetSolve [4] or Ninf [28], which use RPC and are efficient only for coarse-grained applications. Our prototypical implementation confirmed the advantages of the proposed optimizations in the case of Sun's Java RMI, and can thus be viewed as proof of the concept's viability.

The novelty of our work on RMI is that, whereas previous research dealt with single or repeated RMI calls, we focus on an efficient execution of composed method calls, where the result of one call is an argument of another. This situation is very typical of many grid applications, and our work has demonstrated several opportunities to improve the performance of such calls. The concept of hiding latencies using futures was studied e.g., in [35] and implemented in Java (e.g., [32, 16, 7]). However, these approaches lack the ability to send futures to remote servers and thus can not realise server/server communication. This feature can be found in [37], where RMI calls are optimized using call aggregation and where a server can invoke methods on another server directly. While this approach optimizes RMI calls by reducing the amount of data, the method invocations are not asynchronous as in our implementation, instead they are delayed to find as much optimization possibilities as possible.

An important advantage of our approach is that it is orthogonal to the underlying RMI implementation. Our optimizations are thus directly applicable to these faster RMI systems, too, and can be used along with them without any changes being made.

The performance analysis of portable code, e.g., Java bytecode, has only recently begun to be studied. Initial research efforts [9, 11] are concerned with the high-level analysis of bytecode, i.e., the problem of counting how often an instruction is executed in the worst case. We have presented a novel mechanism for performance estimation using automatically generated test programs. Our experimental results with the tridiagonal system solver confirm the high quality of the achievable time estimates, allowing us to predict the performance of grid programs during the design process, and also to control the efficient assignment of remote methods to the compute servers of the grid system.

References

[1] *MPI Forum Homepage*, http://www.mpi-forum.org

[2] M. Alt, H. Bischof, and S. Gorlatch, Program Development for Computational Grids Using Skeletons and Performance Prediction, *Parallel Processing Letters* 12(2), 157–174 (2002)

[3] M. Alt, J. Dünnweber, J. Müller, and S. Gorlatch, HOCs: Higher-order Components for grids, in *Component Models and Systems for Grid Applications*, ed. by V. Getor and T. Kielman (*Saint-Malo, France*, 2004)

[4] D. Arnold, S. Agrawal, S. Blackford, J. Dongarra, M. Miller, K. Seymour, K. Sagi, Z. Shi, and S. Vadhiyar, *Users' Guide to Netsolve v1.4.1*, Innovative Computing Dept. Technical Report ICL-UT-02-05, University of Tennessee, June 2002

[5] P. Atanassov, P. Puschner, and R. Kirner, *Using Real Hardware to Create an Accurate Timing Model for Execution-time Analysis*, International Workshop on Real-Time Embedded Systems RTES 2001, London, UK, Dec. 2001

[6] B. Bacci, S. Gorlatch, C. Lengauer, and S. Pelagatti, *Skeletons and Transformations in an Integrated Parallel Programming Environment*, in Parallel Computing Technologies (PaCT-99), LNCS 1662, (Springer-Verlag, 1999), pp. 13–27

[7] L. Baduel, F. Baude, and D. Caromel, *Efficient, Flexible, and Typed Group Communications in Java*, in Proceedings of the 2002 joint ACM-ISCOPE conference on Java Grande (JGI-02) Seattle, November 2002. (ACM, 2002), pp. 28–36

[8] G. Baker, J. Gunnels, G. Morrow, B. Riviere, and R. van de Geijn, *PLAPACK: High Performance Through High Level Abstraction*, in ICPP98, 1998

[9] I. Bate, G. Bernat, G. Murphy, and P. Puschner, *Low-level Analysis of a Portable WCET Analysis Framework*, in 6th IEEE Real-Time Computing Systems and Applications (RTCSA2000) pp. 39–48, December 2000

[10] F. Berman et al, The GrADS Project: Software Support for High-level Grid Application Development, *Int. J. of High Performance Computing Applications* 15(4), 327–344 (2001)

[11] G. Bernat, A. Burns, and A. Wellings, *Portable Worst Case Execution Time Analysis Using Java Bytecode*, in Proc. 12th EUROMICRO Conference on Real-time Systems, June 2000

[12] H. Bischof and S. Gorlatch, *Parallelizing Tridiagonal System Solver by Adjustment to a Homomorphic Skeleton*, in Proc. of the 4th International Workshop on Advanced Parallel Processing Technologies, ed. by S. Jähnichen and X. Zhou, 2001

[13] H. Bischof and S. Gorlatch, Double-scan: *Introducing and Implementing a New Data-parallel Skeleton*, in Euro-Par 2002, vol. 2400 of *LNCS*, ed. by B. Monien and R. Feldmann, pp. (Springer), 640–647.

[14] H. Casanova and J. Dongarra, NetSolve: *A Network-enabled Server for Solving Computational Science Problems*, *Int. J. of Supercomputing Applications and High Performance Computing* 3(11), 212–223 (1997)

[15] M. Danelutto and P. Teti, Lithium: *A Structured Parallel Programming Enviroment in Java*, in Proceedings of Computational Science - ICCS, number 2330 in Lecture Notes in Computer Science (Springer-Verlag), pp. 844–853

[16] K.K. Falkner, P. Coddington, and M. Oudshoorn, *Implementing Asynchronous Remote Method invocation in Java*, in Proc. of Parallel and Real Time Systems (PART'99), pp. 22–34

[17] I. Foster and C. Kesselmann, (eds), *The Grid: Blueprint for a New Computing Infrastructure* (Morgan Kaufmann, 1998)

[18] V. Getov, G. von Laszewski, M. Philippsen, and I. Foster, Multiparadigm Communications in Java for Grid Computing, *Communications of the ACM* 44(10), 118–125 (2001)

[19] Globus Alliance, Globus toolkit http://www.globus.org/toolkit/

[20] S. Gorlatch, Send-receive Considered Harmful: Myths and Realities of Message Passing, *ACM TOPLAS* 26(1), 47–56 (2004)

[21] S. Gorlatch and H. Bischof, A Generic MPI Implementation for a Data-parallel Skeleton: Formal Derivation and Application to FFT, *Parallel Processing Letters* 8(4), 447–458 (1998)

[22] C. Herrmann, *The Skeleton-based Parallelization of Divide-and-Conquer Recursions*. Logos Verlag Berlin, Berlin, 2000. Dissertation, Universität Passau

[23] K. Kennedy et al, *Toward a Framework for Preparing and Executing Adaptive Grid Programs*, in Proceedings of NSF Next Generation Systems Program Workshop (International Parallel and Distributed Processing Symposium 2002), Fort Lauderdale, April 2002

[24] F.T. Leighton, *Introduction to Parallel Algorithms and Architectures: Arrays, Trees, Hypercubes* (Morgan Kaufmann, 1992)

[25] J. Maassen, R. van Nieuwpoort, H. Bal, T. Kielmann, and R. Hofman, *Ibis: An Efficient Java-based Grid Programming Environment*, in Proc. of the joint ACM-ISCOPE conference on Java Grande, November 2002

[26] S. Matsuoka, H. Nakada, M. Sato, and S. Sekiguchi, *Design Issues of Network Enabled Server Systems for the Grid*. GridForum, APM WG whitepaper, 2000

[27] J. Meyer and T. Downing, *Java Virtual Machine* (O'Reilly, 1997)

[28] H. Nakada, M. Sato, and S. Sekiguchi, Design and Implementations of Ninf: Towards a Global Computing Infrastructure, *FGCS* 15(5-6), 649–658 (1999)

[29] M. Philippsen, B. Haumacher, and C. Nester, More Efficient Serialization and RMI for Java, *Concurrency: Practice and Experience* 12(7), 495–518 (2000)

[30] W.H. Press, S.A. Teukolsky, W.T. Vetterling, and B.P. Flannery, *Numerical Recipes in C: The Art of Scientific Computing* (Cambridge University Press, 1992)

[31] F.A. Rabhi and S. Gorlatch, (eds), *Patterns and Skeletons for Parallel and Distributed Computing* (Springer, 2003)

[32] R. Raje, J. Williams, and M. Boyles, An Asynchronous Remote Method Invocation (ARMI) Mechanism in Java, *Concurrency: Practice and Experience*, 1997

[33] T. Richert, *Using Skeletons to Implement a Parallel Multigrid Method with Overlapping Adaptive Grids*, in Proc. of PDPTA 2000, vol. 3 (CSREA, 2000)

[34] J.E. Savage, *Models of Computation: Exploring the Power of Computing* (Addison Wesley-Longman, 1998)

[35] E.F. Walker, R. Floyd, and P. Neves, *Asynchronous Remote Operation Execution in Distributed Systems*, in Proc. of the Tenth International Conference on Distributed Computing Systems, May 1990

[36] R. Wolski, N. Spring, and J. Hayes, The Network Weather Service: A Distributed Resource Performance Forecasting Service for Metacomputing, *Journal of Future Generation Computing Systems* 15(5-6), 757–768 (1999)

[37] K.C. Yeung and P.H.J. Kelly, Optimising Java RMI programs by Communication Restructuring, in *ACM/IFIP/USENIX International Middleware Conference*, ed. by D. Schmidt and M. Endler, (Springer-Verlag, 2003)

Chapter 6

A Review of Grid Portal Technology

6.1 Introduction

The Grid [14] has emerged as a distributed computing infrastructure for providing pervasive, ubiquitous access to a diverse set of resources ranging from high-performance computers (HPC) to tertiary storage systems, and from large-scale visualization systems to expensive and unique instruments, including telescopes and particle accelerators. The Grid has shifted its focus from the high performance aspects towards virtual organizations [1], which provide flexible, secure, coordinated resources sharing among collections of individuals, institutions, and resources. Currently the focus of Grid development is moving toward the Open Grid Services Architecture (OGSA) [42], which enables the integration of services and resources across distributed, heterogeneous, dynamic virtual organizations—whether within a single enterprise or extending to external resource-sharing and service-provider relationships. With a service-oriented view, the Grid is in its progress toward a utility like the electricity power grid to provide computation-related services on demand to Grid users.

There are mainly two classes of Grid users, system developers and end users. System developers are those who build systems using Grid middleware toolkits such as Globus [47], Unicore [48], or Condor [49]. The end users are typically scientists or engineers who use the Grid to solve their domain-specific problems via a Grid portal. A Grid portal is a Web-based gateway that provides seamless access to heterogeneous backend resources. In general, a grid portal provides end users with a customized view of software and hardware resources specific to their particular problem domain. It also provides a single point of access to Grid-based resources that they have been authorized to use. An objective of Grid portals is the provision of transparent and easy access to these backend resources by the end users. This will allow scientists or engineers to focus on their problem area by making the Grid a transparent extension of their desktop environment. Many Grid portals have been implemented to help end users to access the Grid. The Grid portals currently in use include XCAT Science Portal [17], Gateway [18], Mississippi Computational Web Portal [19], NPACI Hotpage [20], JiPANG [25], The DSG Portal [52], Grappa [56], and ASC Grid Portal [87], and many others.

The rapid increase in the volume and variety of data used in e-science, mirrored by that in e-commerce and e-government, means that any supporting infrastructure must provide a set of core semantic services. These core services must be able to equip data with meaning and generate a surrounding semantic context in which data can be meaningfully interpreted. Fundamental research into Semantic Web [8], knowledge systems and service-oriented architectures has pushed the Grid to move from the current data-centric view to a semantic one, with domain-specific problem solvers and a range of knowledge-based services. The authors in

[2] describe the Semantic Grid as a service-oriented architecture (SOA) in which *entities* provide *services* to one another under various forms of *contract*. The Semantic Grid can provide not only computational services, but information and knowledge ones as well. In such an environment it is essential that information relating to user and applications needs, the resource providers and their resources, are easily discovered via interfaces, and have defined semantic meanings that can be used by higher-level services to effectively use their resources.

It is envisioned that the successful deployment of the Grid will largely depend on the usability of Grid portals because the majority of users are end users. To make the Grid a utility like the electricity power grid, there needs a lot of work to be done for the development of Grid portals. A future Grid portal toolkit should hide the complexity of the backend Grid services from users as much as possible. When building a Grid portal, users should be easily able to add customization, for example, adding or removing a service. In addition, a future Grid portal should provide not only computational services, but also domain problem-solving services and knowledge services as well. If a user has a domain-specific problem, it is better for the user to find a domain problem solver, specify a problem-solving policy such as a high priority or a low priority, how to pay the service, and then get the problem solved on the Grid, all via a Grid portal.

In this chapter, we review the state-of-the-art of Grid portal research and development. The review classifies Grid portals into three generations. The first generation is being used predominantly today, where a Grid portal is tightly coupled with grid middleware tools such as Globus. The second generation makes use of technologies such as portlets to provide a more flexible solution. The third generation is associated with the emergence of the Semantic Grid, where Grid portal facilities take advantage of semantic meanings to provide advanced knowledge-based services. Based on the introduction of PortalLab, a Web Services toolkit for building Semantic Grid portals, we discuss the features of third generation Grid portals. We argue that Grid portals supporting semantics are crucial for the evolution from the current data centric grid to the one where semantic capabilities provide powerful knowledge-based services. By comparing the features of Grid portals in each generation, we are able to conclude that a Semantic Grid portal toolkit, such as PortalLab, will play an important role in the widespread uptake of the Grid.

The rest of the chapter is organized as follows. In Section 6.2, we describe first generation grid portals; this section includes a discussion of a three-tiered architecture generally adopted and the implementation techniques used. We discuss four representative portal toolkits, GridPort [15], GPDK [3], Ninf Portal [16], and the XCAT Science Portal. In Section 6.3, we discuss second generation Grid portals that are built from portlets to help solve the typical "stovepipe" problems often incurred in the first generation of Grid portals. We review the status of Web portal toolkits using portlets and provide a comparison of their use in building Web Portals. In Section 6.4, we present a toolkit for building third generation grid portals. We discuss its software architecture and explain the features of Grid portals in the third generation. We compare the features of the three generations of grid portals in terms of portal services, portal usability, portal interoperability, and portal intelligibility. In Section 6.5, we conclude the chapter and give some recommendations in building a fully functional Grid portal toolkit for the emerging Grid architecture.

6.2   First Generation Grid Portals

In this section, we describe the development of the first generation Grid portals from the points of view of architecture, services, implementation techniques, and toolkits that can be used. Most Grid portals currently in use belong to the category.

6.2.1 A Three-tiered Architecture

First generation Grid portals usually follow a three-tiered architecture as adopted by the DSG Grid portal as shown in Fig. 6.1. The authors in [4] summarize that most grid portals in the first generation share the following characteristics:

- A typical three-tiered architecture, consisting of a first tier of Web Browsers, a middle tier of Web Servers, and a third tier of backend resources such as databases, high performance computers, storages, and specialized devices.
- A user makes a secure connection from a Web Browser to a Web Server.
- The Web Server then obtains a certificate from a proxy certificate server and uses that to authenticate the user.
- When the user completes defining the parameters of the task they want to execute, the portal Web Server launches an application manager, which is a process that controls and monitors the actual execution of the grid task(s).
- The Web Server delegates the user's proxy credentials to the application manager so that the application manger may act on the user's behalf.

6.2.2 Portal Services

First generation Grid portals usually provide the following Grid services:

- Authentication and Authorization

Authentication identifies who is connecting to the system; Authorization is the action of identifying the resources that an entity is permitted to interact with. A Grid portal, typically, provides a single sign-on mechanism [28] that allows users to access multiple remote resources after authentication has occurred.

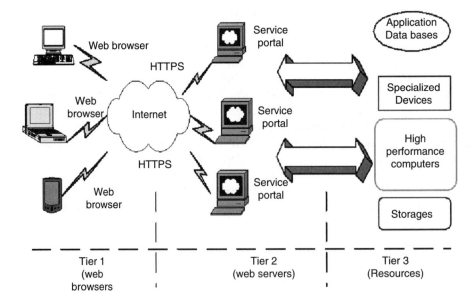

FIGURE 6.1. The three-tiered architecture of first generation Grid portals.

- Job Management

A Grid portal provides users with the ability to manage their tasks (sequential or parallel jobs), i.e., launching their applications via the Web Browser in a reliable and secure way, monitoring the status of tasks and pausing or canceling them if necessary.

- Data Transference

A Grid portal allows users to upload input data sets that need to accompany tasks that are to be executed on remote resources. Similarly the Grid portal enables results sets and other data to be downloaded via a Web Browser to a local desktop.

- Information Services

A Grid portal uses resource discovery mechanisms to discover resources that needed and are available for a particular task. Information that can be collected about resources includes the current load status, CPU configuration, free memory, operating system type, file system information, and network status. In addition, other details such as job status and queue information can also be retrieved.

6.2.3   First Generation Grid Portal Implementations

Most Grid portals in the first generation are implemented with the following technologies.

- A portal GUI is based on HTML pages, with Java Server Pages (JSP) or JavaScript support to provide users dynamics.
- The secure connection from a Web Browser to a Portal Server is via HTTPS.
- Typically, a Java Servlet or a Java Bean on the Web Server receives requests from a user and accesses backend resources.
- Myproxy [21] and Globus GSI [22] are used for user authentication and authorization. MyProxy allows a portal to use the GSI to interact with resources in a standard, secure manner.
- Globus GRAM [23] is used for job submission.
- Globus MDS [24] is used for gathering information on backend resources.
- Globus GSIFTP [50] or Globus GridFTP [51] for data transfer.
- The Java CoG [5] provides the access to the corresponding Globus services for Java programs.

The first generation of Grid portals relied heavily on the Globus toolkit to provide Grid services. The main reasons for this are that Globus provides a complete package and a standard way in building Grid-enabled systems. Globus is open source based and is being jointly developed by many international research efforts. The other reason is the OGSA, promoted by the Globus group and the Global Grid Forum (GGF) [86], is becoming a de facto standard in building services-oriented Grid systems. Currently the Globus toolkit 3 (GT3) has been released and are fully compliant with the OGSA. A Grid portal can be built from scratch using the techniques as mentioned in Section 2.3, or using a toolkit to speed up the construction and integration process.

6.2.4   First Generation Grid Portal Toolkits

In this section, we describe four representative Grid portal toolkits GridPort, GPDK, Ninf Portal, and the XCAT Science Portal. The toolkits can be used to assist system developers in building first generation Grid portals.

6.2.4.1 GridPort

GridPort is a Grid portal toolkit developed by the San Diego Supercomputer Center (SDSC) and the University of Texas. Early versions of GridPort were implemented using Perl CGI scripts. The purpose of GridPort was to facilitate the easy development of application-specific portals. Users can use GridPort in two ways. The first approach requires that Globus should be installed, because GridPort scripts wrap the C-based Globus command line tools in the form of Perl CGI scripts. The second approach to use GridPort does not require Globus, but relies on the CGI scripts that have been configured to use a primary GridPort Portal as a proxy for access to Grid-Port services, such as user authentication, job submission, and file transfer.

6.2.4.2 Grid Portal Development Kit (GPDK)

The GPDK is a Java-based Grid portal toolkit that provides several reusable components for accessing various Grid services. It provides a customizable interface that allows users to perform a variety of operations, including remote application submission, and querying information services. The GPDK gives users the ability to access Grid services in the form of Java Beans via JSP. A user can build a functional portal with the templates pages provided by GPDK.

6.2.4.3 Ninf Portal

The Ninf Portal is designed to facilitate the development of Grid portals by automatically generating a portal frontend that consists of JSP and Java Servlets from a Grid application interface definition language (IDL) defined in XML. The Ninf Portal then utilizes a GridRPC system, such as Ninf-G [6] to interact with Grid backend services.

6.2.4.4 The XCAT Science Portal

The XCAT Science Portal (XCAT-SP) toolkit does not use a centralized Web Server on a remote machine. The XCAT-SP is based on the idea of an "active document," which can be thought of as a "notebook" containing pages of text and graphics describing the science of a particular application and pages of parameterized, executable scripts. These scripts launch and manage the application, and results are dynamically added to the document in the form of data or links to output results and event traces. Grid portals are designed using a notebook of typical Web pages, input forms, and execution scripts. Notebooks have an interactive script/forms editor based on Jpython [57] that allows access to other toolkits such as Java CoG Kit and the Common Component Architecture Toolkit (CCAT) [29].

6.2.4.5 Limitations of First Generation Grid Portal Tools

The first generation Grid portals tools as mentioned above can assist Grid system developers in quickly building portals, but they have the following limitations.

• System Developers Oriented

System developers who build Grid portals normally use these tools. They provide assistance in the form of APIs or scripts that are difficult for naïve end users to get started. A good Grid portal tool should hide as much as possible the underlying complexity of the Grid from the users especially the end users.

- Poor Interoperability

The authors in [18] argue that a major shortcoming of the three-tiered Portal design is its lack of interoperability. The three-tiered architecture results in a classic "stovepipe" problem: user interfaces are locked into particular Grid middle tiers, which in turn are locked into specific backend systems. It is hard to integrate Grid services from different Grid-enabled technologies in a Grid portal of the first generation.

6.2.5   A Summary on First Generation Grid Portals

First generation Grid portals focus on providing basic task-oriented Grid services, such as user authentication and authorization, job submission, monitoring, and data transfer. They are typically tightly coupled with Grid middleware tools and rely heavily on Globus. These early Grid portal tools are mainly implemented and deployed by Grid system developers as the level of knowledge and expertise required for this process is beyond the capability of most naïve end users. However, the experiences and lessons learned in developing the first generation of Grid portals have paved the way towards the second generation Grid portals.

6.3   Second Generation Grid Portals

In this section, we discuss the development of second generation Grid portals. To overcome the "stovepipe" problem incurred in the first generation of Grid portals, portlets have been promoted for use in building second generation Grid portals. Currently, portlets are receiving more and more attentions both from the Grid community and industry. Projects from academia such as XPortlet [53], GridSphere [55] are underway, and aim to provide a framework for building Grid portals with portlets. We review the current status of portlet-oriented portal toolkits both from industry and academia, and give a comparison on their features in creating portlets. First we discuss the concepts behind portlets and explain the benefits that portlets could bring in.

6.3.1   Portlets

From a user's perspective, a portlet is a window in a portal that provides a specific service or information, for example, a calendar or news feed. From an application development perspective, portlets are pluggable modules that are designed to run inside the portlet container of a portal server. The portlet container provides a runtime environment in which portlets are instantiated, used, and finally destroyed. Portlets rely on the overall portal infrastructure to access user profile information, participate in window and action events, and communicate with other portlets, access remote content, lookup credentials, and store persistent data. The portlet container is not a stand-alone container like the Java Servlet container; instead, it is implemented as a thin layer on top of the Java Servlet container, and it reuses the functionality provided by the Java Servlet container.

6.3.1.1   The Concepts Behind Portlets

Portlets are a specialized and more advanced form of Java Servlet. They run in a portal server environment, which is a layer that runs on top of a Web application server. The portal server collects many portlets into a single portal, so users can access these portlet applications from one place. The portal server also provides many useful services for portlets to use. Like Java Servlets, portlets process HTTP requests and produce HTML output (using JSPs), but their HTML output is only a small part of a Web page. The portal server fills in the rest of the page with headers, footers, menus, and other portlets.

Compared with Java Servlets, portlets are administered in a dynamical and flexible way. The following updates can be applied without having to stop and restart the portal server.

- A portlet application, consisting of several portlets, can be installed and removed using the portal administration user interface.
- An administrator with appropriate access rights can change the settings of a portlet.
- Portlets can be created and deleted dynamically, for example, the clipping portlet can be used to create new portlet instances whenever an administrator creates a new clipping.

Portlets also have many standard features that are not available to Java Servlets. One key feature is the built-in support to automatically use different JSP pages for different user devices. This lets users write portlets that work on many devices, including desktop computers with modern Web Browsers, older, or palmtop computers with limited Web Browsers, personal digital assistants (PDAs), and Web-enabled wireless phones. Users do not need to provide portability via the lowest common denominator. They can provide multiple interfaces for different device types reusing the same underlying business logic, and the portal server will choose the most appropriate one for each user. Users can even have multiple portlet controllers, which allows different page/action sequences to be used for each device type.

Figure 6.2 shows how to access Web services from a Web Portal via a portlet. When a Web Portal receives a servlet request, it generates and dispatches events to the portlet using parameters in the request and then invokes the portlet to be displayed through the portlet invocation interface (PII). The portlet internal design normally follows the MVC model [7], which separates the portlet functionality into a controller receiving incoming requests from the PII, invoking commands operating on a model that encapsulates application data and logic to access backend Web content or applications, and finally calling views for presentation of the results.

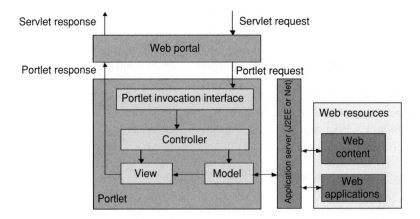

FIGURE 6.2. Access Web services in a Web Portal via a portlet.

6.3.1.2   Portlet Specifications

It is important for portlets developed from independent vendors to interoperate with each other. It is in an urgent need to have a standard for developing portlets. Currently, there are two working groups that work on the standardization of portlets. One is Organization for the Advancement of Structured Information Standards (OASIS) [58]. The other is Java Community Process (JCP) [59].

6.3.1.2.1   OASIS WSRP

The OASIS is a worldwide consortium that drives the development, convergence, and adoption of e-business standards. The consortium has more than 400 corporate and individual members in 100 countries. The Web Services for Remote Portals (WSRP) technical committee has been formed through OASIS. According to OASIS, the objective of WSRP is to define an XML and Web services standard that will allow the plug-and-play of visual Web services with portals or other intermediary Web applications.

6.3.1.2.2   JCP JSR

The JCP is an open organization of international Java developers and licensees whose charter is to develop and revise Java technology specifications, reference implementations, and technology compatibility kits. Java Specification Requests (JSRs) are the actual descriptions of proposed and final specifications for the Java platform.

The JSR168 [60] is the Portlet specification that would enable interoperability between portlets and portals. This specification will define a set of Portlet API for portal composition addressing the areas of aggregation, personalization, presentation and security.

6.3.1.2.3   The Relationship Between WSRP and JSR168

JSR168 defines the Portlet API to build portlets. When used in a remote environment, it is the standard interface that a Java-based WSRP service exposes. Although they are being governed by different standards bodies and review processes, WSRP and JSR168 are complementary specifications.

6.3.2   Portlet Oriented Portal Toolkits

In this section, we review some leading portal toolkits or frameworks that make use of portlets to build portals. The notables are Microsoft SharePoint Server [80], Plumtree Corporate Portal [81], Viador E-Portal [82], IBM WebSphere Portal Server [79], Sun ONE Portal Server [83], Apache Jetspeed [54], GridSphere [55], and Oracle Portal Development Kit [89]. We give a comparison on these tools in terms of usability, support for the Portlet API, providing prebuilt portlets, scalability, multiplatform support, and open source.

6.3.2.1   Microsoft SharePoint Server

Microsoft SharePoint Server is a portal solution for those who want to create, manage, and share content within Microsoft platforms. It is document centric, providing document sharing and document workflow. It has prebuilt Web Parts (portlets), but no support for the Portlet API. SharePoint is aimed at the intranet/e-workplace market and is not advisable for those with more ambitious or open requirements for e-portals. It has some good collaboration, document/work-flow and version control features.

6.3.2.2   Plumtree Corporate Portal

Personalization and enterprise application integration (EAI) are the two main strengths of the Plumtree Corporate Portal, which is primarily targeted at intranet/e-workplace or collaborative implementations. It provides over 300 gadgets (portlets) and Gadget APIs, and scale well for enterprise portals.

6.3.2.3   Viador E-Portal

Viador E-Portal is a Java based tool for building portals. It provides more than 50 portlets and links to backend databases. However, it is hard to set up and has limited collaboration tools.

6.3.2.4   IBM WebSphere Portal Server

WebSphere is an extensible framework for building and delivering portals providing the ability to access and interact with internal and external resources, which can include applications, content, people, and processes. The look and feel of each portal, its behaviour, and resources can be customized. In addition, users can personalize and organize their own view of the portal, manage their own profiles, and publish and share their documents. The WebSphere Portal provides core portal services including single sign-on, security, Web content publishing, search, personalization, collaboration services, enterprise application integration, support for mobile devices, and site analytics. WebSphere is based on OASIS WSRP standard, and provides a functional and integrated development environment (IDE) for building portals with portlets.

6.3.2.5   Sun ONE Portal Server

The Sun ONE Portal Server (formerly the iPlanet Portal Server) provides the key services required to build portals, including aggregation, presentation, security, personalization, integration, and identity management. Plus, it delivers centralized identity services for managing users, policy, and security.

The Sun ONE Portal Server includes point-and-click "wizards" to aggregate various types of content—XML, HTML, RSS (Rich Site Summary), WSDL [67], JSP, and Java Servlets. Prebuilt portlets are also available from various Sun partners, including syndicated and location-based content providers, as well as reporting, legacy, and content management vendors.

The Sun ONE Portal Server is open and extensible. Java APIs are available to access and extend various portal services, such as logging, authentication, or presentation. Deployment is straightforward through the use of a utility that enables a developer to deploy a portlet in a standard way to any portal server. Also, the deployment of portlets is dynamic, and new portlets are available to end users without the need to reboot the server.

6.3.2.6   Jetspeed

Jetspeed is an open source project from the Apache Software Foundation for building portals with portlets. It runs on the Tomcat Web Server and uses the Cocoon XML publishing framework for processing XML information via XSLT. Jetspeed is the source of the Portlet API. Jetspeed supports the Rich Site Summary (RSS) and Open Content Syndication (OCS) formats. The RSS is an XML format used for syndicating Web headlines. The OCS format describes multiple-content channels, including RSS headlines.

Whilst it comes with prebuilt portlets for OCS, RSS, and for embedding HTML sources, creating portlets for other information sources requires Java programming. Modifying the look and feel of a portal from the Jetspeed default also requires JSP or XSLT programming. Jetspeed makes connections to external data and content feeds to retrieve and display the data. Users can implement a portal and access it from a Web Browser or a wireless device (such as a WAP phone or Palm device). Jetspeed supports built-in services for user interface customization, caching, persistence, and user authentication, eliminating the need implement these services.

6.3.2.7   GridSphere

GridSphere is both an implementation of the Portlet JSR and an architecture for supporting the development of reusable portlets and portlet services. It includes a set of core portlets and portlet services that provide the basic infrastructure required for developing and administering Web Portals. A key feature of the design of GridSphere is that it builds upon the Web Application Repository (WAR) deployment model to support third-party portlet Web applications. GridSphere itself is deployed as a WAR and serves as a portlet container for other Portlet WARs that conform to the Portlet API and to the GridSphere deployment model. In this way, portlet developers can easily distribute and share their work with other portal projects that use GridSphere to support their portal development.

GridSphere aims to develop portlet applications that allow endusers make use of backend Grid technologies. GridSphere enables users to upload their Grid credentials and use them to gain access to a variety of Grid services. Moreover, GridSphere contains reusable portlet services that can support different implementations provided by different Grid technologies. The support of Grid services in GridSphere is still ongoing.

6.3.2.8   Oracle Portal Development Kit

Oracle Portal Development Kit (PDK) is a framework for seamless integration into Oracle9i AS Portal. The PDK allows users to develop portlets in any Web language including Java, XML, ASP, Perl, PL/SQL, and via Web Services. There are three types of portlets in the Oracle PDK—prebuilt, database, and Web. The Portal framework includes the services such as end-user personalization, session storage, context, security, logging, and error handling.

6.3.3   A Comparison of Portlet Oriented Portal Toolkits

Table 6.1 shows a comparison of portlet oriented portal toolkits in terms of their usability, support for the Portlet API, prebuilt Portlets, scalability, multiplatform support and open source.

From the points of usability and functionality, IBM WebSphere is the best portal development tool. However, it is not free downloadable thereby denying research groups in Grid community the ability to use the software for research in building Grid portals with portlets. Jetspeed is an open-source framework. It is the source of the Portlet API promoted by the JSR168, and it provides comprehensive functionalities in building portlets. Currently, Jetspeed has been widely used in Grid community to build Grid portals with portlets.

TABLE 6.1. A comparison of portlet oriented portal tools.

	Microsoft sharepoint	Plumtree portal	Viador E-Portal	IBM websphere	Sun ONE portal server	Jetspeed	GridSphere	Oracle PDK
Easy to use	✓			✓				
User customization	✓	✓		✓		✓	✓	✓
Powerful portlet API		✓	✓	✓		✓	✓	✓
Prebuilt portlets	✓	✓	✓	✓	✓	✓	✓	✓
Scalable		✓	✓	✓	✓	✓	✓	✓
Multiplatform support		✓		✓	✓	✓	✓	✓
Open source						✓	✓	

6.3.4 Building Grid Portals with Portlets

Building Grid portals with portlets is gaining attentions from the Grid community to overcome problem encountered in earlier portal development frameworks and toolkits. A portlet in a Grid portal is not just a normal portlet that can be plugged into a portal; it is also associated with a backend Grid service. We define a portlet associated with a Grid service, called a Grid Portlet. Figure 6.3 shows how to access a Grid service from a Grid portal via a Grid Portlet. The model in a Grid Portlet interacts with a Grid service provided by a Grid middleware tool such as Globus to access backend Grid resources. Grid Portlets provide portals with the ability to integrate services from different Grid technologies providers. However, no such tool currently exists that could provide an integrated development environment in which a Grid portal can be easily built with portlets, and integrate Grid services.

The Alliance Portal project [53] is an ongoing project on building the second generation Grid portals. It is based on Jetspeed and targeted at the construction of Grid portals with Grid portlets. Currently the Alliance Portal can provide the following Grid portlets that are leveraged from existing Grid services.

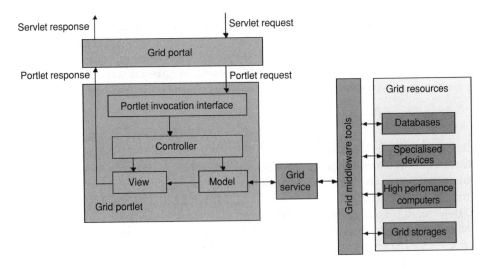

FIGURE 6.3. The Grid portlet concept.

- Interoperability

An SOA, first and foremost, stresses interoperability. That means that each service must provide an interface that can be invoked through a payload format and protocol that is understood by all of the potential clients of the service.

- Dynamic Discovery and Use

A service is design to be interoperable and it may be dynamically discovered and used. Services are deployed over a network; and a client on the network must be able to invoke and use the service.

6.4.3   The Software Architecture of PortalLab

PortalLab is an ongoing research project that aims to build the third generation Grid portals. Although it is still at an early stage, it has shown some features of the third generation Grid portals, which will be described through the section. Figure 6.5 shows the software architecture of PortalLab. Each component is described in detail in the following subsections.

6.4.3.1   Portlets in PortalLab

Portlets in PortalLab include normal portlets and Grid Portlets. Normal portlets are used to display contents on a Grid portal page. Apart from providing computational services such as job submission and monitoring, user authentication and authorization, data transferring, Grid Portlets

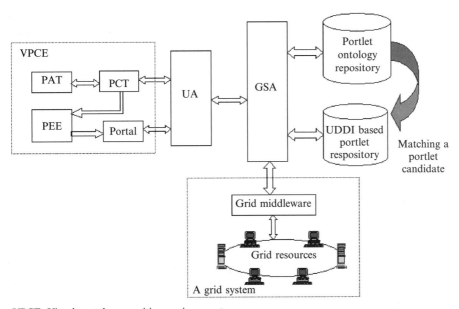

VPCE: Visual portal composition environment
PAT: Portal analysis tool,   PCT: Portal composition tool, PEE: Portal execution environment,
UA: User agent,   GSA: Grid system agent

FIGURE 6.5. The software architecture of PortalLab.

in PortalLab also provide domain problem solving services (solvers) and knowledge-related services such as extracting knowledge from a dataset using a data-mining algorithm. We define a Grid Portlet with semantic capabilities as a Semantic Grid Portlet (SGP). An SGP in PortalLab has a WSDL to describe how to use the portlet, the input/output parameters. The communication between the portlet and the Grid service associated is done through SOAP, via a SOAP proxy and an SOAP wrapper. Through an SOAP wrapper, a Grid service is exposed as a Web service that is independent of location, platform, and programming language. For example, an SGP may use Java CoG to interact with a Grid service provided by Globus toolkit 2 (GT2). In addition, each SGP has an XML description to define its semantic capabilities. Figure 6.6 shows the structure of an SGP in PortalLab.

Each SGP is defined in a context-independent way in terms of its interface, rather than its implementation. For example, a job submission Grid Portlet can be implemented by direct submittal to a queuing system or using Globus. A composite Grid Portlet can be constructed by binding together the interfaces of their constituent Grid Portlets to achieve another higher-level service. This approach is similar to that adopted in the Visual Component Composition Environment [9]. In this way, a Grid portal can be easily composed by plugging and playing independent Grid Portlets.

Since an existing Grid service provided by a Grid middleware toolkit can be leveraged to a uniform SOAP wrapper accessed via an SGP, a Grid portal in PortalLab can integrate Grid services from a variety of Grid systems and thus provides end users the ability to access federated Grid services at a portal level. Figure 6.7 shows a Grid portal consisting of three Grid Portlets leveraged from three Grid Services provided by Globus, Condor, and Myproxy respectively.

Portlets in PortalLab are defined in WSDL and registered with a UDDI-based Portlet Repository (UddiPR). Portlets in the UddiPR can be either private or shared; shared portlets act like libraries which can be used across portals, whereas private portlets are specific to particular portals and are defined by a particular user or user group. Users can also write or import their own portlets through wrappers and incorporate them into the UddiPR, and into a portal. These

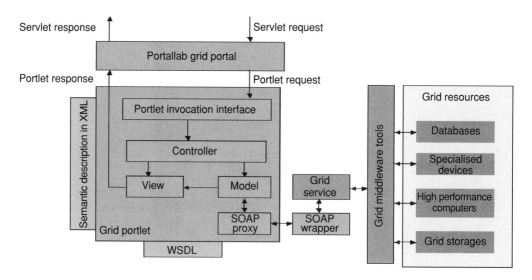

FIGURE 6.6. The Semantic grid portlet concept.

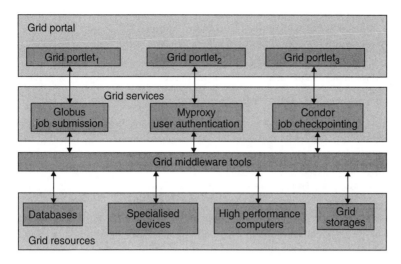

FIGURE 6.7. A Grid portal composed of three Grid portlets.

approaches give users a simple and flexible way to construct a Grid portal from a collection of reusable portlets. Users can produce portlets that they place in the UddiPR that are visible to just themselves, to a group of specified collaborators, or to everyone. The operations in the UddiPR include the registration of a portlet, discovery of an existing portlet, and removal of an obsolete portlet. The WSDL of a job submission portlet using Globus is shown in Fig. 6.8.

6.4.3.2   Enriching Semantics with Portlets in PortalLab

Each SGP in PortalLab has an interface specified in WSDL and a unique registry in a Portlet Ontology Repository (POR) defining their semantic capabilities. The primary target of the UDDI is the integration and semiautomation of business transactions in B2B e-commerce applications. It provides a registry for advertising businesses and the services on offer. These are described according to an XML schema defined by the UDDI specification. The UDDI search mechanism relies on pre-defined categorization through keywords and does not refer to the semantic content of the service registration. The registry functions in a fashion similar to white or yellow pages, where businesses can be looked up by name or by standard service taxonomies already used within the industry. However, UDDI does not support semantic descriptions of services. Currently users can program to search the UDDI registry and retrieve service descriptions; but a human needs to be involved to make sense of the descriptions, and to program actual access to the service.

To enhance the semantic support of Grid services in UddiPR, each Grid system has a POR describing the semantic capabilities of the SGPs of its domain. Here an ontology is defined as a set of knowledge-based terms, including the vocabulary, the semantic interconnections, and some simple rules of inference and logic for some particular topic [10]. Each POR is organized in a tree structure and defined in XML. Each registry in the POR has a unique entry in the UddiPR, which can be used to bind a core Grid service defined in WSDL. Each node in POR has a name and one or more related items of which each has a "match" degree to define the semantic relationship with the node. Figure 6.9 shows an ontology sample of a numerical problem solving SGP.

```
<?xml version="1.0" encoding="UTF-8"?>
<definitions
    name="GlobusJobSubmissionPortlet"
    targetNamespace="/home/eestmml/wsdl"
    xmlns:tns="urn:xmltoday-delayed-quotes"
    xmlns:xsd="http://www.w3.org/1999/XMLSchema"
    xmlns:soap="http://schemas.xmlsoap.org/wsdl/soap/"
    xmlns="http://schemas.xmlsoap.org/wsdl/">
    <message name="SubmissionRequest"/>
        <part name="RSL"type="xsd:string"/>
    <message name="SubmissionResponse"/>
    </message>
    <portTypename="GlobusJob"
        <operation name="Submission">
            <input message="tns:SubmissionRequest"/>
            <output message="tns:SubmissionResponse"/>
        </operation>
    </portType>
    <binding name="GlobusJobSOAPBinding"type="tns:GlobusJob">
        <soap:bindingstyle="rpc"transport=http://schemas.xmlsoap.org/soap/http/>
        <operation name="Submission">
            <soap:operation soapAction="submission"/>
            <input>
                <soap:body
                use="encoded"
                namespace="um:GlobusJobSubmission"
                encodingStyle=http://schemasxmlsoap.org/soap/encoding//>
            </input>
        </operation>
    </binding>
    <service name=GlobusJobSubmissionPortletService>
        <port name="GlobusJob"binding="tns:GlobusJobSOAPBinding">
        <soap:address location="http://localhost:8080/axis/services/GlobusJob"/>
        </port>
    </service>
</definitions>
```

FIGURE 6.8. The WSDL of a job submission portlet.

6.4.3.3   The Visual Portal Composition Environment (VPCE)

The VPCE in PortalLab provides an integrated environment for composing, compiling and executing portal services. It has three components, a Portal Composition Tool (PCT), a Portal Analysis Tool (PAT), and a Portal Execution Environment (PEE). The PCT provides a visual environment that allows users compose a Grid portal by plugging and playing portlets. The PAT displays the hierarchical structure of each portlet in an UddiPR, and gives information about its purpose, interface, and internal structure. After the portal has been constructed, the PEE will generate a task flow related to the portal and send it to a Grid System Agent (GSA) as described below.

6.4.3.4   Agents in PortalLab

In PortalLab, each SGP has a semantic description defined in a POR. A service consumer, such as an end user, needs to negotiate with a service provider about the terms under which services can be provided. The underlying complexity of the Semantic Grid infrastructure and the speedy interaction required, make software agents the most likely candidate to handle these negotiations.

is also significant, albeit, surprisingly, not always larger than in the relatively smaller-scale Grids: 1–2 TeraBytes per day in file sharing systems as of end of 2001 [34], amounting to less than half the data transferred in the D0 Experiment [35], which spans 73 institutions in 18 countries, with thousands of scientists involved, of which hundreds access its resources (data and computers) simultaneously. The amount of activity, on the other hand, can be large. For example, during the first half of 2002, about 300 D0 users submitted 2.7 million requests and retrieved 824 TeraBytes of data.

- Services and Infrastructure

The technologies used to develop Grid and P2P applications differ both in the specific services provided and in the emphasis placed on persistent, multipurpose infrastructure. The term *persistent* indicates that services are operated by participants over extended periods as critical and often highly available infrastructure elements, like DNS servers; and *multipurpose* indicates that the same services are used for many purposes (e.g., the same monitoring and discovery service [36] is used by a wide range of higher-level functions, such as computation scheduling, data replication, and fault detection). Services on the Grid include user authentication and authorization, job submission and monitoring, scheduling and coscheduling, data/file transferring, and many others. In contrast, P2P systems focus on the integration of simple resources and provide services mainly on file sharing. JXTA [73], XtremWeb [37], and BOINC [11] have been proposed as standard service infrastructure for P2P systems but, to date, have seen little adoption and no interoperability.

While the Grid and P2P differ in some aspects, they complement each other. Grid technologies can be applied to a P2P system where resources are heavily used. The P2P technologies can be applied to a Grid system where the environment is highly dynamic. The main features that P2P computing can bring to the Grid are cost sharing/reduction, resource aggregation and interoperability, and dynamism. It is envisioned that more and more Grid systems will appear in the future with each focusing on services of different domains. In PortalLab, each UA interacts with a GSA and multiple GSAs work in a P2P model. When building a Grid portal, a UA will ask a GSA to find the SGPs required. If a GSA does not have a required SGP, it may send a request to other GSAs to ask for the requested SGP. In this way, a Grid-portal built from PortalLab may use SGPs provided by different Grid systems which form a Grid-enabled P2P community. Figure 6.12 shows the Grid-enabled P2P architecture. The benefits the P2P paradigm could bring to the Grid, in this case, are portlets interoperability/aggregation, and the easy management of a large Grid environment, which may involve several VOs.

6.4.3.6   Integrating PortalLab with OGSA

Extended and refined from Web Services, OGSA, led by the Globus research group and IBM, has been receiving lots of attentions from the Grid community through the GGF. It is now becoming the de facto standard for building service-oriented Grid systems. While Web Services technologies address the discovery and invocation of persistent services, the Grid needs to tackle transient service instances. In order to become a Grid service, a Web service has to support a set of predefined interfaces and has to comply with certain conventions. The interfaces that are supported facilitate the discovery, creation, and lifetime management of transient services instances; they further facilitate a notification mechanism to enable the dynamic management of services. The conventions deal primarily with global naming services using Grid Service Handle (GSH) and Grid Service Reference (GSR). Based on these interfaces and conventions, standard semantics

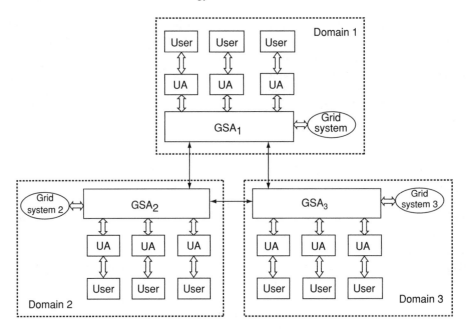

FIGURE 6.12. A Grid enabled P2P model in PortalLab.

for interacting with Grid service are defined: for example, how services are created (via a factory), how their lifetime is determined, and how to invoke functions of a service instance.

It is expected that many different environments, especially application server environments like J2EE or .NET will evolve to support OGSA-oriented Grid services. This would mean that the application servers might provide a special container for hosting these services or that existing containers are modified to support the semantics of these services (Grid service container). The authors in [44] describe the design of such a container based on both, native Java as well as on J2EE.

In this section, we first present an OGSA-oriented environment stack for the third generation Grid portals. We then describe how to leverage the SGPs in PortalLab to be OGSA compliant.

6.4.3.6.1 An OGSA-based Grid Portal Service Stack

Based on the Grid services environment stack presented by the author in [38], Fig. 6.13 shows an OGSA-based Grid portal service stack for building the third generation Grid portals.

An OGSA service container running on top of a Web server such as Sun One Web Server or Apache Tomcat [88] provides Grid services, such as registry, discovery, lifecycle management, services factory, notification, and handles. An OGSA does not place requirements on how a service is implemented, such as the implementation models, programming languages, and execution environments. Therefore, an OGSA-oriented Grid services can be hosted on application servers such as .Net or J2EE. A portlet container in a portal server provides a runtime environment in which portlets including Web portlets and Grid portlets are instantiated, used, and finally destroyed. The Grid portlets are implemented with backend OGSA-oriented Grid services. A third generation Grid portal built from OGSA-compliant portlets could provide services such as eCluster, eWorkflow, and eUtility to end users:

- To enable a variety of economic models with these services but not to explore the economic models themselves.

It is envisioned that there will be a market for trading portlets on the Grid. Renting and hiring a portlet will become popular in the near future, which will share the cost of development and reuse of portlets. Many service requestors do not have their own resources with which to develop sophisticated software or purchase the high-end machinery necessary to accomplish their tasks. For a specific domain problem, they may hire portlets to build a Grid portal to access Grid resources that solve their domain problems. To rent or hire a portlet on the Grid, a service provider or consumer needs to sign an SLA with a Grid center. The hiring of a portlet means that the executable of a portlet can be dynamically downloaded and started where it is needed. One important issue in renting a portlet is the service management of the portlet in term of usage charging. A reimbursement model can be "pay-as-you-use" or "rental" for a period.

References

[1] I. Foster, C. Kesselman, and S. Tuecke: The Anatomy of the Grid: Enabling Scalable Virtual Organizations, *International Journal of High Performance Computing Applications* 15(3), 200–222(2001)

[2] D. Roure, N. Jennings, N. Shadbolt: The Semantic Grid: A Future e-Science Infrastructure, in *Grid Computing: Making the Global Infrastructure a Reality*, ed by F. Berman, G. Fox, and A.J.G. Hey (Wiley, 2003), pp. 437–470

[3] J. Novotny, The Grid Portal Development Kit, *International Journal of Concurrency and Computation: Practice and Experience* 14(13–15), 1129–1144

[4] D. Gannon, R. Bramley, G. Fox, S. Smallen, A. Rossi, R. Ananthakrishnan, F. Bertrand, K. Chiu, M. Farrellee, M. Govindaraju, S. Krishnan, L. Ramakrishan, Y. Simmhan, A. Slominski, Y. Ma, C. Olariu, N. Rey-Cenvaz, Programming the Grid: Distributed Software Components, P2P and Grid Web Services for Scientific Applications, *Cluster Computing* 5(3), 325–336 (2002)

[5] G. Laszewski, I. Foster, J. Gawor, P. Lane, A Java Commodity Grid Kit, Concurrency and Computation: Practice and Experience, 13(8-9), 645–662 (2001)

[6] H. Nakada, M. Sato, S. Sekiguchi, Design and Implementations of Ninf: Towards a Global Computing Infrastructure, Future Generation Computing Systems, 15(5-6), 649–658. Metacomputing (1999)

[7] G. Krashner, S. Pose, A Cookbook for Using the ModelViewController User Interface Paradigm in Smalltalk80, *Journal of Object-Oriented Programming* 1(3), 27-49 (1998)

[8] L. Lee, J. Hendler, O. Lassila, *The Semantic Web*, Scientific American, May 2001

[9] D. Walker, M. Li, O. Rana, M. Shields, Y. Huang, The Software Architecture of a Distributed Problem-Solving Environment, *Concurrency: Practice and Experience* 12(15), 1455-1480 (2000)

[10] J. Hendler, Agents and the Semantic Web, *IEEE Intelligent Systems* 16(2), 30-37 (2001)

[11] D.P. Anderson, J. Kubiatowicz, The Worldwide Computer, *Scientific American* (2002) (3)

[12] T.R. Gruber, A translation Approach to Portable Ontology Specifications, *Knowledge Acquisition* 5(2): 199–220 (1993)

[13] R. Buyya, D. Abramson, J. Giddy, H. Stockinger, Economic Models for Resource Management and Scheduling in Grid Computing, Special Issue on *Grid Computing Environments, Concurrency and Computation: Practice and Experience* 14 (13-15) (2002)

[14] I. Foster, C. Kesselman, The Grid, Blueprint for a New Computing Infrastructure (Morgan Kaufman, San Francisco, CA, 1999)

[15] M. Thomas, S. Mock, J. Boisseau, M. Dahan, K. Mueller, D. Sutton, *The GridPort Toolkit Architecture for Building Grid Portals*, in Proceedings of the 10th IEEE Intl. Symptom on High Performance Distributed Computing (HPDC10), San Francisco, CA, Aug 2001, IEEE Press

[16] T. Suzumura, H. Nakada, M. Saito, S. Matsuoka, Y. Tanaka, S. Sekiguchi, *The Ninf Portal: An Automatic Generation Tool for the Grid Portals*, in Proceedings of Java Grande 2002, Seattle, Washington, (ACM, 2002)

[17] S. Krishnam, R. Bramley, D. Gannon, M. Govindaraju, R. Indurkar, A. Slominski, The XCAT Science Portal, in Proceedings of Super Computing (SC), Denver, Colorado, (IEEE Press, 2001)

[18] M. Pierce, C. Youn, G. Fox, The Gateway Computational Web Portal: Concurrency and Computation: *Practice and Experience*, 14(13–15) (2002)

[19] T. Haupt, P. Bangalore, G. Henley, *A Computational Web Portal for the Distributed Marine Environment Forecast System*, in Proceedings of HPCN 2001, Amsterdam, (2001), Lecture Notes in Computer Science, (Springer Verlag, 2001), pp. 104–113

[20] M. Thomas, S. Mock, J. Boisseau, *Development of Web Toolkits for Computational Science Portals: The NPACI HotPage*, in Proceedings of Ninth IEEE International Symposium on High Performance Distributed Computing (HPDC-11), Pittsburgh, Pennsylvania, (IEEE Press, 2000), 308–309

[21] J. Novotny, S. Tuecke, V. Welch, *An Online Credential Repository for the Grid: MyProxy*, in Proceedings of the Tenth International Symposium on High-Performance Distributed Computing (HPDC-10), San Francisco, California, (IEEE Press, 2001)

[22] I. Foster, C. Kesselman, G. Tsudik, S. Tuecke,; *A Security Architecture for Computational Grids*, in Proceedings of fifth ACM Conference on Computer and Communications Security Conference, San Francisco, California, (ACM, 1998), pp. 83–92

[23] K. Czajkowski, I. Foster, N. Karonis, C. Kesselman, S. Martin, W. Smith, S. Tuecke,; *A Resource Management Architecture for Metacomputing Systems*, in Proceedings of JSSPP'98, Lecture Notes in Computer Science (Springer-Verlag, 1998), pp. 62–82

[24] K. Czajkowski, S. Fitzgerald, I. Foster, C. Kesselam,; *Grid Information Services for Distributed Resource Sharing*, in Proceedings of the Tenth IEEE International Symposium on High-Performance Distributed Computing (HPDC-10), (IEEE Press, 2001)

[25] T. Suzumura, S. Matsupka, H. Nakana, JiPANG: *A Jini Based Computing Portal System*, in Proceedings of Super Computing 2001 (SC01), Denver, Colorado (IEEE Press, 2001)

[26] M. Pierce, G. Fox, C. Youn, S. Mock, K. Mueller, O. Balsoy, *Interoperable Web Services for Computational Portals*, in Proceedings of Super Computing 2002 (SC02) (IEEE Press, 2002)

[27] Sarmenta, L.: Bayanihan Computing .NET, *Grid Computing with XML Web Services*, in Proceedings of CCGrid 2002, Berlin, Germany, (IEEE Press, 2002)

[28] K. Keahev, V. Welch, *Fine-Grain Authorization for Resource Management in the Grid Environment*, in Proceedings of Grid2002 Workshop, (2002)

[29] R. Bramley, K. Chiu, S. Diwan, D. Gannon, M. Govindarju, N. Mukhi, B. Temko, M. Yechuri, *A Component Based Services Architecture for Building Distributed Applications*, in Proceedings of HPDC 2000, Pittsburgh, Pennsylvania (IEEE Press, 2000)

[30] M. Li, P. Santen, D. Walker, O. Rana, M. Baker, PortalLab: *A Web Services Toolkit for Building Semantic Grid Portals*, in Proceedings of IEEE/ACM International Symposium on Cluster Computing and the Grid (CCGrid 2003), Tokyo, Japan, (IEEE Press, 2003)

[31] L. Sarmenta, S. Chua, P. Echevarria, J. Mendoza, R. Santos, S. Tan, *Bayanihan Computing .NET: Grid Computing with XML Web Services*, in Proceedings of the second CCGrid 2002, Berlin, Germany (IEEE Press, 2002)

[32] I. Foster, A. Iamnitchi, *On Death, Taxes, and the Convergence of Peer-to-Peer and Grid Computing*, in Proceedings of the second International Workshop on Peer-to-Peer Systems (IPTPS'03), Berkeley, CA, USA (2003), Lecture Notes in Computer Science (Springer Verlag, 2003)

[33] Laic, G. Medvunsky, B.C. Neuman, *Endorsements, Licensing, and Insurance for Distributed System Services*, in Proceedings of the second ACM Conference on Computer and Communication Security, (1994), Fairfax, Virginia, (ACM Press, 1994)

[34] S. Sen, J. Wang, *Analyzing Peer-to-Peer Traffic Across Large Networks*, in Proceedings of Internet Measurement Workshop, Marseille, France, (ACM Press, 2002)

7.2   Fraunhofer Resource Grid

The Fraunhofer Resource Grid is a initiative of five Fraunhofer institutes funded by the German federal ministry of education and research with the main objective to develop and to implement a stable and robust distributed computing infrastructure within the Fraunhofer–Gesellschaft, to integrate available resources, and to provide internal and external users with an easy-to-use interface for controlling distributed applications and services [13]. The component environment supports loosely coupled applications where each software component represents an executable file that reads input files and writes output files (atomic job) [16]. The communication between the atomic jobs is realized via file transfer. Legacy code can be integrated easily using shell scripts to encapsulate the program. Up to now, the workflow architecture does not support tightly coupled schemes like CORBA, MPI, or HLA, but such applications can be included as a whole like an atomic job. Most of the software developed within the FhRG will be made Open Source (GPL) under the label *eXeGrid* [10].

Figure 7.1 depicts the general architecture of the FhRG, that is built on top of the Globus Toolkit 2.4 [38]. The user has four different alternatives to access resources within this architecture:

1. The user can directly use the standard **Globus services** like GRAM or GridFTP in order to run simple Globus jobs (atomic jobs) on a specified node.
2. If the user wants to run a predefined Grid job, he can use the **Grid Job Handler Web Service**. In this case, the user must provide a document that specifies the Grid job (GJobDL, see Section 7.3 and 7.4). The selection of suitable resources is done during runtime on current information.

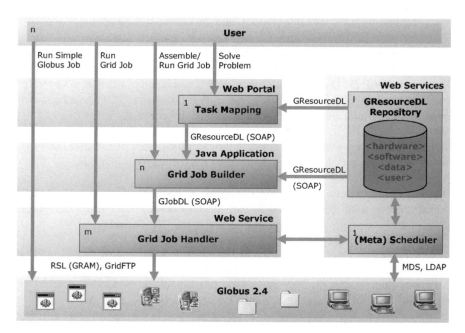

FIGURE 7.1. The layered architecture of the Fraunhofer Resource Grid. The numbers in the upper left corners denote the cardinality.

3. The user may use the graphical **Grid Job Builder** to assemble and configure the resources to form a coupled Grid job that is defined by a GJobDL document.
4. If the user does not have the information which resources to use in order to solve his problem, he may invoke the **Task Mapping** of the Web portal. There, the user navigates through a task tree in order to restrict the application area of the problem and to map it onto a suitable set of resources.

7.3   Describing Grid Resources

One basic service in state-of-the-art Grid computing environments is resource mapping or resource brokerage, which is responsible for finding resources that match specified resource requests. Special solutions already exist for various kinds of resource requests, such as the Storage Resource Broker [33], the implementation of Set-Matching algorithms [26], and the Globus Resource Broker in the Globus Toolkit [12]. Our approach is a more general one. To describe the properties and requirements of resources, we have developed a generic and extensible family of XML-based languages. The objective of this Grid Application Definition Language (GADL) is to assemble and to define complex-distributed applications on an abstract level with the aim of automatically mapping these applications onto the available and suitable hardware and software resources, and to control the workflow and dataflow during the execution. The GADL consists of four major parts each covering a different scope:

GResourceDL: The Grid Resource Definition Language is used to describe and to categorize resources. The term "resource" comprises hardware resources (computers, measuring devices, etc.) as well as software components and data. The GResourceDL delegates some special parts of the resource description to the GInterfaceDL and the GDataDL (see below).

GInterfaceDL: Currently, the Grid Interface Definition Language is mostly a placeholder for descriptions of advanced interfaces of software components that incorporate technologies such as CORBA [31] or SOAP [15] for communication. Web Service interfaces that incorporate SOAP are currently described by the Web Service Description Language [3]. Simple communication techniques via standard IO and files are included in the GResourceDL.

GDataDL: The Grid Data Definition Language provides the description of data that is available as resources or data streams that are exchanged between software components.

GJobDL: The Grid Job Definition Language is used to describe Grid jobs, i.e., a set of resource descriptions together with the definition of their dependencies and logical interrelations. The description of the participating resources is delegated to the GResourceDL.

In order to support task-mapping mechanisms for problem-solving environments and resource discovery with regard to the dependencies between resources, it is mandatory to have suitable metadata about the resources involved in the Grid job. Therefore, the Grid Resource Definition Language (GResourceDL) supports the description of six basic resource types:

concrete software components (type="software"),
software classes (type="softwareClass"),
concrete hardware resources (type="hardware"),

hardware classes (type="hardwareClass"),
concrete data (type="data"), and
data classes (type="dataClass").

The distinction between concrete instances of objects on the one hand, and classes of objects on the other hand is very useful when resolving the dependencies between resources during the resource mapping. Here, we use the term *instance* for objects that actually possess a physical (or logical) location represented by a unique location tag, e.g., the IP number of a hardware resource or the URI of a data file. A *class* of objects does not possess a unique location tag, though. A hardware class could be a certain type of processor (e.g., AMD Athlon) or the minimal amount of memory (e.g., RAM > 512MB). A software class, for example, could be the operating system "Linux" or the library "glibc-2-3." Another design principle applied to the GResourceDL—besides the distinction between instances and classes—is the concept of extension by inheritance, thus allowing the recursive formulation of complex and nested resource descriptions with a small set of basic language elements. This is achieved by introducing a language element that allows us to define dependencies between different resource descriptions. The syntax of declaring relationships between resources has been borrowed from the Advanced Package Tool (apt) provided by Debian GNU/Linux [5]. Four types of dependencies are currently supported by the GResourceDL:

depends is used to declare that one resource absolutely depends on one or more others, e.g., the software component "lagrange" depends on the software classes "linux," "glibc-2-3," and the hardware class "x86."

provides is used to declare that one resource provides or contains one or more others. The resource inherits the properties of the resource provided and may extend it by further properties, e.g., the resource "linux-kernel-2-4-18" provides and extends the software class "linux."

conflicts is used to declare that one resource must not be used together at the same time with other resources.

suggests is used to declare that one resource may be more useful with one or more others.

GResourceDL excerpt of a software and hardware resource description:

```
<resource id="lagrange" type="software">
<dependencies type="depends">
    <resourceRef id="linux" type="softwareClass" />
    <resourceRef id="glibc-2-3" type="softwareClass" />
    <resourceRef id="x86" type="hardwareClass" />
</dependencies>
...
</resource>

<resource id="gridNode15" type="hardware">
<dependencies type="provides">
    <resourceRef id="x86" type="hardwareClass" />
    <resourceRef id="network-ethernet-100"
```

```
                        type="hardwareClass" />
        <resourceRef id="linux-kernel-2-4-18"
                        type="softwareClass" />
        <resourceRef id="glibc-2-3" type="softwareClass" />
    </dependencies>
    <location>
        <url>
        x-gram://gridNode15.fhg.de:2119/jobmanager:
        /O=Fraunhofer/O=Globus/CN=host/gridNode15.fhg.de
        </url>
    </location>
    <parameter name="memory.freeVirtual" unit="MB">
        <timestamp unit="iso8601">
        2003-05-15T08:45:00Z
        </timestamp>
        <value type="int" op="eq">1027</value>
    </parameter>
    ...
    </resource>
```

In the above example, the hardware resource "gridNode15" matches the requirements of the software resource "lagrange" if the software class "linux-kernel-2-4-18" provides the resource "linux." The element <resourceRef>   defines a reference to a resource that is already declared in another place. The GResourceDL includes two different approaches to declare the properties of the resources. The first approach is provided by including a generic element "parameter." The value of each parameter is defined by the child element "value" and its attribute "op" ∈ {=, >, ≥, <, ≤}. The name of the parameter is declared by its attribute "name." This generic approach has the disadvantage that the names and types of the parameters cannot be specified in advance and typing errors may consequently result in runtime errors. Another shortcoming is the overhead needed to categorize and search specific properties. Therefore, we include a second approach in the GResourceDL, declaring frequently-used properties by own element tags that can be checked directly by means of a validating XML parser. Frequently-used resource properties that are needed in a distributed environment are, e.g., the resource location, the execution location, the input and output ports, as well as accounting and authorization information.

7.4   Grid Job Orchestration

In the Grid computing community, there are several approaches to execute; not only single tasks on single resources but also to support workflow schemes that enable the composition and execution of complex distributed applications. Advanced job orchestration tools support the user in defining Grid jobs independently of the hardware infrastructure and implementation-specific details. The user should be able to focus on the functionality and the data he wants to include in the Grid job.

The composition framework we describe in this section considers loosely coupled software components; the communication is achieved using standard IO and file transfer. The main advantage of this approach is that it does not require any modification or recompilation of the software components, so existing legacy code can be included easily in the framework. The coordination and synchronization of the execution of multiple application tasks is done by an external driver called *Grid Job Handler* (see Section 7.5) that acts as a higher-level service on top of existing middleware. This technique is different from other computing frameworks, which use tighter coupling schemes, such as MPI [30], CORBA [31], or Cactus [36], where remote procedure calls or message passing function calls are often included directly in the source code of the software component. Of course, our approach would be inadequate for certain high-performance applications, but by not requiring internal modifications on integration it is superior when bringing a broad range of applications to the Grid.

There are several possibilities to provide a workflow management that coordinates the execution of Grid jobs. Either the workflow is defined inherently by the software components themselves, or by software agents that act on behalf of the software components, resulting in a self-organizing or hard-wired Grid job. Another alternative is to define the workflow on a metalevel on top of the software components, providing a complete view of the workflow. To describe this kind of workflow, it is very important to have suitable semantics. There are three main approaches to achieve the workflow description: it may be based on scripting languages (e.g., GridAnt [23], and JPython in XCAT [21]), on graphs (e.g., Condor DAGman [4], and Symphony [27]), or on a mixture of both (e.g., WSFL [25], XLANG [35], BPEL4WS [2], UNICORE [9], and GSFL [22]). Although the scripting language approaches may be very convenient for skilled users, they are not really intuitive and are limited by the vocabulary provided by the scripting language as every type of workflow needs other language elements (e.g., for sequential or parallel execution, loops, conditions, etc.).

In our approach, we use a Petri-net-based workflow model that allows the graphical definition of arbitrary workflows with only few basic graph elements—just by connecting data and software components. Figure 7.2 shows a screenshot of the Grid Job Builder, a Java application providing a graphical user interface for assembling Grid jobs. The output of the Grid Job Builder is a GJobDL document, which defines the Grid job. This GJobDL document can be stored as a file or be transmitted directly to the Grid Job Handler Web Service in order to enact the workflow.

The GJobDL description of a Grid job contains the resource descriptions of the basic resources that are required to define it and a model of the workflow and dataflow using the concept of Petri nets [32]. In many other projects, the workflow of coupled-distributed applications is modeled using Directed Acyclic Graphs (DAG) (see Fig. 7.3). One example for this approach is UNICORE, where so-called AbstractJobs are defined on the basis of DAGs [9]. Other prominent projects using DAGs are Condor [4], [34], Cactus [36], and Symphony [27]. The DAGs are widely spread due to their simple structure they possess, however, some relevant disadvantages: DAGs are acyclic, so it is not feasible to explicitly define loops (while...do), and they only describe the behavior, but not the state of the system. The DAGs generally describe either the workflow or the dataflow but not both of them. Because of these limitations we decided to use Petri nets (see Fig. 7.3) instead of DAGs. The idea to use Petri nets to control the workflow of complex applications has been borrowed from the Graphical Simulation Builder that is being developed by the Potsdam Institute for Climate Impact Research (C. Ionescu, personal communication) The author in [29] describes a similar approach in his book about internet-based workflow management.

Petri nets are a special class of directed graphs. The type of Petri nets we introduce here corresponds to the concept of Petri nets with individual tokens (colored Petri net) and constant

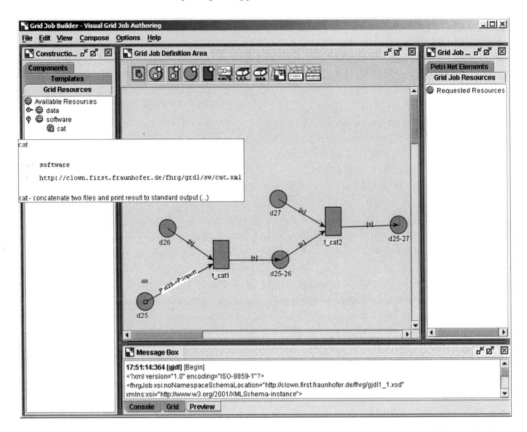

FIGURE 7.2. A screenshot of the Grid Job Builder, developed by Fraunhofer IGD. The Grid Job Builder includes a resource browser (*left*), a composition panel for Petri-net-based workflows (*middle*), a job inspector (*right*), and a message box (*bottom*). The Grid Job Builder supports drag and drop to introduce new components to the job workflow.

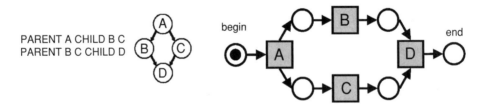

FIGURE 7.3. Example of a Directed Acyclic Graph (DAG) (*left*) and the equivalent Petri net (*right*).

arc expressions which are composed of places, denoted by circles (○); transitions, denoted by boxes (□); arcs from places to transitions (○ → □); arcs from transitions to places (□ → ○); individual and distinguishable objects that flow through the net as tokens (·); an initial marking that defines the objects that each place contains at the beginning, and an expression for every arc that denotes an individual object. A place p is called input place (output place) of transition t if an arc from p to t (from t to p) exists. A brief introduction to the theoretical aspects of colored Petri-nets can be found, e.g., in [20]. The standardization of the Petri-net concept is in progress as an ISO 15909 committee draft [19].

Petri nets can be made Turing complete, e.g., by introducing a single FIFO place. This shows that in principle they are suitable to model arbitrary computing algorithms, but with the disadvantage that complex and huge workflows may result in very complex graphs. A hierarchical Petri net model—where single transitions may act as containers for subPetri nets—could hide this complexity; however this approach would considerable increase the effort of implementing the architecture. The usefulness of the Petri-net model strongly depends on the granularity of the component model that is supported. While Petri nets are very suitable to describe the workflow among coarse-grained components like large-size programs and applications, other approaches, such as XCAT [21], WSFL [25], BPEL4WS [2], MPI [30], CORBA [31], or Cactus [36] may be better suited for fine-grained components consisting of small-size components like functions, modules, and classes.

The workflow of a Petri net is not required to be deterministic. This makes it difficult to predict the runtime of a Grid job, especially for complex graphs that include conditions and loops. In this context, DAGs are easier to handle as every node of the graph will only be reached exactly once, however, it is trivial to map any DAG onto a Petri net with the same properties.

Within the Askalon project, the group of Thomas Fahringer is following another promising approach by using UML activity diagrams in order to model the workflow of Grid jobs [11]. The UML activity diagrams are graph representations similar to Petri nets but with more classes of graph elements that are very common in the software engineering community. In our opinion this approach is very adequate in order to model complex distributed software; however, it would be much more complicated to implement a handler that maps this type of graph automatically onto real resources, and executes the corresponding workflow on the Grid.

Petri nets possess special characteristics that can be defined mathematically and are used to analyze and to classify Petri nets. Terms like *conflict, confusion, contact, pit,* and *deadlock* are well-defined properties of Petri nets that may be helpful when optimizing the workflow of a Grid job. When using Petri nets, it is easy to model all kinds of discrete workflows by means of the three basic components—places, transitions, and arcs. The actual state of the workflow is represented by the marking of the Petri net. An overview of how to describe different workflow patterns using Petri nets can be found in [1]. Petri nets are suitable to describe the sequential and parallel execution of tasks with or without synchronization; it is possible to define loops and the conditional execution of tasks. Conditional transitions are required at every region in the Petri net where two ore more activated transitions share the same input place and compete for the token that is located on that place. This situation is called *conflict.* In our framework, the decision which transition fires is taken by evaluating disjunctive conditions that are referred by the transition.

We use Petri nets not only to *model,* but furthermore to *control* the workflow of Grid jobs. In most cases, the workflow within Grid jobs is equivalent to the dataflow, i.e., the decision when to execute a software component is taken by means of availability of the input data. Therefore, the tokens of the Petri net represent real data that is exchanged between the software components. In this case, we use Petri nets to model the interaction between software resources represented by software transitions, and data resources represented by data places. In some cases, however, the workflow is independent from the dataflow, and in addition to the data places and software transitions we have to introduce control places and control transitions. The corresponding tokens contain the state of the process (e.g., done, failed). Control transitions evaluate logical conditions. For further details about the Petri net approach of the FhRG refer to [17] and [18].

There already exist several approaches to describe Petri nets with XML-based description languages. Widely spread is the Petri Net Markup Language (PNML) developed by the Humboldt–Universität zu Berlin [40]. A dedicated XML syntax, similar to the PNML, is introduced in the GJobDL. The job description consists of the declaration of the places, transitions, and arcs that build the Petri net of the Grid job. Transitions and places may be linked to external or internal GResourceDL descriptions. Control transitions may possess conditions that are evaluated prior to the firing of activated transitions. Places may have an initial marking that defines the initial state of the Grid job.

GJobDL excerpt of the Grid job already displayed in Fig. 7.2:

```xml
<!-- data: d25 -->
<resource id="d25" type="data">
  <location>
    <resourceRef id="gridNode15" type="hardware"/>
    <directory>/home/fhrgdata</directory>
    <filename>d25.dat</filename>
  </location>
</resource>
...
<!-- workflow description -->
<job type="petriNet" id="concatenateIt">
  <place id="d25">
    <resourceRef id="d25" type="data"/>
    <initialMarking>
      <value type="boolean" op="eq">true</value>
    </initialMarking>
  </place>
  ...
  <place id="d25-27">
    <resourceRef id="d25-27" type="data"/>
  </place>
  <transition id="t_cat1">
    <resourceRef type="software" id="cat"/>
  </transition>
  <transition id="t_cat2">
    <resourceRef type="software" id="cat"/>
  </transition>
  <arc id="arc1" type="P2T">
    <placeRef id="d25"/>
    <transitionRef id="t_cat1">
      <inputRef id="input1" type="file"/>
    </transitionRef>
  </arc>
  ...
</job>
```

7.5   Grid Job Execution and Monitoring

The Grid Job Handler is responsible for the execution of each Grid job on a set of suitable hardware resources. Therefore, the Grid Job Handler parses the job description, resolves the dependencies between the resources, and searches for sets of hardware resources that fulfill the requirements of each software component. A meta scheduler (see Fig. 7.1) is used to select the best-suited hardware resource of each set of matching hardware resources, according to a given scheduling policy (fastest, cheapest, etc.). The Grid Job Handler maps the resulting atomic jobs onto the Globus Resource Specification Language (RSL) [37] and submits them via GRAM to the corresponding nodes. For the communication between the Grid Job Handler and the Globus middleware, we use a patched version of the Java Commodity Grid Kit [24]. The Grid Job

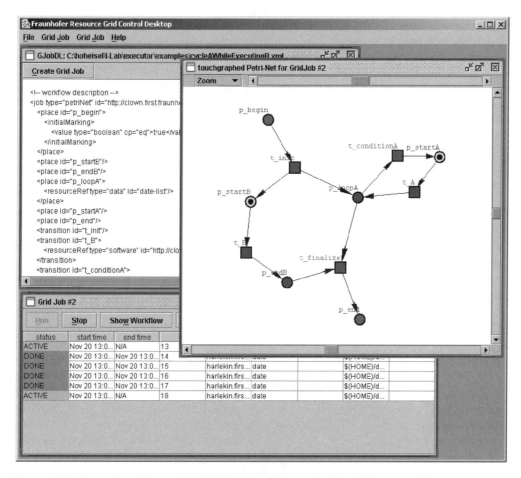

FIGURE 7.4. Screenshot of the graphical Grid Job Handler user interface. The upper left panel displays an excerpt of the GJobDL document. The right panel shows a graphical representation of the corresponding job workflow. The lower left panel lists the atomic jobs that are induced by the Grid job with their actual status.

Handler itself is deployed as a Web Service with possibilities to create, run, and monitor Grid jobs remotely. The desktop version of the Grid Job Handler includes a graphical user interface (see Fig. 7.4) and additional command line tools.

The following steps are iteratively invoked in the kernel of the Grid Job Handler:

1. **Verify** the Petri net (well-formedness, liveliness, deadlocks, pits, etc.).
2. Collect all **activated transitions** of the Grid job.
3. Evaluate the **conditions** of the activated transitions.
4. Invoke **method calls** that are referred by the activated transitions (transfer executable, transfer data, unpack, etc.).
5. If a transition references a software component, invoke the **resource mapping** in order to get a set of matching hardware resources.
6. Ask the **meta scheduler** for the best-suited hardware resource to execute the software component out of the set of matching hardware resources.
7. **Refine** the Petri net if necessary (insert additional data transfer, software deployment, or fault management tasks).
8. **Submit** the **atomic jobs** to the hardware resources using the middleware (e.g., GRAM).
9. A **transition fires**, if the corresponding atomic job is "done" or has "failed." Remove tokens from input places and put tokens containing information about the exit status of the atomic job to the output places.
10. **Repeat 1-9** until there are no more activated transitions left.

Note that it does not matter how complex the distributed application becomes, the kernel of the Job Handler remains the same for every type of workflow.

7.5.1 Dynamic Workflow Refinement

The refinement model of the Petri net theory allows substituting parts of a Petri net by new sub-Petri nets. The Grid Job Handler takes advantage of this feature and supplements the workflow during runtime by introducing additional tasks that are necessary to complete the Grid job. The user is not required to model every detail of the workflow—he just has to include the essential transitions and places that are related to the software components and the data he wants to include in his Grid job. Additional tasks that have to be invoked due to specific properties of the infrastructure (e.g., network topology) are detected by the Grid Job Handler and considered by automatically introducing additional transitions and places before or during runtime of the Grid job.

In the current version of the Grid Job Handler, data transfer tasks and software deployment tasks are automatically added to the workflow if they are missing in the initial Grid job definition provided by the user. A data transfer task may be introduced to transfer files that are not available on the remote computer (Fig. 7.5). A software deployment task may be introduced to

FIGURE 7.5. Software components *A* and *B* are scheduled to different nodes (*left*). A data transfer task is introduced to transfer the output files of *A* to the location where *B* will be executed (*right*).

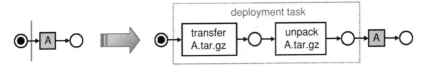

FIGURE 7.6. Software component *A* is to be executed on a node, where it is not yet installed (*left*). A software deployment task is introduced to install the software on the corresponding node (*right*).

automatically install software components (Fig. 7.6). Further Petri net refinements could concern authorization, accounting, billing, and fault management tasks (see next section).

7.5.2 Fault Management

We distinguish between *implicit* and *explicit* fault management. **Implicit fault management** is inherently included in the middleware and is invoked either by lower-level services regarding fault management of atomic jobs or by higher-level services considering the workflow of the Grid job. This type of implicit fault management can be achieved by Petri net refinement as shown in Fig. 7.7, where a fault management task is introduced automatically if the submission or execution of an atomic task fails. **Explicit fault management** in our definition refers to user-defined fault management. Within the Petri net workflow model, the user defines the fault management explicitly by including user-defined fault management tasks in the Petri net of the Grid job. Two examples of user-defined fault management are shown in Fig. 7.8.

We propose that Grid architectures should provide mechanisms for both, implicit and explicit fault management. The implicit fault management guarantees a basic fault tolerance of the system whereas explicit fault management is needed to support arbitrary, user-defined fault management strategies.

7.6 Case Study

An example application that takes advantage of the described workflow framework is the **Environmental Risk Analysis and Management System (ERAMAS)**, developed by *Fraunhofer FIRST* in collaboration with the *Ingenieurbüro Beger für Umweltanalyse und Forschung* and the *Dresdner Grundwasser Consulting GmbH* [6], [39]. The ERAMAS is a simulation-based analysis framework for risks caused by carcinogenic and chemically toxic substances that are

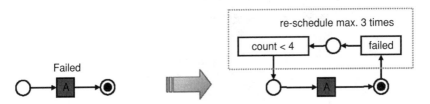

FIGURE 7.7. Example of implicit fault management. If the execution of software component *A* fails (*left*), a fault management task may be introduced into the Petri net (*right*). Here, the fault management task reschedules the software component maximum three times.

FIGURE 7.8. Two examples of explicit, user-defined fault management. If *A* fails, *B* will be executed; if *A* completes successfully, *C* will be executed (*left*). If *A* does not complete after a specified time out, *C* will be executed. If *A* completes in time, *B* will be executed (*right*).

released during accidents in industrial installations, the transport of dangerous goods, or by terrorist attacks. It is designed to be employed for real-time emergency management as well as for preliminary studies concerning approval procedures and emergency plans.

Figure 7.9 shows an overview of the simulation models involved in ERAMAS regarding the different transportation paths in the atmosphere and the ground. Currently ERAMAS includes the following components:

- A *diagnostic wind field model (dwm)* that calculates 3-D realistic wind fields considering topography from sparse input data, e.g., measurements from a weather station such as wind speed and direction, temperature, stability class.
- Several *source modules* for the simulation of the pollutant emission through a chimney, jet release, line source, or evaporation from a puddle. To consider uncertainties in the input data, we use a Monte Carlo Simulation for these source modules.
- A *lagrange model* for the simulation of the pollutant transport in the atmosphere. It calculates from the emissions and the 3-D wind field the spatial and temporal distribution of the pollutants.

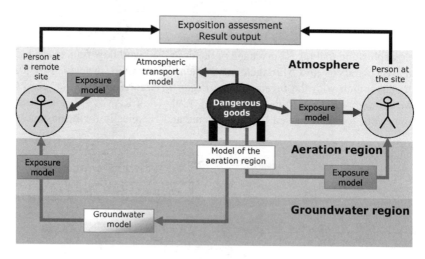

FIGURE 7.9. ERAMAS integrates a variety of physical simulation models in order to calculate the transport of carcinogenic and chemically toxic substances in the atmosphere and the ground and the exposure to human beings.

[18] A. Hoheisel, U. Der, *Dynamic Workflows for Grid Applications*, in Proceedings of the Cracow Grid Workshop '03, Cracow, Poland, (2003) http://www.andreas-hoheisel.de/docs/Hoheisel_and_Der_2003_CGW03.pdf

[19] ISO 15909: *High-level Petri Nets – Concepts, Definitions and Graphical Notation*, Committee Draft ISO/IEC 15909, Version 3.4, (1997) http://www.daimi.au.dk/PetriNets/standardisation/

[20] K. Jensen, An Introduction to the Theoretical Aspects of Coloured Petri Nets, in Lecture Notes in Computer Science, vol. 803 (Springer-Verlag, Berlin Heidelberg New York, 1994) 230–272

[21] S. Krishnan, R. Bramley, D. Gannon, M. Govindaraju, R. Indurkar, A. Slominski, B. Temko, J. Alameda, R. Alkire, T. Drews, and E. Webb, *The XCAT Science Portal, SC 2001*, (ACM SIGARCH / IEEE, Denver 2001)

[22] S. Krishnan, P. Wagstrom, and G. von Laszewski, GSFL: *A Workflow Framework for Grid Services*, Technical Report, The Globus Project, (2002) http://www-unix.globus.org/cog/projects/workflow/gsfl-paper.pdf

[23] G. von Laszewski, K. Amin, B. Alunkal, S. Hampton, and S. Nijsure, *Gridant – white paper*. Technical report, Argonne National Laboratory (2003) http://www.globus.org/cog/grant.pdf

[24] G. von Laszewski, I. Foster, J. Gawor, and P. Lane, A Java Commodity Grid Kit. Concurrency and Computation: Practice and Experience 13, 643–662 (2001)

[25] F. Leymann, Web Services Flow Language (WSFL 1.0). Technical report. IBM Software group (2001)

[26] C. Liu, L. Yang, I. Foster, and D. Angulo, *Design and Evaluation of a Resource Selection Framework for Grid Applications*. in Proceedings of the 11th IEEE International Symposium on High Performance Distributed Computing (HPDC11), Edinburgh, Scotland (2002), 63–72

[27] M. Lorch, and D. Kafura, Symphony—*A Java-based Composition and Manipulation Framework for Computational Grids*, in Proceedings of the CCGrid2002. Berlin, Germany (2002)

[28] T. Mailund, K. Mortensen, *Separation of style and content with XML in an interchange format for high-level Petri Nets*, in Proceedings of the Meeting on XML/SGML based Interchange Formats for Petri Nets, Aarhus, Denmark (2000) 7–12

[29] D.C. Marinescu, *Internet-Based Workflow Management – Toward a Semantic Web* (Wiley, 2002)

[30] Message Passing Interface Forum, *MPI-2: Extensions to the Message-Passing Interface*, (1997) http://www.mpi-forum.org/docs/

[31] Object Management Group, *Common Object Request Broker Architecture*, Core Specification,(2002) http://www.omg.org/technology/documents/corba_spec_catalog.htm

[32] C.A. Petri, *Kommunikation mit Automaten*, Ph.D. dissertation Bonn (1962)

[33] A. Rajasekar, M. Wan, and R. Moore, MySRB and SRB—Components of a Data Grid, in Proceedings of the 11th IEEE International Symposium on High Performance Distributed Computing (HPDC11), Edinburgh, Scotland (2002) 301–310

[34] Thain, D., Tannenbaum, T., Livny, M, Condor and the Grid, in *Grid Computing: Making the Global Infrastructure a Reality*, ed by F. Berman, G. Fox, T. Hey (Wiley, 2002)

[35] Thatte, S.: XLANG: *Web Services for Business Process Design*, Specification, Microsoft Corporation (2001)

[36] *The Cactus Project*, (2003) http://www.cactuscode.org

[37] The Globus Project, *The Globus Resource Specification Language RSL v.1.0*, (2000) http://www-fp.globus.org/gram/rsl_spec1.html

[38] *The Globus Toolkit* 2.4, http://www.globus.org/gt2.4/download.html (2003)

[39] S. Unger, A. Hoheisel, E. Beger, U. Beims, *ERAMAS – Analyse- und Managementsystem von schadstoffbedingten Umweltrisiken*, Technische Überwachung, vol. 44, No. 4, Springer-VDI-Verlag Düsseldorf, (2003) 46–49 http://www.andreas-hoheisel.de/docs/Unger_et_al_2003_sd403.pdf

[40] M. Weber, E. Kindler, *The Petri Net Markup Language*, in Petri Net Technology for Communication Based Systems, Lecture Notes in Computer Science, Advances in Petri Nets, (2002) http://www.informatik.hu-berlin.de/top/pnml/

Chapter 8

Toward GRIDLE: A Way to Build Grid Applications Searching Through an Ecosystem of Components

8.1 Introduction

Today, the development of Grid applications is considered a nightmare, due to lack of Grid programming environments, standards, off-the-shelf software components, etc. Nonetheless, several researchers believe that economic principles will guide the future development of the Grid: an open market of services and resources will become available to developers, who will choose to use computing time and software solutions from different vendors, sold at different prices, with different performance and QoS.

Standardization efforts on component models, integration platforms, and business domain concepts based on XML will accelerate the usage and spreading of blocks for building component-based Grid services and applications. We can expect that, in a very near future, there will be thousands of open-market components available on the Grid. Grid programming will consist of selecting, coordinating and deploying *components* chosen from this large software market: the problem will be to find the best component that fits the requirements and with the best performance/price trade-off.

Two essential requirements for a software market-place have been slow to emerge: (1) standard, interchangeable *components*, orchestrated according to complex job *workflows*, and (2) the consumers' ability to *search* and *retrieve* the right parts for the job at hand. While we can register several activities in the Grid community directed toward the definition of a standard for high performance components, the effort to develop searching and retrieving services for software Grid components has been limited.

In this contribution, we will discuss the preliminary design issues of GRIDLE, a Grid component search service, which will follow the direction of using the mature technology of Web search engines to discover software components on the Grid. GRIDLE, a *Google^{TM}-like Ranking, Indexing and Discovery service for a Link-based Eco-system of software components*, is thought as the key tool in a more modern and natural framework for application development.

Nowadays, a typical process of application development may look as follows:

the programming environment offers a repository (*palette*) of possible components, from which developers can choose the most appropriate ones for their purpose. These components are locally developed, or these are remote, but explicitly and perfectly known: the programmer, or the environment, knows the availability of trusted components, their location in the Grid, their interfaces and their behavior. The developer can build complex workflows, according to which components can be deployed, and their ports can be interconnected appropriately.

We envision a different approach:

a Grid programmer needs to fulfill a complex job. S/he starts the application development by specifying a *high-level workflow plan*: for each needed component, s/he specifies functional and not functional requirements, which are used to query the search service. GRIDLE will start a search session and present the user a ranked list of components that are partially/totally matching the requirements. The programmer is then in charge of adapting interfaces or making the component compatible with the run-time system supported by her/his computing environment. Using a suitable cost and performance model, and the information offered by the components themselves, the framework tries to predict the overall cost of the application, and its expected performance. It should also verify, on behalf of the developer, the credentials of the chosen components (with suitable security technology). With this information, the user can be driven to a cost-effective solution.

In other words, GRIDLE will work like a Web search engine, i.e., offering a simple interface to a large, evolving market of components. As will be shown in the next sections, a user should be given the opportunity to find the needed software components simply through a short description of his/her requirements.

Looking at the evolution of search engine technology, which will constitute the basis for the design of GRIDLE, we can observe the increasing importance of the adoption of new ranking methods for pages, besides the well-known Information Retrieval models.

In particular, search engines make use of the link structure of the Web to calculate a quality ranking for each Web page. For example, Google interprets a link to a given page as a vote. These votes produce a ranking method called PageRank, which can be thought as an objective measure of a web page's importance that corresponds well with people's subjective idea of importance. In other terms, PageRank works because we can imagine the Web as an *ecosystem* of hyper-linked data contents, in which such contents *cooperate* – i.e., these are hyper-linked to each other in order to offer more complete information – and *compete* – i.e., they publish information and try to make themselves more visible than others. From this Darwinian process, only the most important pages become accessible through a Web search engine. Note that, similar to a real ecosystem, the winners in this competing environment will be those who will be chosen as a partner (linked to) by a large number of other information providers (Web pages).

We believe that a similar process will happen for Grid components and their ecosystem. They will *cooperate* – i.e., they will be composed by means of specific workflows – and *compete* – i.e., they will try to make themselves more visible than others in the large component marketplace. So, we envision that workflows will play a role similar to hyperlinked pages in the Web, i.e., a means to improve the visibility of available components on the Grid. In practice, workflows can be considered as particular documents with hyperlinks to the components involved: GRIDLE could exploit them to improve the precision of a search. We also believe that Web pages describing components and related features will be also made available, and thus the more traditional Web search engine methods will continue being adopted in combination with this new technology.

This contribution is organized as follows. In the next section, we describe emerging issues related to the creation and publication of software components, with special attention to the wrapping of existing code: we compare several component-oriented frameworks, and we highlight some key features. Then, we comment on some standards of application description. Starting from these, in section 8.4, we give our vision of a new way to build applications starting from software components available on the Grid. We then conclude, summarizing the most challenging research problems, which we plan to address in the future.

8.2   Component-Based Grid Programming

When Unix introduced pipes in 1972 [1], new opportunities for software engineering became available: nobody before thought seriously about building *software solutions* out of existing tools, and designing them as *filters* so that they could be easily used as building blocks for larger tasks: currently, all Unix programmers design chains of pipes for their needs, instead of writing new applications from scratch, as part of their daily routine.

Unix filters and the pipe composition model represent the first successful example of a component-based design. It offers several important features, among which *substitutability*, i.e., the pieces building up a complete application are designed to be added, removed, and replaced with cheaper, faster, more robust ones; *customization*, because through some user interface (e.g., the Unix command line) the components offer a certain degree of configurability; *heterogeneity*, since tools developed with different languages can interoperate through a well-known, common interface (Unix text stream).

In literature, "a component is a unit of composition with contractually specified interfaces and explicit context dependencies only. A component can be deployed independently and is subject to composition by third parties [2]". In a growing Grid market, the way software components are defined and modeled has a strong impact on the speed of a transition to a component-oriented application design. In this section, we describe the state of the art of software component design, describing some existing component frameworks. Then, we consider pros and cons of the existing approaches, with some quantitative analysis. Next, we highlight our proposal of a new approach to component modeling and linking, with a brief overview of tools for automatic wrapping.

8.2.1   Component-Oriented Frameworks

Here, we analyze the state of the art of software component design. In particular, we focus on two frameworks that are representative, in our opinion, of two opposite approaches to component modeling: CCA [3] and Java Beans [4]. CCA is based on the use of an Interface Definition Language (IDL). Java Beans is based on Java's most modern features (introspection, object-oriented design...) to provide a simple and portable programming environment.

8.2.1.1   The Common Component Architecture

Common Component Architecture (CCA) [3] is a proposed standard aimed at promoting the integration of heterogenous software components, by defining a minimal set of required services that every component should feature: *Port, getPort, setServices.*

In the CCA vision, a component is a software entity that allows different languages, different hardware/software architectures to co-operate. It supports a structured, modular approach to software development, very useful in the case of third-party libraries and external services. A component can be built out of a library or a class (object type), but it can exist only with the support of a framework, responsible for connecting the interfaces of the different components, in order to build a complete application.

Every component exports one or more input and output ports (*uses* and *provides* ports), identified by their type. Inheritance and specialization allows the programmer to refine definition and semantics of a component. Also, multiple ports can offer a different point of view of the same service.

The CCA is implemented by a variety of frameworks, offering different programming models: CCAffeine is targeted to SPMD (Single Program, Multiple Data) parallel applications, based on the connection of locally available components [5]; CCAT/XCAT is more suitable to Grid/distributed applications, as it can connect component located on remote machines (e.g., in a Globus-based Grid) [6]; SCIRun supports parallel multi-threaded application, based on local connection [7]; finally, Decaf is aimed at offering language interoperability for a sequential application.

In the next paragraphs, we will discuss in detail CCAffeine and Babel, a tool used by CCAffeine and other CCA framework to support language heterogeneity.

The CCAffeine Framework   CCAffeine [5] is a CCA-compliant framework oriented to SPMD (or SCMD—Single Component Multiple Data) applications. It can assemble together heterogeneous, internally parallel components. As an example, in Figure 8.1, three parallel components, each composed of five parallel processes, build up an application. Intra-processor communication, among different components (vertical arrows) is managed by the framework: it is responsible for data conversion if the components are heterogeneous. On the other side, inter-processor communication, within a parallel component (horizontal arrows), is responsibility of the component developer, who can use the tool of his/her choice (MPI, PVM, RPC, shared memory or any other communication library).

CCAffeine offers a basic GUI (see Figure 8.2) to deploy and connect components: a *palette* listing the available components is shown to the user, who can pick up the needed functions from it. Using a simple drag-and-drop interface, s/he can connect them into a graph that describes the

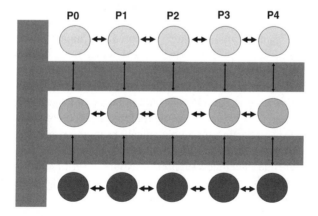

FIGURE 8.1. Communications among and within components. Five machines (P0 through P4) are running an application composed of three parallel components.

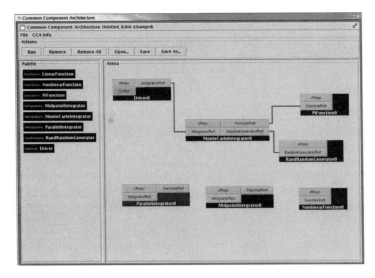

FIGURE 8.2. CCAffeine graphical interface.

complete application. The framework is responsible for instantiating a copy of the application graph on every machine in the computing environment. CCAffeine internally uses MPI and creates the requested components on all machine in the MPI world. The *run* command will start, in parallel, execution on each machine.

Over all, CCAffeine offers a language-independent wrapping to parallel components (mostly, MPI-based). Thus, it supports the usage of heterogenous development environments (SO shared-object libraries can be easily connected), leveraging the services of Babel.

Babel   Babel [8] is a tool suite featuring an interface-description language oriented to high-performance scientific programming. It is aimed at supporting the co-operation of software written with different languages. It offers a set of functionalities similar to CORBA [9], but enriched by scientific features, among which support for dynamic multi-dimensional arrays, complex numbers, in-process optimizations, support to C, C++, Fortran-77, Java, Python, Fortran-90.

The usage of Babel SIDL is similar to that of other IDL-based tools. Given the interface description, the Babel parser creates: *IOR files* with the Internal Object Representation (IOR) of the needed data structures; *Skel files*, responsible for the conversion of the IOR to the native data representation; *Impl files*, collecting the implementation, in any supported language; and *Stub files*, needed to connect to the Babel support libraries.

Babel creates server- and client-side support: it exports a set of stubs to be used to call the implemented object from a program written in any other supported language. In our experience, Babel does not seem to use effective shortcuts when implementing communication among homogeneous components: we observed that two C++ components need to go through the slower run-time support of abstracted data, which is needed by heterogeneous components, instead of using the native format. In Table 8.1, we show the call stack for a simple program, completely written

TABLE 8.1. The call stack for a simple program. The *go()* method (line #9) activates the *integrate()* function (#5), which calls then *evaluate()* (#0).

#0	functions::PiFunction_impl::evaluate() at functions_PiFunction_Impl.cc:47
#1	skel_functions_PiFunction_evaluate () at functions_PiFunction_Skel.cc:32
#2	functions::Function::evaluate() at functions_Function.cc:236
#3	integrators::MonteCarloIntegrator_impl::integrate() at integrators_MonteCarloIntegrator_Impl.cc:134
#4	skel_integrators_MonteCarloIntegrator_integrate () at integrators_MonteCarloIntegrator_Skel.cc:48
#5	integrators::Integrator::integrate() at integrators_Integrator.cc:237
#6	tutorial::Driver_impl::go() at tutorial_Driver_Impl.cc:100
#7	skel_tutorial_Driver_go () at tutorial_Driver_Skel.cc:45
#8	gov::cca::ports::GoPort::go() at gov_cca_ports_GoPort.cc:244
#9	BabelOpaqueGoPort::go() at BabelOpaqueGoPort.cc:28
#10	ConnectionFramework::goOne() at ConnectionFramework.cxx:1139
#11	DefaultBuilderModel::goOne() at DefaultBuilderModel.cxx:222
#12	CmdActionCCAGo::doIt() at CmdActionCCAGo.cxx:55
#13	CmdParse::parse() at CmdParse.cxx:564
#14	CmdLineBuilderController2::parse() at CmdLineBuilderController2.cxx:118
#15	CmdLineClient::main() at CmdLineClient.cxx:861
#16	main () at CmdLineClientMain.cxx:318
#17	__libc_start_main () from /lib/tls/libc.so.6

in C++ (thus, no heterogeneity is present). The call of *evaluate()* by *integrate()* is mediated by several layers of framework support.

This is a problem common to other IDLs: their run-time support does not provide effective shortcuts to use native data structures, and the language-independent data abstraction needs to be used, with an evident performance overhead.

The process of creating a CCA component, in particular a CCAffeine component, from the Babel interface requires a complex series of steps:

1. Definition of component interfaces using Babel
2. Implementation of component algorithms in the Babel-generated Impl files (in any supported language)
3. Definition of CCA ports in the Impl files
4. Creation of a wrapper and a CCA definition file
5. Creation of a suitable makefile

In our experience, this process could cause problems of software engineering and is potentially error-prone. In particular, there are some naming conventions that needs to be respected in the development of the wrapper and CCA files (fourth step), which can be missed and are not recognized properly by the development tools.

Performance   As said, the main goal of CCAffeine is to improve the inter-operability of software components. High performance is responsibility of the application developer, who has to tune computation, communication, and data placement to this goal.

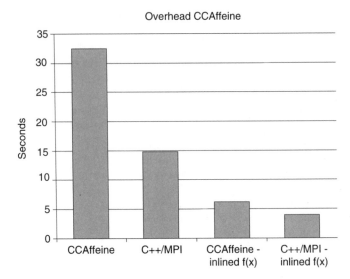

FIGURE 8.3. Comparison of CCAffeine and native code. The first column is CCAffeine implementation; the second is C++/MPI; the third is CCAffeine with inlined function; the fourth is C++/MPI with inlined function.

In our tests, we observed huge performance overhead when homogeneous components were communicating. In Figure 8.3, a comparison of a C++ implementation vs. a component implementation of a simple integration program is shown. A parallel MPI integrator distributes function evaluations among a set of workers. Partial results are then *reduced* to compute the final sum. The data flow for the CCAffeine implementation is: a driver component invokes the services of a generic parallel integrator, which invokes the method *evaluate()* of a function component. The parallel integrator is responsible for orchestrating the final reduction. In the C++ version, components are replaced by functions, and service invocations are replaced by function calls. A second version was tested, where the function was inlined in the integrator body. When the function to be integrated is an autonomous component, a large overhead for the function call can be observed. When the function is inlined, the framework start-up time dominates.

Tests were performed on a cluster of eight dual-Pentium machines, running Linux RedHat, Babel 0.8.4, and CCAffeine 0.4.1.

The overall performance of CCAffeine is strongly affected by the features of the underlying run-time support of Babel. We want here to highlight an important feature of Babel arrays. As well known, an important factor affecting performance when manipulating matrices is the ordering of column and rows. If the order is correct, elements can be accessed sequentially, otherwise a more complex access is needed. Babel SIDL allows the programmer to define the order to be used by the data passed to a component: a component can choose to access row-major or column-major matrices. In row-major mode, rows can be scanned sequentially, increasing the column number. We tested the performance of a simple matrix multiplication, with different matrix ordering. In Table 8.2, one can compare the costs for some choices of orders for the matrices A, B, and C (with $C = A \times B$). R stands for row-major, and C for column-major.

TABLE 8.2. Matrix multiply with different orderings. Time in seconds.

Size	RCR	CRR	CRC	Transpose
16	0.06	0.02	0.02	0.00
32	0.08	0.03	0.03	0.00
64	0.12	0.1	0.09	0.10
128	0.37	0.31	0.29	0.31
256	1.62	2.99	2.65	2.30
512	12.11	54.95	54.13	62.32

The last column indicates what the cost is when a matrix is transposed because it does not match the parameter definition: if, at the moment of call, the data in the actual parameter are ordered differently from what is expected, the system is responsible for transposing it, a costly operation for large matrices. This operation has a high cost, and the programmer is not warned about this.

Also, we have to emphasize that components have to use the Babel SIDL array data abstraction, and there is no automatic optimization: if the matrices are defined with a sub-optimal ordering, the code will have bad performance, as it can be seen in the second and third columns, where the matrix ordering does not match the natural structure of the multiplication algorithm.

According to the developers, component overhead is "negligible [...] for component implementation and abstract interfaces when using appropriate levels of abstraction." Nonetheless, they also measure that parameter passing can be three times slower than native code [10]. More data to compare this framework with native code are given in Section 8.2.2.

8.2.1.2   Java Beans

Java Beans API [4] is a mature software standard developed by a consortium, led by SUN, with the goals of designing a portable, simple, high-quality API for component software development. Concretely, a Java Bean is a reusable software component that can be manipulated visually in a builder tool. While visual manipulation is an important part of software development, and many beans have important GUI functionalities (scrolling bars, editing windows...), beans can be more complex and can be used to model larger software entities: data-bases, observational instrumentations, and visualization facilities can be modeled as beans and integrated into the development framework.

The most advanced and useful features of beans are introspection, customization, and the event-driven programming model.

Introspection is a very powerful tool for component publication and connection: Java classes are able to analyze their own structure, and publish their interface. This is present in a very basic form in any Java class, which can dump its own identity to a string, when asked to perform the method `toString()`. Also, `Serializable` classes are able to store their state to a stream.

Java Beans offer a more advanced set of information methods, able to retrieve the name of the relevant methods, the set of fired events, the interesting properties. If desided, an explicit `BeanInfo` service can be provided by the Bean, e.g., if the internal properties of the Bean are to be hidden or abstracted. Also, a *design-time customizer* can be offered with the Bean. This tool will be invoked by the design tool, instead of the standard configuration interface.

Java Beans are mostly event-driven. This means that they can react asynchronously to particular circumstances that happen during application execution, for example clock ticks or user input. More advanced message-driven beans are also possible, using the run-time support offered by `Java 2 Enterprise Edition` (J2EE) [11] and similar software packages. Moreover, Beans can be multi-threaded, and can operate on multiple requests at a time.

8.2.1.2.1 Design Time and Run Time

Java Beans recognize two important moments in the application development. *Design time* is the moment when the bean is manipulated, customized, and composed into an application. Customization tools offered by the bean (called `Customizer`) are invoked at design time by the design framework. When the application is completed, and it is packaged to run (*run time*), the design-time code is stripped out, and only the run-time code is kept in the application code. `Customizers` are available for complex beans that require long, detailed customization, or when the internal implementation needs to be abstracted or hidden.

This strategy can be very good, in general, for complex component: versatile configuration tools can be packaged along with the main code, and then stripped out to reach performance at run-time.

8.2.1.2.2 Design Conventions

The Java standard is highly based on naming and coding conventions, usually called, in Java Beans terminology, *design patterns* [4] that simplify and co-ordinate the interaction of software components: these standards are highly suggested (but not mandatory) and are exploited at the moment of interaction. Java Beans frameworks look for these naming conventions in the class signature, and use them to extract some semantic information.

For example, when two methods, `PropertyType getSomeProperty()` and `void setSomeProperty(PropertyType s)` are found, a property `someProperty` of type `PropertyType` is defined, and presented to the user at design time.

This set of standards allow automatic tools to present suitable customizing tools for the object's properties. For instance, `BeanBox` and `BeanBuilder` will present a palette for a color attribute, a list of choice for an enumeration type and so on (see Figure 8.4).

8.2.1.3   Other Component-Based Environments

The *CORBA Component Model* [9] is an extension of CORBA with the goal of defining component interfaces, and objects with persistent state. The CORBA is a powerful tool to perform method invocation on objects running on remote servers based on an IDL. PARDIS [12] extends CORBA in another direction, so as to allow sequential and parallel clients (SPMD and MPMD) to interact with sequential and parallel servers. With similar goal, further results have been reached by PAWS [13] and Ligature [14].

Web Services are another standard to define and represent software components. The OGSI (Open Grid Service Infrastructure) forum has enriched the standard to include some more

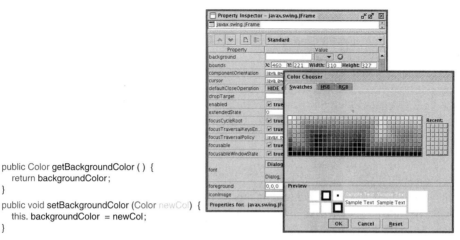

```
public Color getBackgroundColor ( ) {
    return backgroundColor;
}

public void setBackgroundColor (Color newCol) {
    this. backgroundColor = newCol;
}
```

FIGURE 8.4. Example of design convention: when a pair of *get-set* methods are found, the framework can identify a property and offer the correct customization tool.

Grid-oriented services [15]. The design of a Web service is quite straightforward and highly automated starting from Java classes. Tools are also available for other languages (mostly, C++).

Another emerging framework is Microsoft .NET [16], which presents an integrated model of component-oriented software and Web-based services. We will consider its features in the comparison presented below.

8.2.2   A New Approach. What Is Needed

We want, here, to summarize pros and cons of the discussed environments, in order to define the requirement of a new approach to software component design. First, we give a qualitative comparison of the critical features of the two main approaches (CCA and Java Beans) with some considerations about solutions offered by .NET. Then, we compare their performance, with particular attention to the overhead introduced by Babel IDL.

8.2.2.1   Qualitative Comparison.

The two approaches present strong differences in the way they face many issues related to software development.

8.2.2.1.1   Re-use of Legacy Code

In our experience, the process of modifying existing code in order to use the IDL-generated skeletons and stubs is complex and potentially error-prone. An approach following the example of Java, where any class can be quickly transformed into a Bean and then plugged into the framework, is to be preferred.

8.2.2.1.2 Component Publication

With Java Beans, there is no need to define interfaces and to pass them around. The JAR file, storing the code for the component, can be queried: the object is able to introspect and to publish its own methods and data. The CCA Babel interface, instead, needs to be passed around as part of the code documentation with strong problem of component packaging.

8.2.2.1.3 Architecture and Language Portability

Java byte code is designed to run on any platform that offers a Java virtual machine: this includes Sparc, Macintosh, Linux, Windows, and many portable devices. In the context of Grid computing, a component can be moved to and executed on different resources at every run: Java is a very simple way to ensure that the code is portable.

On the other side, components developed with Babel/CCA are expected to run natively, possibly after re-compiling, on any CCA-compliant framework. Also, heterogeneous components can inter-operate.

.NET offers an approach similar to Java, using a virtual machine for Windows system, called Common Language Run-time (CLR), which has been partially ported to Linux by the Mono project team [17]. Also, it can compile a variety of languages to run on the virtual machine, thus allowing heterogeneous components to operate easily together.

8.2.2.1.4 Visual Manipulation

Visual manipulation can be an important part of a component-oriented framework if used by non-expert programmers: this is an interesting feature if the component is to be used in a Problem Solving Environment (PSE) or some computer-aided application designer.

Java Beans and CCA components are both designed to be easily manipulated with graphical tools. Nonetheless, Java Beans offer a more versatile interface (i.e., a specific Customizer for complex Beans), which inherits the flexibility of Java.

8.2.2.1.5 Standardization

Java is one of the most wide-spread software standards. There is large availability of software, and a large number of discussion symposia. CCA is still a proposal of standard, which is competing with several others for large acceptance. .NET is another emerging standard, pushed strongly by Microsoft, but also accepted in the open software community for its advanced features.

8.2.2.1.6 Type Control

CCA offers a very strong type control, based on port typing and object inheritance/specialization. In Java, type matching can be sometimes overridden if methods with no arguments are used: with Java Beans, control on the type of communicating entities is limited. .NET, instead, offers a strong typing system, common to all supported languages, known as Common Type System (CTS). Strong control is needed if the component is to be used by a wide public.

8.2.2.1.7 Performance of numeric applications

Java code running on a virtual machine can have lower performance than optimized C or Fortran code. This is due to the overhead introduced by the virtual machine, to the limits of the compiling

data types, which is independent by the size of the application: even if framework and start-up overhead are smaller with very large applications, the overhead due to data structures is common to any numerical code using this tool.

The Java code, compiled with optimization, reaches a performance comparable to the CCAffeine implementation. As expected, both fall far behind the faster C implementation.

8.2.3   A Choice for a Component Model

As shown, two main ways are available today for component publication and management: one is based on a description language along with compilers to generate stubs and skeletons; the second is based on object introspection and coding conventions and allows a very fast deployment of Java classes.

The use of an interface description language (see Figure 8.6(a)), such as Babel SIDL [8] and CCM description language [9], can be very costly, in term of learning curve, code rewriting, and possibility of errors: in our opinion, present day interface description languages are taking an innatural approach, because they ask the developer to start writing an interface, and then to adapt the existing code to the automatically generated skeleton/stub files. This can be particularly time-consuming with legacy code.

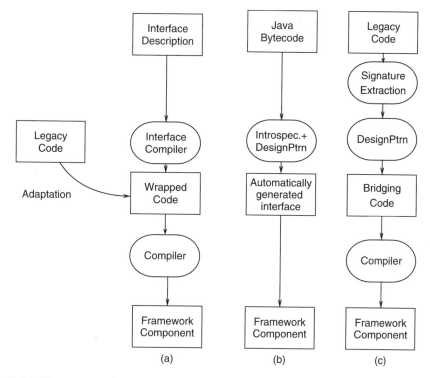

FIGURE 8.6. Different approaches to component development: (a) is based on an IDL compiler; (b) is the one followed by Java Beans; (c) is the one we propose, based on automatic manipulation of legacy code.

As shown in Figure 8.6(b), JavaBeans proposes a different approach, based on introspection. Compiled JavaBeans classes are able to respond to specific queries about the methods they provide, presenting to the framework a full description of the available methods, and their interface (name, arguments, and their type, returned value). Moreover, the Java Beans API sets a standard for more advanced tools, such as an explicit *Customizer*—presented to the designer when s/he wants to customize the Bean—and a redefined *BeanInfo* method, that overrides the automatically collected information.

We strongly believe design standards will emerge naturally with the advent of a Grid economy, in a way similar to what happened with the Web. Any Web-designer is free to design his/her pages in the preferred way, and any Web-browser can open them. Nonetheless, if s/he wants the web site to be discovered easily by a search engine, s/he will adhere to some HTML/XML standards, such as *META* tags, textual *ALT* tags for images, and so on. Moreover, s/he will use some self-explaining description for the information provided: a car-company, for example, should add, somewhere in the Web site, in a clear textual form, the words "car" and "company." Similarly, a component developer will choose to adhere to some well-known interface for the service s/he wants to publish.

We propose a new approach, such as the one in Figure 8.6(c): legacy code is analyzed in order to extract the signature of functions and variables; then, design conventions are recognized in it, and are used to develop the bridging code, needed to link the software unit with the framework and the other components at hand. We explore this opportunity below.

8.2.3.1   Extracting Information from Compiled Code

A direction we are investigating is the possibility of extracting information about methods signature from the compiled code, in a way similar to Java Beans. There are very effective tools for code developed with some modern languages such a C#, Lisp, Java, Visual Basic. For Java, for instance, Mocha [21] can extract full information from the code, because Java byte-code is very rich of information.

Binary code offers a more complex challenge. To reach higher performance, debugging information and many data related to the symbol table are stripped out of the executable file. On the other side, dynamically linked libraries are usually called by name: often function names and types are available in the binary. Also, the headers sometimes offered with libraries can be parsed to reconstruct some of the information needed to use the code. This is clearly a good situation: for old legacy code, headers could be missing.

As a matter of fact, some tools are available also for languages other than Java. *GDB* [22] can retrieve some information, especially if debugging data are kept. Other basic utilities for binary code (known as *binutils* [23]) are available on Unix systems.

The process we envision, is as follows:

- Legacy code is developed with the tools of choice of the development team.
- Compiled code and, if available, source code and headers, are analyzed to extract signatures of interest: methods' names and types are discovered in the code; to understand the basic semantics and the relationships among functions, the system looks for common naming and coding conventions (as for Java Beans design patterns); the application developer is offered the opportunity to choose which methods to publish, and which to keep hidden (if this is not clear from the code).
- This information can be used to generate, automatically, or with some computer-aided process: wrappers in other languages, so to allow inter-operability, featuring the minimal data

conversion needed; WSDL descriptions, so to deploy the functions as Web Services; links to a graphical interface for composing functions.

8.2.3.2 Examples of Automatic Wrapping

Several attempts have been done to perform automatic wrapping of existing code for particular frameworks, with noteworthy results, some of which are listed here.

Taylor et al. developed a way to wrap C function calls in Java components, to be used within the Triana framework [24]: JACAW [25] performs this operation automatically. Before this, Mintchev and Getov [26] wrapped C libraries so as to be used within a Java program: they were able to use a C implementation of MPI from Java. Also, Li et al. [27] wrapped high-performance MPI legacy code (written in C and Fortran) into Java/CORBA components, and were able to maintain very good performance after conversion. A different approach was followed by Stuer et al. [28]: a new pluglet for the H2O framework is able to export and publish all the other loaded pluglets as WSDL and GSDL documents.

We agree that Java is a very versatile tool for software distribution, and the cited works propose effective way to use Java as a standard for interface description and component linking. From the Java description, Web Services can be easily created. Nonetheless, to reach peak performance, in our opinion *ad-hoc* conversion filters among connected components should be automatically generated by the framework.

8.2.4 Components in a Grid Economy

A component-oriented design based on IDLs introduces a high programming overhead in the process of wrapping existing code to be re-used. The CCAffeine framework, taken as an example, requires the manipulation of several files to connect two components for a simple matrix multiplication. This is why we push for a more natural approach, based on automatic extraction of interfaces, and then computer-aided generation of suitable bridging layers. Java Beans offer an interesting example, as they base connection and discovery on interface introspection and design conventions. In our opinion, there is a need for tools able to analyze legacy code, extract signature information, and then generate efficient bridging code. The strong results available in the field of wrapping C into Java components can be a valid starting point.

In the next section, we consider application and activity description. Particular attention needs to be paid to the choice of parameters that are of relevance for a component living in a Grid economy. Components' description should include information that will allow a developer to choose the fittest resource to his/her needs. This can include the following:

- Their names and descriptions, in natural language
- Cost of using the components
- Expected (or guaranteed) performance
- Billing information (bank account...)
- Access requirements (password, licenses...)
- Level of data security and privacy
- Authority certifications
- Quality standards that are met

Along with the above-mentioned information few more standard functional information are as follows:

- Interface, i.e., a formal specification of services provided (used) and related parameters
- Actions, i.e., the modifications of the environment caused by the execution of the component
- Pre-conditions, i.e., expressions that must be true before the action(s) can take place
- Post-conditions, i.e., expressions that must be true after the action(s) do take place
- Communication protocol
- Data format
- Needed computing resources

An application developer should be able, using these parameters, to choose the components that reach the point in the cost/performance trade-off that better fits his/her needs. Also, s/he should be able to use only components which meets some standards in term of design quality, QoS and/or security and privacy. This information should allow the creation of a search engine as of that depicted in section 8.4.

8.3   Application Description and Workflows

A central concept for the deployment of Grid software components is a *workflow* description model to specify the coordination level of the activities caused by component execution. While *activities* are units of work to be performed by agents, computers, communication links, etc., the *process description* of a workflow is a structure describing both the activities to be executed and the order of their execution (see also Marinescu [29]).

Workflows need to name and describe the *activities* to be composed, where activities are usually characterized by several parameters, including their name and description (in natural language), interface signature, pre- and post-conditions. These parameters are going to be used during a component search, as it will be shown in the next section.

Traditionally, workflows are encountered in business management, office automation, or production management. Grid workflows have several peculiar characteristics. For instance, *resource allocation* is a critical aspect of the Grid-based workflow enactment. The Grid provides an environment, where multiple classes of resources, within distinct administrative domains, are available. In addition, there is a large variability of resources in each class.

In this section we want to survey some of the workflow approaches currently followed in the Grid community, and compare these efforts with others in the (business) Web Services community.

8.3.1   Workflow Models for the Grid

In the scientific Grid community, the component model and the related workflow concepts often correspond to merely determining the execution order of sequences of tasks, which simply read/write raw files. Many scientific applications are built, in fact, by composing legacy software components, often written in different languages, where the seamless interface is realized through raw permanent streams (files). The most common Grid workflow can thus be modeled as simple Directed Acyclic Graphs (DAGs) of Tasks, where the order of execution (modeled as odes) is determined by dependencies (in turn modeled as directed arcs). Even if several projects have addressed the composition of specific sequences of Grid tasks, and several groups have developed visual user interfaces to define the linkage between components, currently there is no consensus on how workflow should be expressed.

Within this framework, the most notable example is the Directed Acyclic Graph Manager for Condor, *DAGMan* [30], i.e., the well-known workload management system for compute-intensive jobs. Condor is a major effort to reach *high-throughput computing* on distributed resources. It features resource management and scheduling for jobs and data on large collections of computing elements. It also offers very effective scheduling for parameter-sweep applications. DAGMan is a Condor meta-scheduler, that submits jobs to the high-throughput Condor scheduler in an order represented by a DAG and processes the results.

Besides DAGs, *UNICORE* [31] provides more sophisticated control facilities in the workflow language. Constructs such as Do-N, Do-Repeat, If-then-else, and Hold-Job have been defined and integrated into the abstract job description and the client UNICORE GUI. In particular, Do-N forces the repetition of an activity N times, where N is fixed at submission time, Do-Repeat repeats an activity until a condition evaluated at runtime becomes true, If-Then-Else executes one of two activities depending on a condition evaluated at runtime, while Hold-Job suspends an activity until a given time/date has passed.

Grid programmers have also the necessity to deploy high-performance applications made up of *peer-to-peer components* (P2P), collaborating through high-performance communication channels, characterized by standard interfaces. Unfortunately, we have to observe the lack of a standard model for specifying this kind of composition. A notable contribution to the definition of high-performance Grid components and their composition is the CCA (Common Component Architecture), introduced in the previous section. Within the CCA framework, the application structure is built as a free directed graph of port connection. It does not describe directly the movement of data, or the order of calls, but simply the set of all components which can be activated by any other components. The available commands are limited to instantiation of a component, and to connection of two *uses/provides* ports.

Within the *Java Beans* framework, the application structure can be more complex. Any component can be connected to another in order to react to changes in its status. A component, in particular, can react to user input (keyboard, mouse), time clicks, changes in the value of a property (regardless of the way it changed), explicit messages, fired events, as they appear in another bean. The network of connection can be as complex as desired, with mutual and multiple links among two Beans, including cycles and self-loops. This can built using the graphical interface of *BeanBuilder* or similar tool, and then compiled into a complete, autonomous Java application. Alternatively, the programmer can load and connect the beans with a Java program. In this case, the language used to implement the components is the same used to connect them. As for CCA, the connections describe very loosely the logical flow of data or control dependencies among components.

8.3.2 Workflow Models in the Business Community

We can notice a strong similarity between these research efforts in the Grid community regarding component-based programming, and the current evolution of the Internet/Web scenario, which from a media for merely publishing static data is becoming a media of interacting *Web Services* [32–35]. In this case too, we can observe a large effort to standardize the way in which Web services (components) are published, deployed, searched, and invoked. The final goal is to transform the Internet into a general platform for distributed computing as required for Business-to-Business (B2B) eCommerce. The existence of this standard is considered the central requirement to make this programming approach feasible.

In the commercial Web Service community, there are several research activities aimed to permit the specification/orchestration of a service workflow. For example, the WSFL (Web Service Flow Language) language [35], and its industry evolution BPEL4WS (Business Process Execution Language for Web Services) [36]. Also, there is commercial interest in services and protocols for registering, discovering and integrating Web Services, including the UDDI protocol [34].

An interesting comparison of Grid (CCA) and Web Service (WSDL/WSFL) programming is presented in [37]. In this paper, Gannon et al. discuss how the provides ports of a CCA component can be described by WSDL (Web Service Description Language), and hence can be accessed by any Web Service client that understands that port type. Unfortunately, no *uses* ports can be defined by using WSDL, but a distributed application can still be built by means of WSFL (Web Services Flow Language), thus defining the workflow of the application in terms of the provided WSDL interfaces. The XML-based WSFL script needs to be executed by a centralized *workflow engine* that must mediate each step of application with the various Web Services. In the CCAffeine approach, the only centralization point is the application controller component, aimed to instantiate and connect together a chain of other components. After the application is started, there is no more centralization. If the data traffic between the services is heavy, it is probably not the best choice to require it to go through a central WSFL flow engine. Furthermore, if the logic that describes the interaction between the components is complex and depends upon the application behavior, then putting it in the high level/general purpose workflow may not work. This is an important distinction between application dependent flow between components and service mediation at the level of workflow.

Despite all these problems, several Grid researchers think that it is necessary to adhere to the business standards coming from the Web Service world, trying to solve possible performance problems. For instance, an application described as a composition of Web Services can be optimized by redirecting the output of a service directly to the input of another, without passing through a centralization point. This can be done without breaking the existing standards, but simply through framework optimizations.

8.4 GRIDLE: A Search Engine for a Component-Based Programming Environment

User interactive environments like portals can provide high-level access to Grid services, such as job submission or data movement, or may offer a way to interact with specific application that have been modified to exploit Grid infrastructure. There are several classes of tools that fall into this category.

To date, we can observe that there has been very limited work on Grid-specific programming languages. This is not too surprising since automatic generation of parallel applications from high-level languages usually works only within the context of well-defined execution models [38], and Grid applications have a more complex execution space than parallel programs. As previously discussed, the best results in Grid programming have been reached by scripting

due to the links present between components. Obviously, in order to make these links significant, we must define how a component can be referred (i.e., Unique Identifier, URL, URI, etc.).

The next module is the *Indexer*, whose job is to build the *index* data structure of GRIDLE. This step is very important, because some information about the relevance of the components within the ecosystem must be discovered and stored in the index. In other words, we have to choose the kind of characteristics we consider to be important for the search purposes, such as:

- Functional information, as interfaces and running environment requirements
- Non-functional information, as textual description, performance and billing
- Linking information

The *functional information* refers to a more complex but more precise description of the functionality offered by the component. For example, it may declare the number of published methods, their names, their signature, and so on. For example, the result of the introspection operation applied to a software component. Furthermore, there are other functional features that we can notice: for example, the specification of the requirements for allowing a component to be used (e.g., *Contracts* [41]).

Non-functional information consists of a textual description, in natural language, which describes the main functionalities of a component. Also, cost and performance information can be described here, along with details about guaranteed QoS, licenses that are needed for the use, and so on.

The third characteristic is the information regarding the context where a component can be found. In particular, the *interlinked structure* of metacomponents (workflows) allows for designing smart Ranking algorithms for software components. In particular, we would like to consider the number of in-links of a given component[1] as a factor of high quality (high rank). In addition, we would like to reinforce the quality of a metacomponent on the basis of the importance of the referred components. This last aspect can be better explained using again the example graph of Figure 8.7.

Let us consider the module "Hotel Reservation 3." In the ranking phase of the search process, it will obtain an importance coefficient depending on: (1) the importance of the "Flight Reservation" component, and (2) the importance of the "CAR" component.

The computation of the rank according to (1) can be carried out using the well-known PageRank [42] iterative algorithm. The idea of *ecosystem of components* we introduced before is of fundamental importance for the evaluation of the components' PageRank. The main intuition behind the classical PageRank metric applied to Web Pages is that a page p should receive an importance value proportional to the probability that a random surfer will visit that page starting from another page picked at random. In our case, PageRank should be modified so that *a components will receive a higher importance value if other components are **actually** using it*. Note that in our framework, a component can be related to another either directly or indirectly (i.e., by linking to metacomponents that use that component).

After this phase, following (2) we increase the weight of "Hotel Reservation 3" by a constant factor α proportional to the relevance of "CAR."

The last module of GRIDLE is the *Query Answering* one, which actually resolves the component queries on the basis of the index. The main function carried on by this module is to return a list containing the most relevant components in response to a user's query. The relevance score

---

[1]An *in-link* is a directed link which targets the current component.

is computed by the *ranking module* using the four aspects outlined above as comparison metrics. In principle, the algorithm is simple:

- for each component C previously indexed
  - Compute the distance among C and the place-holder query Q
  - Place the score along with C in a list L
- select from L the r most relevant component with respect to Q.

In this algorithm, the main interesting point is the computation of the distance. In our model, this should come out from a mix of the four relevance judgements given by the above mentioned criteria. Then, the results-set L is presented to the user for further refinements.

8.4.3   Component Search Engines: Related Work

In the last years, thanks to technologies like Internet and the Web, a number of interesting approaches [43,44] to the problem of searching for software components, as well as a number of interesting papers analyzing new and existing solutions [45,46], have been proposed.

In [43], *Odyssey Search Engine (OSE)*, a search engine for Components is presented. OSE is an agent system responsible for domain information (i.e., domain items) search within the Odyssey infrastructure. It is composed of an interface agent *(IA)*, filtering agents *(FAs)*, and retrieval agents *(RAs)*. The IA is the agent responsible for display the search results according to the users' profile. These profiles are modeled by identifying groups of users with similar preferences, stereotypes, and so forth. The FAs match user keywords and the textual description of each component, returning those with the greatest number of occurrences of user keywords. Finally, the RAs are the agents responsible for searching for relevant components among different domain descriptions.

In [44], the *Agora* components search engine is described. Agora is a prototype developed by the Software Engineering Institute at the Carnegie Mellon University. The object of this work is to create an automatically generated, indexed, worldwide database of software products classified by component type (e.g., JavaBean, CORBA or ActiveX control). Agora combines introspection with Web search engines in order to reduce the cost of bringing software components to, and finding components in, the software marketplace. It supports two basic functions: the location and indexing of components, and the search and retrieval of a component. For the first task, Agora uses a number of agents which are responsible for retrieving information through introspection. At the time the paper was written, Agora supported only two kinds of components: JavaBeans, and CORBA components. The task of searching and retrieving components is split into two distinct steps: in the first, a keyword-based search is performed and then, once the results have been presented to the user, s/he can refine or broaden the search criteria, based on the number and quality of matches. One of the most interesting features of Agora is the capability of discovering automatically the sites containing software components. The technique adopted to automatically find components is quite straight-forward but appears to be effective. Agora simply crawls the Web, as a typical Web crawler does, and whenever it encounters a page containing an <APPLET> tag, it downloads and indexes the related component.

In [45], Frakes and Pole analyze the results of an empirical experiment with a real Component Search Application, called *Proteus*. The study compares four different methods to represent reusable software components: attribute-value, enumerated, faceted, and keyword. The authors tested both the effectiveness and the efficiency of the search process. The tests were conducted on a group of thirty-five subjects that rated the different used methods, in terms of preference and helpfulness in understanding components. Searching effectiveness was measured with recall, precision, and overlap values drawn from the Information Retrieval theory [47]. Among others, the most important conclusion cited in the paper is that no method did more than moderately well in terms of search effectiveness, as measured by recall and precision.

In [46], the authors cite an interesting technique for ranking components. Ranking a collection of components simply consists of finding an absolute ordering according to the relative importance of components. The method followed by the authors is very similar to the method used by the Google search engine [48] to rank Web pages: PageRank [42]. In ComponentRank, in fact, the importance of a component[2] is measured on the basis of the number of references (imports, and method calls) other classes make to it.

8.5 Conclusions

In this contribution, we presented our vision of a new strategy to design component-based Grid applications. A three-staged approach, driven by graphical tools and accessible to non-expert programmers, should be as follows:

1. *Application sketching*, based on the definition of an *application workflow*, where *place-holders* describe the needed services
2. *Components discovery*, which is performed by retrieving components matching the place-holders through a component search engine
3. *Application assembling/composition*, the phase when the component interfaces are compared and suitable filters are deployed to make types and protocols match

The main innovation of this approach is the component search service, which allows users to locate the components they need. We believe that in the near future there will be a growing demand for ready-made software services, and current Web Search technologies will help in the deployment of effective solutions. The search engine, based on information retrieval techniques, in our opinion should be able to *rank* components on the basis of: their similarity with the place-holder description, their popularity among developers (something similar to the hit count), their use within other services (similarly to PageRank), etc.

Clearly, it is of primary importance for the existence of a quick, efficient, automatic way to deploy software components out of existing code. In our opinion, there is the need for automatic tools able to extract signature information from legacy code, and able to create the bridging code needed to make the component communicate with other entities, designed with different languages or running on different platforms.

When all these services become available, building a Grid application will become a straight-forward process. A non-expert user, aided by a graphical environment, will give a high-level description of the desired operations, which will be found, and possibly paid for, out of a quickly evolving market of services. At that point, the whole Grid will become as a virtual machine, tapping the power of a vast numbers of resources.

---

[2]Only Java classes are supported in this version.

Acknowledgments. We would like to thank our colleagues at the ISTI High Performance Computing Laboratory, Ranieri Baraglia, Tiziano Fagni, Alessandro Paccosi, Antonio Panciatici, Raffaele Perego, and Nicola Tonellotto for their critical and constructive support during the preparation of this contribution.

This work was partially supported by the Italian MIUR FIRB Grid.it project (RBNE01KNFP) on High-Performance Grid Platforms and Tools, and by the MIUR CNR strategic Project L499/1997-2000 on High-Performance Platforms. Part of our research was performed in collaboration with the Computer Architecture group, led by professors Marco Vanneschi and Marco Danelutto, at the Computer Science Department, University of Pisa.

References

[1] Ritchie, D.M.: The evolution of the UNIX time-sharing system. LNCS **79** (1980).

[2] Szyperski, C., Pfister, C.: WCOP '96 Workshop Report, ECOOP 96 Workshop Reader (1996).

[3] Armstron, R., Gannon, D., Geist, A., Keahey, K., Kohn, S., McInnes, L., Parker, S., Smolinsk, B.: Toward a common component architecture for high-performance scientific computing. In: Conference on High Performance Distributed Computing (1999).

[4] Hamilton, G.: Java beans, api specification, version 1.01-a (1997).

[5] Bernholdt, D.E., Elwasif, W.R., Kohl, J.S., Epperly, T.G.W.: A component architecture for high-performance computing. In: Workshop on Performance Optimization for High-Level Languages and Libraries (2002).

[6] Govindaraju, M., Krishnan, S., Chiu, K., Slominski, A., Gannon, D., Bramley, R.: Xcat 2.0: A component-based programming model for grid web services. Technical Report Technical Report-TR562, Department of Computer Science, Indiana University (2002).

[7] Johnson, C., Parker, S., Weinstein, D., Heffernan, S.: Component-based problem solving environments for large-scale scientific computing. Journal on Concurrency and Computation: Practice and Experience (2002) 1337–1349.

[8] Kohn, S., Dahlgren, T., Epperly, T., Kumfert, G.: Babel scientific interface description language (2002) http://www.llnl.gov/CASC/components/babel.html

[9] Ruiz, D.S.: Corba and corba component model (2003) http://ditec.um.es/ ~dsevilla/ccm/

[10] Katz, D., Rasmussen, C., Kohl, J., Armstrong, R., McInnes, L.: Cca tutorial at the cca forum winter meeting. http://www.cca-forum.org/tutorials/2003-01-15/index.html (2003).

[11] Sun Technologies Inc.: Java 2 enterprise edition 1.3.1 api specification (2003) http://java.sun.com/j2ee/sdk_1.3/techdocs/api/

[12] Keahey, K., Gannon, D.: Pardis: Corba-based architecture for application-level parallel distributed computation. In: Supercomputing '97 (1997).

[13] Beckman, P.H., Fasel, P.K., Humphrey, W.F., Mniszewski, S.M.: Efficient coupling of parallel applications using paws. In: Proc. of 7th IEEE International Symposium on High Performance Distributed Computing (1998).

[14] Keahey, K., Beckman, P.H., Ahrens, J.: Ligature: Component architecture for high performance applications. In: International Journal of High Performance Computing Applications, Special Issue on Performance Modeling — Part 2. Volume 14 (2000).

[15] Snelling, D., Tuecke, S.: The open grid service infrastructure forum (2003) http://www.gridforum.org/ogsi-wg/

[16] Microsoft Corp.: The microsoft .net framework (2004) http://www.microsoft.com/net

[17] Ximian Inc.: The mono project (2003) http://www.go-mono.com/

[18] The Java Grande Forum: http://www.javagrande.org (2003).

[19] Moreira, J.E., Midkiff, S.P., Gupta, M., Artigas, P.V., Snir, M., Lawrence, R.D.: Java programming for high performance numerical computing. IBM Systems Journal **39** (2000).

The first one relies on a location sever which keeps track of the mobile objects in the system. When needed, the server is queried to obtain an up-to-date reference to an active object. After migrating, an object updates its new location.

The second one uses a fully decentralized technique known as *forwarders* [18]. When leaving a site, an active object leaves a special object called a forwarder which points to its new location. Upon receiving a message, a forwarder simply passes it to the object (or another forwarder).

The third one is an original scheme based on a mix between forwarding an location server which provides both performance and fault tolerance.

9.2.4   Group Communications

The group communication mechanism of *ProActive* achieves asynchronous remote method invocation for a group of remote objects, with automatic gathering of replies.

Given a Java class, one can initiate group communications using the standard public methods of the class together with the classical dot notation; in that way, group communications remain typed. Furthermore, groups are automatically constructed to handle the result of collective operations, providing an elegant and effective way to program gather operations.

Here is an example of a typical group creation, based on the standard Java class A presented above:

```
// A group of type "A"  and its 2 members are created at once
// on the nodes directly specified,
//  parameters are specified in params,
Object[][] params = {{...}, {...}};
Node[] nodes = {..., ...};
A ag = (A) ProActiveGroup.newActiveGroup("A", params, nodes);
```

Elements can be included into a typed group only if their class equals or extends the class specified at the group creation. Note that we do allow and handle *polymorphic* groups. For example, an object of class B (B extending A) can be included to a group of type A. However based on Java typing, only the methods defined in the class A can be invoked on the group.

A method invocation on a group has a syntax similar to that of a standard method invocation:

```
ag.foo(...); // A group communication
```

Such a call is asynchronously propagated to all members of the group using multithreading. Like in the *ProActive* basic model, a method call on a group is nonblocking and provides a transparent future object to collect the results. A method call on a group yields a method call on each of the group members. If a member is a *ProActive* active object, the method call will be a *ProActive* call and if the member is a standard Java object, the method call will be a standard Java method call (within the same JVM). The parameters of the invoked method are broadcasted to all the members of the group.

An important specificity of the group mechanism is: the *result* of a typed group communication *is also a group* (see Fig. 9.3). The result group is transparently built at invocation time, with a future for each elementary reply. It will be dynamically updated with the incoming results, thus gathering results. The *wait-by-necessity* mechanism is also valid on groups: if all replies are awaited the caller blocks, but as soon as one reply arrives in the result group, the method call on this result is executed. For instance in:

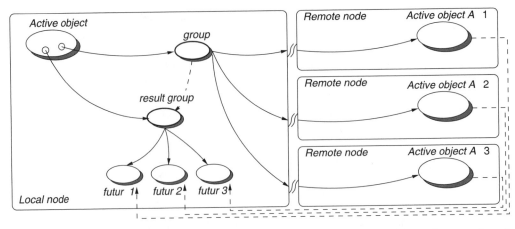

FIGURE 9.3. Execution of an asynchronous and remote method call on group with dynamic generation of a result group.

```
V vg = ag.bar();  // A method call on a group, returning a result
                  // vg is a typed group of "V"
vg.f();           // This is also a collective operation
```

a new f() method call is automatically triggered as soon as a reply from the call ag.bar() comes back in the group vg (dynamically formed). The instruction vg.f() completes when f() has been called on all members.

Other features are available regarding group communications: parameter dispatching using groups (through the definition of *scatter* groups), hierarchical groups, dynamic group manipulation (add, remove of members), group synchronization and barriers (waitOne, waitAll, waitAndGet); see [3] for further details and implementation techniques.

9.2.5 *Abstracting away from the Mapping of Active Objects to JVMs: Virtual Nodes*

Active objects will eventually be deployed on very heterogeneous environments where security policies may differ from place to place, where computing and communication performances may vary from one host to the other, etc. As such, the effective locations of active objects must not be tied in the source code.

A first principle is to *fully* eliminate from the source code the following elements:

- machine names,
- creation protocols,
- registry and lookup protocols,

the goal being to deploy any application anywhere without changing the source code. For instance, we must be able to use various protocols, rsh, ssh, Globus, LSF, etc., for the creation of the JVMs needed by the application. In the same manner, the discovery of existing resources or the registration of the ones created by the application can be done with various protocols such as RMIregistry, Jini, Globus, LDAP, UDDI, etc. Therefore, we see that the creation, registration, and discovery of resources has to be done externally to the application.

A second key principle is the capability to abstractly describe an application, or part of it, in terms of its conceptual activities. The description should indicate the various parallel or distributed entities in the program or in the component. As we are in a (object-oriented) message passing model, to some extent, this description indicates the maximum number of address spaces. For instance, an application that is designed to use three interactive visualization nodes, a node to capture input from a physic experiment, and a simulation engine designed to run on a cluster of machines should somewhere clearly advertise this information.

Now, one should note that the abstract description of an application and the way to deploy it are not independent piece of information. In the example just above, if there is a simulation engine, it might register in a specific registry protocol, and if so, the other entities of the computation might have to use that lookup protocol to bind to the engine. Moreover, one part of the program can just lookup for the engine (assuming it is started independently), or explicitly create the engine itself.

To summarize, in order to abstract away the underlying execution platform, and to allow a *source-independent deployment*, a framework has to provide the following elements:

- an abstract description of the distributed entities of a parallel program or component,
- an external mapping of those entities to real *machines*, using actual *creation, registry*, and *lookup* protocols.

Besides the principles above, we want to eliminate as much as possible the use of scripting languages, that can sometimes become even more complex than application code. Instead, we are seeking a solution with XML descriptors, XML editor tools, interactive ad hoc environments to produce, compose, and activate descriptors (see Section 9.4).

To reach that goal, the programming model relies on the specific notion of Virtual Nodes (VNs), i.e.,

- it is identified as a name (a simple string),
- it is used in a program source,
- it is defined and configured in a deployment descriptor (XML) (see Section 9.4 for further details),
- it after activation, it is mapped to one or to a set of *actual* ProActive *Nodes*.

Of course, distributed entities (active objects), are created on Nodes, not on Virtual Nodes. There is a strong need for both Nodes and *Virtual Nodes*. *Virtual Nodes* are a much richer abstraction, as they provide mechanisms such as *set* or *cyclic mapping*. Another key aspect is the capability to describe and trigger the mapping of a single VN that generates the allocation of several JVMs. This is critical if we want to get at once machines from a cluster of PCs managed through Globus or LSF. It is even more critical in a Grid application, when trying to achieve the coallocation of machines from several clusters across several continents.

Moreover, a Virtual Node is a concept of a distributed program or component, while a Node is actually a deployment concept: it is an object that lives in a JVM, hosting active objects. There is of course a correspondence between Virtual Nodes and Nodes: the function created by the deployment, the mapping. This mapping can be specified in an XML descriptor. By definition, the following operations can be configured in such a deployment descriptor (see Section 9.4):

```
ProActiveDescriptor pad =
            ProActive.getProActiveDescriptor(String xmlFileLocation);
//---- Returns a ProActiveDescriptor object from the xml file
VirtualNode dispatcher = pad.getVirtualNode("Dispatcher");
//---- Returns the VirtualNode Dispatcher described
//      in the xml file as a java object
dispatcher.activate()
//---Activates the VirtualNode
Node node = dispatcher.getNode();
//-----Returns the first node available among nodes mapped
//      to the VirtualNode
C3DDispatcher c3dDispatcher = newActive("C3DDispatcher", param, node);
.......................
```

FIGURE 9.4. Example of a *ProActive* source code for descriptor-based mapping.

- the mapping of VNs to Nodes and to JVMs,
- the way to create or to acquire JVMs,
- the way to register or to lookup VNs.

Now, within the source code, the programmer can manage the creation of active objects without relying on machine names and protocols. For instance, the piece of code given in Fig. 9.4 will allow to create an active object onto the Virtual Node `Dispatcher`. The Nodes (JVMs) associated in a descriptor file with a given VN are started (or acquired) only upon activation of a VN mapping (`dispatcher.activate()` in the Fig. 9.4).

9.3   Composing

9.3.1   Motivation

The aim of our work around components is to combine the benefits of a component model with the features of *ProActive*. The resulting components, that we call "Grid components," are recursively formed of either sequential, parallel and/or distributed subcomponents, that may wrap legacy code if needed, and that may be deployed but further reconfigured and moved—for example, to tackle fault tolerance, load balancing, or adaptability to changing environmental conditions.

Here is a typical scenario illustrating the usefulness of our work. Consider complex grid software formed of several services, say of other software (a parallel and distributed solver, a graphical 3-D renderer, etc). The design of this grid software is highly simplified if it can be considered as a hierarchical composition (recursive assembly and binding): the solver is itself a component composed of several components, each one encompassing a piece of the computation. The whole software is seen as a single component formed of the solver and the renderer. From the outside, the usage of this software is as simple as invoking a functional service of a component (e.g., call *solve-and-render*). Once deployed and running on a grid, assume that due to load balancing purposes, this software needs to be relocated. Some of the ongoing computations may just be moved (the solver for instance); others depending on specific peripherals that may not be present at the new location (the renderer for instance) may be terminated and replaced by a new instance adapted to the target environment and offering the same service. As the solver is itself a hierarchical component formed of several subcomponents, each encompassing an activity, we trigger the migration of the solver as a whole, without having to explicitly move each of its subcomponents, while references toward mobile components remain valid. Eventually, once the new graphical renderer is launched, we rebind the software, so as it now uses this new configuration.

9.3.2   Component Model

Observing the works done so far on component software, including standardized industrial component models, such as CCM, EJB, or COM, some researchers concluded that there was still missing an appropriate basis for the construction of highly flexible, highly dynamic, heterogeneous distributed environments. They consequently introduced a new model[5], based on the concepts of encapsulation (components are black boxes), composition (the model is hierarchical), sharing,[1] life–cycle (a component lives through different phases), activities, control (this allows the management of nonfunctional properties of the components), and dynamicity (this allows reconfiguration). This model is named Fractal.

The Fractal model is somewhat inspired from biological cells, i.e., plasma surrounded by membranes. In other words, a component is formed out of two parts: a *content* and a set of *controllers*. The content can be recursive, as a component can contain other components: the model is hierarchical. The controllers provide introspection capabilities for monitoring and exercising control over the execution of the components. A component interacts with its environment (notably, other components) through well-defined *interfaces*. These interfaces can be either client or server, and are interconnected using *bindings* (see Fig. 9.5).

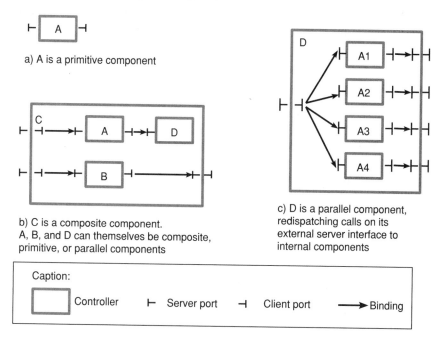

a) A is a primitive component

b) C is a composite component.
A, B, and D can themselves be composite,
primitive, or parallel components

c) D is a parallel component,
redispatching calls on its
external server interface to
internal components

Caption:

☐ Controller   ⊢ Server port   ⊣ Client port   ⟶ Binding

FIGURE 9.5. The three types of components.

---

[1] Sharing is currently not supported in the *ProActive* implementation

Fractal is a component model conceived to be simple but extensible. It provides an API in Java, and offers a reference implementation called Julia. Unfortunately, Julia is not based on a distributed communication protocol (although there exists a Jonathan personality, i.e., a set of RMI Fractal components), thus hindering the building of systems with distributed components.

Besides, *ProActive* offers many features, such as distribution, asynchronism, mobility or security, that would be of interest for Fractal components.

We therefore decided to write a new implementation of the Fractal API based on *ProActive*, that would benefit from both sides, and that would ease the construction of distributed and complex systems.

9.3.3   ProActive *Components*

A *ProActive* component has to be parallelizable and distributable as we aim at building grid-enabled applications by hierarchical composition; componentization acts as a glue to couple codes that may be parallel and distributed codes requiring high performance computing resources. Hence, components should be able to encompass more than one activity and be deployed on parallel and distributed infrastructures. Such requirements for a component are summarized by the concept we have named *Grid Component*.

Figure 9.5 summarizes the three different cases for the structure of a Grid component as we have defined it. For a composite built up as a collection of components providing common services (Fig. 9.5.c), *group communications* (See Section 9.2.4) are essential for ease of programming and efficiency. Because we target high performance grid computing, it is also very important to efficiently implement point-to-point and group method invocations, to manage the deployment complexity of components distributed all over the Grid and to possibly debug, monitor, and reconfigure the running components.

A synthetic definition of a *ProActive* component is the following:

- It is formed from one (or several) Active Object(s), executing on one (or several) JVM(s)
- It provides a set of server ports (Java Interfaces)
- It possibly defines a set of client ports (Java attributes if the component is primitive)
- It can be of three different types:

1. primitive: defined with Java code implementing provided server interfaces, and specifying the mechanism of client bindings.
2. composite: containing other components.
3. parallel: also a composite, but redispatching calls to its external server interfaces towards its inner components.

- It communicates with other components through one-to-one or group communications.

A *ProActive* component can be configured using:

- an XML descriptor (defining use/provide ports, containment, and bindings in an Architecture Description Language style)
- the notion of virtual node, capturing the deployment capacities and needs

Finally, we are currently working on the design of specialized components encapsulating legacy parallel code (usually Fortran-MPI or C-MPI). This way, *ProActive* will allow transparent collaboration between such legacy applications and any other Grid component.

9.3.4   Example

We hereby show an example of how a distributed component system could be built using our component model implementation. It relates to the scenario exposed in Section 9.3.1.

C3D, an existing application, is both a collaborative application and a distributed raytracer: users can interact through messaging and voting facilities in order to choose a 3-D scene that is rendered using a set of distributed rendering engines working in parallel. This application is particularly suitable for component programming, as we can distinguish individual software entities and we can abstract client and server interfaces from these entities. The resulting component system is shown in Fig. 9.6: Users interacting with the dispatcher component can ask for the scene motion, and can see the evolution of the ray-tracing. The dispatcher delegates the calculation of the scene to a parallel component (renderers). This parallel component contains a set of rendering engines (R1, R2, R3), and distributes calculation units to these rendering engines thanks to the group communication API (scatter feature, see Section 9.2.4). The results are then forwarded (from the client interface i of the renderers component) as a call-back to the dispatcher (server interface d), and later to the users (from client interface g of the dispatcher to server interface b of the clients). These relations result in cyclic composition of the components. During the execution, users (for instance user1 represented on the figure) can dynamically connect to the dispatcher and interact with the program. Another dynamical facility is the connection of new rendering engine components at runtime: to speedup the calculations, if the initial configuration does not perform fast enough, new rendering engines can be added along with R1, R2, R3. Besides, components being active objects, they can also migrate for load-balancing or change of display purposes, either programmatically or interactively using tools such as IC2D (see Section 9.4.3). Interaction between users, like votes, is not represented here.

There are two ways of configuring and instantiating component systems: either programmatically, or using an architecture description language (ADL). The ADL can help a lot, as it automates the instantiation, the deployment, the assembly, and the binding of the components. The following examples correspond to the configuration of the C3D application. The ADL is composed of two main sections. The first section defines the types of the components (User-Type, Dispatcher-Type, and Renderer-Type), in other words the services the components offer and the services they require:

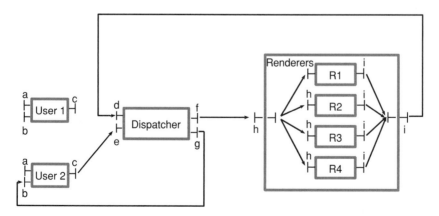

FIGURE 9.6. A simplified representation of the C3D component model.

```
<types>
   <component-type name="User-Type">
       <provides>
           <interface name="a" signature="package.UserInput"/>
           <interface name="b" signature="package.SceneUpdate"/>
       </provides>
       <requires>
           <interface name="c" signature="package.
           UserSceneModification"/>
       </requires>
   </component-type>
   <component-type name="Dispatcher-Type">
       <provides>
           <interface name="d" signature="package.
           UserSceneModification"/>
           <interface name="e" signature="package.CalculationResult"/>
       </provides>
       <requires>
           <interface name="f" signature="package.CalculateScene"/>
           <interface name="g" signature="package.SceneUpdate"/>
       </requires>
   </component-type>
   <component-type name="Renderer-Type">
       <provides>
           <interface name="h" signature="package.Rendering"/>
       </provides>
       <requires>
           <interface name="i" signature="package.CalculationResult"/>
       </requires>
   </component-type>
</types>
```

The second section defines the instances of the components, the assembly of components into composites, and the bindings between components:

```
<components>
    <primitive-component implementation="package.User"
                    name="user1" type="User-Type"
                    virtualNode="UserVN"/>
    <primitive-component implementation="package.User"
                    name="user2" type="User-Type"
                    virtualNode="UserVN"/>
    <primitive-component implementation="package.Dispatcher"
                    name="dispatcher" type="Dispatcher-Type"
                    virtualNode="DispatcherVN"/>
    <parallel-component name="parallel-renderers"
                    type="Renderer-Type"
                    virtualNode="parallel-renderers-VN">
        <components>
            <primitive-component implementation="package.Renderer"
                    name="renderer" type="Renderer-Type"
                    virtualNode="renderers-VN"/>
```

```
              <!-- the actual number of renderer instances
              depends upon the mapping of the virtual node -->
          </components>
          <!-- bindings are automatically performed
          inside parallel components -->
      </parallel-component>
  </components>
  <bindings>
      <binding client="dispatcher.c" server="parallel-renderers.c"/>
      <binding client="renderers.r" server="dispatcher.r"/>
      <binding client="user1.i" server="dispatcher.i"/>
      <binding client="dispatcher.g" server="user2.b"/>
      <!-- bindings to clients can also be performed dynamically
      as they appear once the application is started
      and ready to receive input operations -->
  </bindings>
```

Bindings connect components at each level of the hierarchy, and are performed automatically inside parallel components. The primitive components contain functional code from the class specified in the implementation attribute.

Each component also exhibits a "virtual node" property: the design of the component architecture is decoupled from the deployment (see Section 9.4.2) of the components. This way, the same component system can be deployed on different computer infrastructures (LAN, cluster, Grid).

In conclusion, the benefits of the componentization of the C3D application are—at least— threefold. First, the application is easier to understand and to configure. Second, the application is more evolutive: for instance, as the rendering calculations are encapsulated in components, one could improve the rendering algorithm, create new rendering engine components and easily replace the old components with the new ones. Third, the application is easier to deploy, thanks to the mapping of the components onto virtual nodes.

9.4   Deploying, Monitoring

9.4.1   *Motivation*

Increasing complexity of distributed applications and commodity of resources through grids are making the tasks of deploying those applications harder. There is a clear need for standard tools allowing versatile deployment and analysis of distributed applications. We present here concepts for the deployment and monitoring, and their implementation as effective tools integrated within the *ProActive* framework. If libraries for parallel and distributed application development exist (RMI in Java, jmpi [19] for MPI programming, etc.) there is no standard yet for the deployment of such applications. The deployment is commonly done manually through the use of remote shells for launching the various virtual machines or daemons on remote computers, clusters, or grids. The commoditization of resources through grids and the increasing complexity of applications are making the task of deploying central and harder to perform.

Questions such as "are the distributed entities correctly created ?", "do the communications among such entities correctly execute ?", "where is a given mobile entity actually located ?", etc., are usually left unanswered. Moreover, there is usually no mean to dynamically modify the execution environment once the application is started. Grid programming is about deploying processes (activities) on various machines. In the end, the security policy that must be ensured for those processes depends upon many factors: first of all, the application policy that is needed, but also, the machine locations, the security policies of their administrative domain, and the network being used to reach those machines.

Clearly said, the management of the mapping of processes (such as JVMs, PVM, or MPI daemons) onto hosts, the deployment of activities onto those processes have generally to be explicitly taken into account, in a static way, sometimes inside the application, sometimes through scripts. The application cannot be seamlessly deployed on different runtime environments.

To solve those critical problems, the quite classical and somehow ideal solutions we propose follow 4 steps:

1. abstract away from the hardware and software run-time configuration by introducing and manipulating in the program virtual processes where the activities of the application will be subsequently deployed,
2. provide external information regarding all real processes that must be launched and the way to do it (it can be through remote shells or job submission to clusters or grids), and define the mapping of virtual processes onto real processes,
3. provide a mean to visualize, complete, or modify the deployment once the application has started,
4. provide an infrastructure where Grid security is expressed outside the application code, outside the firewall of security domains, and in both cases in a high level and flexible language.

9.4.2 Deployment Descriptors

We solve the two first steps by introducing XML-based descriptors able to describe activities and their mapping onto processes. Deployment descriptors allow to describe: (1) virtual nodes, entities manipulated in the source code, representing containers of activities, (2) Java virtual machines where the activities will run and the way to launch or find them, (3) the mapping between the virtual nodes and the JVMs. The deployment of the activities is consequently separated from the code; one can decide to deploy the application on different hosts just by adapting the deployment descriptor, without any change to the source code.

Descriptors are structured as follows:

```
virtual nodes
        definition
        acquisition
deployment
        security
        register
        lookup
        mapping
        jvms
infrastructure
```

9.4.2.1   Virtual Nodes

As previously stated (see Section 9.2.5), a virtual node is a mean to define a mapping between a conceptual architecture and one or several nodes (JVMs), and its usage in the source code of a program has been given on Fig. 9.4.

The names of the virtual nodes in the source code has to correspond to the names of the virtual nodes defined in the first section. There are two ways of using virtual nodes. The first way is to name them (and further explicitly describe them):

```
<virtualNodesDefinition>
    <virtualNode name="User"/>
</virtualNodesDefinition>
```

The second way is to acquire virtual nodes already deployed by another application:

```
<virtualNodesAcquisition>
    <virtualNode name="Dispatcher"/>
</virtualNodesAcquisition>
```

9.4.2.2 Deployment

The deployment section defines the correspondence, or mapping, between the virtual nodes in the first section, and the processes they actually create.

The security section allows for the inclusion of security policies in the deployment (see Section 9.4.4):

```
<security file="URL">
```

The register section allows for the registration of virtual nodes in a registry such as RMIRegistry or JINI lookup service:

```
<register virtualNode="Dispatcher" protocol="rmi">
```

This way, the virtual node "Dispatcher," as well as all the JVMs it is mapped to, will be accessible by another application through the rmi registry.

Symmetrically, descriptors provide the ability to acquire a virtual node already deployed by another application, and defined as acquirable in the first section:

```
<lookup virtualNode="Dispatcher" host="machineZ" protocol="rmi"/>
```

The mapping section helps defining:

- a one virtual node to one JVM mapping:

```
<map virtualNode="User1">
    <jvmSet>
        <currentJvm protocol="rmi"/>
        <!-- currentJvm is the Jvm of the file parsing process -->
    </jvmSet>
</map>
```

- a one virtual node to a set of JVMs mapping:

```
<map virtualNode="Renderer">
    <jvmSet>
        <vmName value=Jvm1/>
        <vmName value=Jvm2/>
        <vmName value=Jvm3/>
        ...
    </jvmSet>
</map>
```

- the collocation of virtual nodes, when two virtual nodes have a common mapping on a JVM.

Virtual nodes represent sets of JVMs, and these JVMs can be remotely created and referenced using standard Grid protocols. Each JVM is associated with a creation process, that is named here but fully defined in the "infrastructure" section. For example, here is an example where Jvm1 will be created through a Globus process that is only named here, but defined in the infrastructure section:

```
<jvms>
    <jvm name="Jvm1">
        <acquisition method="rmi"/>
        <creation>
            <processReference refid="GlobusProcess"/>
        </creation>
    </jvm>
    ...
</jvms>
```

9.4.2.3   Infrastructure

The infrastructure section explicitly defines which Grid protocols (and associated *ProActive* classes) to use in order to create remote JVMs.

The remote creation of a JVM implies two steps: first, the connection to a remote host; second, the actual creation of the JVM.

Let us start with the second step. Once connected to the remote host, the JVM can be created using the JVMNodeProcess class:

```
<processDefinition id="jvmProcess">
    <jvmProcess class="org.objectweb.proactive.core.process.
        JVMNodeProcess"/>
    <processReference refid="localJvmCreation"/>
```

The first step, the connection process, can itself invoke other processes. For example, the connection to LSF hosts requires beforehand a ssh connection to the frontal of the cluster, then a bSub command to reach the hosts inside the cluster. When connected, the previously defined localJvmCreation process is called:

```
<processDefinition id="bsubInriaCluster">
    <bsubProcess
        class="org.objectweb.proactive.core.process.lsf.
            LSFBSubProcess">
        <processReference refid="localJvmCreation"/>
        <bsubOption>
            <processor>20</processor>
        </bsubOption>
    </bsubProcess>
</processDefinition>
<processDefinition id="sshProcess">
    <sshProcess
        class="org.objectweb.proactive.core.process.ssh.SSHProcess"
        hostname="sea.inria.fr">
        <processReference refid="bsubInriaCluster"/>
```

```
        </sshProcess>
    </processDefinition>
```

Other protocols are supported, including: rsh, rlogin, ssh, Globus, PBS. Here is an example using Globus:

```
<processDefinition id="globusProcess">
    <globusProcess
        class="org.objectweb.proactive.core.process.globus.
            GlobusProcess"
        hostname="globus.inria.fr">
        <processReference refid="localJvmCreation"/>
        <globusOption>
            <count>15</count>
        </globusOption>
    </globusProcess>
</processDefinition>
```

More information about the descriptors and how to use them is given in [20].

9.4.2.4   Deployment of Components

The ADL used for describing component systems associates each component with a virtual node (see Section 9.3.4). A component system can be deployed using any deployment descriptor, provided the virtual node names match. The parallel components take advantage of the deployment descriptor in another way. In the example of Section 9.3.4, consider the parallel component named "renderers." It only defines one inner component "renderer," and this inner component is associated to the virtual node "renderers-VN." If "renderers-VN" is mapped onto a single JVM A, only one instance of the renderer will be created, on the JVM A. But if this "renderers-VN" is actually mapped onto a set of JVMs, one instance of the renderer will be created on each of these JVMs. This allows for large scale parallelization in a transparent manner.

9.4.3   Interactive Tools

We solve the third step mentioned in Section 9.4.1 by having a monitoring application: *IC2D* (Interactive Control and Debugging of Distribution). It is a graphical environment for monitoring and steering distributed *ProActive* applications.

9.4.3.1   Monitoring the Infrastructure and the Mapping of Activities

Once a *ProActive* application is running, *IC2D* enables the user to graphically visualize fundamental distributed aspects such as topology and communications (see Fig. 9.7).

It also allows the user to control and modify the execution (e.g., the mapping of activities onto real processes, i.e., JVMs, either upon creation or upon migration. Indeed, it provides a way to interactively **drag-and-drop any running active object** to move it to any node displayed by *IC2D* (see Fig. 9.8). This is a useful feature in order to react to load unbalance, to expected unavailability of a host (especially useful in the context of a *desktop grid*), and more importantly in order to help implementing the concept of a *pervasive grid*: mobile users need to move the frontend active objects attached to the on-going grid computations they have launched, on their various computing devices so as to maintain their grid connectivity.

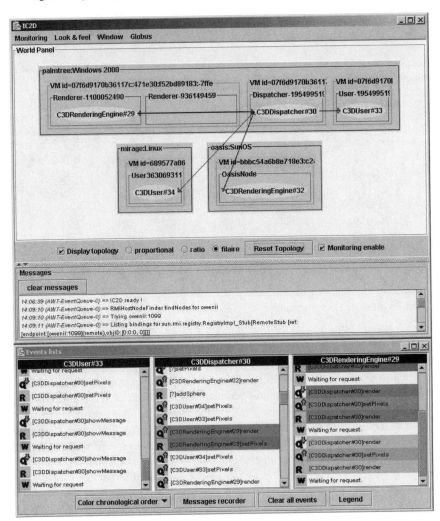

FIGURE 9.7. General view of what *IC2D* displays when an application is running.

Moreover, it is possible to trigger the activation of new JVMs (see Fig. 9.9) adding dynamicity in the configuration and deployment.

9.4.3.2   Interactive Dynamic Assembly and Deployment of Components

IC2D compose and *IC2D deploy* are two new interactive features we are planning to add to the *IC2D* environment.

The idea is to enable an integrator to graphically describe an application: the components, the inner components, and their respective bindings. The outcome of the usage of *IC2D compose* would be an automatically generated ADL. At this specific point, we need to provide the integrator with several solutions for composing virtual nodes. Indeed, as each *ProActive* component is attached to one virtual node, what about the virtual node of the composite component that

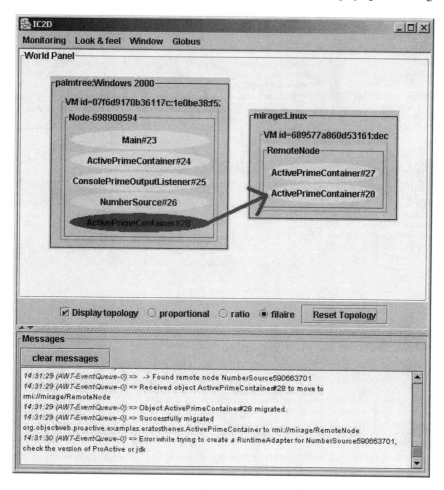

FIGURE 9.8. Drag-and-drop migration of an active object.

results from the composition of several subcomponents? Should the resulting component still be deployed on the different virtual nodes of its inner components; or, on the contrary, should those virtual nodes be merged into one single virtual node attached to the composite? The decision is grounded on the fact that merging virtual nodes is an application-oriented way to enforce the collocation of components.

Besides, *IC2D deploy* will be an additional tool that graphically would enable to trigger the deployment then the starting of an application based upon its ADL; this of course requires the complementary usage of a deployment descriptor attached to this application, so as to first launch the required infrastructure. Once the application has been deployed, *IC2D deploy* would enable to dynamically and graphically manage the life–cycle of the components (start, stop), and interface with *IC2D compose* so as to allow the user modify their bindings and their inclusion. Of course, the *IC2D* monitor itself is still useful so as to visualize the underlying infrastructure and all activities. At this point, we will need to extend the *IC2D* monitor, so as to provide a way to

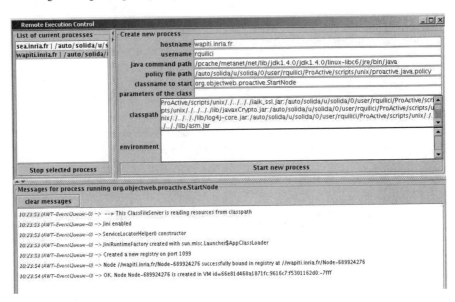

FIGURE 9.9. Interactive creation of a new JVM and associated node.

graphically show all activities that are part of the same component: in this way, it will be possible to trigger the migration of a component as a whole, by using the usual drag-and-drop facility.

9.4.4   Security Enforcement

We now describe the fourth step mentioned in Section 9.4.1. Grid applications must be able to cope with large variations in deployment: from intradomain to multiple domains, going over private, to virtually private, to public networks. In the same way as the deployment is not tied up in the source code, we provide a similar solution regarding the security, so as it becomes easily configurable in a flexible, and abstract manner. Overall, we propose a framework allowing:

- declarative security attributes (Authentication, Integrity, Confidentiality), outside any source code and away from any API;
- policies defined hierarchically at the level of administrative domain,
- dynamic security policy, taking into account the nature (private or public) of the underlying networks;
- dynamically negotiated policies (for multiprincipals applications),
- policies for remote creation and migration of activities.

9.4.4.1   A Hierarchical Approach to Grid Security

A first decisive feature allows to define application-level security on Virtual Nodes, those application-level deployment abstractions: **Virtual Node Security:** Security policies can be defined at the level of Virtual Nodes. At execution, that security will be imposed on the Nodes resulting from the mapping of Virtual Nodes to JVMs, and Hosts.

As such, virtual nodes are the support for intrinsic application level security. If, at design time, it appears that a process always requires a specific level of security (e.g., authenticated and encrypted communications at all time), then that process should be attached to a virtual node on which those security features are imposed. It is the designer's responsibility to structure his/her application or components into virtual node abstractions compatible with the required security. Whatever deployment occurs, those security features will be maintained.

The second decisive feature deals with a major Grid aspect: deployment-specific security. The issue is actually twofold:

1. allowing organizations (security domains) to specify general security policies,
2. allowing application security to be specifically adapted to a given deployment environment.

Domains are a standard way to structure (virtual) organizations involved in a Grid infrastructure; they are organized in a hierarchical manner. They are the logical concept allowing to express security policies in a hierarchical way.

Declarative Domain Security: Fine grain and declarative security policies can be defined at the level of *Domains*. A Security Domain is a domain to which a certificate and a set of rules are associated.

This principle allows to deal with the two issues mentioned above:

(1) the administrator of a domain can define specific policy rules that must be obeyed by the applications running within the domain. However, a general rule expressed inside a domain may prevent the deployment of a specific application. To solve this issue, a policy rule can allow a well-defined entity to weaken it. As we are in a hierarchical organization, allowing an entity to weaken a rule means allowing all entities included to weaken the rule. The entity can be identified by its certificate;
(2) a Grid user can, at the time he runs an application, specify additional security based on the domains being deployed onto, directly in his deployment descriptor for those domains.

Finally, as active objects are active and mobile entities, there is a need to specify security at the level of such entities.

Active Object Security: Security policies can be defined at the level of Active Object. Upon migration of an activity, the security policy attached to that object follows.

In open applications, e.g., several principals interact in a collaborative Grid application, a JVM (a process) launched by a given principal can actually host an activity executing under another principal. The principle above allows to keep specific security privileges in such case. Moreover, it can also serve as a basis to offer, in a secure manner, hosting environments for mobile agents.

9.4.4.2 Interactions Definition

Security policies are able to control all the *interactions* that can occur when deploying and executing a multiprincipals Grid application. With this goal in mind, interactions span over the creation of processes (JVM in our case), to the monitoring of activities (ActiveObjects) within processes, including, of course, the communications. Here is a brief description of those interactions:

- JVMCreation (JVMC): creation of a new JVM process
- NodeCreation (NC): creation of a new Node within a JVM (as the result of Virtual Node mapping)
- CodeLoading (CL): loading of bytecode within a JVM
- ActiveObjectCreation (AOC): creation of a new activity (active object) within a Node

- ActiveObjectMigration (AOM): migration of an existing activity object to a Node
- Request (Q), Reply (P): communications, method calls, and replies to method calls
- Listing (L): list the content of an entity; for Domain/Node provides the list of Node/Active Objects, for Active Object allows to monitor its activity.

One must be able to express policies in a rather declarative manner. The general syntax to provide security rules, to be placed within security policy files attached to applications (for instance, see the `security` tag within the deployment descriptor), is the following:

```
Entity[Subject]  -> Entity [Subject]
                              : Interaction # [SecurityAttributes]
```

Being in a PKI infrastructure, the subject is a certificate or credential. Other "elements" (Domain, Virtual Node, Object) are rather specific to Grid applications and, in some cases, to the object-oriented framework. An "entity" is an element on which one can define a security policy. "Interaction" is a list of actions that will be impacted by the rule. Finally, security attributes specify how, if authorized, those interactions have to be achieved.

In order to provide a flavor of the system, we consider the following example.

```
Domain[inria.fr]  -> Domain[ll.cnrs.fr]  : Q,P # [+A,+I,?C]
```

The rule specifies that between the domain *inria.fr* (identified by a specific certificate) and the parallel machine *ll.cnrs.fr*, all communications (reQuests, and rePlies) are authorized, they are done with *authentication* and *integrity*, *confidentiality* being accepted but not required.

9.4.4.3   Security Negotiation

As a Grid operates in decentralized mode, without a central administrator controlling the correctness of all security policies, these policies must be *combined*, *checked*, and *negotiated* dynamically.

During execution, each activity (Active Object) is always included in a *Node* (due to the Virtual Node mapping) and at least in one *Domain*, the one used to launch a JVM (D_0). Figure 9.10

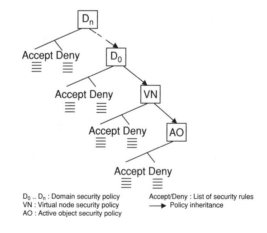

FIGURE 9.10. Hierarchical security levels.

hierarchically represents the security rules that can be activated at execution: from the top, hierarchical domains (D_n to D_0), the virtual node policy (VN), and the Active Object (AO) policy. Of course, such policies can be inconsistent, and there must be clear principles to combine the various sets of rules.

There are three main principles: (1) choosing the *most specific rules* within a given domain (as a single Grid actor is responsible for it), (2) an interaction is valid only if all levels accept it (absence of weakening of authorizations), (3) the security attributes retained are the most constrained based on a partial order (absence of weakening of security). Before starting an interaction, a *negotiation* occurs between the two entities involved.

In large scale Grid applications, migration of activities is an important issue. The migration of Active Objects must not weaken the security policy being applied. When an active object migrates to a new location, three cases may happen:

- the object migrates to a node belonging to the same virtual node and included inside the same domain. In this case, all already-negotiated sessions remain valid.
- the object migrates to a known node (created during the deployment step) which belongs to another virtual node. In this case, all already-negotiated sessions can be invalid. This kind of migration imposes reestablishing the object policy, and upon a change, renegotiating with interacting entities.
- The object migrates to an unknown node (not known at the deployment step). In this case, the object migrates with a copy of the application security policy. When a secured interaction will take place, the security system retrieves not only the object's application policy but also policies' rules attached to the node on which the object is to compute the policy.

9.5   Conclusion and Perspectives

In summary, the essence of our proposition, presented in this chapter, is as follows: a distributed object-oriented programming model, smoothly extended to get a component-based programming model (in the form of a 100% Java library); moreover this model is "grid-aware" in the sense that it incorporates from the very beginning adequate mechanisms in order to further help in the deployment and runtime phases on all possible kind of infrastructures, notably secure grid systems. This programming framework is intended to be used for large scale grid applications. For instance, we have succeeded to apply it for a numerical simulation of electromagnetic waves propagation, a non embarrassingly parallel application [21], featuring visualization and monitoring capabilities for the user. To date, this simulation has successfully been deployed on various infrastructures, ranging from interconnected clusters, to an intranet grid composed of approximatively 300 desktop machines. Performances compete with a previous existing version of the application, written in Fortran MPI. The proposed object-oriented approach is more generic and features reusability (the component-oriented version is under development, which may further add dynamicity to the application), and the deployment is very flexible.

We are conducting further works in several but complementary directions that are needed in grid computing, mainly:

- checkpointing and message logging techniques are in the way of being incorporated into the *ProActive* library. Indeed, we will as such be able to react to versatility of machines and network connections, without having to restart all the application components. Several similar works are under way ([22] for instance). The original difficulty we are faced with, is that it is possible to checkpoint the state of an active object only at specific points: only between the service of two requests (for the same reason which explains why the migration of active objects is weak). Nevertheless, we provide an hybrid protocol combining communication induced checkpointing and message logging techniques, which is adapted to the nonpreemptibility of processes. This protocol ensures strong consistency of recovery lines, and enables a fully asynchronous recovery of the distributed system after a failure.

- *ProActive* components that wrap legacy codes, and in particular, parallel (MPI) native codes, are being defined and implemented (see [23] for related approaches). Of course, the design aims at enabling such components to interact with 100% *ProActive* components.

Overall, we target numerical code coupling, combination of numerical simulations and visualization, and collaborative environments in dedicated application domains (see [24]), etc. The aim is to use our grid component model as a software bus for interactions between some or all of the grid components.

Indeed, the presented approach does not specifically target high-level tools appropriate for scientists or engineers who may not have a computer science background. In this respect, our objective is to succeed to incorporate the *IC2D* tools suite into grid portals, such as the Alliance portal [25]. An other complementary on-going work for this class of users is to enable *ProActive* components to be published as Web services (and enable those Web service enabled components interact using SOAP). Notice that it does not prevent a service to be implemented as one or several hierarchical ProActive components, i.e., as the result of a recursive composition of 100% *ProActive* components, internally interacting only through *ProActive*. Then, within such portals, end users could rely on workflow languages such as WSFL or BPEL4WS to compose applications by simply integrating some of the published components at a *coarse-grain level*.

In this way, those coarse-grain web service enabled components could provide the usual service-oriented view most users are familiar with. But as those instanciated components may use stateful resources, encompass possibly complex compositions of activities and data, we claim that the object and component oriented programming model we propose is adequate to 'internally' program and deploy those hierarchical components.

References

[1] F. Baude, D. Caromel, F. Huet, L. Mestre and J. Vayssière, *Interactive and Descriptor-based Deployment of Object-Oriented Grid Applications*, in 11th IEEE International Symposium on High Performance Distributed Computing (2002), pp. 93–102

[2] I. Attali, D. Caromel, A. Contes, *Hierarchical and Declarative Security for Grid Applications*, in 10th International Conference on High Performance Computing, HIPC, vol. 2913, LNCS (2003), pp. 363–372

[3] L. Baduel, F. Baude, D. Caromel, *Efficient, Flexible, and Typed Group Communications in Java*, in Joint ACM Java Grande - ISCOPE 2002 Conference (ACM, 2002) pp. 28–36

[4] F. Baude, D. Caromel, M. Morel, *From Distributed Objects to Hierarchical Grid Components*, in On the Move to Meaningful Internet Systems 2003: CoopIS, DOA, and ODBASE - OTM Confederated International Conferences, CoopIS, DOA, and ODBASE 2003, vol. 2888, LNCS (2003), pp. 1226–1242

[5] E. Bruneton, T. Coupaye, J.B. Stefani, *Recursive and Dynamic Software Composition with Sharing*, in Proceedings of the 7th ECOOP International Workshop on Component-Oriented Programming (WCOP'02), (2002)

[6] E. Bruneton, T. Coupaye, J.B. Stefani, *Fractal Web Site*, (2003)
    http://fractal.objectweb.org

[7] D. Gannon, R. Bramley, G. Fox, S. Smallen, A.R. I, R. Ananthakrishnan, F. Bertrand, K. Chiu, M. Farrellee, M.G. Indaraju, S. Krishnan, L. Ramakrishnan, Y. Simmhan, A. Slominski, Y. Ma, C. Olariu, N. Rey-Cenvaz, Programming the Grid: Distributed Software Components, P2P and Grid Web Services for Scientific Applications, *Cluster Computing* 5 (2002)

[8] G. Fox, M. Pierce, D. Gannon, M. Thomas, Overview of Grid Computing Environments, (2003) Global Grid Forum document, http://forge.gridforum.org/projects/ggf-editor/document/GFD-I.9/en/1

[9] A. Grimshaw, and W. Wulf, The Legion Vision of a World-wide Virtual Computer, *Communications of the ACM* 40 (1997)

[10] M. Humphrey, *From Legion to Legion-G to OGSI.NET: Object-based Computing for Grids*, in NSF Next Generation Software Workshop at the 17th International Parallel and Distributed Processing Symposium (IPDPS2003), Nice, France (IEEE Computer Society, 2003)

[11] R. Bramley, K. Chin, D. Gannon, M. Govindaraju, N. Mukhi, B. Temko, M. Yochuri, *A Component-based Services Architecture for Building Distributed Applications*, in 9th IEEE International Symposium on High Performance Distributed Computing (2000)

[12] A. Denis, C. Pérez, T. Priol, Achieving Portable and Efficient Parallel CORBA Objects, *Concurrency and Computation: Practice and Experience* 15, 891–909 (2003)

[13] A. Denis, C. Prez, T. Priol, A. Ribes, PADICO: *A Component-based Software Infrastructure for Grid Computing*, in 17th IEEE International Parallel and Distributed Processing Symposium (IPDPS2003), (2003)

[14] D. Caromel, F. Belloncle, Y. Roudier, The C++// Language, in *Parallel Programming Using C++*, (MIT, 1996), pp. 257–296 73118-5.

[15] F. Baude, D. Caromel, D. Sagnol, Distributed Objects for Parallel Numerical Applications, Mathematical Modelling and Numerical Analysis Modelisation, special issue on Programming tools for Numerical Analysis, EDP Sciences, *SMAI* 36 837–861 (2002)

[16] J. Bull, L. Smith, L. Pottage, R. Freeman, *Benchmarking Java Against C and Fortran for Scientific Applications*, in Joint ACM Java Grande - ISCOPE 2001 Conference, Palo Alto, CA (ACM, 2001)

[17] D. Caromel, Toward a Method of Object-oriented Concurrent Programming, *Communications of the ACM* 36 90–102 (1993)

[18] J. Maisonneuve, M. Shapiro, P. Collet, Implementing References as Chains of Links, in 3rd Int. Workshop on Object-orientation in Operating Systems (1992)

[19] K. Dincer, *Ubiquitous Message Passing Interface Implementation in Java: JMPI*, in Proc. 13th Int. Parallel Processing Symp. and 10th Symp. on Parallel and Distributed Processing (IEEE, 1999)

[20] OASIS: ProActive web site, (2004) http://www.inria.fr/oasis/ProActive/

[21] L. Baduel, F. Baude, D. Caromel, C. Delbe, N. Gama, S.E. Kasmi, S. Lanteri, A Parallel Object-oriented Application for 3d electromagnetism, in IEEE International Symposium on Parallel and Distributed Computing, IPDPS (2004)

[22] A. Bouteiller, F. Cappello, T. Herault, G. Krawezik, P.L. Marinier, F. Magniette, A Fault Tolerant MPI for Volatile Nodes Based on the Pessimistic Sender Based Message Logging, in ACM/IEEE International Conference on Supercomputing SC 2003, (2003)

[23] M. Li, O. Rana, D. Walker, Wrapping MPI-based Legacy Codes as Java/CORBA Components, *Future Generation Computer Systems* 18 213–223 (2001)

[24] M. Shields, O. Rana, D. Walker, A Collaborative Code Development Environment for Computational Electro-magnetics, in IFIP TC2/WG2.5 Working Conference on the Architecture of Scientific Software (Kluwer, 2001), pp. 119–141

[25] The Alliance Portal, (2004)   http://www.extreme.indiana.edu/xportlets/project/index.shtml

Chapter 10

ASSIST As a Research Framework for High-Performance Grid Programming Environments

10.1 Introduction: High-Performance Application Development and Grids

The research activity of our group at the Department of Computer Science, University of Pisa, is focused on programming models and environments for the development of high-performance multidisciplinary applications. The enabling computing platforms we are considering are complex distributed architectures, whose nodes are parallel machines of any kind, including PC/workstation clusters. In general such platforms are characterized by heterogeneity of nodes, and by dynamicity in resource management and allocation. In this context, Grid platforms at various levels of integration [25] are of main interest, including complex distributed structures of general and dedicated subsystems, private heterogeneous networks, and systems for pervasive and ubiquitous computing. In the following, we shall speak of Grids to refer to such architectural scenario.

A Grid-aware application must be able to deal with heterogeneity and dynamicity in the most effective way (adaptive applications), in order to guarantee the specified level of performance in spite of the variety of run-time events causing modifications in resource availability (load unbalancing, node/network faults, administration issues, emergencies, and so on). This is true for any kind of Grid applications. But it is an even more important feature in case we are interested in high performance Grid-aware applications, i.e., in applications, both have to be run on Grids and need to achieve high performances in order to be actually useful. With respect to traditional platforms, now it is much more important to rely on application development environments and tools that guarantee high-level programmability and application compositionality, software interoperability and reuse, and, at the same time, to be able to achieve high performance and capability to adapt to the evolution of the underlying technologies (networks, nodes, clusters, operating systems, middleware, and so on) [8, 11, 24, 33, 37, 38, 42]. Achieving this high-level view of Grid application development is the basic goal of our research, notably in the *Grid.it* national project [31] and associated initiatives at the national and European level.

Though the programming environment and infrastructure must take into account outstanding issues in domain administration and security too, in this chapter we concentrate on the very fundamental issue of the programming model and its implementation. Our view of Grid

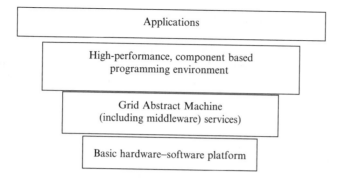

FIGURE 10.1. The role of programming environment in Grid application development.

application development is summarized by the level structure shown in Fig. 10.1. This schema is independent of the kind of applications taken into account. It simply provides a useful way to structure tools and programmer responsibilities.

The Programming Environment is centered on the existence of a high-level, high-performance programming model and related development tools. A high-level view of compositionality, inter-operability, reuse, performance, and application adaptivity characterizes the Programming Environment we advocate. Applications are expressed entirely on top of this level. The level denoted by *Grid Abstract Machine* (GAM) includes all the functionalities to support the preparation, loading and execution of the applications expressed in the formalism of the programming environment and transformed by the compiling tools. The GAM includes the functionalities that, in the current view of Grids, are provided by the Middleware tools and services, e.g., moving bottom-up: the Connectivity (microkernel), Resource (resource management services) and Collective (collective and dynamic resource control and allocation) levels [26]. This Middleware may be one of the current/standard products (Globus Toolkit and its evolutions [25–28]), or a subset of the services performed by them.

The GAM exploits a subset of the Middleware services and adds critical functionalities that support the programming model and the development tools, including all the strategies for resource management and scheduling and rescheduling, allocation and reallocation, as well as all the actions concerning the application structuring and restructuring. By replacing the old-fashioned OS-like view—according to which the application development occurs directly on top of the Middleware, by the view centered upon the Programming Environment and the Grid Abstract Machine, We wish to stress the programming-model based approach to system design, and, at the same time, to minimize the amount and variety of functionalities that are present in the underlying levels: i.e., these functionalities must be limited just to the support to the programming model and tools used to build Grid-aware, adaptive applications. Potentially, this approach leads to achieve a much better trade-off between programmability and interoperability on one side, and performance on the other side.

From the discussion above, it follows that the fundamental research issues, to design innovative platforms for Grid-aware applications, are the programming model and its implementation strategies. Other notable research projects [8, 11, 12, 19, 20, 24, 33, 37, 38, 42] propose to follow a similar approach, each one with its own characterization.

In this chapter, we illustrate how A Software development System based upon Integrated Skeleton Technology (ASSIST) [1–3, 43] is a valid research vehicle to pursue this programming-model driven line. An ASSIST is a programming environment oriented to the development of parallel and distributed high-performance applications according to a unified approach. It is supported by projects funded by the Ministry of University and Research, National Research Council, and Italian Space Agency. Most of the results discussed in this work are supported by the experiences made using ASSIST by different research groups participating in this project. In particular, these groups developed applications including Image Processing: iso-surfaces extraction, decimation, compression (IMATI-CNR, Genova), Earth Observation: SAR, Interferometry (Italian Space Agency), Computational Chemistry: molecular dynamics (ISTM-CNR, Perugia), MPEG2 parallel encoder (the authors' Department), Knowledge Discovery in semi structured data sets (parallel query execution engine), Question Answering, Search Engines (the authors' Department), and a Data Mining framework for Customer Relationship Management platforms. This complex application, developed by our group in the SAIB Project (MIUR and SEMA SpA), will be illustrated later on in this chapter.

In Section 10.2, we discuss the conceptual framework for Grid-aware programming environments, based upon structured parallel programming and components technology, anticipating how ASSIST possesses the essential features required by such framework. In Section 10.3, we summarize the ASSIST programming model, showing its evolution, along the line of structured parallel programming, to solve critical problems of expressive power, flexibility, interoperability and efficiency. Section 10.4 illustrates the modular compiler model and the current implementation for heterogeneous platforms and Globus-based Grids. In Section 10.5, we show the features that allow ASSIST programs to be used in CORBA infrastructures that represent our basic starting point towards interoperability in Grid applications. Section 10.6 extends the presentation of Section 10.3 about the ASSIST-based frameworks for dynamically adaptive applications. Section 10.7 summarizes the current status of our research and its fundamental steps in the next two years.

10.2 Programming Model: Distribution, Parallelism, Interoperability and Adaptivity

Currently, Grid applications are often designed according to a low-level approach (i.e., by relying on the Middleware services directly, possibly through a Grid portal) and, in many cases, they consist in single jobs or in limited forms of job composition (e.g., DAGs). Parallelism, where present, is limited inside single jobs, in a way that does not affect the overall workflow of the application (e.g., a job may be an MPI program). The result is that Grid applications are rarely highly optimized for high-performance.

As discussed in the previous section, our point of view is radically different. It is based on the definition and realization of a programming model with the following features:

1. applications are expressed as compositions of high-performance components,
2. a uniform approach is followed for distributed and parallel programming: in general, components exploit internal parallelism and are executed in parallel with each other,
3. the strategies to drive the dynamic adaptation of applications are expressed in the same high-level formalism of the programming model.

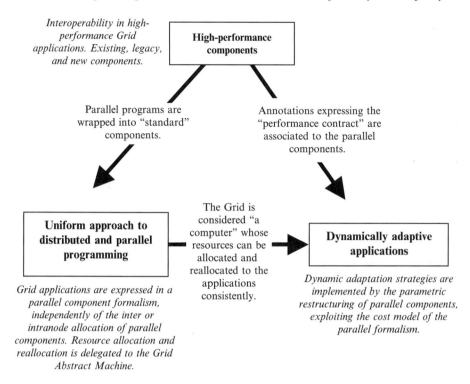

FIGURE 10.2. The conceptual framework for Grid-aware programming environments.

Figure 10.2 summarizes their interrelationships, which form the conceptual frameworks on which we found our research approach. A programming model implementing this set of features will be able to automatically implement proper and effective optimizations that depend on the kind of target architecture (nodes) considered, thus relieving the programmer from such an heavy and error prone duty. As both parallel execution of components and internally parallel components are taken into account, our "high performance" keyword does not (only) refer to the classical high performance computing framework, but rather it refers to a pervasive attention to the implementation of very efficient mechanisms supporting Grid-aware application execution.

We will show that the ASSIST model, in the current version and according to its foreseen evolution, is a research vehicle which is consistent with the requirements of such frameworks.

10.2.1 Grid-aware Applications as Compositions of High-Performance Components

Feature 1 is based on the proper exploitation of the component technology [10]. In our view, components are the basic mechanism to achieve compositionality by guaranteeing software interoperability and reuse. Here, we assume that the basic features of this software technology are known to the reader.

Achieving high performance in component technology is currently an important research issue [6, 13, 32, 36, 37, 38]. Currently, we are evaluating how the existing standards (CCA [13, 30], Java Beans [41], CCM [17], Web Services [18, 28, 45]) can be assumed as starting points to define and realize a robust component-based high-performance programming model, that can be widely accepted and that is able to interoperate in many application areas.

As we shall see, ASSIST provides the abstraction of high-performance components and high-performance composition of components, independently of any commercial standard. This allows us to understand the basic features that high-performance components should possess, in particular from the point of view of computation structuring, parallelism exploitation and modularity. These features will be properly merged with one or more commercial standard, or their future high-performance versions, in order to achieve extensive interoperability and reuse. The merging of high-performance programming and component technology must allow the designer to structure the application as the proper composition of components, i.e., some of which may be already existing/legacy (possibly in binary form), and other ones are programmed from scratch (e.g., written in ASSIST) or as the combination of existing software into new parallel structures.

Version 1.2 of ASSIST supports heterogeneity and the interoperability with several current standards, in particular the *CORBA* interoperability [17, 35], i.e., an ASSIST program can act as a client of a CORBA server, but also ASSIST programs can be easily defined as, and automatically transformed into, CORBA servers invoked by any CORBA client. The performance penalties introduced by the CORBA infrastructure, with respect to pure ASSIST programs, are quite acceptable for many applications with reasonable granularity. Though referred to as an object-oriented approach, this experience proves that interoperability features can be merged into the ASSIST model, in order to design applications as composition of components, some of which are possibly parallel.

10.3   Uniform Approach to Distributed and Parallel Programming for Grid-aware Applications

Despite the current limitations in Grid application development, Grid applications have to be distributed in the real meaning of the word. With Feature 2 of the conceptual framework we further characterize this concept: we design a Grid application as a parallel program described by the parallel composition of parallel components (and possibly existing components). *No* distinction is made a priori between parallelism and distribution, i.e., between modules to be executed in the same (possibly parallel) Grid node or in distinct Grid nodes. In the same way, we do not restrict the application to be a single (sequential or internally parallel) job or a DAG of jobs. In general, the structure of the application can be any graph whose nodes are (parallel) components and the arcs are the mechanisms for their composition and interaction. The programming model of ASSIST is based on this concept.

At this point, it is important to clarify that modeling a Grid application as a parallel program does not necessarily mean that we are considering a Grid merely as a parallel machine, though in some cases this is a meaningful and effective view. There may be applications in which we could not be interested in intercomponent parallelism or in optimizing such potential parallelism, possibly exploiting the parallelism at the intracomponent level and forcing distinct components to be allocated onto distinct Grid nodes.

However, there are strong reasons in support to a uniform view of distributed programming and parallel programming, notably:

1. Provided that the module granularity is determined properly, there are many applications that can greatly benefit from internode parallelism, while additional performance is gained at the

intranode level. We point out that, because of the heterogeneous and dynamic nature of Grid platforms, the a priori distinction between inter and intranode types of parallelism may be difficult or, by forcing it in some way, it may cause a sensible degradation in performance or fault tolerance. Instead, we believe that the distinction between inter and intranode parallelism must be delegated to the programming tools, both at compile- and at run-time: as said in Section 10.1; it is for this reason that the resource management, scheduling, and allocation functionalities must belong to the Programming Environment support (the GAM), and in particular to the support of the programming formalism.

2. As a consequence, an approach that does not limit the parallelism opportunities is characterized by much more flexibility and performance: notably, it must be possible to adapt applications, with little or no modifications, to changes and evolutions in the underlying platform, such as in node architecture and multiplicity, communication latency/bandwidth, processor power, operating system facilities, and so on. This aspect is consistent with the trends in component technology, e.g., application versioning according to different requirements of users and/or availability of system resources.

10.4   Dynamically Adaptive Applications

The considerations of the previous points 1 and 2 are generalized to the possibility of developing dynamically adaptive applications, i.e., applications whose resource allocation varies at run-time to guarantee a desired level of performance. Rescheduling and reallocation of resources should occur because of node unavailability or node unbalancing, or because an increase in performance is required in response to an emergency (e.g., in an Earth Observation application for landslip detection, the response to some events may require a very large increase in computing power that can be rendered available by a large collection of Grid-connected machines).

Currently, despite some interesting ongoing projects [8, 11, 12, 19, 20, 24, 31, 33, 40, 42, 44, 46] try to find innovative solutions, when this problem is addressed only partial solutions are mentioned: notably, dynamic code/data movement.

In general, the problem does not consist merely in finding a better allocation of the same code and data, instead we need to take into account other more complex actions that imply a transformation of the executable version of the program, such as a different degree of parallelism, different data distribution and partitioning, and also alternative versions of the program implementing the same functionality, i.e., a different implementation of the same component or composition of components.

A rigorous approach to the adaptivity problem can be based upon the following points:

- several modalities of expressing the structuring and restructuring of a computation must be available in the programming formalism,
- these modalities must be characterized by a cost model (performance model) that can drive the structuring and restructuring phases with reasonable complexity and overhead.

These modalities can correspond to the usage of different (combinations of) parallelism forms, or parallelism paradigms, as it normally happens in structured parallel programming models based upon the skeletons concept [4, 7, 14, 22, 43]. In such models a consistent set of parallelism forms is provided to the programmer to structure/restructure the application at hand, e.g., pipelines, farms or divide&conquer (D&C) are typical task–parallel (stream–parallel) paradigms, while map, reduce, prefix, scan, and stencil are typical data–parallel paradigms. In structured parallel programming, a coordination language is adopted that acts as a metalanguage used to compose codes expressed in any standard language (C, C++, Java, and FORTRAN). These codes may be already existing, e.g., they may be existing programs, libraries, or components themselves.

Skeletons are associated both with a semantic model and a cost model that make this approach very promising also for Grid programming; because of the existence of the cost model, the static and dynamic implementation of each skeleton is parametric with respect to few parameters. For example, the actual degree of parallelism or the actual number of data partitions can be varied dynamically without affecting the code of the run-time support.

An ASSIST is based on the structured parallel programming approach [43]. Beyond the "classical" skeletons, the ASSIST programming model contains several features (graphs, parallel modules, external objects) that sensibly increase flexibility and expressive power, including the possibility to design adaptive program structures (see the previous consideration about the need for alternative versions of the same computation). The ASSIST features will be presented in Section 10.6.

In other words, we have seen that parallelism (and structured parallelism in particular) is not only useful per se (i.e., to exploit higher performance of a certain code, possibly allocated onto the same Grid node), but also it has an utilization which is much more consistent with the dynamically adaptive nature of Grid-aware applications: in fact, in our model structured parallel programming is a way to specify the strategy for structuring and for restructuring a component or a composition of components. Components are internally expressed in ASSIST, with the addition of proper scripting annotations for specifying the "performance contract" of the component (e.g., performance metrics, critical events, and so on). Notice that, in general, processes of the same component could be rescheduled onto different Grid nodes. These issues will be discussed in Section 10.6.

10.5   Interrelationships of Programming Model Features

As shown in Fig. 10.2, Features 1, 2, and 3, which we advocate for the definition of a Grid programming model, are strongly interrelated. Feature 1, that implies interoperability, is fundamental for being able to structure complex application that include existing and/or predefined software components, and their "glue" is made possible and easy by the structured parallel programming approach. This feature is also fundamental to allow "legacy code" usage in Grid programs.

Feature 3 requires that components of an application can be rescheduled and restructured dynamically: in turn, this requires Feature 2 (uniform approach to distributed and parallel programming) because processes of the same parallel component could be restructured and reallocated onto different and distinct nodes, even in the case that at launch time this component has been allocated onto the same node in a sequential or differently parallelized fashion. The parametric feature of structured parallel programming makes the realization of a performance model for the dynamic restructuring of applications feasible.

To sum up, a Grid-aware application can be designed as a parallel program, properly "wrapped" into a component structure (together with some possibly preexisting components), without distinguishing between inter or intranode parallelism at the implementation level. Provided that an initial allocation of the components is done at launch time, the allocation of parts of the same components can be modified at run-time (both in identities of nodes and in amount of nodes) to deal with the dynamic adaptation strategies expressed in the same parallel formalism. Finally, we observe that dealing with the complexity of the Grid programming model has beneficial effects on the same parallel programming principles per se. In fact, the possibility to express dynamically adaptive computations also contributes to the solution of irregular and dynamic problems in parallel programming, i.e., computations that cannot efficiently be expressed according to predefined paradigms and/or that need substantial modifications according to some data values known at run-time (e.g. parallel Barnes–Hut algorithm), including some interactive applications. An ASSIST aims to be a solution to these problems too, since it goes beyond the typical limitations of "classical" skeletons in dealing with irregularity, dynamicity, and interactivity.

10.6   The ASSIST Programming Model

Structured parallel programming, based on the skeletons model, is an approach to deal with the complexity in the design of high-performance applications. The validity of this approach has been proved, in the last few years, for homogeneous parallel machines (MPP, Clusters, and Clusters of SMP). As discussed in the previous section, the basic features of structured parallel programming are much more valid for complex heterogeneous, dynamic platforms, like Grids.

The validity of the skeletons model can be summarized by the following elements:

1. parallel programs are written, by means of a coordination language, as compositions of predefined parallel paradigms, called skeletons. In the past experiences of our group (parallel languages P^3L and SkIE [7], Lithium [4]), they are the stream parallel skeletons pipeline, farm (also known as master-worker or parameter sweeping) and data–flow loop, and the data–parallel skeletons map (independent virtual processors), reduce and comp (sequential composition of map–reduce combinations). In other skeletal language, similar constructs are adopted. The "host" languages, i.e., the languages with which the sequential parts are written, are all the standard ones (C, C++, Java, Fortran) with their compilers;
2. owing to its clear semantics, for each skeleton it is known that a set of implementation templates and a cost model, both parametric, that can be used to optimize the compilation and the run-time support taking into account the composition characteristics. The optimization of the composition is largely dependent upon the knowledge of the possible compositions, and also on some equivalence properties of the composition themselves;
3. from points 1 and 2 it follows that, often, writing structured parallel programs is rather easy and fast, since the most complex decisions related with the parallel implementation are delegated to the compiling and run-time tools.

The intensive experiences with skeletal languages have shown that, in many parallel programs, the performance measures are satisfactory, and comparable with those of the same programs expressed in lower level formalism, such as MPI, or in other parallel languages when possible (HPF for data–parallel computations only). For example this result is achieved by the parallel program depicted graphically in Fig. 10.3, that expresses a parallel version of the Data Mining a priori algorithm [15] as a pipeline composition of six stages, two of which are farms and the other four are sequential modules (mainly performing file transfer).

The partitioned parallel a priori requires two scans of the input to compute the set of frequent sets. The two phases have the same skeleton representation. Sequential module Ph1 reads in the input and sends data partitions to the workers W. Module R1 is a sequential reduction (union of the result sets). The same schema is repeated with different sequential modules (Ph2, W, and R2)

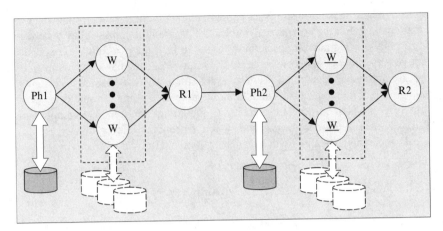

FIGURE 10.3. Skeleton structure of partitioned a priori algorithm.

to produce the result. The application scales well with database size; however, modules Ph1 and Ph2 are I/O bound, and the efficiency of the structure can be improved by forms of shared data access from within the workers.

Despite many advantages, the classical skeleton approach has several drawbacks in terms of expressive power and efficiency for complex applications, flexibility in adapting to a variety of combinations of parallel paradigms, as well as in terms of interoperability and suitability to component-based programming for Grid applications.

An ASSIST is an evolution of the classical skeleton model aiming to act as a research vehicle in this complex scenario. In the following, we summarize the main features of the ASSIST programming model (ASSIST–CL: ASSIST Coordination Language) through their relationship with significant problems to be solved. For an extensive presentation of the ASSIST–CL syntax, semantics and implementation, the reader is referred to [1–3, 43].

10.7   High-performance Programs as Graphs

In several applications, the computation structures that can be expressed by the classical skeletons are not adequate. Notably:

1. many applications can be conceived in terms of the composition of independently developed components, without a predefined structure;
2. the composition structure may follow a data–flow or, alternatively, a nondeterministic model (event driven computations) in which the components, in general, can have an internal state. Many Work Flow models and their extensions have these features;
3. components can interact by means of several communication patterns, notably streams (sequences of typed objects), events, or single invocations, possibly in a remote procedure call (RPC) fashion;
4. many parallel algorithms can be expressed in a D&C style. Though a D&C specific skeleton can be defined [4, 14], its performance may be low in general, because of the large variety of configurations and situations in which this paradigms occurs. The solution, adopted in SkIE, making use of parallel compositions (e.g., pipelines, farms, and map–reduce) inside

a data–flow loop, has a similar drawback because a general implementation of the data–flow loop cannot be optimized for all the situations. Many irregular and dynamic parallel algorithms have similar features.

In ASSIST, a parallel program can be structured as a generic graph, whose nodes correspond to parallel or sequential modules, and arcs correspond to communication channels over which streams of typed values are transmitted. Thus, in our case streams are the general composition mechanism for components. Other communication patterns (single invocation, RPC, and so on) can easily be expressed as particular cases of streams or implemented in a stream-based formalism. A computation, applied to the values of an input stream, terminates when the stream ends. Modules can have a state that is initialized at the beginning of the computation, and that is significant until the computation terminates. Each module can have any number of different input and output streams. In general, input streams are selected nondeterministically in a CSP-like fashion (i.e., by means of guards and priorities like in the Communicating Sequential Processes model). Alternatively, a node may have a data–flow behavior driven by all the input streams, or, in the most general case, a mixed nondeterministic and data–flow behavior.

The choice of graphs and streams in ASSIST is not only more general, but it also eliminates the performance penalties mentioned in point 4. In fact, streams are explicitly controlled by program, and it is much more feasible to achieve an efficient implementation of simple communication channels and guarded commands, with respect to the complex communication patterns which are needed by D&C and irregular/dynamic computations.

Figure 10.4 shows the structure of an ASSIST program for a parallel implementation of the Data Mining C4.5 algorithm according to a D&C solution. Conquer and Computing (the Divide functionality, i.e., the core of the computation) are ASSIST parmods (see Section 10.3.2); the streams convey (references to) training set and decision tree objects. The description will be detailed in Section 10.3.5. It can be shown [15] that this parallel program has a performance comparable to the solution written directly in MPI or other lower-level libraries. This proves the

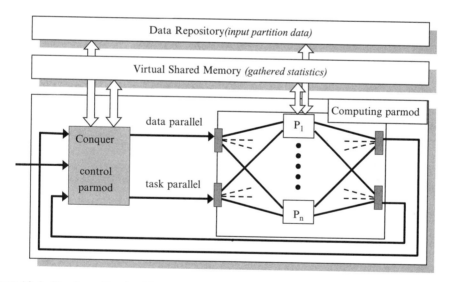

FIGURE 10.4. Structure of a classifier (sequential code based on C4.5) made up of two interconnected parmods exploiting external objects.

validity of the implementation of streams and parallel modules also in computations structured as complex cyclic graphs.

In the component version of ASSIST, single nodes of the program graph, or entire subgraphs, correspond to components, whose interfaces are expressed in terms of streams activating internal operations of the modules. For example, "provides" and "uses" ports, as well as events or other kind of interfacing mechanism [13, 17, 18, 30, 41, 45], can be mapped onto the ASSIST composition mechanisms. This issue is currently investigated and the precise definition of the ports–streams mapping will depend on the specific component model that will be adopted. However, structuring ASSIST programs in terms of graphs and streams (and in terms of external objects, see Section 10.3.3) is sufficient to capture the essential semantics of high-performance components, in a way that is largely independent of the specific component technology.

10.8   A Generic Skeleton: Parallel Module (parmod)

Every classical skeleton correspond to a specialized paradigm to express parallelism. Though in many algorithms they are exactly what the programmer needs, there are some applications which need much more flexible structures for expressive power and/or efficiency reasons. Notable examples are:

a. stream–parallel farms with an *ad hoc* task scheduling strategy (master), workers having some form of internal state or additional communications, or specific task ordering strategy;
b. data–parallel algorithms with various kind of stencils that can be statically recognized (fixed or variable stencils), or dynamic stencils;
c. specific data distribution strategies, ranging from on-demand scheduling to scatter, multicast, broadcast;
d. no limitation in the number of input/output streams, controlled according to a nondeterministic or data–flow style, or both;
e. existence of internal state, considered significant for the duration of the computation, which is usually prohibited by the classical completely functional semantics of data–flow skeletons,
f. proper combinations of stream– and data–parallel paradigms in the same module (e.g. in systolic computations),
g. modules that are able to behave according to different paradigms in different phases of run-time behavior, e.g., the Divide module in the C4.5 implementation of Fig. 10.4 may have a data–parallel behavior or a farm-like behavior in order to optimize load balancing during phases that, because of the multiplicity of data, have significantly different requirements.

All these situations can be emulated by means of specialized skeletons, but at the expense of code complexity and/or efficiency. For example, often the solution could consist in combining specific skeletons in parallel data-flow loop structures; however, besides the loop implementation, serious overhead sources are represented by the operations providing data transformation and redistribution necessary for the correct combination of skeletons (e.g., a pipeline combination of farm and data–parallel skeleton).

The ASSIST solution is a generic skeleton, which is a general-purpose construct that can be tailored, for each application instance, in order to deal with all the features needed to solve problems *a–g*). This construct, called parallel module or parmod, must possess the feature that, when it describes the computations equivalent to specialized skeletons, it does not incur in a perceptible overhead due to its generality.

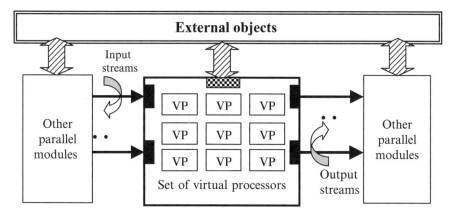

FIGURE 10.5. Elements of a parallel module (parmod).

A parallel module is defined as follows (see Fig. 10.5):

- a set of *virtual processors* with internal state. The set has declared a certain topology to provide names to virtual processors, when needed, e.g., an array topology or a "none" topology (meaning that there is no explicit topology: virtual processors are anonymous in this case);
- a set of typed input streams controlled in a data-flow and/or nondeterministic fashion. Once selected, the data of an input stream may be preprocessed, and are sent to the virtual processors according to the scatter, multicast, broadcast, or on-demand strategies. The chosen distribution strategy is expressed by program through a proper declaration;
- a set of output streams controlled independently by means of collective operations on the state value of the virtual processors. Postprocessing on the data to be sent to other modules can be performed collectively.

It is easy to see that all the known specialized stream– and data–parallel skeletons can be expressed directly in ASSIST. More important, no performance penalty is paid with respect to the equivalent specialized skeletons. Several kernels have been tested in ASSIST to verify the comparison of parmod performance with respect to the specialized skeletons. The result [1, 2] is that the parmod performance is comparable to, or better than, the performance of specialized skeletons or programs written in data–parallel languages. For example, the ASSIST program corresponding to the a priori computation of Fig. 10.3 is expressed by a graph, where the two farm nodes are expressed by parmods with *none* topology and on-demand distribution, while the other nodes are sequential modules (e.g., parmods with only one virtual processor, but with all the parmod features about the control of input/output streams). The speed-up of the ASSIST program [1, 2, 15] is equal or better than the corresponding SkIE program (using specialized skeletons) and comparable to the MPI version.

Analogous considerations apply to the evaluation of parmods implementing data–parallel skeletons. In these cases, the comparison is done with respect to data–parallel languages (HPF), for fixed and variable stencils. Finally, the cases in which ASSIST achieves higher performance are those computations where a sophisticated combination of various parallel paradigms is needed within a same module. Notable examples are the adaptive version of C4.5 and systolic algorithms. Other significant cases derive from the combined utilization of parmods and external objects (see next Section).

An important observation concerns the cost model. In the specialized skeletons approach, analytical cost models are derived for some skeletons, especially stream parallel or simple data parallel ones. What is the position of ASSIST from this point of view? First of all, the implementation of a parmod can be optimized in the same way that it happens for simple skeletons: the capability to optimize the run-time support is the true strength of structured parallel programming. From this point of view, ASSIST is not different from the approaches based on specific skeletons.

Moreover, especially in complex applications and Grid platforms, we have to consider the issue of cost model in a much more general way, that is according to the capability to express a cost of a parallel component or any combinations of parallel components in a context that is strongly variable and dynamic. Dynamically adaptive Grid applications must have associated a performance contract, specifying information to evaluate the application performance and, possibly, to drive the application restructuring (see Sections 10.2.3 and 10.6). In this context, we have to know a library of cost models for various structures, both elementary and composed; such library could be enriched according to the past history of the system or application field. For ASSIST, this library is known, at least in the same way that it was known with specific skeletons (e.g., in SkIE); we know the cost model of a parmod when it is equivalent to a farm or to a map/reduce, or similar simple skeletons. In addition, we know or can derive the cost models of a rich variety of data–parallel structures with fixed and variable stencils, as well as of some notable combinations of stream– and data–parallel (e.g., systolic), or with graphs with specific structures. All such information will be inserted in the annotation of the components of a Grid-aware application (Section 10.2.3), and exploited by the GAM at launch time and at run time. In conclusion, ASSIST has (at least) all the features of a structured parallel programming model from the point of view of the cost model and its utilization.

10.9 External Objects

Another feature to increase both flexibility and efficiency of ASSIST programs are the so-called external objects. A module (sequential or parallel) of an ASSIST program can refer to external objects according to the interfaces/methods or APIs of such objects. This is a mechanism to exploit (import) the functionalities of possibly existing objects defined outside the application.

External objects are also a mechanism to cooperate with other modules of the same application, in addition to the stream mechanism. While streams can be used only at the beginning and at the end of activation (i.e. a stream input variable does not change during the activation of a Virtual Processor), an external object can be referred to by a parmod in any phase (input, virtual processors processing, output).

In general, the goals of including in the programming model and of supporting external objects are the following:

1. to provide a powerful mechanism to import/export abstract objects in commercial standards,
2. to provide a standard modality to interact with system functionalities (servers),
3. to optimize scalability when the by-reference communication is more efficient than the by-value one;
4. to overcome the limitations of the single node resources (notably, memory capacity) in distributed architectures,
5. to make the management of dynamic and/or irregular program/data structures easier.

Three kinds of external objects are distinguished:

- Shared variables: a first kind of external object is defined just in terms of the same data types of ASSIST–CL. Any variable can be defined as shared by modules of an ASSIST application. This can be interpreted as an extension of the concept of internal state of modules: now the state can also be shared between distinct modules.
- Integration of Distributed Shared Memory libraries: in many problems, the goals 3-5 mentioned above can be met by means of external objects expressed by abstractions of shared memory. In particular, we integrated libraries for Distributed Shared Memory (DSM) and for abstract objects implemented on top of some DSM. While on shared variables we can only execute the operations corresponding to the ASSIST–CL types, on the shared memory objects the proper set of operations is defined for expressing powerful strategies of allocation, manipulation, and synchronization.
- Remote objects: they enable an ASSIST program to interact with external services through their specific interfaces (e.g., parallel file systems, databases, GUIs, other—possibly parallel—programs or libraries), using an object-oriented formalism, provided for example by a distributed object middleware like CORBA. The interoperability with CORBA has been introduced in Section 10.2.1 and will be described in Section 10.12.

The use of shared variables and shared objects is a further mechanism to increase the expressive power and efficiency of ASSIST programs. The preliminary experiences with the addition of shared objects to specialized skeletons [15] have proved the feasibility and effectiveness of this mechanism. A first example has been shown about the C4.5 algorithm (Fig. 10.4), where the heaviest data structures are shared by the virtual processors of the Divide parmod, while the streams convey references to such data structures.

Another significant example is shown in Fig. 10.6. It is an ASSIST version of the Barnes–Hut N–Body algorithm, using a proper combination of parmods and shared objects (vector of bodies and other control structures).

Owing to the utilization of shared objects, the modules are combined in a noncyclic structure, exploiting both nondeterminism and data-flow behavior. Streams convey just reference to the shared objects that are created and scheduled by the Emitter module and processed by the Farm module.

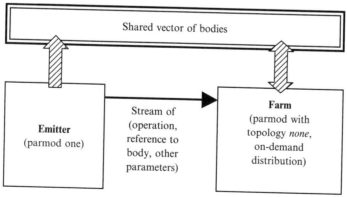

FIGURE 10.6. ASSIST version of Barnes–Hut algorithm using proper combinations of parmods and shared objects.

While the performance of this algorithm expressed by specialized skeletons is rather low, the performance of this ASSIST version is quite satisfactory: the efficiency lies between 70 and 80% with 8–16 processors for rather small data sets (100K, 1000K bodies). The achieved result is comparable with a dedicated MPI version computing the same data sets. Due to the usage of Shared Objects, which are built on top of a distributed virtual shared memory library, the ASSIST version of the program is able in principle to handle data sets not completely fitting in the memory of a single machine. However, the MPI version was not able to handle this feature and this is way the comparison has been made on these small data sets. In particular, the overhead introduced by the ASSIST support in communication, nondeterminism and sharing is negligible with respect to the corresponding primitive underlying mechanisms. This and other benchmarks prove that ASSIST is able to express efficiently many irregular and dynamic/adaptable computations, though by adopting a high-level structured approach to parallel programming.

10.10 Example of Complex Application in ASSIST: A User Modeler Server for Customer Relationship Management Platforms

System for Internet Banking Applications (SAIB) is a large research project which brings together some Italian academic institutions and industrial partners in the effort of producing an open-source based Customer Relationship Management (CRM) solution for financial applications. We describe part of the User Modeler Server (UMS), a parallel Knowledge Discovery in Databases (KDD) system designed to be integrated within the SAIB system. Among the requirements there are flexibility and programmability, as well as high-performance customer profiling functionalities.

Our KDD system provides to the marketing analysts the Data Mining (DM) services needed to build customer profiles from a customer database. Knowledge models can then be deployed to the CRM main core, where they can be used to customize user interaction at different levels. The UMS performs both batch operations (heavyweight Data Mining algorithms out of the main business flow) and on–line ones (per-user knowledge queries), which are subject to near–real-time constraints.

In developing a parallel KDD system we are faced with different issues:

- to deal with databases of several gigabytes in size;
- to develop efficient parallel mining algorithms, managing both sustained and irregular demands of I/O and computation, scalable with available computing resources to higher performance and throughput;
- to ensure a high internal degree of integration of the system, as well as simplicity and performance of the interaction between the parallel mining algorithms, data management, and KDD support modules for knowledge management and visualization
- to ensure system interoperability and ease of cooperation with different software technologies. Industry standard languages and technologies like XML, Java/EJB, and ODBC have to be exploited to integrate advanced parallel modules within larger applications.

In the architecture of the UMS, these goals were accomplished with a portable, high-level software design thanks to the programming approach of ASSIST, to the features of its coordination language and of its supporting environment. The architecture of the UMS, shown in Fig. 10.7, is made up of a few basic elements, namely: (1) Activity Scheduler, i.e., control and visualization

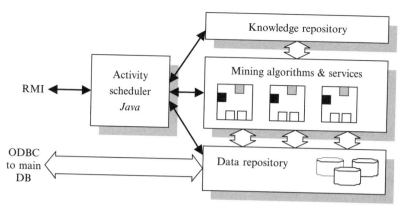

FIGURE 10.7. Overall architecture of the UMS module.

interface (UI, the User Interface), (2) a set of mining algorithms (MA), (3) data management module (DR, the Data Repository) and (4) knowledge and metadata management module (KR, the Knowledge Repository). The system is more thoroughly described in <articolo Europar>, we only summarize here the importance of exploiting ASSIST features.

The User interface in our case is a gateway to the rest of the SAIB system, with no visualization and low-level user interaction tasks. It cooperates with the rest of the UMS by means of Java native methods, file system I/O and calls to the ASSIST program loader.

The set of MAs contains ASSIST parallel programs, some of them described later on, which perform actual mining tasks, and simpler ones used to manage the DR data (e.g., selection and sorting). We reused parallel mining applications designed in our previous research [15], which were based on skeleton structures and data-flow stream cooperation, and we extended them with new functionalities. Taking advantage of the modular structure of ASSIST programs, we have evolved them so that they (1) interface to the DR module for most of the I/O, and (2) benefit from more sophisticated features like external objects, or control of nondeterminism.

The DR module is implemented as an external object of ASSIST, and it is built on top of the PVFS Parallel File System. It provides high performance I/O support for large files with a simple record structure of typed fields (the kind of regular data tables we have to host in a mining warehouse), and a mechanism of block-oriented views to allow large grain, parallel operation on the same file. This design exploits parallel file system performance and bandwidth from within portable ASSIST programs.

The KR module manages the knowledge extracted by the mining algorithms, represented using the standard PMML 2.0 language. A client-side linked library provides ASSIST programs with XML parsing and serialization on models, as well as interface to the KR server.

In composing the UMS modules we have exploited the features of interoperability of ASSIST, mixing Java, C and C++ code, stream and RMI cooperation. We describe some of the parallel modules performing the Data Mining functions. High performance and dynamic adaptiveness of these parallel applications rely on the parallel structure that is described at high level, supported by the ASSIST run-time.

Classification is performed with a decision tree induction algorithm, shown in Fig. 10.4. After a first, data parallel phase of the execution, we should switch to a task-parallel behavior and below a certain node size to sequential computation. We have evolved the structure reported in [15] following the idea outlined before and in [43]. The same parmod implements all the different functionalities related to the Divide part of the algorithm. Another parmod with "one" topology acts as a controller and performs the Conquer steps. Dynamic load balancing in the task-parallel case is granted by the on-demand distribution. Stream guards controlled by shared variables make it clear and manageable the transition among the different behaviors. Access to the data is supported by the external object paradigm, both in distributed shared memory (node statistics are kept there) and in the DR module (which provides the input data).

Association Rules are computed by an a priori-like algorithm. Its parallelization [15] is based on the partitioning method, which requires two phases of anonymous workers with load balancing. Its structure has been shown in Fig. 10.3, expressed with traditional skeletons: actually, the farm and sequential skeletons are replaced by corresponding parmods. On the other hand, by exploiting the DR External Object, the input dataset is accessible to all the processes, removing the file transfer bottleneck, with relatively minor changes to the code.

The Clustering application is built around the association rules module. Following [34], we group together records that satisfy the most popular association rule of a dataset. Rules are mined again and again on unclustered records until a given threshold is reached. The parallel implementation fully reuses the association rule ASSIST modules. The program graph becomes cyclic, a controller module is in charge of recycling data (also applying a rearranging strategy to enhance locality and reduce the amount of I/O), and nevertheless the change can be kept hidden to the contained modules.

10.11   ASSIST Implementation

10.11.1   Modular Design of ASSIST Compiler

The ASSIST environment has been designed both to produce fast object code and to be easily modifiable if needed. It has been designed and implemented exploiting well-known software engineering techniques that have enabled the easy extension of programming environment features along several ASSIST versions.

Overall, the ASSIST compiler (namely astcc) produces code for plain POSIX/TCP workstation networks/clusters. We briefly outline the ASSIST implementation structure. The whole ASSIST–CL compiling tools have a three–tier design:

- front-end (the top tier) parses ASSIST–CL syntax and produces an internal representation of the program;
- core (the middle tier) that is the compiler core. It translates the internal representation of a program into the "task code." The task code can be seen as a C++ template-based, high-level and parallel assembly language. The step transforming internal representation into task code is completely implemented exploiting design pattern technology [29]. A façade pattern decouples compiler internals from the compiler engine; a builder is being used to actually produce the task code;
- back-end (the bottom tier) compiles task code down to the ASSIST abstract machine (CLAM, the Coordination Language Abstract Machine) object code. The CLAM is built on top of POSIX processes/threads and communication (SysV and TCP/IP sockets) primitives. All those primitives are used via the Adaptive Communication Environment (ACE) library [39].

The whole compilation process is illustrated in Fig. 10.8. The result of compilation consists of two distinct items:

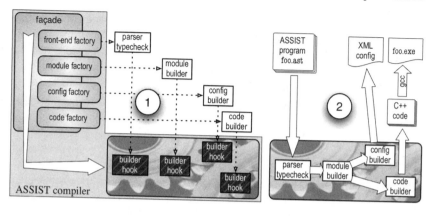

1) ASSIST builders are generated through proper factories and arranged in a workflow. Compiler features may be easily extended adding new builders (e.g., a F90 code builder producting Fortan code). 2) The ASSIST program is processed by all builders producing an XML configuration file and a number of source and object files. Eventually they are compiled through suitable standard compilers.

FIGURE 10.8. ASSIST compiler at work.

comp 1) a set of object code/DLLs including the code needed to execute all application modules and run-time support. Each code may be produced in different version, each of them targeting a different platform;

comp 2) a configuration file including module and run-time "coordination" information. Coordination information is represented in XML format; they include two main classes of information: static and dynamic. Static information includes parallel activities description, the description of (initial) modules graph, external libraries description, and their bindings to modules. Dynamic information includes machine names, parallel degree of parallel modules, and modules–machines mapping.

A CLAM master process scans the XML configuration file produced by astcc compiler and arranges things in such a way that the CLAM slave processes, running on the target architecture processing nodes, load and execute the suitable code (either coming from ASSIST–CL source code or belonging to external libraries properly named by the programmer in the ASSIST–CL source code). A detailed description of the ASSIST implementation can be found in [1, 3]. As CLAM (and the object code itself) access POSIX features via ACE wrappers, and as ACE is available on different operating systems (such as Linux, MacOSX, and Windows), CLAM actually behaves as the fourth tier of the compile/run process and guarantees a high degree of portability of the whole programming environment.

The compiler design allows efficient code to be generated, as each tier may take the most appropriate and efficient choices related to object code production. Furthermore, the heavy usage of well-known software engineering techniques, such as the design patterns, insulate all the individual parts of the compiler in such a way that modifications in one compiler part neither affect the whole compilation process (but for the new features introduced/modified) nor require changes in other compiler parts. Eventually, ASSIST–CL compiled code is run by means of a dedicated loader (the assistrun command), that in turn activates CLAM run-time support.

A first example of modifiability of the ASSIST support has been represented by the integration of mathematical MPI libraries belonging to the ScaLAPACK, FFTW and PAMIHR packages, directly in ASSIST, i.e., they are available to the programmer as ASSIST constructs [21]. The whole library code has then been wrapped in such a way that it looks like a normal parmod code to the programmer.

10.11.2 Supporting Heterogeneity

The first design of ASSIST was targeted to homogeneous clusters of Linux machines. The items needed to produce code for heterogeneous architectures were basically two: the inclusion of some kind of external data representation (XDR) wrapping messages flowing between heterogeneous processing elements, and the generation of proper makefiles to compile final object code. Both these problems have been solved exploiting the ASSIST–CL compiling tools structure. The astcc compiler uses a builder pattern both to generate the actual task code and to generate the makefiles needed to compile task code to object code. Thanks to this modularity, the only interventions needed to support Operating System and Hardware heterogeneity was to modify these builders in the following way:

- on the one side, communication routines are produced that either process memory communication buffers with XDR routines during marshaling and unmarshaling, or do not process them with XDR. The former routines will be used in case processing elements using different data representations (e.g., little/big endian machines) are involved in the communication. The latter routines instead will be used in those cases when homogeneous processing elements are involved in the communications. Proper makefiles are generated consequently;
- on the other side, the XML configuration file is arranged in such a way that XDR communication libraries are used when different architectures are involved and nonXDR routines are used in all the other cases.

Currently, heterogeneous clusters of Intel Linux and MacOSX platforms are supported. However, the technique we rely on is fully general: in order to add yet another architecture, it is sufficient to add the builder that produces code suitable for the new architecture. In the case this architecture includes a POSIX API, the proper builder may be produced with minor revisions of existing ones.

From the performance viewpoint, we experienced a fairly limited impact of marshaling routines on overall application code. Current benchmarks experience a slowdown of normalized performances, ranging from 1% (short messages) to 15% (long messages), for heterogeneous architectures with respect to homogenous ones.

10.11.3 ASSISTconf and the Grid

As seen, the ASSIST compiler divides data needed to run compiled applications in two main classes, denoted by *comp1* and *comp2* in Section 10.4.1. Exploiting this feature, ASSIST–CL programs can be run on a Grid performing the following three steps:

1. the XML configuration file (comp 2) is analyzed and the resources needed to execute the program are identified;

2. the resources needed to execute the program are gathered, and reserved, using the normal Grid middleware tools (e.g., those provided by the Globus toolkit);

3. the XML file is modified in such a way that the resources gathered are used to run the ASSIST code.

We developed the ASSISTconf tool [9], in collaboration with the group of ISTI–CNR to validate this approach. An ASSISTconf supports such kind of manipulation of the original XML configuration file. Currently, the tool supports decisions taken directly by the programmer via a GUI: starting from information gathered from the Grid, the tool proposes to the programmer a set of choices. Afterward, the tool produces a new XML configuration file describing the new mapping of program entities onto Grid resources.

An ASSISTconf represents an intermediate step toward full Grid support in ASSIST. In order to automatically and effectively targeting the Grid, many factors have to be taken into account, which are traditionally handled by expert programmers: resource coallocation, code and data staging, task scheduling, and the alike. We are experimenting with a first prototype of tool directly/automatically taking care of these steps currently in charge of the programmer in ASSISTconf.

The extension to the general automated solution is allowed by the global approach to the Grid programming environment stressed in this document, and by the design methodology of the ASSIST definition and implementation modularity. The structure of the existing ASSIST programming environment is exploited as follows:

1. resource coallocation is decided on the basis of the contents of the XML configuration file produced by the ASSIST–CL compiling tools. In particular, the compiler already devises the number and the kind of resources needed to execute the code, mostly exploiting user provided parameters. A CLAM version targeting the Grid can easily process the XML configuration file in such a way that the proper resources are selected;

2. code and data staging are also managed by the CLAM setup process. Also on clusters, the first phase in the execution of an ASSIST–CL program consists in deploying the proper object/library code to the interested processing nodes;

3. task scheduling is completely under the control of CLAM and follows the directives taken from the XML configuration file.

The first results achieved in the development of the fully automated ASSISTconf are encouraging, in that they confirm that the structure of the ASSIST programming environment can be exploited to effectively automate tasks that otherwise must be completely put in charge to the programmer. In particular, we are experimenting different strategies to coallocate tasks on Grid nodes. The different strategies can be easily implemented due to the completely modular and design pattern based implementation of the fully automated ASSISTconf module. We are assuming, at the moment, that Grid nodes can be reserved for the (possibly nonexclusive) execution of ASSIST tasks without any kind of intermediate scheduler. In turn, the ASSIST support is able to figure out how to properly dispatch ASSIST tasks to the discovered/reserved nodes in such a way that the features of these nodes are correctly taken into account and exploited. The fact that the resources can be busy (that is the consequence of considering them not managed by specific schedulers that guarantee mutually exclusive access) is handled by the part of the ASSIST support dealing with dynamicity, that is, the one described in Section 10.6.

10.12   ASSIST–CORBA Interoperability

An ASSIST provides various opportunities for interoperability, owing to its definition and implementation. For example, in Section 10.3.5 we saw the possibility of effectively mixing Java, C and C++ code, stream and RMI cooperation in complex parallel applications.

An ASSIST provides full interoperability with CORBA objects. In this way we have achieved a first concrete result that combines the benefits of software reuse and interoperability with those of high-level parallel programming. CORBA, a distributed object-based middleware, is a well-established commercial standard, and offers interoperability with several sequential languages. Recent studies recognized that CORBA technology could be leveraged to support the development of advanced Grid applications [37, 38]: the CORBA CoG kit [36], for example, provides CORBA applications with access to the Grid services provided by the Globus Toolkit.

The ASSIST can easily import (or use) other pieces of software encapsulated in external CORBA objects, as in a traditional sequential language (i.e., C++). Most important for the sake of this paper, ASSIST can export parallel algorithms and applications as well. For example, a computation intensive component of a large application can be conveniently expressed in ASSIST to exploit parallelism and achieve good performance; it can be automatically encapsulated in a CORBA object, so that it can interact (e.g., be invoked) with the rest of the application (coded in any language supported by CORBA) by means of standard CORBA invocation mechanisms. This enables the construction of complex, scalable applications in an easy way.

We devised two possible ways of interconnecting an ASSIST subprogram to a distributed application, to address two different classes of problems:

a) RMI-like synchronous invocation of a subprogram (with arguments and return values), when the task that should be carried in parallel is well defined and insulated;
b) stream-like asynchronous data passing (realized using the standard CORBA event channel mechanism), when the production of data can be overlapped with the elaboration, or when we want to deal with partial data or results (for example when rendering images or videos).

An ASSIST subprogram, in order to be exported to the CORBA world, must be a composition of ASSIST modules (at the extreme, it can be a single module) in which one input stream and one output stream are left unconnected and are elected to be the input and output of the entire component. In the RMI-like case, a further constraint to be satisfied (that cannot be statically checked) is that, for every datum received from the input source, the program must produce one and only one datum on the output stream.

The process of exporting an ASSIST program in the CORBA world has been automated: the ASSIST program undergoes an initial phase in which it is analyzed to verify that the conditions stated earlier are met. It is transformed ("wrapped"), according to the option RMI-synchronous (a) versus stream-asynchronous (b) interaction chosen by the programmer, adding support code to interact with the CORBA runtime and services:

case a) The program is exported as a CORBA object with a single method: a module that acts as a bridge towards CORBA is attached to the program input and output stream; it implements the method invocation by delivering every request to the program input stream and then waiting for a response from the output stream, that will be returned to the caller;

case b) The program interacts through CORBA event channels: two modules are added, one that intercepts ingoing events and sends them to the input stream of the program, and the other that receives messages from the output stream and forwards them as outgoing events.

As a final step, suitable CORBA IDL interfaces are generated. This process is simplified by the fact that, in the module interfaces, ASSIST recognizes the standard CORBA types, which are mapped to native types following the standard CORBA type mapping. The generated interfaces, then, can be processed by CORBA compliant IDL compilers, to produce suitable stub code to invoke the ASSIST CORBA object (RMI-like case), or to publish or subscribe the events that are recognized as inputs or produced as outputs by the ASSIST component (stream-like case).

Two basic experiments demonstrate that the methodology is a viable solution to parallel software integration:

i) we have compared the service time of a data–parallel algorithm expressed in ASSIST and exported as a CORBA object (invoked from an external C++ application) to an equivalent solution expressed in the ASSIST–CL language. The ASSIST program is a synthetic data–parallel algorithm, operating on large matrices (the argument and result are 700 x 700 floats) in order to estimate the overhead introduced by CORBA communication mechanisms. The algorithm performs a $O(n^3)$ computation involving transcendental function evaluation;

ii) to evaluate the event-based asynchronous interaction, we have compared a stream–parallel algorithm expressed in ASSIST and exported via CORBA with an ASSIST implementation that uses only ASSIST native streams. The ASSIST program is a classical Mandelbrot set computation as a task farm, in which each task is a set of contiguous points that must be evaluated.

In both cases, the overhead introduced by the program transformation is comparable in absolute value to the one in the sequential case; this means that the implementation does not introduce inefficiencies. Moreover, the overhead affects the service time for a small percentage, allowing a good speed-up up to 16 processors (<5% degradation).

The whole experience gained with this CORBA interoperability experiment demonstrates that the overall design of ASSIST helps supporting interoperability with completely diverse, independent programming frameworks. In addition to this, the whole CORBA experience has been exploited when components have been taken into account and we implemented the support for the CORBA Component Model interoperability, i.e., when we start considering existing, assessed component models and we made experiments to evaluate their efficiency when used to implement the component-based, Grid-aware version of ASSIST.

10.13   Dynamically Adaptive Applications

Let us now come back to the discussion of Sections 10.2.3 and 10.2.4 about the possibility of using ASSIST not only for parallelizing single components, but also, more in general, for expressing the global dynamic adaptation strategies in Grid-aware applications.

The research project *Grid.it* will develop, on top of available standard services (GT), a GAM (see Section 10.1) based on an Application Manager (AM) for parallel and distributed applications according to the Grid-awareness principles. An AM that logically is a centralized entity whose implementation may be decentralized, will exploit the functionalities made available by

- Performance Model
- Monitoring
- Resource Discovery
- Scheduling strategies, both local to single nodes and global to Grid
- Allocation strategies of codes and data.

The current implementation of ASSIST for heterogeneous networks and Grids, described in Section 10.4, will be extended in order to support the dynamic allocation of ASSIST programs [22, 23]: this affects the run-time support of parmod and of shared objects, so that parts of the same parallel components can be reallocated dynamically to different nodes according to the decisions of AM.

As discussed in Section 10.2, subgraphs of ASSIST programs will be wrapped into standard components and, in general, made interoperable with other non-ASSIST components in order to build Grid applications. Moreover, each component will provide a scripting annotation about the "performance contract" to be established with the GAM.

The following example could serve to clarify the ASSIST-based approach to the design of dynamically adaptive applications (a more detailed discussion of the features of ASSIST dealing with dynamicity can be found in [47]. The example here is just to outline how dynamic reconfiguration of ASSIST applications can be achieved exploiting the knowledge derived from the application structured source code). The application consists of the component composition shown in Fig. 10.9.

a) Component C1 is an interface towards a Grid memory hierarchy, that virtualizes and transforms data sets available on the Grid into two streams of objects: the one (whose elements have an elementary type) is sent to C2 and the other (whose elements have array type) is sent to C3. Component C1 may be an existing component available on the Grid, virtualized by an ASSIST program, e.g., by using external objects and/or the CORBA facility.

b) Component C2 encapsulates an ASSIST program. The "performance contract" of C2 specifies that

- *by default* C2 is a sequential module (parmod with topology one) executing a certain function F;
- when the Monitoring and Performance Model services generate the event that signals the need or opportunity to adjusting the current performance level (*on restructuring*), C2 is transformed into a farm computation (parmod with topology none and data distribution on-demand) whose workers execute the same function F. An AM of the GAM determines the actual number of workers and their allocation to Grid resources: these may belong to the same Grid node (cluster) or to different Grid nodes. This is consistent with our conceptual framework (Section 10.2, Fig. 10.2), according to which the high-level version of the application is expressed by the structured parallel formalism with annotations, and all the allocation strategies are delegated to the GAM.

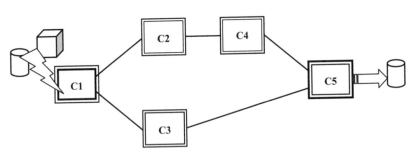

FIGURE 10.9. Example of an adaptive application expressed by parallel components.

c) Component C3 encapsulates an ASSIST data-parallel program operating on each stream element of array type (parmod with topology array, proper distribution for the specific data parallel algorithm, and possibly a stencil expressed in the virtual processors section). Similarly to the approach described for C2, the "performance contract" of C3 specifies that, *by default*, the ASSIST program has to be executed on a single Grid node with cluster internal architecture, while *on restructuring* it can modify (increase) the parallelism degree (amount of real processors onto which the virtual processors are mapped). The re-allocation may exploit resources belonging to one Grid node or to distinct Grid nodes.

d) Component C4 encapsulates an ASSIST program which, *by default*, is a sequential module, while *on restructuring* it is transformed into a parmod operating on the input stream according to a data–parallel or a farm style, depending on the values of the parmod state and on the input values themselves. In this case the adaptation principle is applied at two levels: at the program level and at the allocation level.

e) Component C5 encapsulates an ASSIST program operating nondeterministically on the input values received from C3 or C4, and transforming the two streams into a data set. The "performance contract" of C5 specifies that C5 can be allocated and executed only on a certain Grid node and that no reconfiguration can occur. This may be due to security, or privacy, reasons, or to requirements related to the specific resource kinds needed to operate on the data set.

Let us assume that at a certain time C2 is becoming a bottleneck that causes a substantial degradation of performance of the whole application. An AM provides to transform C2 into a version with the proper parallelism degree and to reschedule and reallocate this new version, assuming that, interacting with the Grid Resource Management services, the necessary resources can be found. In case of restructuring of data–parallel components, the AM strategy must be applied also to the redistribution of the data constituting the internal state of parmod.

10.14   Current and Future Work

We have shown how ASSIST can be used as a valid research framework in the definition and realization of innovative programming environments for high-performance Grid platforms. Our current research activity includes:

i) experiments on standard component frameworks, notably CCM and Web services. Several benchmarks will be tested in order to verify the performance features especially when components are used to wrap ASSIST programs;

ii) realization of the full ASSIST implementation on top of the Globus toolkit, as discussed in Section 10.4.3.

The result of these short-time experiments have been or will be exploited in the main tracks of our research:

a) dynamic ASSIST; i.e., definition and realization of ASSIST support to achieve the dynamic reallocation and restructuring of ASSIST programs on the Grid nodes. Recent experiences have proven the feasibility of this track [22, 23];

b) performance model for Grid-aware applications: performance models that, relying upon the cost model of ASSIST-structured parallel programs, evaluate the performance of the Grid application. For this purpose, basic Middleware mechanisms, such as monitoring, will be exploited;

c) Application Manager: definition and realization of this fundamental component of the GAM, according to the ASSIST-based approach introduced in this paper;

d) the results of activities *a)*, *b)*, and *c)* will be exploited into the design, according to the principles stated in Section 1 and 2, of the first version of the *Grid.it* programming environment, whose beta release is available since July 2005 and the first stable release is expected to be released by the autumn of 2005.

References

[1] M. Aldinucci, S. Campa, P. Ciullo, M. Coppola, S. Magini, P. Pesciullesi, L. Potiti, R. Ravazzolo, M. Torquati, M. Vanneschi, and C. Zoccolo, *The Implementation of ASSIST, an Environment for Parallel and Distributed Programming*, in Proc. of Euro-Par2003: Parallel and Distributed Computing, *LNCS* n. 2790 (Springer, 2003)

[2] M. Aldinucci, S. Campa, P. Ciullo, M. Coppola, M. Danelutto, P. Pesciullesi, R. Ravazzolo, M. Torquati, M. Vanneschi, and C. Zoccolo. *ASSIST Demo: A High Level, High Performance, Portable, Structured Parallel Programming Environment at Work*, in Proc. of Euro-Par2003: Parallel and Distributed Computing, LNCS n. 2790 (Springer, 2003)

[3] M. Aldinucci, S. Campa, P. Ciullo, M. Coppola, M. Danelutto, P. Pesciullesi, R. Ravazzolo, M. Torquati, M. Vanneschi, and C. Zoccolo. *A Framework for Experimenting with Structured Parallel Programming Environment Design*, in Proc. of Intl. Conference ParCo2003: Parallel Computing, Dresden, Germany, September 2003

[4] M. Aldinucci, M. Danelutto, and P. Teti. An Advanced Environment Supporting Structured Parallel Programming in Java. *Future Generation Computer Systems* 19(5), 611–626, (2003)

[5] M. Aldinucci, S. Campa, M. Coppola, M. Danelutto, D. Laforenza, D. Puppin, L. Scarponi, M. Vanneschi, and C. Zoccolo, *Components for High-Performance Grid Programming in Grid.it*, Proceedings of the Workshop on Component Models and Systems for Grid Applications, St. Malo, France, 2004, satellite workshop of ICS'04 (in press).

[6] R. Armstrong, D. Gannon, A. Geist, K. Keahey, S. Kohn, L. McInnes, S. Parker, and B. Smolinski. *Toward a Common Component Architecture for High Performance Scientific computing*, Proc. 8th High Performance Distributed Computing (HPDC'99), 1999

[7] B. Bacci, M. Danelutto, S. Pelagatti, and M. Vanneschi. SkIE: A Heterogeneous Environment for HPC Applications, *Par. Computing* (25), 1827–1852 (1999)

[8] H E. Bal, Ibis: A Java-based Grid Programming Environment, in Proc. of Euro-Par2003 (invited talk), *LNCS* n. 2790 (2003).

[9] R. Baraglia, M. Danelutto, D. Laforenza, S. Orlando, P. Palmerini, P. Pesciullesi, R. Perego, and M. Vanneschi. *AssistConf: A Grid Configuration Tool for the ASSIST Parallel Programming Environment*, in Proc. of 11th Euromicro Conference on Parallel Distributed and Network based Processing (Euro-PDP'03), Genova, Italy, February 2003, pp. 193–200

[10] G. Beneken, U. Hammerschall, M. Broy, M.V. Cengarle, J. Jürjens, B. Rumpe, and M. Schoenmakers, *Componentware—State of the Art 2003*. Background paper for the Understanding Components Workshop, Venice, 7–9 October 2003

[11] F. Berman, R. Wolski, H. Casanova, et al., Adaptive Computing on the Grid using AppLeS. *IEEE Trans. on Parallel and Distributed Systems* 14 (5), (2003).

[12] E. Bruneton, T. Coupaye, and J.B. Stefani, *The Fractal Composition Framework*, the Object Web Consortium, Interface Specification, July 2002

[13] CCA Forum home page, http://www.cca-forum.org/

[14] M. Cole, *Algorithmic Skeletons: Structured Management of Parallel Computation* (MIT, Cambridge, MA, 1989).

[15] M. Coppola and M. Vanneschi, High Performance Data Mining with Skeleton-based Structured Programming, *Parallel Computing* 28, 793-813, (2002) special issue on Parallel Data Intensive Algorithms, Elsevier Science

[16] M. Coppola, P. Pesciullesi, R. Ravazzolo, and C. Zoccolo *A Parallel Knowledge Discovery System for Customer Profiling*, Proceedings of Euro-Par 2004, LNCS 3149 (2004)

[17] The CORBA & CCM home page, http://ditec.um.es/~dsevilla/ccm/

[18] F. Burbera et al., Unraveling the Web Services Web: An introduction to SOAP, WSDL, and UDDI. *IEEE Internet Computing* 6(2), 86–93 (2002)

[19] H. Dail, F. Berman, and H. Casanova. A Modular Scheduling Approach for Grid Application Development Environments, *Journal of Parallel and Distributed Computing* 63(5), (2003)

[20] H. Dail, O. Sievart, F. Berman, H. Casanova, A. Yarkahn, S. Vadhiyar, J. Dongarra, C. Liu, L. Yang, D. Angulo, and I. Foster. Scheduling in the Grid Application Development Software Project, in *Grid Resource Management* (Kluwer, 2003)

[21] P. D'Ambra, M. Danelutto, D. Di Serafino, and M. Lapegna. *Integrating MPI-based Numerical Software into an Advanced Parallel Computing Environment*, Euromicro Conference on Parallel, Distributed and Network-based Processing, Genova IEEE (2003)

[22] M. Danelutto, Efficient Support for Skeletons on Workstation Clusters, *Parallel Processing Letters* 11(1), 41–56 (2001)

[23] M. Danelutto, *Adaptive Task Farm Implementation Strategies*, Euromicro Conference on Parallel, Distributed and Network-based Processing, La Coruna (IEEE, 2004), pp. 416–423.

[24] B. Ensink, J. Stanley, and V. Adve. Program Control Language: A Programming Language for Adaptive Distributed Applications, *Journal of Parallel and Distributed Computing* (in press)

[25] I. Foster and C. Kesselman (eds.), *The Grid: Blueprint for a New Computing Infrastructure* (Morgan Kaufmann, San Francisco, CA, 1999.)

[26] I. Foster, C. Kesselman, and S. Tuecke. The Anatomy of the Grid: Enabling Scalable Virtual Organization, *The International Journal of High Performance Computing Applications* 15(3), 200–222, (2001).

[27] I. Foster, C. Kesselman, J. Nick, and S. Tuecke. *The Physiology of the Grid: An Open Grid Services Architecture for Distributed Systems Integration*, 2002 http://www.globus.org/research/papers/ogsa.pdf

[28] I. Foster et al., Grid Services for Distributed System Integration, *Computer* 35(6), 37-46 (2002)

[29] E. Gamma, R. Helm, R. Johnson, and J. Vissides. *Design Patterns: Elements of Reusable Object-oriented Software* (Addison Wesley, 1994).

[30] M. Govindaraju, S. Krishnan, A. Slominski K. Chiu, D. Gannon, and R. Bramley, *XCAT 2.0: A Component-based Programming Model for Grid Web Services*. Technical Report TR562, Department of Computer Science, Indiana University, 2002

[31] Grid.it Project, *Enabling Platforms for High-performance Computational Grid Oriented to Scalable Virtual Organizations*, MIUR, FIRB National Research Programme, November 2002

[32] K. Keahey and D. Gannon. *PARDIS. A Parallel Approach to CORBA*, 6th IEEE Int. Symp. on High Performance Distributed Computing, 1997, pp. 31-39

[33] K. Kennedy, M. Mazina, J. Mellor-Crummey, K. Cooper, L. Torczon, F. Berman, A. Chien, H. Dail, O. Sievert, D. Angulo, I. Foster, D. Gannon, L. Johnsson, C. Kesselman, R. Aydt, D. Reed, J. Dongarra, S. Vadhiyar, and R. Wolski, *Toward a framework for preparing and executing adaptive Grid programs*, in Proc. of NSF Next Generation Systems Program Workshop (IPDPS 2002), 2002

[34] W.A. Kosters, E. Marchiori, and A.A.J. Oerlemans, *Mining Clusters with Association rules*, in Advances in Intelligent Data Analysis, LNCS 1642 ed. by D. Hand, J. Kok, M. Berthold (1999), pp. 39–50

[35] Object Management Group, *The Common Object Request Broker: Architecture and Specification*, (2000) Minor revision 2.4.1, http://www.omg.org

[36] M. Parashar, G. Laszewski, S. Verma, J. Gawor, K. Keahey, N. Rehn. A CORBA Commodity Grid Kit, *Concurrency Practice and Experience*, special issue on GRID Computing Environments 14, 1057–1074 (2002)

[37] C. Prez, T. Priol, A. Ribes, *PaCO++: A Parallel Object Model for High Performance Distributed Systems*, in Distributed Object and Component-based Software Systems, Hawaii Int. Conf. On System Sciences, IEEE (2004)

[38] T. Priol, *Programming the Grid with Distributed Objects*, in Proc. of Workshop on Performance Analysis and Distributed Computing (PACD 2002), 2002

[39] D. C. Schmidt, The ADAPTIVE Communication Environment: *An Object-oriented Network Programming Toolkit for Developing Communication Software*, in Proc of Sun User Group conferences, San Jose, CA, USA, December, 1993 and San Francisco, CA, USA, June 1993

[40] J.M: Schopf, *Structural Prediction Models for High-performance Distributed Applications*, Cluster Computing Conference (1997)

[41] Sun M.sys, *JavaBeans home page*, http://java.sun.com/products/javabeans

[42] D. Thain, T. Tannenbaum and M. Livny, *Condor and the Grid*, Grid Computing: Making the Global Infrastructure a Reality, ed. by F. Berman and G. Fox, and T. Hey (2002)

[43] M. Vanneschi, *The Programming Model of ASSIST, an Environment for Parallel and Distributed Portable Applications*, Par. Computing 28(12),1709–1732 (2002)

[44] F. Vraalsen, R. Aydt, C. Mendes, and D. Reed. *Performance Contracts: Predicting and Monitoring Grid Application Behaviour*, TR, Comp. Sc. Dept, Univ. Illinois at Urbana-Champaign, 2001

[45] W3C. *Web Services home page*, http://www.w3.org/2002/ws/

[46] R. Wolski, N. Spring, and J. Hayes. *The Network Weather Service: A Distributed Resource Performance Forecasting Service for metacomputing*, Journal of Future Generation Computing Systems, 15 (5-6), (1999)

Chapter 11

A Visual Programming Environment for Developing Complex Grid Applications

11.1 Introduction

Grids are receiving even more attention by a significant number of scientific, industrial, and economical bodies, thanks to their capability to enable collaborations, even cross-organizational, based on large-scale resource sharing and performance orientation.

Presently, Grids researchers and professionals have been concerned with the development of a series of experiments and demonstrations aimed at showing basic Grid features and potentials. Large-scale Grids were deployed to solve computational or data intensive problems as well as to perform complex simulations. Presently, Grids are widely recognized as the next generation computing architecture, the natural evolution of the Web toward the delivery of computing power, information, and knowledge.

Now, Grid community's efforts are focused to make that technology robust, reliable, and available to those interested in adopting it. The recent involvement of companies like IBM, Sun, and Microsoft is a clear symptom of the relevance the matter is going to assume in the near future. Belonging to this trend, providing high-level environments and advanced instruments able to support end users and developers, is of main importance to explore many of the Grid-related benefits not yet fully exploited.

In the Grid era, people have not to worry about the acquisition of powerful computers or expensive instruments, but rather the key aspect is the capability of effectively exploit shared resources through high-level environments providing the needed abstractions and facilities. Indeed, today this scenario is still not realistic due to research and technological challenges that must be faced, but it should lead scientists and professionals to provide more abstract techniques and tools for supporting Grid computing.

Most problems addressed by Grids are not simply solved through the execution of a specific ad hoc "program," but often require several software modules, most likely interacting each others, to run separately and/or concurrently over a given set of inputs. During a certain period of time Grid Portals have been the most advanced instrument for the solution of this kind of problems. But they represent still a limited programming approach and are often tailored to specific application domains.

Till today not much work has been done to build high-level design facilities for complex Grid applications in which many programs and data sets are involved. This class of applications are quite common in several domains, such as knowledge management, computational science, and e-business; in addition, they share common traits with software component-based applications.

Software component technology is now a standard part of many software design practices. Microsoft COM and much of .NET [1] are based on component concepts, as well as Enterprise Java Beans [2], that is another important technology for building large scale e-commerce applications. A software component model is a system for assembling applications from smaller units called components. The system defines a set of rules that specify the precise execution environment provided to each component, the rules of behavior, and special design features components may have. A component is then nothing more than an object (or collection of objects) that obey the rules of the component architecture. A component framework is the software environment that provides the mechanisms to instantiate components, compose and use them to build applications. The software component model can be effectively used in Grid applications integrating legacy code and new software modules.

In this chapter we present a high-level Grid programming environment that shares some common features with the software component paradigm. The system we discuss here is VEGA - *Visual Environment for Grid Applications*. A VEGA provides a unified environment comprising services and functionalities ranging from information and discovery services to visual design and execution facilities. The VEGA was designed and implemented to support users in the design of data-intensive Grid applications as part of the Knowledge Grid [6], a software infrastructure for developing knowledge discovery applications. However its high-level features make it useful in the development of a large class of Grid applications.

The remainder of the chapter is organized as follows. Section 11.2 presents the design aspects and the main features of VEGA; Section 11.3 introduces the visual language used to design an application in VEGA; Section 11.4 illustrates the architecture of the environment; and Section 11.5 goes more deeply into some implementation aspects. Several enhancements and additional features under development are presented in Section 11.6, where "open issues" are discussed. Section 11.7 presents two case studies and Section 11.8 discusses some of the major related projects. Finally, Section 11.9 concludes the chapter.

11.2   Main Features and Requirements

The main goal of VEGA is to offer a set of visual functionalities that give the users the possibility to design complex software, such as complex solving environments and knowledge discovery applications, starting from a view of the present Grid status (i.e., available nodes and resources), and composing the different steps inside a structured environment, without having to write submission scripts or resource description files.

The high-level features offered by VEGA are intended to provide the user with easy access to Grid facilities with a high level of abstraction, in order to leave her/him free to concentrate on the application design process. To fulfill this aim, VEGA builds a visual environment based on the component framework concept by using and enhancing basic services offered by the Knowledge Grid and the underlying Grid middleware.

To date, a Grid user willing to perform a Grid application must know and handle a number of detailed information about involved resources (computing nodes, software, data, etc.), such as their names and locations, software invocation parameters, and other details. Thus, in the absence of high-level tools the planning and submission of an application could result in a long and annoying work, exposed even to failures due to user mistakes in writing allocation scripts with a given syntax, wrong memory about resources details, etc.

As a first feature, VEGA overcomes these difficulties by interacting with the *Knowledge Directory Service* (KDS) of the Knowledge Grid to know available nodes in a Grid and retrieve additional information (metadata) about their published resources. Published resources are those made available for utilization by a Grid node owner by means of the insertion of specific entries in the *Grid Information Service*. Therefore, when a Grid user starts to design its application, she/he needs first of all to obtain from KDS *metadata* about available nodes and resources. After this step, she/he can select and use all found resources during the application design process (as described in the following). This first feature aims at making available useful information about Grid resources, showing the user their basic characteristics and permitting her/him to design an application.

The application design facility allows the user to build typical Grid applications in an easy, guided, and controlled style, having always a global view of the Grid status and the overall building application. A VEGA offers the users a way to look at Grid resources as a collection of typed resources and a set of defined "relationships" between them. This can be identified as the core functionality of VEGA. To support structured applications, composed of multiple sequential stages, VEGA makes available the *workspace* concept, and the *virtual resource* abstraction. Thanks to these entities it is possible to compose applications working on data processed in previous phases even if the execution has not been performed yet (useful in many knowledge discovery applications).

Once the application design has been completed, resulting job requests are to be submitted to the proper Grid Resource Allocation Manager (GRAM). A VEGA includes in its environment the execution service, which gives the designers the possibility to execute an application and to view its output.

Another important feature is the monitoring of the jobs execution, needed to allow the user to get information about the different jobs running on different machines as originated by the application execution.

A Grid-based application is often more complex with respect to a similar one based on classical computing systems. Issues like distribution of software, data, and computers themselves have to be addressed. The availability of computing nodes able to host a given computation is related to strict constraints about performance and platform requirements, as well as specific policies about access to resources, as defined by the related *virtual organization* [4].

In addition, a Grid application seeks out to take advantage of all benefits coming from the distributed and potentially parallel environment. For that reason some other problems may arise. In complex applications, large simulations and especially knowledge discovery applications, collaborations and interchanges between several concurrent or sequential stages of the overall computation are very common and able to boost up their capabilities and performance.

To conclude about the design properties and choices that guided us in the design of VEGA, here we list a set of properties that we identified to draw up the general requirements for a high-level Grid programming environment:

- the environment has to provide a set of useful abstractions about Grid resources and basic and enhanced actions supported by them;
- an abstract model for defining relationships among Grid resources and constructs for composing an applications must be provided;
- an advanced use of information about resources availability and status is fundamental to allow for a dynamic adaptation of applications to the changing conditions of the Grid;

- the system architecture must be as much as possible independent from low-level mechanisms used to gather information about resources, allocate jobs, etc.; but at the same time,
- more specialized and high level services must be compatible with low-level basic Grid services, so as to facilitate the implementation and take advantage of the underlying middleware;
- when the planning of an application implies choices that may affect its performance, the system needs to implement the right combination between a user-driven and a system-driven policy in taking decisions.

11.3   A Visual Language to Specify Applications

A structured way to model and express the variety of constraints and implications of complex Grid applications is needed. We believe that a way to address discontinuities (in systems characteristics as well as domain policies) and problems related to the scattered nature of resources is to look at a Grid application as a collection of resources and a set of well-defined relationships among them.

A VEGA, rather than devise a set of customized syntactical rules, makes available a *visual language* to express "relationships" among "resources," and to describe with a graphical representation the overall computation.

A VEGA provides developers with a set of graphical objects representing different kinds of resources they can select and use to compose an application. In particular, there are three types of graphical objects:

- *hosts*,
- *software*, and
- *data*.

Each of these objects represents a physical resource in the Grid. The user can insert several instances of the same resource into a *workspace* of the current project if needed. A *workspace* is thus a working area of the VEGA environment, in which objects representing resources are hosted to form a particular stage of the application. When a resource is inserted in a workspace, a label containing the name of the related physical resource is added to the corresponding graphical object.

Several relationships, indicating interactions between resources, can be defined. Relationships are represented in VEGA as graphical links between the resources which they refer to. Through relationships it is possible to specify one or more desired actions on resources included in a workspace. In other words, it is possible to describe one or more jobs (see Fig. 11.1).

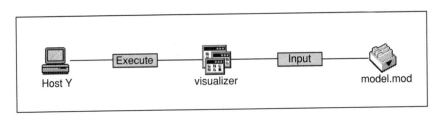

FIGURE 11.1. Objects and links in VEGA.

A common definition of "Grid job" states that it is *the execution of a given software on a specific Grid node*, with its input and output parameters/files specified as well. Relationships available to describe jobs are:

- *execution* of a given software on a given host,
- *file transfer*, of a certain software or dataset on a specified host
- *input*, (a given dataset as input for a software) and
- *output* (a given file as collector of a software output).

The file transfer relationship is a special kind of job, since it can be viewed as the execution of a file transfer program which parameters are the file to be moved, the destination host, etc. Thus, in VEGA *a job is a software execution or a file transfer*.

While introducing relationships between resources, some rules must be followed, in order to make the composition have sense. For instance, an execution relationship (link) cannot be inserted between a data object and a host object. Moreover, no link can be inserted between objects of the same type.

The set of admissible links is listed in Table 11.1, with enclosed the meaning each one takes in the specific context. Objects refer to specific resources offered by Grid nodes included in the deploying project; they can be linked with resources owned by the same node as well as with resources of a different node. In the latter case a *staging* operation is implicitly defined. If, for instance, a software component *SW* owned by the host *H*1 is linked with an execute link with a host *H*2, then the executable associated to *SW* will be first transferred to *H*2, and will be deleted from there after the execution.

A computation is generally composed by a number of different sequential or parallel steps. In VEGA it is possible to distinguish sequential and parallel execution of jobs through the *workspace* concept. All jobs that can be executed concurrently are to be placed inside the same workspace, whereas different workspaces can be used to specify a priority relationship. It is worth noting that when different sets of jobs are placed into different workspaces often they share common data, on which they make different computations.

As an example, let us consider a typical execution of the data mining tool DM-tool on the specific Grid node Host_X, taking as input the pre-processed.dat file, and producing as result the file classes.dat. This job (say simple submission) is described in the VEGA *visual language* by linking the objects representing the resources as showed in Fig. 11.2-A. A multiple submission, that is the parallel execution of the same software component on more than a Grid node, is quite similar to a simple execution, the only exception is that the same software object is linked with more hosts (see Fig. 11.2-B). Similarly, different submissions, i.e., two different, software to be executed on different hosts, may share the same dataset, like in Fig. 11.2-C.

The design of an application is obtained through the composition of a graphical model representing it. This is accomplished by using some graphical objects on which several actions (like

TABLE 11.1. Admissible links between resources.

Resource1	Resource2	Link	Meaning
Data	Software	Input	**indicates the software input**
Data	Software	Output	**indicates the software output**
Data	Host	File Transfer	**data transfer to the host**
Software	Host	File Transfer	**software transfer to the host**
Software	Host	Execute	**software execution on the host**

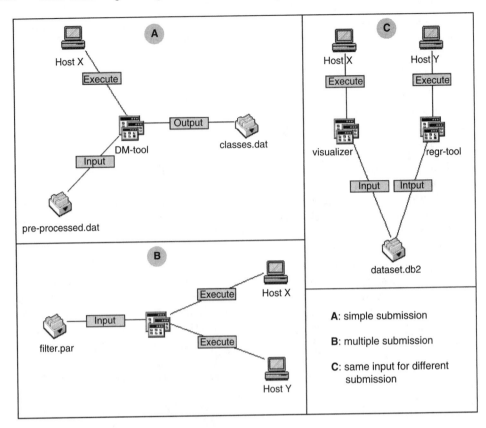

FIGURE 11.2. Some jobs in the VEGA visual language.

insertion in a workspace, linking with other objects, specification of attributes and properties, etc.) can be invoked, given that they assure consistency and logic sense to the computation. All this happens giving always freedom to the user in choosing how to build its application and the ordering of the actions applied to graphical objects.

A fundamental characteristic is the possibility to model the designing application through a visual language offering a set of abstractions as flexible as possible and able to describe a significant part of the typical Grid scenarios and applications. In this approach lies the novelty and the power of an environment like VEGA, because until now the community was lacking such a reference model and structured operational way on which to model a Grid application.

Moreover, it should be noted that although a set of predefined *links* are employed, there are several specific attributes and parameters that contribute to increase the expressiveness and the flexibility of the visual language.

11.4   Architecture

This section outlines how the VEGA environment works on top of the Knowledge Grid and the underlying Grid middleware, basic relationships, and interchanges among these entities are also explained.

The *Knowledge Grid* is a software infrastructure for distributed data mining and extraction of knowledge in Grid environments. The Knowledge Grid accomplishes its objectives through the implementation of a set of basic services and high-level tools designed to support geographically distributed high-performance knowledge discovery applications [6].

The set of services and functionalities offered by VEGA is composed basically by two categories: design facilities and execution handling. The first ones are concerned with functions for designing and planning a Grid application, whereas the others make possible to execute the application. Figure 11.3 shows hierarchies and some basic interactions between them and the Knowledge Grid and Grid services. In particular, the design facilities make use of the *knowledge directory service*, implemented by the Knowledge Grid, to discover resources and their properties, whereas basic Grid services are used during the authentication and the execution phases.

There are at least four steps a user must follow to execute one or more jobs employing Grid resources:

- *definition* of involved resources and specifications of the relationships among them;
  - *checking* of the planned actions consistency;
  - *generation of the job set* to be submitted to one or more Grid resource allocation managers;
  - *execution* of the jobs and *monitoring* of their life cycle.

The job submission procedure in VEGA can be divided in the previous four steps. Figure 11.4 shows the VEGA software modules implementing them together with the needed data exchanges.

The visual composition phase is useful to the user during the application design. It is accomplished by the Graphic Composer software module and its submodules. To design her/his application a user may compose graphical objects representing resources (datasets, software components, computing nodes). These objects are composed through visual facilities, aimed to specify existing relationships among them, to form a graphical representation of each job of the entire computation, accordingly with the rules discussed in the previous section.

Namely, this task is accomplished by the following submodules: Workspace *Manager*, *Object Manager*, and *Resource Manager*.

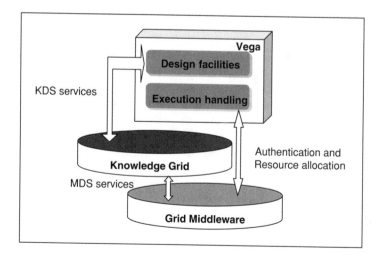

FIGURE 11.3. VEGA overall architecture.

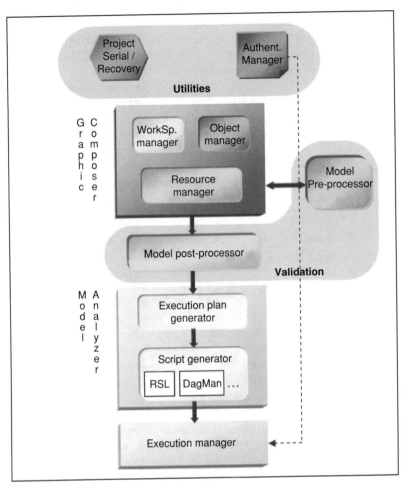

FIGURE 11.4. VEGA software modules.

The Resource Manager (RM) is concerned with the browsing of a local cache called *Task Metadata Repository* (TMR), where metadata about retrieved resources are stored, in order to allow the selection of resources to include in the designing computation. The Resource Manager is divided into two sections, directly showed to the user: the first one contains the list of the chosen computing nodes (hosts); the second one contains the resources belonging to the currently selected host, divided into two categories, data and software, on the basis of the content of associated metadata (see Fig. 11.5). Such a structure gives an overall view of the available hosts and related resources, permitting, at the same time, to include them inside a workspace of the current project.

Additional information about these resources are retrieved through the *Knowledge Directory Service*, a system able to include customized metadata into the *Grid Information Service*, and to delivery them to each user of the Grid when requested. Metadata used in the Knowledge Grid are constituted by XML-encoded information describing software and data resources. The analysis of the Knowledge Grid information system functioning is out the purposes of this chapter (details can be found in [6] and [7]). For what concerned with the operations of the RM, it is enough to know that XML documents specify some resources attributes among which: owner host, file name, and related path.

To import a resource in a workspace the user can drag and drop it. When the RM detects the *drag-started* event, it provides the OM with all the information found in the resource metadata document, so that the graphical object for that resource can be created.

The WM performs a preliminary analysis of the composing computation, to discover conditions that may originate virtual resources, like the presence of a file transfer operation, or the presence of an output resource generated by a job in the computation. When such a condition holds, the WM generates appropriate metadata and put them in the TMR, marking them as temporary entries (waiting for the real execution of the application). Metadata about virtual resources are homogeneous to ones about "real" resources and can be thus managed by the RM. Temporary entries, created during the design phase, will become permanent only when the execution is performed and it terminates successfully. Otherwise, if the user exits the working session without executing the application, they will be removed from the TMR. The user interface of the WM is basically constituted by a tabbed pane that allows for selecting the workspace on which to operate (see Fig. 11.5). The WM accomplishes also the task of building the *internal model* of the computation on the basis of the graphical composition made by the user and constituted by the workspaces sequence. The construction of the internal model takes place together with its graphical definition by the user.

The *OM* can be thought as a "service module," in fact it has not a specific corresponding element in the user interface and most part of the code implementing it is distributed in several *listeners*. Java implements the *events-driven programming paradigm*, in which listeners are classes notified of the occurrence of particular events (e.g., mouse and keyboard activities); these classes contain methods to handle such events.

The internal model consistency checking ensures that the model to be passed to the Model Analyzer is correct and without inconsistencies, that is, able to represent coherently a Grid application. The *Model preprocessor* operates during the application composition. Its main objective is to prevent the planning of jobs in a wrong or incomplete fashion. To this end, it supervises the links insertion, checking for the right association (see Table 11.1) between resource types and links.

When no type of link is admitted for a given couple of resources, each attempt to insert any link will fail. Whereas when one or more links are admitted, a generic link with a "no type" label is first traced, afterwards the user will specify the actual type by choosing among those available in a *popup menu*.

At the end of the design session, the user may have defined one or more workspaces. Although the workspaces composition has been guided by the Model pre-processor, there are some ambiguous situations that can be only recognized when the designing phase is over. Main constraints verified by the *Model postprocessor* are:

- at least one host must be present in each workspace;
- all inserted links must have a specified type;
- each software component must be linked with at least one host;
- every resource must be linked with at least another one.

As previously mentioned, the *execution plan* is coded in XML and represents the application at a high level of abstraction; it is generated to make aware the Knowledge Grid Execution Plan Management Service (EPMS) of the computation structure (the formalism is well described in [10]). To generate the execution plan, the EPG analyzes the internal model of the computation to individuate all the jobs planned by the user.

Execution and file transfer jobs are described in the *execution plan*, accordingly with a set of well-defined rules. In particular, they originate a set of Computation and DataTransfer elements, comprising attributes of the jobs and references to metadata of involved resources. To specify priority relationships among these jobs some `TaskLink` elements are used.

The *script* generation takes place on the basis of the execution plan and the information provided by metadata referred in it. All jobs in the execution plan are translated into requests expressed into the specific scripting language. For example, in the *RSL script generator* this is accomplished by assigning proper values to specific Globus RSL attributes. Details about Globus RSL tags can be found in [11]. Main attributes used by the VEGA *RSL script generator* are:

- `resourceManagerContact`, the node to which the request is to be submitted;
- `executable`, path and name of the program to run;
- `arguments`, a set of arguments to be passed to the program through the command line.
- `stdout`, the file to redirect standard output of the program to (if required by the user).

`Computation` elements in the execution plan are translated into job requests specifying the execution of a given executable with some inputs and outputs; as already mentioned, all details on executable inputs and outputs are retrieved in the referred XML files. `DataTransfer` elements are processed using as an executable the file transfer program provided by the Grid middleware, with source and destination parameters as indicated in the execution plan. If the middleware used is Globus all file transfer operations may be carried out using the GridFTP protocol [12] implemented by the file transfer program `globus-url-copy`. To reflect the workspace sequence in the jobs execution, job requests present in different workspaces are placed in separated script files and will be submitted to execution in strict sequence by the Execution Manager.

After the script files are generated, they will be executed through the proper submission command (i.e., `globusrun` in Globus). It is invoked by the VEGA Execution Manager taking into consideration each script file and allocating a new process for it on the machine which the user is working on. In addition, to provide the user with a feedback about the computation execution, standard output and error streams of that process are redirected to the EM and showed as well.

During this phase the Job Monitor gathers information about the activated jobs. The Job Monitor operates in strict relation with the middleware component in charge of the resource allocation, the GRAM. It periodically queries each node involved in the application about the status of the activated jobs, and update a set of information about the total execution time, the execution time of each job, its current status, the history of the statuses of each job, with enclosed the amount of time elapsed before a status change. This information is shown to the user in a table; moreover the user can clean up or kill each single job if needed, and eventually she/he can choose to save all this information into a report file.

11.6   Open Issues

In the current VEGA implementation workspaces can be connected in a pipelined fashion. This may represent a limitation of representing some computation patterns, even if complex patterns can be designed inside a single workspace. To make more flexible the way of composing workspaces, the sequential workspace composition is going to be replaced by an acyclic graph model.

In a varying and discontinuous environment such as a Grid, users' requests cannot be always deterministic in all details. It would be unacceptable, and flexibility loss leading, to pretend the user to specify all the details about the resources involved in a computation. Therefore, when the user does not worry about which will be the target machine for a given job, provided that it is able to satisfy a set of expressed requirements, it should be up to the system to find a suitable host and to assign it the job execution.

This could be also a powerful mechanism that can give the user the opportunity to design applications independent from the particular Grid on which they will be executed, hence, reusable upon different Grid systems and over time.

To this purpose the concept of *"abstract resources"* has been designed to be introduced in VEGA, This concept allows for specifying resources by means of constraints (i.e., required main memory, disk space, CPU speed, operating system version, etc.). In addition, a *metascheduler* will also be included to instantiate abstract resources. After the appropriate matching of abstract resources with physical ones and an optimization phase, the system can submit for execution all the jobs defined in the application design on the basis of the application structured layout.

A VEGA defines in a particular way "file transfer" jobs, permitting also to specify and configure a particular protocol to be used in the transferring, this because the file transfer has been historically a fundamental mechanism of communications between team of scientists and the most used one in Grid applications. The existence of specific services and features such as those provided by the so-called "Data Grids" confirms the particular importance of this matter.

Nevertheless, there are a lot of applications that need to operate on streams of data coming from a sensor or more generally from a network connection. Moreover, some other applications might achieve best performances, even if filebased, if it was possible for them to start their computations while the stream of data is reaching the Grid node to be stored on the file system (see Section 11.7.2 for an example).

11.7   Case Studies

This section presents two case studies through which the main features and potentials of VEGA will be better explored. At the same time a practical use of VEGA will be shown and some issues that may arise in this kind of applications will be analyzed. The first one consists of a Grid-enabled version of a knowledge discovery application, the second one is an example of a general purpose data intensive application.

11.7.1   Distributed Bank Scoring

This example takes into consideration the evaluation process done by banks when approving a loan. Loan officers must be able to identify potential credit risks and decide whether grant the money, and, in that case, the amount of the loan. Usually this is accomplished by evaluating information about people to whom the institution previously loaned money (such as debt level, income level, marital status, etc.).

Let us consider the case of three banks whose purpose is to join their efforts and extract a loan-scoring prediction model, based on the information each of them own about their clients. Since preserving client's privacy is a must for credit institutes, the treatment of this information by third parts is often prohibited or subject to restrictions. To overcome this problem the banks decide to make the computations locally, at each of the three sites, and to transfer on a centralized location only the obtained models.

In this way, no sensitive information has to be accessed by unauthorized organizations, but only the data models have to be shared. Privacy commitments are thus assured, because the data models are constituted by coded information about aggregated data.

When a decision is based on several factors, a decision tree can help to identify which factors to consider and how each factor has historically been associated with different outcomes of the decision. A decision tree creates a model as either a graphical tree or a set of text rules that can predict (classify) each applicant as a good or bad credit risk. The training process that creates the decision tree is usually called *induction*. One important characteristic of the tree splitting algorithm is that it is greedy. Greedy algorithms make decisions locally rather than globally. When deciding on a split at a particular node, a greedy algorithm does not look forward in the tree to see if another decision would produce a better overall result. This allows for creating partial models from subsets of the data that can be then joined into a global model.

Prior to integrating any decision tree into a business process as a predictor, a test and a validation of the model using an independent dataset is generally performed. Once accuracy has been measured on an independent dataset and is determined to be acceptable, the tree (or a set of production rules) is ready to be used as a predictor. The testing phase in this example is done after the combination of the three models.

To summarize, the entire application is composed of two main phases (see Fig. 11.6 for a graphical schema): the induction of the decision trees performed locally at each of the three banks, and the models combination and validation operated at one of the three sites after the others' models have been produced and moved there.

Let the Grid nodes made available by the banks be: k1.cs.icar.cnr.it, k2.cs. icar.cnr.it, and k3.cs.icar.cnr.it. The application design and submission will be performed on the Knowledge Grid node k1 that will be also the node on which the final model will be obtained from the partial ones. All nodes contain a dataset about the clients of the bank and a parameters file with a description of the structure of the dataset, this file is used by the inductor also to determine which the dependent variable is and which columns have to be considered as independent variables. The datasets are named respectively dataset1.data,

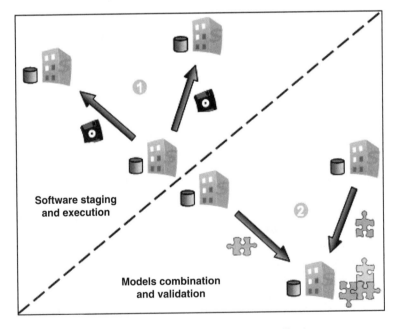

Software staging and execution

Models combination and validation

FIGURE 11.6. Distributed bank scoring application.

dataset2.data, and dataset3.data; while the associated parameters files are parameters1.par, parameters2.par, and parameters3.par. On k1 the software components DT-inductor and DT-combiner are also present.

The design of the application using VEGA produces four workspaces. First of all, it is necessary to transfer a copy of the software used for the induction to nodes k2 and k3 (where it is not available); this step is planned in workspace1 (see Fig. 11.7). Afterwards, the trees induction can take place at each of the three hosts by executing DT-inductor with the dataset and parameters file as inputs, see workspace 2 in Fig. 11.8. As a result of the computations in workspace 2, three files (tree1, tree2, tree3) containing the resulting partial trees will be obtained on each host. The subsequent stage performs the transferring of tree2 and tree3 to k1, so as to have all the trees on the same node (see Fig. 11.9). The combination of the partial trees into a global one will next happen on k1 by means of the DT-combiner tool, as can be seen in Fig. 11.10.

From workspaces 3 and 4, it is possible to note that as a direct consequence of the transfer of tree1 and tree2 to k1 in workspace 3, they are shown in workspace 4 as data resources of k1, even if the execution of the application has not been performed yet. This outcome is due to the intervention of the Workspace Manager that creates the needed virtual resources so as to allow for the use of this data in subsequent computations.

A VEGA generates four Globus RSL script files (bank_scoring0.rsl, bank_scoring1.rsl, bank_scoring2.rsl, bank_scoring3.rsl), one for each workspace, containing the formal description of the jobs to be executed. When requested by the user, the execution will be launched by the environment submitting the generated RSL files in sequence to the Globus GRAM.

Figures 11.11, 11.12, and 11.13 present the content of the Globus RSL files. From a quick look it is easy to understand the difference between the VEGA programming model and the low-level

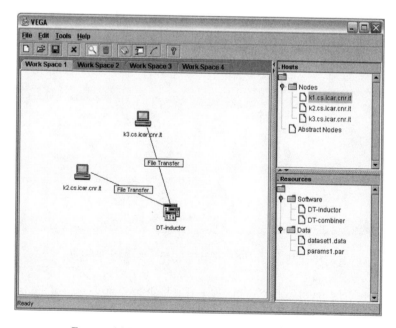

FIGURE 11.7. Distributed bank scoring: Workspace 1.

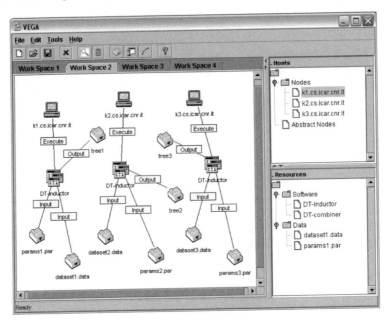

FIGURE 11.8. Distributed bank scoring: Workspace 2.

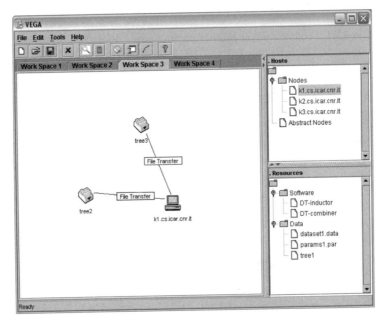

FIGURE 11.9. Distributed bank scoring: Workspace 3.

programming model offered by the Globus RSL. The high-level properties of the visual approach bring several benefits to developers both in terms of structured approach, easy programming, and code reuse.

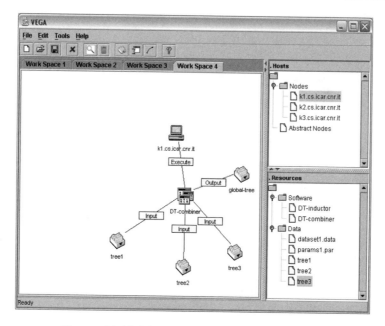

FIGURE 11.10. Distributed bank scoring: Workspace 3.

```
+
( &(resourceManagerContact=k2.cs.icar.cnr.it)
   (label=subjob1)
   (executable=$(GLOBUS_LOCATION)/bin/globus-url-copy)
   (arguments=-vb -notpt gsiftp://k1.cs.icar.cnr.it/tools/bin/DT-inductor
           gsiftp://k2.cs.icar.cnr.it/tools/bin/DT-inductor
   )
)
( &(resourceManagerContact=k3.cs.icar.cnr.it)
   (label=subjob2)
   (executable=$(GLOBUS_LOCATION)/bin/globus-url-copy)
   (arguments=-vb -notpt gsiftp://k1.cs.icar.cnr.it/tools/bin/DT-inductor
           gsiftp://k3.cs.icar.cnr.it/tools/bin/DT-inductor
   )
)
```

FIGURE 11.11. file bank_scoring0.rsl.

11.7.2   A Video Conversion Application

This example has been taken from a demo developed at IBM laboratories [17], and is aimed at showing main advantages coming from the use of a visual environment such as VEGA in respect of the classical approach, as well as the ability of VEGA to deal with general purpose Grid applications.

The application starts from a home video tape and converts it to a Video-CD that can be played on DVD players supporting this format. Depending on the quality level, a typical one hour tape can create over 10 GB of video data, which needs to be compressed to approximately 650 MB

```
+
( &(resourceManagerContact=k1.cs.icar.cnr.it)
    (label=subjob1)
    (executable=/tools/bin/DT-inductor)
    (arguments=   -d /data/dataset1.data
                  -p /data/params1.par
                  -o /data/tree1
    )
)
( &(resourceManagerContact=k2.cs.icar.cnr.it)
    (label=subjob2)
    (executable=/tools/bin/DT-inductor)
    (arguments=   -d /data/dataset2.data
                  -p /data/params2.par
                  -o /data/tree2
    )
)
( &(resourceManagerContact=k3.cs.icar.cnr.it)
    (label=subjob3)
    (executable=/tools/bin/DT-inductor)
    (arguments=   -d /data/dataset3.data
                  -p /data/params3.par
                  -o /data/tree3
    )
)
```

FIGURE 11.12. file bank_scoring1.rsl.

to fit on a Video-CD. The compression stage is CPU intensive, since it creates an MPEG data stream by encoding the frames after a matching process performed on all parts of adjacent video frames containing similar subpictures. The audio is compressed as well.

The compression process can take even more than one day, depending on the quality level and the speed of the system being used. For commercial DVD quality, conversions are typically done by a service company that has developed higher quality conversion algorithms. Such conversions may take weeks. Hence, Grid technology is ideal for improving the process of video conversion.

Sending many gigabytes of data from one computer to another takes a considerable amount of time, even with a 100 MB Ethernet connection. Thus, for Grid applications processing large amounts of data, it is crucial to understand the network topology and to keep the data near the processing node that needs to use it.

Let us assume that all packages and libraries required for performing the acquisition, the compression, and the CD burning have been already installed and properly configured on related machines. Since, each phase of the application makes use of several calculations carried out by different software, to simplify the comprehension, instead of executing them directly, some shell scripts invoking these tools will be used (namely, videocapture.sh, videoconversion.sh and videocd.sh).

In this example the acquisition node is the grid node griso.deis.unical.it, whereas the nodes used to execute the compression of the split video files are minos.cs.icar.cnr.it, icarus.cs.icar.cnr.it and telesio.cs.icar.cnr.it.

After the capture phase, the video file is then split into a number of smaller files. These files are sent via Globus to Linux-based grid systems for compression. The compressed segments are then

```
+
( &(resourceManagerContact=k1.cs.icar.cnr.it)
    (label=subjob1)
    (executable=$(GLOBUS_LOCATION)/bin/globus-url-copy)
    (arguments=-vb -notpt gsiftp://k2.cs.icar.cnr.it/home/data/tree2
                gsiftp://k1.cs.icar.cnr.it/home/data/tree2
    )
)
( &(resourceManagerContact=k1.cs.icar.cnr.it)
    (label=subjob2)
    (executable=$(GLOBUS_LOCATION)/bin/globus-url-copy)
    (arguments=-vb -notpt gsiftp://k3.cs.icar.cnr.it/home/data/tree3
                gsiftp://k1.cs.icar.cnr.it/home/data/tree3
    )
)
```

FIGURE 11.13. file bank_scoring2.rsl.

reassembled and a CD is written in the VCD format. Figure 11.14 gives a conceptual schema of the entire process.

Following a classical approach to grid problems, a set of operations have to be executed to prepare and start the execution of the processing jobs on the grid nodes. These operations are shown in the shell script of Fig. 11.15, in which the different phases are marked in bold (video files creation, transfer of the video files and the conversion software, compression, retrieving of the compressed files, CD burning).

When the same application is designed using VEGA, it originates the workspace sequence reported by Fig. 11.16 to Fig. 11.21. Workspaces 1 and 2 are used to record the video files and to move them and the videoconversion.sh script to the hosts on which the conversion will take place. Workspace 3 executes concurrently the compression on the nodes minos, icarus and telesio; workspace 4 moves the resulting files to griso, the origin node. Finally, workspaces 5 and 6 create a unique file and write it on a recordable CD.

Making a comparison of the two approaches, it is possible to notice that while the logical phases that form the application are, obviously, the same, there is a fundamental difference in how the application will be executed. The shell script is replaced in the VEGA version of the application by pure RSL scripts, since all the operations required to configure and run the video conversion application are performed using Globus services.

This means that such an application is really architecture independent, because it is based on Globus services. Hence it is reusable on different Grids and over time. In addition, thanks to this representation it would be simple, by using VEGA, to reconfigure the application to fit with a different Grid context or simply to change some parameters.

There are some changes that can be made to improve the performance of the video conversion application. One of these changes is to begin the video file transfer during the capture phase. Once the first video file is obtained, it can be staged to the remote machine and the conversion can begin. Furthermore, using MDS, it may be possible to locate on the Grid the machine with a low CPU load and send the video file to it. To this end, the considerations made in the open issues section are of primary importance and could provide support for application able to better exploit the Grid infrastructure.

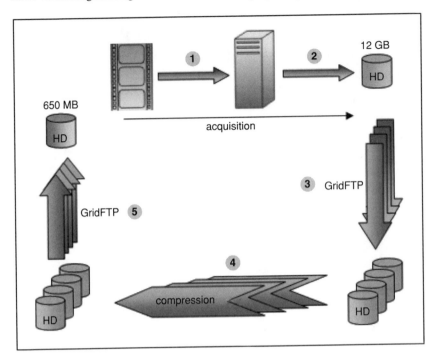

FIGURE 11.14. The video conversion application.

11.8   Related Work

This section briefly describes some related projects and tools, giving also a short comparison of the common and distinctive features between them and the environment we presented here.

A Grid-based knowledge discovery environment that shares some goals with the Knowledge Grid is *Discovery Net* (D-Net) [13]. The D-Net main goal is to design, develop, and deploy an infrastructure to support real-time processing, integration, visualization, and mining of massive amount of time critical data generated by high-throughput devices. The building blocks in Discovery Net are the so-called *Knowledge Discovery Services* (*KDS*), distinguished in *Computation Services* and *Data Services*. The former typically comprise algorithms, e.g., data preparation and data mining, while the latter define relational tables (as queries) and other data sources. Both kinds of services are described (and registered) by means of *adapters*, providing information such as input and output types, parameters, location and/or platform/operating system constraints, *factories* (objects allowing to retrieve references to services and to download them), *keywords*, and a *description*. The KDS are used to compose moderately complex data-pipelined processes. The composition may be carried out by means of a GUI which provides access to a library of services. The XML-based language used to describe processes is called *Discovery Process Markup Language*. The D-Net is based on an open architecture using common protocols and infrastructures such as the Globus Toolkit.

The *Parallel Application WorkSpace* (PAWS) [14] is a software infrastructure for connecting separate parallel applications within a component-like model. A PAWS provides also for dynamically coupling of applications and supports efficient communication of distributed data structures. The PAWS Controller coordinates the coupling of applications, manages resources, and

```
#!/bin/sh
#First, capture video from DVcamera
./videocapture.sh
#set environment variables
target_dir=/home/globususer
curdir=`pwd`
#stage code and video to remote machines
ndx=1
# List machines to be used here and below (one conversion
per machine):
for target_host in minos.cs.icar.cnr.it
icarus.cs.icar.cnr.it telesio.cs.icar.cnr.it
do
echo Setting up demo on host $target_host
globus-url-copy file:${curdir}/videoconversion.sh
gsiftp://${target_host}:2811${target_dir}/videoconversion.sh
echo sending video ${curdir}/videocap00${ndx}.avi
globus-url-copy file:${curdir}/videocap00${ndx}.avi \
gsiftp://${target_host}:2811${target_dir}/videocap00${ndx}.avi
globus-job-run ${target_host}/bin/chmod 755 videoconversion.sh
echo Building RSL for $target_host
echo +>demo_rsl${ndx}
echo "( &(resourceManagerContact="${target_host}")" >> demo_rsl${ndx}
echo " (subjobStartType=strict-barrier)" >> demo_rsl${ndx}
echo " (label="videocap00${ndx}")" >> demo_rsl${ndx}
echo " (executable= ${target_dir}/videoconversion.sh)" >> demo_rsl${ndx}
echo " (arguments = videocap00${ndx}.avi )" >> demo_rsl${ndx}
echo ' (stdout= $(GLOBUSRUN_GASS_URL) \
# "'$curdir/videocap00${ndx}.out'")' \>> demo_rsl${ndx}
echo ' (stderr= $(GLOBUSRUN_GASS_URL) \
# "'$curdir/videocap00${ndx}.err'")' >> demo_rsl${ndx}
echo ")" >> demo_rsl${ndx}
# Jobs submission
echo submiting job to $target_host
globusrun -w -f demo_rsl${ndx} &
ndx=`expr $ndx + 1`
done
echo waiting for all conversions to complete
wait
echo getting result files now
rm -f videocap.mpg
# Getting compressed files
ndx=1
for target_host in minos.cs.icar.cnr.it icarus.cs.icar.cnr.it
        telesio.cs.icar.cnr.it
do
globus-url-copy
gsiftp://${target_host}:2811${target_dir}/videocap00${ndx}.
avi.mpg \file:${curdir}/videocap00${ndx}.avi.mpg
cat videocap00${ndx}.avi.mpg >> videocap.mpg
rm -f videocap00${ndx}.*
rm -f demo_rsl${ndx}
ndx=`expr $ndx + 1`
done
# Now create the video cd (VCD)
./videocd.sh
```

FIGURE 11.15. Shell script for the video conversion application.

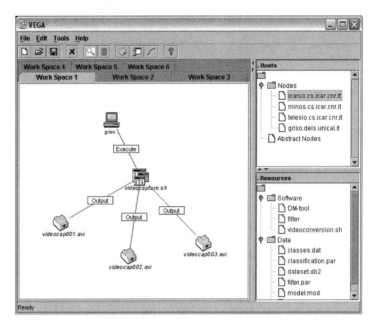

FIGURE 11.16. Video conversion: Workspace1.

handles user authentication. Heterogeneity issues in PAWS are handled by the underlying Nexus library. Currently, PAWS is a C++ library (C and Fortran interfaces are under development). Applications written in any language that may incorporate such libraries can be interconnected with PAWS and may communicate exploiting the common PAWS layer. A PAWS is designed to coordinate a parallel execution of multiple, interconnected programs; to this end multiple communication channels are exploited. For employing optimized communication schedules, PAWS requires information on the layout, the location, and the storage type of the data, all of which has to be provided by the user through appropriate PawsData objects.

Recently, a few general purpose grid programming tools have been developed or are going to be developed. *Graph Enabled Console COmponent* (GECCO) is a graphical tool developed at Argonne National Laboratory [15][16]. The GECCO is based on the Globus CoG Kit [5] and provides facilities to specify and monitor the execution of sets of tasks with dependencies between them. Specifically it allows to specify the jobs dependencies graphically, or with the help of an XML-based configuration file, and execute the resulting application. Each job is represented as a node in a graph. A job is executed as soon as its predecessors are reported as having successfully completed. It is possible to set up the specification of the job while clicking on the node: a specification window pops up allowing the user to edit the RSL, the label, and other parameters. Editing can also be performed at run-time (job execution), hence providing for simple computational steering.

These systems show how problems and issues of Grid-based generic, parallel and knowledge discovery applications are addressed and solved in various contexts. It can be noted that some approaches are similar to that defined into the Knowledge Grid architecture and used by VEGA, like the composition of tasks and the employment of an XML-based formalism to represent the structure of the application. On the other hand, several differences are also present, above all the

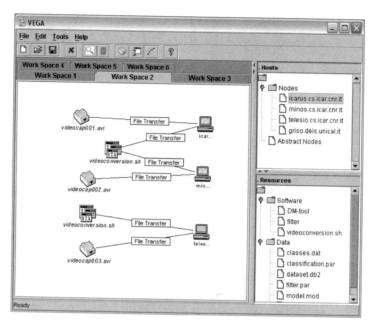

FIGURE 11.17. Video conversion: Workspace 2.

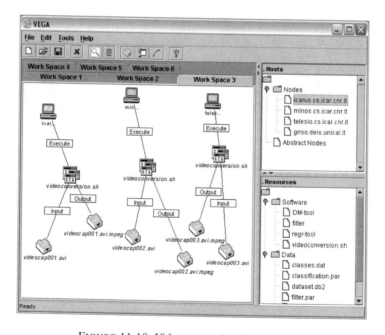

FIGURE 11.18. Video conversion: Workspace 3.

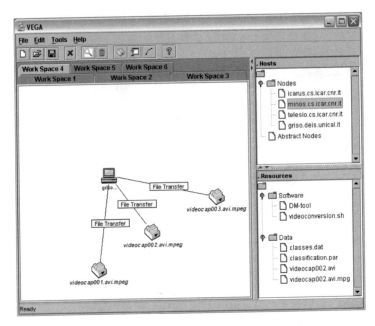

FIGURE 11.19. Video conversion: Workspace 4.

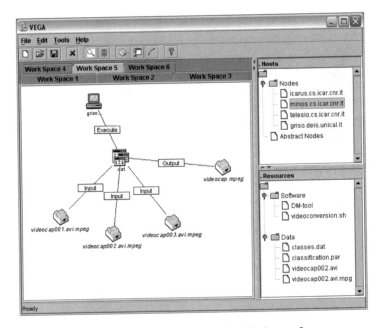

FIGURE 11.20. Video conversion: Workspace 5.

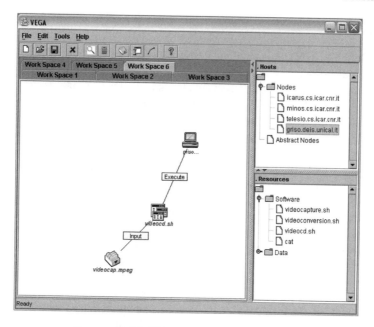

FIGURE 11.21. Video conversion: Workspace 6.

role and structure of the *execution plan* and the use in VEGA of a metadata based *information system* (KDS) from which extracting information about grid nodes and datasets characteristics.

The VEGA, as part of the Knowledge Grid, provides access to a set of services for generic and knowledge discovery applications. An application running into the VEGA environment does not contain any limitation about the processing strategy to employ (i.e., move data, move model, etc.), neither about the number and the location of the grid nodes that will perform a mining process. The integration and use of new data access methods or processing algorithms, as well as entire commercial suite or software components coming from preexistent sequential or parallel systems, is simple and does not require any customization. It is obtained by their publication in the KDS, which will provide the system with all needed information to use that component inside an application (i.e., invocation syntax, component requirements, etc.). The XML-based approach used in the Knowledge Grid and VEGA to define metadata is going to be the most used in several Grid-based environments and also the new version of the Globus Toolkit (GT3) exploits XML-based metadata for handling resource management.

11.9   Conclusion

A condition to bring Grid computing to a mature phase is the availability of high-level supporting tools and development environments that allows users and developers to effectively exploit Grid features in designing advanced applications. Here we presented VEGA, a high-level *Visual Environment for Grid Application* designed to support the design and execution of complex applications upon Grid environments.

A VEGA offers the users a programming model that represents Grid resources as a collection of typed resources and a set of defined "relationships" between them. As part of the implementation of the Knowledge Grid, VEGA interacts with some of its services. In particular, the *knowledge directory service* is widely used to retrieve basic information about Grid resources. The key concepts in the VEGA approach to the design of a Grid application are the *visual language* used to describe the jobs constituting an application, and the methodology to group these jobs in *workspaces* to form a specific stage. These are also the features that make the environment provided by VEGA adhere to the *software component framework*, that is, a system for composing application from smaller software modules.

The software modules composing the VEGA architecture implement a set of functionalities able to simplify the planning and submission of complex applications, providing an easy access to Grid facilities with a high level of abstraction. These functionalities range from *design facilities* to *consistency checking, execution management, credentials management*, and *projects management*.

All these features have been developed specifically to support the design of data analysis and knowledge discovery applications, but are suitable to satisfy the requirements of most general purpose applications. The case studies presented in Section 11.7 are intended to show a practical use of VEGA, as well as to demonstrate how VEGA can handle a typical Grid application and to illustrate the main benefits in comparison with the still predominant low-level approach.

The open issues section discussed some improvements (part of which are already under development) that could be added to the system. In particular the *acyclic graph* hypothesis for the workspaces and the *abstract resources* concept are key features to open the way towards larger and more complex classes of applications.

References

[1] Microsoft Corporation, ".*NET*", see http://www.microsoft.com
[2] A. Thomas, "Enterprise JavaBeans Technology: Server Component Model for the Java Platform", http://java.sun.com/products/ejb/white_paper.html, 1998
[3] I. Foster and C. Kesselman, "Globus: A Metacomputing Infrastructure Toolkit," *Int. Journal of Supercomputing Applications* 11, 115–128 (1997)
[4] I. Foster and C. Kesselman, "The Anatomy of the Grid: Enabling Scalable Virtual Organizations," *Int. Journal of Supercomputer Applications*, 15(3), (2001)
[5] The Globus Project, "*Java Commodity Grid Kit*," see http://www.globus.org/cog/java
[6] M. Cannataro and D. Talia, "KNOWLEDGE GRID: An Architecture for Distributed Knowledge Discovery," *Communications of the ACM* (2003).
[7] C. Mastroianni, D. Talia and P. Trunfio, "*Managing Heterogeneous Resources in Data Mining Applications on Grids Using XML-based Metadata*," Proc. IPDPS 12th Heterogeneous Computing Workshop, Nice, France, April 2003
[8] The Apache Software Foundation, "*Xerces Java Parser 2.0.0*," available at http://xml.apache.org
[9] World Wide Web Consortium, "*Document Object Model (DOM) Level 3 XPath Specification*," see http://www.w3.org/TR/DOM-Level-3-XPath
[10] M. Cannataro, A. Congiusta, D. Talia and P. Trunfio, "A *Data Mining Toolset for Distributed High-Performance Platforms*," Proc. 3rd Int. Conference Data Mining 2002, WIT Press, Bologna, Italy, September 2002, (WIT), pp. 41–50.
[11] The Globus Project, "*The Globus Resource Specification Language RSL v1.0*," see http://www.globus.org/gram/rsl_spec1.html
[12] W.Allcock, "*GridFTP Update January 2002*," available at http://www.globus.org/datagrid/deliverables/GridFTP-Overview-200201.pdf

[13] V. Curcin, M. Ghanem, Y. Guo, M. Kohler, A. Rowe, J. Syed and P.Wendel, "Discovery Net: Towards a Grid of Knowledge Discovery," Proc. Eighth ACM SIGKDD Int. Conf. on Knowledge Discovery and Data Mining, Edmonton, Canada, 2002

[14] P. Beckman, P. Fasel, W. Humphrey, and S. Mniszewski, *Efficient Coupling of Parallel Applications Using PAWS*," Proceedings HPDC, Chicago, IL, July 1998

[15] G. von Laszewski, "A Loosely Coupled Metacomputer: Cooperating Job Submissions Across Multiple Supercomputing Sites," *Concurrency, Experience, and Practice* (2000)

[16] G. von Laszewski and I. Foster, "*Grid Infrastructure to Support Science Portals for Large Scale Instruments*," Distributed Computing on the Web Workshop (DCW), University of Rostock, Germany, June 1999

[17] IBM Grid computing, see http://www.ibm.com/grid/

Chapter 12

Solving Computationally Intensive Engineering Problems on the Grid Using Problem Solving Environments

12.1 Introduction

The present rapidly changing state of Grid computing is that the technologies, resources, and applications used in grid computing all have tremendous diversity [1]. In particular the applications are diverse and encompass many different computing techniques. The common theme between them all is that computing power away from local resources is required, and that these applications envisage the need to use distributed resources. With any application the results achieved should be the most important part, and Grid technologies should be employed to facilitate getting faster results to harder problems.

Grid applications which are computationally intensive and collaborative in terms of the scientific community examining the results lead to two important questions [2]. First, how can knowledge and insight be acquired quickly from an application that may be running on a distributed resource rather than on the users' desktop machine. The second, how can these results be effectively shared between potentially geographically disparate scientists who may well have very different areas of expertise. Both of these questions are particularly relevant when the Grid application is being run by non traditional users who may not have computational science backgrounds, and who may be from a broad range of disciplines.

While a commonly held belief in the Grid community is that the Web Portal will allow applications to be run from any computer, it may also be true that the Web need not be the only portal into the Grid. The Web interface may be simple, but the outputs returned are constrained by the same "bare bones" nature of the environment. Users from all backgrounds are now used to high quality 3-D visualizations, from graphics on news programmes to high quality animations shown during talks. The Grid has the ability to provide these same quality outputs, but the interaction method may need to be driven by the demands of visualization software which provides an important way of extracting knowledge from large datasets. In this work we describe the stages necessary to provide real-time desktop visualization of results for a parallel Grid application computed via problem-solving environments (PSEs). Apart from the visualization, the biggest advantage of using a PSE is the ability to use computational steering. In traditional applications, the input parameters are set and not often changed while the code is running. By making the input parameters available in the PSE, it is possible to change the problem being solved after the simulation has been started. This means that the visual feedback from the output visualizations can help to guide further inputs, either away from failing computations or toward better investigation of more exciting parameter regions. The benefits of computational steering as a means of improving the solution procedure go back to one of the first demonstrations of steering by Haber and McNabb [3] in 1989.

Recent work by Brodlie et al. [4] shows how collaboration between scientists using PSEs can be achieved through various methods such as (i) sharing the display of the PSE, (ii) sharing the output visualisations once they have reached the PSE, and finally (iii) sharing the access to the simulation allowing steering from any user. The first of these can be done using technologies such as Virtual Network Computing,[1] (VNC) which allows any internet connected computer to view and interact with the desktop on a single machine. This can be useful for shared demonstrations such as in Access Grid Ref here sessions, where conversation may revolve around the computed results. Sharing of data is possible through technologies such as COVISA [5], which has a client-server approach enabling sharing of parameters, formatted datasets, or even geometry within IRIS Explorer. In this work we focus on the third type of collaboration in the final section of the chapter.

Although the example used here is computationally demanding and lends itself to parallel solution techniques, the approach taken here will be to illustrate, through the code development, the use of distributed and shared memory parallelization techniques as will the use of Grid job management. Using the Grid as HPC on-demand for large, complex applications will inevitably involve the use of parallel programming techniques within the application [6]. The Grid will be presented in terms of getting seamless, interactive, on-demand access to high-performance computing (HPC) resources, and how applications may be extended beyond conventional HPC considerations.

The rest of the chapter describes the series of stages necessary to transform a typical application into a fully Grid-enabled one, operating from within a problem-solving environment. These stages will be further explained with a series of example PSEs outlining the technical enhancements necessary for transforming an engineering code into one which fully exploits the benefits of Grid technology.

In Section 12.2, the basic components of a PSE are described in detail, along with some consideration of the options available in choosing the package within which the PSE is to be built. The case studies focus on IRIS Explorer and SCIRun, although other options exist including the use of packages such as Cactus,[2] MATLAB,[3] AVS,[4] and OpenDX.[5] These are a mixture of open source and proprietary software, but the principles for developing in one system transfer well into the others. Other example PSEs using these systems can be found in work by Brodlie et al. [7] for IRIS Explorer; Johnson et al. [8] for SCIRun; Allen et al. [9] for Cactus; Kierzenka

---

[1]http://www.realvnc.com or http://www.tightvnc.com

[2]http://www.cactuscode.org

[3]http://www.mathworks.com/products/matlab

[4]http://help.avs.com/AVS5

[5]http://www.opendx.org

and Shampine [10] for MATLAB; and, Treinish [11] for OpenDX. More tailor-made solutions include the ICENI project [12], and the RealityGrid project using VTK[6] [13].

In Section 12.2.1, we describe how a traditional code for a demanding mechanical engineering problem has been embedded for use within a PSE. In this study we also consider some of the issues to do with like, how embedded simulations are managed. This example is not necessarily Grid-aware, but sets up the necessary framework for the later applications discussed.

The idea of running the PSE on the Grid and doing the rendering locally, as described in the second example, does not optimise the resources effectively. The greatest leap in Grid computing for PSEs comes when the local machine running the PSE, authenticates with a Grid resource and handles the communication with this separate resource. We describe the mechanisms for doing this in Section 12.4 and in the accompanying PSE Example. Particularly relevant here are the measures for communicating input and output data between the desktop PSE and Grid simulation.

The final stage in the evolution of the Grid-enabled PSE is to remove the dependencies between the desktop and the Grid processes. This is done through the launched process having an extra library attached which handles all the communication with the simulation. This means that once launched, the Grid process need not have any "listeners" but equally it may have many who will be able to see the same results and steer the application. These extensions are described in Section 12.5. The final example describes how such a simulation may be set up, and why such an application is ideally suited for a Grid environment beyond traditional HPC needs.

We conclude in Section 12.6 and consider some of the features which still need implementing. The most obvious issue which we are not attempting to cover in this work is that of brokering. Intelligent brokering, the automatic choice of the best Grid resource for the particular application is still some way off, although many test projects are considering these issues. We have only considered the case that the PSE user can use the standard tools to make the choice of resources, coupled with personal knowledge of the resources required for the application in question.

12.2   Problem-solving Environments (PSE)

One aspect of the advent of Grid computing is that users are now able to access much more powerful resources to perform larger simulations. Since the number of people performing such calculations is not decreasing, then the contention for these resources is also increasing. If the Grid moves to a "commodity computing" phase where each CPU second is chargeable then effective management of simulations will also become an economic factor.

Problem-Solving Environments (PSEs) combine several important processes into one body. The actual application, be it a numerical solver, as used in this chapter, or data–Grid style search, e.g. [14], is only one component in an environment, which has access to visualization tools for the output results generated. It also has the ability to set input parameters for the application, and hence can provide a user-friendly interface to a complex problem. The PSE therefore has synchronous computation and visualization. There are three ways in which even basic PSEs are advantageous: the input parameters can all be set, or adjusted at run time; the solver is included as an important part of the PSE and hence it can be possible to change solution methods, if appropriate; and finally the visualization is an innate component of the package, and results can be visualized and studied as the calculation proceeds. Computational steering gives the PSE

---

[6]http://public.kitware.com/VTK

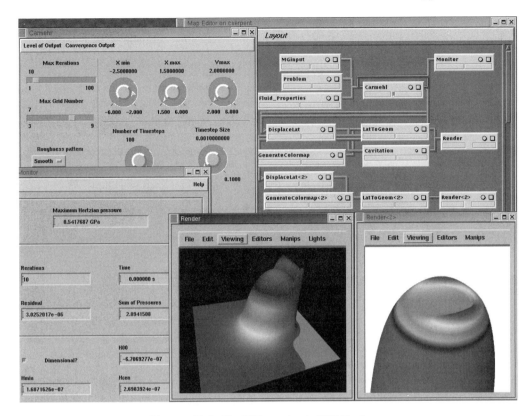

FIGURE 12.1. The PSE running in IRIS Explorer.

codes for complete control of the module's firing pattern and communication of data through the workflow pipeline, and these require no alteration by a developer.

Computational steering is implemented in IRIS Explorer using the looping mechanisms provided. Rather than saving results to disk at the end of a run, the work arrays inside the software can be declared as static and hence the previous results are automatically available for use on the next run. A solution used in this manner may provide a good initial estimate for a differently loaded case, or be interpolated for a change of domain size.

The use of the Hyperscribe module [25] would allow another layer of steering to be included. This module stores datasets or variables on disk for future usage, at the user's discretion. If the entire work arrays, previously saved as static, were stored based on the problem's input characteristics then a suite of previously calculated solutions could be created for future invocations of the PSE on separate occasions, or even by other users.

12.3   Parallel PSE Applications

The style of PSE creation described in the previous section is appropriate for applications which run on a standard PC, where the solution process is sufficiently quick so that the desired steering can produce visible changes instantly, e.g., the pollution demonstrator described in Walkley et al. [26]. It is, however, the basic building block for the rest of the work described here on constructing Grid-enabled PSEs. Interactivity has been obtained, visualizations rendered, and theoretically trivial parallelism on the PSE level may have occurred since the different simulation and visualization processes should be occurring independently, hence, a multiprocessor machine should enable simultaneous execution. The next stage has to allow the simulation itself to be run in parallel.

Working in the framework of the simulation as an embedded module means that far greater consideration must be given to the actual fabric of the environment in which the PSE is built. For example, as was explained above, IRIS Explorer has each module in the dataflow pipeline as a separate process. Since these processes are launched internally from IRIS Explorer and the processes themselves are wrapped in generated code to communicate with the IRIS Explorer user interface, then launching one of these modules using MPI [27] is not an option currently available. Instead shared memory techniques have been used. In this section the use of shared memory parallelism using SCIRun will be explored.

12.3.1 Parallel Shared Memory Computation within SCIRun

The SCIRun has been developed by the SCI group at the University of Utah as a computational workbench for visual programming [17] and has now been released as open-source software. SCIRun was developed originally for calculations in computational medicine [28], but has since been extended to many other applications.

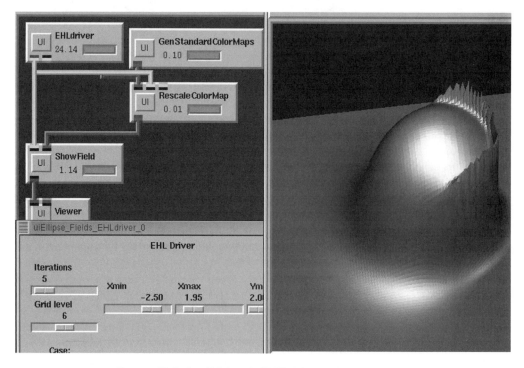

FIGURE 12.2. Parallel threaded EHL PSE running in SCIRun.

The overall appearance of SCIRun is similar to that of IRIS Explorer, as can be seen in Fig. 12.2, where the implementation of the EHL problem explained in Example PSE 1, can be seen working. The module firing algorithm in SCIRun probes the workflow diagram from the desired point of execution so that all elements have all the information they need to run, before then sending the information downstream and firing those modules. This means that upstream elements will be fired if they need to supply information to any other element. Similarly all the downstream modules directly affected by the firing will be made aware that new data will be coming.

A SCIRun is a multi-threaded program, and hence a single process, with (at least) one thread for each launched module. Therefore, every module can have access to all same data without the use of shared memory. This has the advantage that there is more memory available for the generation of datasets to pass between modules, and the disadvantage that any operating system limits on the memory available to a single process apply to the entirety of SCIRun, meaning that calculation and visualization are all included in the same maximum space allocation defined by the system. It also means that any variables declared as static in one invocation of a module will be the same as used in other invocations, since the operating system cannot differentiate between the two.

Parallelism can be easily achieved on SCIRun, thanks to its threaded structure. SCIRun has its own implementation of threads that can be easily incorporated into a user's code. The use of threads means a shared memory machine must be used, but within these constraints the parallel performance for numerical calculations is very good. Next generation packages, such as Uintah [29], use a combination of MPI and threads to achieve massively parallel scientific computations on terascale computing platforms.

Since SCIRun is written as a single threaded process, it has added flexibility with regard to the rewiring of workflow elements during execution. For the EHL problem, when a transient case is run, the output datasets are prepared and released down the pipeline for visualization at the end of each time step. With more than one solution variable being solved for, there is obviously a choice as to what is visualized at anytime. In SCIRun, these changes can be made "on the fly." For example, if the pressure solution was being visualized, then it is possible to change to a surface geometry plot between time steps. This is an important feature since it allows the user to learn and experiment interactively, whilst still making excellent use of the allocated Grid resources.

12.3.2   Shared Memory Parallel Computation Grid Architecture

In developing the shared memory Grid software architecture, it should be noted, however, that running the entire PSE remotely is not always a good idea. The main reason for this is that the final rendering should be done locally whenever possible to allow full utilization of the local graphics hardware. Minimizing the network traffic between simulation and display is another factor which must be considered. For examples, with large datasets for visualization, then doing this work on a Grid resource will be very advantageous. Considering the size of datasets to be transferred over the intervening network between generation, visualization and rendering are very important, as are the connectivity rates. This can be illustrated by the scenario demonstrated in Fig. 12.3. Here we are imagining the computationally intensive part being done on Grid Resource 1, but the visualization is done on Grid Resource 2. Often, all communication with nodes of such resources has to be channelled through a head node. Within the resource the communication will use the fast interconnects, or shared memory, but between resources the

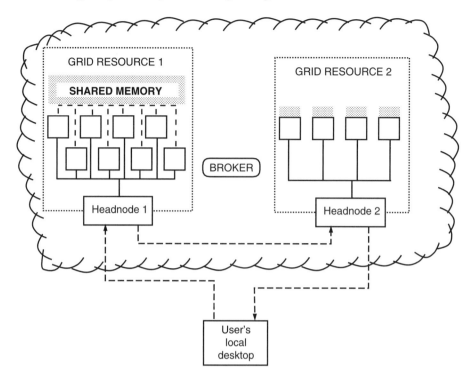

FIGURE 12.3. Example Grid architecture diagram, with different workflow elements on distributed resources.

communication will be at a lower rate. If the native architecture of Grid Resource 1 can be used for the visualization tasks, too, then the overall performance of the application may be substantially enhanced. This scenario emphasizes the difficulties in accurately brokering the entire Grid application, as the broker would need some idea of the data transfer rates between the machines, the size of the datasets to be generated, and an idea of the regularity of the rate at which these are produced.

One way in which manual distribution of work between resources has been implemented in IRIS Explorer is through the use of remote hosts. Work by Wood et al. [20] has extended the standard access methods to include secure Grid-aware authenticated connections.

12.4 Grid-enabled Workflow

To extend the parallelism options available away from shared memory, it must be possible to launch jobs onto remote distributed resources. These resources will now, typically be managed by Grid-aware scheduling software, and hence interaction with this middleware must be done as transparently to the user as possible.

The methods described here use the standard Globus[9] [30] tools for Grid job management, including file input and output. We shall assume that the necessary Globus certification process has already been undertaken before launching the PSE. The brokering is, as described previously, done through user selection based on knowledge of the resources currently available.

The key remaining steps to getting the PSE having elements run on distributed resources are (i) launching the job onto a remote resource, (ii) communicating information back to the PSE detailing the location where the job is running, and (iii) communication of steering and output information to and from this job. These three steps are possible using a variety of approaches, of which we shall describe two.

In order to launch the job onto the resource it is often necessary to have a good understanding of the specification of that resource, and knowledge of the schedulers on that resource. For example, a parallel job launched through Globus requires extra information for the local scheduler to best use the native MPI or shared memory options. Unfortunately, the idea of Globus providing transparent access to heterogeneous resources through a simple command is reliant on the application writer to have enough information about the options to write the user interface and to hide the unnecessary details from the user. A good example of this is shown in Fig. 12.4 below where all the authentication details have been hidden behind the "Use Globus" button.

The communication, the location of the running application from the Grid resource back to the PSE is a surprisingly nontrivial operation. Assuming the job has been submitted using Globus, typically it will be scheduled from the headnode to one or more nodes under its control. This internal node will then be the location with which the PSE will need to communicate information. This location will then need to be passed out of the Grid resource, such that the PSE can obtain the information and commence communication of data. This is typically done either with a direct socket connection, or by using a Web service. The Web service directory approach has the advantage that the location will be available for other users to connect to, or for a central store of running applications with separate input and output streams which the PSE may wish to connect to, and steer, independently. Using a Web service is also useful when the Grid job may be waiting in a queueing system. The advantage of the direct connection is that the connection back to the PSE can be instantaneous on job startup rather than requiring the polling of the Web service. The security of each of these methods is reliant on either the socket connection being encrypted or secure authentication to the web service. The direct socket style of connection is described in Example PSE 3, with the Grid directory style in Section 12.5.

---

[9]http://www.globus.org

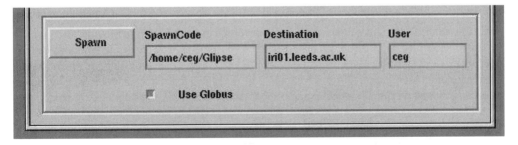

FIGURE 12.4. Grid enabling options for an IRIS Explorer PSE.

The final stage is the communication between the PSE and the Grid application. Again it is possible to do this using direct connections or using a Web services approach. The biggest disadvantage of using the latter is that the Web service must be polled to discover if any new output data has been posted, rather than the direct connection method which can wait "listening" for a new dataset to start arriving. It is this latter method which is considered in the rest of the chapter.

One final consideration needs to be given to Grid resources where the internal nodes are not visible to the network outside. In this scenario it is necessary to build a proxy service which manages authenticated connections for services running on that resource. This will run on the headnode, such as shown in Fig. 12.3, and will manage connections for all services on that resource. Such communication bottlenecks are unfortunate, but it is hoped that in future systems, administrators will be able to design more efficient, secure solutions.

12.4.1 Grid-enabled Simulation Using IRIS Explorer

This section describes the expansion of the embedded serial implementation from Section 12.2.1 to a distributed memory, parallel version, as described in Goodyer et al. [31], which is Grid-enabled. To the user, the user interface in IRIS Explorer will still look identical to that shown in Fig. 12.1. The change to the PSE is all implemented within the application module, which is now solely the user interface to the simulation running on the Grid. The additional Grid information required are all confined to only a few extra inputs, such as shown in Fig. 12.4. These are namely the destination, i.e., the selected Grid destination, which we typically have as a user choice from the available resources [32]; the destination executable, to choose which of the available services to run; and, finally the username, which simply acts as an identifier tag in any Web service directory produced.

When the job on the remote machine is started, communication between the launching IRIS Explorer module and the launched Grid process is done through sockets. The launched process knows where to connect to, by means of extra flags passed to it when it is started. Once contact has been established, the launched process then is the dominant communicator, with the launcher as the listener. When the launched process needs data from the PSE, e.g., control parameters for the simulation, it sends a request to the listener who packs the values up into a data array of predefined size and structure, and sends it to the Grid process.

Similarly, output data is packaged by the Grid process and sent to the listener. The received data is then formatted into the relevant output data types which are released down the pipeline for visualization.

Extra input modules are added before the Grid module poses few problems. The incoming data is packed into arrays which are sent to the Grid module, as with the control parameters. Since these input modules need not always be present, then there must be a default set of parameters for cases where they are not connected so that the application can operate accordingly.

Having completed the requested number of job, the Grid process does not terminate but regularly polls the associated PSE module until it is requested to perform the computation. This eliminates the cost of starting up a job on the Grid, and also means that results from the previous iteration can still be stored in local memory or filestore, for future use.

During computationally intensive simulations it used to be the case that the simulation module spent considerable amounts of time "firing." Since the work is being done outside the PSE, this is no longer the case and, so firings only occur when new data is received, be it from changes to input parameters or through the receipt of output data. Whereas input data was only ever available to the simulation at the start of execution it may now be requested at any time, and hence the opportunity for steering the calculation is increased. This may not always be sensible, so care must be taken when constructing the communication over which parameters can be allowed to change during the solution process.

Part of the rationale for use of the Grid is to gain access to remote-parallel machines. Information about the parallel requirements can be incorporated into the launching mechanism. To accomplish this, two more options must be added to the user interface: one detailing the number of processors and one confirming the launch process for the parallel job. As was explained in the previous section, parallel Grid jobs using Globus do need substantially more information at startup, and sensible communication back to the PSE must only be attempted from one of the processors. The attempt, as ever, in developing PSEs, is to try and hide as much of this as possible away from users.

12.5   Asynchronous Steering of Grid Applications

The method of Grid enabling the PSE described in the previous section with direct socket connections from Grid resource to PSE works well, provided that the simulation you are running is sufficiently fast and that results are available whilst the user watches. The additional demands from Grid-enabled PSEs come when the job has a long initial set up, or when the chosen resource is too busy to schedule the job for immediate execution. This leads to the idea of wanting to launch the job and then having the ability to connect to it later on, potentially allowing asynchronous steering. The functionality required to do this means that the job must be running in a known location, and must be ready to accept new users as well as to continue when said users leave the PSE.

These abilities have been central to the gViz project [20], which is part of the UK e-Science Core Programme. The central theme is that a gViz library is attached to the running simulation. This spawns extra threads for "listening" to incoming communication, and "output" of datasets while the main application generates the results as before. This is intended to act as a much more generic environment for programming Grid-enabled applications.

The PSE modules that attach to the Grid also have the gViz library attached and are able to interact with the simulation by posting and receiving messages via the gViz library. The local-to-remote communication is again done via either sockets or Web services.

Resource discovery and job launching is accomplished using the methods described in Section 12.4. The posting of the socket address or other access information to a Web service provides a central way for any new users to connect to previously running simulations. These options are very useful if there are multiple jobs running or a distributed resource is being used.

Output data from the simulations is expected to be stored centrally with the application. This means that whenever a user joins the simulation they get all the relevant output data as well as the current steering parameters. Since this data is stored in a raw format and the "packaging up" into appropriate formats for output is done at the client end, it has been possible to simultaneously connect a single simulation running on a Grid resource to PSEs in-built using IRIS Explorer, SCIRun, and VTK. The updating of steering parameters, when one side changes a value, can be done transparently and the data is flushed down the map (network) when new data is generated by the application. In this way the simulation and the PSE are now almost disjoint entities but the PSE still retains in full control.

12.5.1 Fully Distributed Grid Applications

In this section we will expand the numerical solver presented earlier to be the full engineering environment used by Shell, as described in [33, 34]. This application is an optimization problem intended to best match experimental results against numerical simulation of lubricant behaviour. This involves typically thousands of evaluations of groups of, between 36 and 100 independent test parameters.

The independent nature of these calculations makes this type of application ideal for parallelism at the solver level. The small amounts of communication necessary between runs make the Grid setting a very appropriate resource. The optimizer itself can be greatly helped by using the PSE to guide the solutions out of local minima and this, in turn, will improve the performance and increase the effective power of the Grid.

The overall schematic of the optimizer is shown in Fig. 12.5. This indicates the distributed nature of the entire application. Whilst only one person needs to authenticate via Globus and start the Grid job, other collaborators may connect direct to the Grid job once they know where it has been launched. The Grid Master process handles all the connections to steering and output information, and is the central point for the distributed application underneath to communicate back to. Each individual instance of the numerical solver can still be running in parallel with communication between instances only between the smaller groups of head nodes. The parallelization of this work is described fully in [34] with just the gViz-enabled PSE described below.

For Grid applications, perhaps the most interesting part comes from the ability to utilize metacomputing techniques. Through the use of MPICH–G2 [35], the Globus-enabled, Grid-aware version of the message passing standard [27], it is possible to exploit the Grid as a collection of smaller resources to accomplish large HPC tasks. The MPICH–G2 passes messages in a manner which reflects the topology of the Grid to maximize efficiency of communication. This means that each instance of the computationally expensive, communication heavy numer-

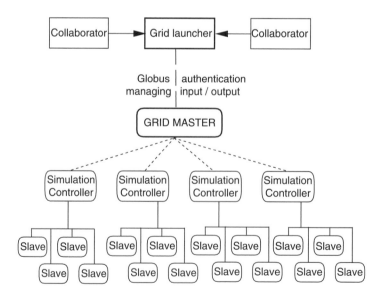

FIGURE 12.5. Schematic of the Grid-enabled Optimisation PSE.

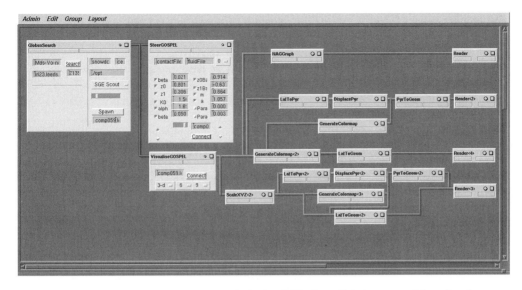

FIGURE 12.6. IRIS Explorer map of the optimisation PSE. Data–flow represented by wires between modules.

ical solver can be run on a single resource with all the messages handled by the fast-internal mechanisms; whereas the less frequent, synchronization communications at the end of each optimization iteration can be performed using the slower TCP/IP messages. In this manner it is possible to fully utilize many much smaller resources than would be typically available in traditional HPC applications.

An example of a typical map for the PSE is shown in Fig. 12.6, where the data–flow pipeline, generally from left to right is clearly visible. The majority of the modules are used in the visualization process and hence only the three modules on the left are described here.

The first module in the map interrogates a Grid information (GIIS) server to analyze the available resources and their current statuses [32]. The user can then select a resource and choose a suitable launch method, including launching the job onto the Grid using Globus. For this work we have extended the gViz library to include parallel launch mechanisms, including writing a parallel job submission script or Globus resource specification language (RSL) script which then gets submitted to Sun Grid Engine for scheduling onto a suitable node. When the job is spawned a socket connection back to the PSE is made telling the launching application which node of the Grid resource the simulation will be communicating from. Information about this node and port is then passed to the next two modules in the map which handle the steering inputs, and the receipt of the data for visualization. Knowledge of where the simulation is running also allows any other user access to the simulation through the gViz libraries. This means that one person, with Grid certification, say, can start the simulation and other collaborators around the world can then all see the results of that simulation and help to steer the computation [26, 32]. In fact, the person who originally launched the Grid job need not actually be involved from that point on.

The steering module has several uses. Firstly it shows the current best set of values found by the simplex, along with $\mathcal{R}_F$. This allows a user access to individual numbers from the simulation rather than much larger data sets for visualization purposes. These numbers can also be used for steering. For example it is possible to resubmit this current best set to the optimizer once a minimum has been found. The NAG library will then build a new simplex around this previous minimum potentially allowing it to escape from local minima. Similarly, a different point in the search space can be specified away from where the optimizer has previously searched. Finally, as mentioned, the accuracy can be changed. A method we have implemented here is the ability to turn on (or off) the thermal components of the solution. The thermal solve is much more expensive but adds greater accuracy to the friction results obtained, especially for cases where more heat is generated [36].

Communication from the PSE to the simulation is done through the gViz libraries. At suitable points the simulation will check if any new input data has been received. If a steering request is for additional accuracy, say, then these changes can be introduced without changing the points of the current simplex and would therefore only apply to future calculations. If, on the other hand, a new simplex was requested then the NAG libraries do not allow movement of the current simplex points and hence use of the communication flag inside the routine will cause the optimization routine to drop out of the NAG routines and then the new simplex is submitted.

The visualization module communicates with the simulation to receive all the data sets for visualization. These are then packaged up into standard IRIS Explorer data types and sent down the rest of the map for visualization. When the full data sets are being shown then more information needs to be returned from the parallel nodes than is necessary for just the optimization process. The root process which is communicating with any attached users also needs to retain full copies of all output data previously generated so that any listeners joining the simulation later get the full set of results rather than just those generated from that stage.

The full optimization run generates hierarchies of multivariate data. Full descriptions of the data sets returned are described in [34], along with how the different techniques give added information to the user. Here we will content ourselves to simply show how the effect of steering can improve the quality of solutions obtained. In Fig. 12.7, we see the behavior of the variables changed by the optimizer over the course of the entire process. The first graph shown has the optimizer progressing without any steering, the second has a new simplex formed after the 30th improvement to the best point in the simplex. It can be clearly seen how this has encouraged the optimizer to a very different point in the search space which turns out to be a better overall result.

12.6   Conclusions and Future Directions

The use of problem-solving environments provide a visually striking and powerful tool for both developers and users of application code. The visualizations provided allow real-time evaluation of the results generated, and computational steering enables interactivity with running simulations. The use of PSEs will grow as even computationally light applications benefit from such techniques.

The use of Grid technologies increases the usefulness of the PSE as it potentially allows access to a much richer computational space which may provide the opportunity to learn about the application more quickly. More work is obviously required in the middleware between the PSE and the simulation. Projects such as gViz are providing these interfaces in a way which should be as transparent to the user as possible.

Future challenges relating to PSEs and the Grid mirror those issues affecting general Grid use: resource discovery, resource access, and security. These future directions are discussed briefly below.

Discovery of resources requires more than just knowing what machines are available. Knowledge of the architecture itself governs which executables will and will not run, but further knowledge is required for use of library functions, etc. Brokering of the resource choice will always be an issue, but if varying pecuniary charging models are applied to different resources then these considerations will need to be built in too.

The challenges regarding access extend beyond the authorization to use a resource. When a PSE job is submitted, it may be sensible for immediate access to be provided. This may require special queueing arrangements to be introduced on local machines, rather than the job scheduling software starting the job in the middle of the night, potentially waiting for input. Access is also an issue regarding the connectivity between the PSE and the resource: if the nodes where the job is running are not visible from the desktop, an intermediary staging server should be provided at the interface between the systems. Access to information regarding running simulations will need a standard location, such as a Web service, on each resource to enable users to fully know what is available.

Finally, security of access to information has not been fully developed thus far in the construction of the PSEs. Whilst secure transfer of data between PSE and Grid is possible, authenticated via Globus certificates, this encryption is computationally expensive. Also, since the infrastructure has been built in gViz to allow multiple collaborators, then the issues concerning who will have access to any running simulations needs to be fully addressed. This authorization should probably be tied to the information in the Web service listing of the jobs. Thus, while the use of Grid-based PSEs with computational steering and parallelism is an attractive way to solve computationally intensive problems, there remain many challenges to be addressed before such a paradigm is routinely and widely used.

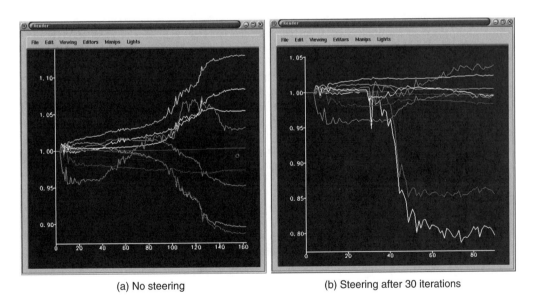

(a) No steering   (b) Steering after 30 iterations

FIGURE 12.7. Progression of optimizer showing relative change of best solution found to initial guess. Each line represents a different variable.

Acknowledgments. This work was funded by EPSRC and through the UK e-Science Core Programme. Thanks are also due to Jason Wood for providing the gViz library used in this work, and Laurence Scales from Shell Global Solutions for work on the lubrication project.

References

[1] I. Foster, and C. Kesselman, The Grid 2: The Blueprint for a New Computing Infrastructure (Elsevier, 2004)

[2] F. Berman, G.C. Fox, and A.J.G. Hey, Grid Computing: Making the Global Infrastructure a Reality (Wiley, 2003)

[3] R.B. Haber, D.A. McNabb, Eliminating Distance in Scientific Computing: An Experiment in Televisualization, International Journal of Supercomputer Applications 4, 71–89 (1990)

[4] K.W. Brodlie, D.A. Duce, J.R. Gallop, J.P.R.B. Walton, and J.D. Wood, Distributed and collaborative Visualization—State of the Art Report, *Computer Graphics Forum* 23, 223–251 (2004).

[5] J. Wood, H. Wright, and K.W. Brodlie, *Collaborative Visualization*, in Proceedings of IEEE *Visualization 97* (1997), pp. 253–259

[6] C.E. Goodyer, M. Berzins, *Eclipse and Ellipse: PSEs for EHL solutions using IRIS Explorer and SCIRun*, in Computational Science, ICCS 2002 Part I, Lecture Notes in Computer Science, Vol. 2329, ed. by Sloot, P.M.A., Tan, C.J.K., Dongarra, J.J., Hoekstra, A.G. (Springer, 2002), pp. 521–530

[7] K.W. Brodlie, A. Poon, H. Wright, L. Brankin, G. Banecki, A. Gay, *GRASPARC—A Problem-solving Environment Integrating Computation and Visualization*, in IEEE Visualization (IEEE, 1993), pp. 102–109

[8] C.R. Johnson, M. Berzins, L. Zhukov, R. Coffey, *SCIRun: Application to Atmospheric Dispersion Problems Using Unstructured Meshes*, in Numerical Methods for Fluid Mechanics VI. ICFD '98, Oxford ed. by Banies, M.J. (1998), pp. 111–122

[9] G. Allen, E. Seidel, J. Shalf, *Scientific Computing on the Grid*, Byte 24–32 Spring (2002)

[10] J. Kierzenka, F., S.L.: A BVP Solver Based on Residual Control and the Matlab PSE, *ACM Transactions on Mathematical Software* 27, 299–316 (2001)

[11] L.A, Treinish, *Interactive, Web-based Three-dimensional Visualizations of Operational Mesoscale Weather Models*, in Proceedings of the Eighteenth International Conference on Interactive Information and Processing Systems for Meteorology, Oceanography and Hydrology, American Meteorological Society (2002), pp. J159–161

[12] N. Furmento, W. Lee, A. Mayer, S. Newhouse, J. Darlington, *ICENI: An Open Grid Service Architecture Implemented with Jini*, in Proceedings of SuperComputing 2002 (2002)

[13] J. Chin, J. Harting, S. Jha, P. Coveney, A. Porter, S.Pickles, *Steering in Computational Science: Mesoscale Modelling and Simulation*, Contemporary Physics 44, 417–434 (2003)

[14] P. Watson, Databases and the Grid, in *Grid Computing : Making the global infrastructure a reality0*, ed. by. Berman, F., Fox, G.C., Hey, A.J.G., (Wiley, 2003), pp. 363–384

[15] S.G. Parker, C.R. Johnson, *SCIRun: A Scientific Programming Environment for Computational Steering*, in Proceedings of Supercomputer '95, New York, ed. by Meuer, H.W. (Springer-Verlag, 1995)

[16] J.P.R.B. Walton, *Now You See It—Interactive Visualisation of Large Datasets*, in Applications of Supercomputers in Engineering III, ed. by Brebbia, C.A., Power, H. (Computatational Mechanics Publications/Elsevier Applied Science, 1993)

[17] Scientific Computing and Imaging Institute (SCI), SCIRun: *A Scientific Computing Problem solving Environment (2002)*, http://software.sci.utah.edu/scirun.html

[18] J.D. Mulder, J.J. van Wijk, R. van Liere, A Survey of Computational Steering Environments, *Future Generation Computer Systems* 15, 119–129 (1999)

[19] J.M. Brooke, P.V. Coveney, J. Harting, S. Jha, S.M. Pickles, R.L. Pinning, A.R. Porter, Computational steering in RealityGrid, in Proceedings of the All Hands Meeting 2003, EPSRC, ed. by Cox, S. (2003), pp. 885–888

[20] J.W. Wood, K.W. Brodlie, J.P.R. Walton, gViz: Visualization and Computational Steering for e-Science, in, ed. by Cox, S. Proceedings of the All Hands Meeting 2003, EPSRC (2003), 164–171

[21] D. Dowson, P. Ehret, *Past, Present, and Future Studies in Elastohydrodynamics*, in Proceedings of the Institution of Mechanical Engineers Part J, *Journal of Engineering Tribology* 213, 317–333 (1999)

[22] C.H. Venner, A.A. Lubrecht, *Multilevel Methods in Lubrication* (Elsevier, 2000)

[23] C.E. Goodyer, Adaptive Numerical Methods for Elastohydrodynamic Lubrication. PhD thesis, University of Leeds, Leeds, England (2001)

[24] H. Wright, K.W. Brodlie, T. David, *Navigating High-dimensional Spaces to Support Design Steering*, in VIS 2000 (IEEE, 2000), pp. 291–296

[25] H. Wright, J.P.R.B. Walton, HyperScribe: *A Data Management Facility for the Data–flow Visualization Pipeline*, Technical Report IETR/4, NAG (1996)

[26] M.A. Walkley, J. Wood, K.W. Brodlie, *A distributed collaborative problem-solving Environment*, in Computational Science, ICCS 2002 Part I, Lecture Notes in Computer Science, Vol. 2329, ed. by Sloot, P.M.A., Tan, C.J.K., Dongarra, J.J., Hoekstra, A.G., (Springer, 2002), pp. 853–861

[27] Message Passing Interface Forum, MPI: A Message-passing Interface Standard, *International Journal of Supercomputer Applications* 8, (1994)

[28] C.R. Johnson, S.G. Parker, *Applications in Computational Medicine Using SCIRun: A Computational Steering Programming Environment*, in Proceedings of Supercomputer '95, New York, ed. by Meuer, H.W. (Springer-Verlag, 1995), pp. 2–19

[29] D. de St. Germain, J. McCorquodale, S. Parker, C.R. Johnson, *Uintah: A Massively Parallel Problem Solving Environment*, in Ninth IEEE International Symposium on High Performance and Distributed Computing (2000)

[30] I. Foster, C. Kesselman, Globus: A Metacomputing Infrastructure Toolkit, *International Journal of Supercomputer Applications* 11, 115–128 (1997)

[31] C.E. Goodyer, J. Wood, M. Berzins, *A parallel Grid-based PSE for EHL problems*, in Applied Parallel Computing, Proceedings of PARA '02, Lecture Notes in Computer Science, Vol. 2367, ed. by Fagerholm, J., Haataja, J., Järvinen, J., Lyly, M., Råback, P., Savolainen, V., (Springer, 2002), pp. 523–532

[32] K.W. Brodlie, S. Mason, M. Thompson, M.A. Walkley, J.W. Wood, *Reacting to a Crisis: Benefits of Collaborative Visualization and Computational Steering in a Grid Environment*, in Proceedings of the All Hands Meeting 2002 (2002)

[33] C.E. Goodyer, R. Fairlie, D.E. Hart, M. Berzins, L.E. Scales, *Adaptive Techniques for Elastohydrodynamic Lubrication Solvers*, in Transient Processes in Tribology: Proceedings of the 30th Leeds-Lyon Symposium on Tribology, ed. by Dalmaz et al. (Elsevier, 2004)

[34] C.E. Goodyer, M. Berzins, P.K. Jimack, L.E. Scales, *Grid-based Numerical Optimization in a Problem-solving Environment*, in Proceedings of the All Hands Meeting 2003, EPSRC, ed. by Cox, S. (2003), pp. 854–861

[35] N. Karonis, B. Toonen, I. Foster, MPICH-G2: A Grid-enabled Implementation of the Message Passing Interface, *Journal of Parallel and Distributed Computing* 63, 551–563 (2003)

[36] R. Fairlie, C.E. Goodyer, M. Berzins, L.E. Scales, *Numerical Modelling of Thermal Effects in Elastohydrodynamic Lubrication Solvers*, in Trobological Research and Design for Engineering Systems, Proceedings of the 29th Leeds-Lyon Symposium on Tribology, ed. by D. Dowson et al. (Elsevier, 2003), pp. 675–683

Chapter 13

Design Principles for a Grid-enabled Problem-solving Environment to Be Used by Engineers

13.1 Introduction

The Grid offers to engineers access to distributed resources which have potential benefits for a variety of engineering applications [1–3]. For example: seamless access to distributed compute resources may facilitate the adoption of computationally intensive optimization techniques in engineering design [4].

One of the technical issues that must be addressed in order to realize the potential offered by the Grid is the ease with which it can be exploited by the enduser. This determines the engineer's ability to incorporate the use of Grid resources into their working practices. Consequently, the existence of suitable tools and computing environments is essential to promote the adoption of Grid technologies by endusers [5].

The Problem Solving Environment (PSE) concept, of a *"compute system that provides all of the facilities required to solve a target class of problems efficiently,"* was developed to facilitate access to advanced software libraries by the average scientist and engineer [6]. An ideal PSE incorporates a user interface, access to appropriate software libraries, integration facilities, and user support in the form of a knowledge base. The PSE model is easily extended to incorporate the Grid paradigm [5], and provides a blueprint for the design of an application-specific Grid computing environment for engineering disciplines.

In this chapter we discuss the design and implementation of a PSE for Engineering Design Search and Optimisation (EDSO) over the Grid by the Geodise project [7]. In doing so we discuss experiences that may be valuable to developers of Grid enabled PSEs in other fields, and those design choices driven by the problem domain of EDSO.

Design search and optimization involves the modeling and analysis of engineering problems to yield improved designs. It is a tool that is valuable at a number of stages in the development of a product. The design spiral in Fig. 13.1 depicts examples of the many aspects of a product that must be addressed during the design process. The EDSO may be employed in the analysis of computational models which are used to evaluate different aspects of the product; such as the strength and performance of a design, or its environmental impact. The EDSO techniques may also be employed across a variety of engineering disciplines. For example they have been applied to engineering design involving Computational Fluid Dynamics (CFD) [4, 8], structural analysis [9], and Computational Electromagnetics (CEM) [10].

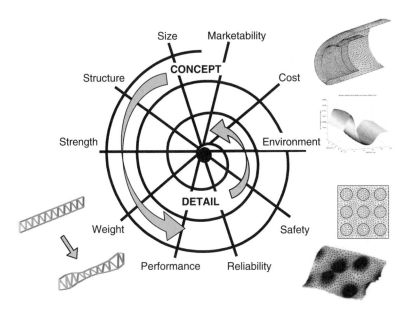

FIGURE 13.1. The design spiral depicted here involves the consideration of a multitude of aspects of the product. The end-to-end development of the product may require a number of analysis techniques to be employed across a range of scales. Applications for EDSO include aircraft nacelle aerodynamics (top right, courtesy of Rolls-Royce) [4], satellite truss design (bottom left, courtesy of A.J. Keane) [9] and photonic devices (bottom right) [10].

An EDSO begins with a process of problem definition, during which the engineer identifies the design parameters that may be modified to improve the design, and a measure of the quality of a particular design (the objective function). The objective function must be computed with an appropriate model. The engineer may also define constraints that determine the suitability of candidate designs.

A number of design search algorithms may then be used to yield information about the behavior of the model over the parameter space, and to maximize/minimize the objective function to improve the quality of the design. This process may involve repetitive calculations to obtain the value of the objective function with respect to the design variables at a number of points.

It is crucial that during the design process the engineer makes decisions based upon models that have an appropriate fidelity to the underlying physics. Where a high fidelity analysis is required the model may become computationally expensive, for example when using detailed CFD analysis. To perform the numerous solutions necessary for extensive parameter exploration may require access to significant computational resources. Engineering design search is also data intensive as valuable data may be generated by each of the software packages required to calculate the properties of a design.

These characteristics make EDSO well suited to Grid computing. The Grid may enable the engineer to perform investigations that are unfeasible upon local resources. The need to coordinate the seamless access to distributed compute and data resources poses new, and difficult, challenges to the engineer. To undertake Grid-enabled EDSO the engineer requires a supportive environment to perform modeling, analysis, and design improvement.

13.2   Design Principles

The literature on PSE development delineates a number of themes relevant to the construction of Grid computing environments. These include modularity, legacy systems [11], and user interface design [12,13]. Here we summarize the key motivations that prompted design choices during the development of the Geodise system. Our priorities in the construction of a PSE for EDSO are encapsulated by the following design principles:

1. An emphasis upon the usability of the PSE.
2. Integration of existing Grid resources and applications.
3. Facilitation of collaboration by promoting the sharing and reuse of components, workflows, results, and knowledge.

13.2.1   Usability

Ease of use is fundamental to the PSE paradigm. With this objective Bramley et al. [12] suggest that a human-centered view should be central to architectural decisions in PSE design. In the development of the Geodise PSE we considered the requirements, skills and expectations of the end user.

We divide the end users of the Geodise system into three overlapping classes: expert, intermediate, and novice. The novice user of the PSE has little or no knowledge of optimization techniques and must be assisted to compose EDSO workflows by being guided through a suitable template. Whereas the expert user of the system has sufficient expertise to design EDSO workflows from scratch, and expects the ability to customize the settings of the optimization algorithms and other components of the workflow. Intermediate users can customize existing templates, whilst benefiting from experts' knowledge. In this way the end users should be supported to use the system, without restrictions upon the functionality available to them. Support for users with differing levels, and domains of expertise is required from a knowledge base and design advice system.

A PSE for EDSO must meet several requirements. The EDSO *workflows*, which represent the relationships between all of the activities required during the EDSO process, are multilayered and may be very complex. For example Keane [8] describes a complex optimization strategy involving a parallel Design of Experiments followed by an iterative process during which the model is repeatedly approximated and evaluated to determine the best design.

Aspects of the EDSO workflow pertaining to problem definition will be specific to the engineer's individual problem, incorporating a user-defined model of the quality of a design, and perhaps unusual constraints. The engineer, therefore, requires an environment sufficiently expressive to describe these workflows.

In addition the engineer expects that the tools to be used are both robust and polished, with documentation and a look-and-feel comparable to other software packages on his desktop. It is essential for the developer of the PSE to meet these requirements in order to provide a tool that the engineer is able, or willing, to use.

13.2.2   Integration

A PSE for EDSO must support the engineer to integrate the existing software and computing infrastructure that they wish to exploit in the design process. This may include third party applications which represent the industry standard analysis or preprocessing software, or hardware resources that are intimately associated with a crucial legacy application. The provision of commercial Grid services, such as access to computational resources, as commodity services means that financial influences may ultimately determine the resources that the engineer wishes to use. As a consequence, the Grid resources that the engineer needs to incorporate into EDSO workflows will be a heterogeneous and unpredictable collection.

The PSE must be flexible enough to meet the changing requirements of the user throughout its lifetime. Consequently, a PSE that is not extensible will have built-in obsolescence. Therefore, it is a priority that the Geodise system be easily maintainable with a low cost to any additional development that is required to meet the needs of the engineer.

Ideally, from the perspective for the end user, the adoption of Grid technologies would not mean abandoning the tools, computing environments, or *ways of working* that represent their daily practice. Whilst it would be unrealistic to expect every application on the user's desktop to become "Grid-enabled," it is important to understand the investment that the engineer's current practice represents. Agrawal et al. [14] assert that for this reason the integration with existing scientific computing environments is essential to promote the uptake of Grid technologies by research professionals (and engineers).

The need to facilitate access to Grid resources from existing software is met, in part, by the Commodity Grid (CoG) kits [15] which provides client functionality to a number of "commodity technologies." These include CoG kits for Java [16], Python, CORBA [17], and Perl. By using client software to Grid services written for these commodity technologies, the developer of a PSE is able to remain independent of platform and operating system.

13.2.3   Share and Reuse

To be of benefit to the engineer, a PSE must reduce the end-to-end solution time of the design process. The end-to-end solution time includes code development, workflow execution, and the analysis of results. In this respect the PSE model is valuable as it can provide an integrated environment for all of these activities. However the PSE may be less helpful if it precludes suitable activities, or if it leads the engineer to use lengthy or unsuitable procedures.

To assist the engineer to work as efficiently as possible the Geodise PSE should seek to promote the reuse of components and workflows, data, and the expert knowledge of the users of the PSE.

The reuse of components and EDSO workflows can potentially reduce the development time during the design process. For example, the engineer's problem may be defined in terms of a parameterized geometry that is manipulated by a number of predefined components representing mesh generation, CFD analysis or pre/post-processing [7]. Similarly, well designed EDSO work flows represent a valuable investment which could be applied to classes of problems that share a number of common features.

When the execution time for the design model is high, for example if the objective or constraint function requires a lengthy CFD analysis, the cost of standard optimization routines may be prohibitive. In this situation it may be beneficial to reanalyse existing data sets, for example by building a Response Surface Model of the behaviour of the model in an area of parameter space sampled by a set of computational expensive data points [8]. By encouraging the reuse of existing data where appropriate, the PSE can help the engineer to avoid unnecessary computation. Through data management the reuse of components, workflows, and data can also provide benefits for auditing the design process, to establish the provenance of a design and the process of the design.

The Grid has been defined as an infrastructure for *"coordinated resource sharing and problem solving in dynamic, multiinstitutional virtual organizations"* [18]. In this context Grid computing environments have a role as the interface through which scientists and engineers collaborate in the problem solving process. Sophisticated technologies exist for collaborative visualization and computational steering [19], or high-quality video conferencing [20] to support human interaction across the grid. However, scientists and engineers also collaborate at another level by sharing resources, data, and experience.

By promoting the sharing and reuse of components, results and expert knowledge, these tools can facilitate the users of the PSE to work in collaboration. For example, members of a virtual organization collaborating in the design process using the Geodise PSE will share a window onto the designs, their results, and the code used to explore them.

13.3   Implementation

During the implementation of the Geodise PSE the requirements and priorities motivated a number of design choices.

13.3.1   Scripting Components

The engineer's requirement to integrate existing applications into complex EDSO workflows means that the programming model must necessarily support the control of heterogeneous resources. The Grid programming model [21] that best meets these characteristics is a loosely coupled "coordination model." Using the coordination model a number of heterogeneous components are integrated into a single application that can execute on parallel and distributed systems. The coordination model tackles the issue of heterogeneity by separating the coordination of the components from the details involved in the execution of the component parts. This approach allows an agnostic approach toward the middleware which is used to expose the Grid resources.

In the development of a PSE for engineering design search and optimization, we require a medium to capture and execute these complex workflows. A common solution to the workflow problem that has been adopted when building Grid computing environments has been to use an XML workflow language (such as WSFL or BPEL4WS) to invoke components in sequence [5]. This approach is sufficient for simple workflows. However, for the diverse and complex workflows involved in EDSO, we needed a more expressive representation than is possible with current XML workflow languages. Rather we use a high-level scripting language to express user-defined workflows.

Scripting languages are typically interpreted, and often use a grammar and syntax similar to a human language (so-called fourth-generation languages) [22]. They are frequently used to support the rapid development of applications, allowing users to glue components together. Beazley and Lomdahl [23] describe the flexibility and control which becomes possible by using the Python scripting language to develop large-scale scientific simulations from modular components. In addition, scripting languages typically support a great deal of high-level functionality, which increases the ease and efficiency of development of scripts that encapsulate the logic of the user's workflow.

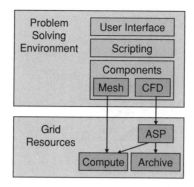

FIGURE 13.2. Scripting of components provides transparent access to Grid resources from the PSE.

By adopting scripting languages we have taken a pragmatic approach which delivers the greatest flexibility. Potentially, scripts could be generated automatically by a GUI (Fig. 13.2), with support from Geodise knowledge services, but these scripts could also be edited and reused by expert users. We consider this flexibility to be important since ideally the engineer should not be limited by the tools with which they are provided.

Scripting languages reconcile the competing requirements of quick application development, and the capture and reuse of the valuable logic contained within the script. We believe that it is important that the final expression of the engineer's workflow is in a form that is human readable, and has a value beyond the PSE.

By using the constructs available within modern scripting languages, such as exception handling, the user is easily able to cater for a wide range of conditions, including the failures that are, unfortunately, often a feature of both CFD and Grid computing. The top-level PSE becomes as flexible as the scripting language that it supports.

We support the Matlab scripting language [24] which is widely used within the engineering community, and therefore familiar to many of our users. The language is accessible, and is sufficiently expressive to describe these workflows. The Matlab environment for technical computing provides a large number of toolboxes, including those for visualization and data analysis. The NetSolve system [14], which uses a client–server architecture to expose platform dependent software libraries, has also successfully adopted Matlab as a user interface, leveraging the contribution that Matlab makes to the productivity of its users.

Matlab also integrates seamlessly with Java classes that contain the client functionality to our Grid services. Java is a modern high-level programming language that is widely supported. By implementing much of the logic required by the PSE in Java, the cost of development is low, and the system can easily be extended to meet the requirements of the end user.

Similarly, we have been able to offer client functionality to Grid services from Jython [25], a Java implementation of the Python scripting language. This allows engineers to script access to Grid resources when the Python scripting language is preferred, or more appropriate, to the Matlab environment.

In this way we supply the basic building blocks required by the engineer for design search and optimisation on the Grid. The functionality required to utilize computational and data resources on the Grid is supplied through several Matlab toolboxes [7].

```
% Create a Globus proxy certificate
gd_createproxy

% Define the Globus resource
host = 'grid-compute.oesc.ox.ac.uk';
% Define the computational job
RSL = '&(executable="./myexecutable")(stdout="results.out")';

% Submit the job for execution
jobhandle = gd_jobsubmit(RSL, host);
% Poll the job until completion
gd_jobpoll(jobhandle)

% Retrieve the output of the job using GridFTP
gd_getfile(host,'results.out','results.txt');
```

FIGURE 13.3. The submission of a compute job to a National Grid Service [28] cluster using the Geodise computational toolbox [7].

For example, the Geodise computational toolbox provides client functionality to Globus Grid services [26] that are widely used to expose computational resources to the Grid. Matlab functions within this toolbox allow engineers to script file transfer and job submission activities with a familiar and straightforward syntax (Fig. 13.3). The toolbox provides a number of other functions supporting rich user interactions with Globus resources. The Geodise computational toolbox is built upon the Globus client API provided by the Java CoG [16]. Similar client functions have been produced for other resources that the engineer may wish to access, including the Condor workload management system [27].

The low level functionality provided by these toolboxes can then be incorporated into higher level functions that comprise the component parts of the EDSO workflows (Fig. 13.4). Development at this level can be undertaken by domain experts in the Matlab scripting language.

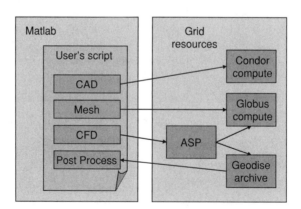

FIGURE 13.4. EDSO workflows can be scripted within the Matlab environment to access a heterogeneous collection of resources. These may include computational resources, data management services, or integrated Application Service Providers (ASPs).

13.3.2   Data Management

The share and reuse of components, workflows, and data within the Geodise PSE is supported through a data management system which allows users to annotate, archive, query, and retrieve data [29]. The data management system provides this functionality to the engineer through the Matlab environment using a familiar syntax, thus allowing data management to be easily integrated into the EDSO workflows.

The Geodise data management system implements *write-once read-only* archive functionality which is designed to provide an enduring record of the EDSO process. Using this system the engineer can archive the data files that are produced by applications invoked during the evaluation of a design. Data files are archived to a file server, and are associated with standard and custom metadata that is stored in a relational database. Alternatively the engineer can directly archive variables from the Matlab workspace. These Matlab variables are transparently converted into XML [30] and placed in the database. Archived items are then given a unique identifier which can later be used to retrieve them.

Jiao et al. [29] describe functions that are available to allow the engineer to associate items in the archive to form datagroups, or to annotate items with custom metadata which can later be used to locate items in the archive. These functions use syntax that is intuitive to users familiar with the Matlab environment. Custom metadata may be defined by the engineer as a Matlab structure which associates values to fieldnames. This structure is stored by the data management system as native XML in the database.

Users of the PSE can query across the standard and custom metadata that is associated with items in the archive, or they can directly query the contents of archived Matlab variables. Searches can be automated from the Matlab environment using scripted queries. Alternatively, a GUI is provided which allows the engineer to browse the contents of the archive by using hyperlinks to explore the associations between the items and datagroups. An engineer is able to authorize other members of the virtual organization to have access to items which they have archived.

The simple script in Fig. 13.5 demonstrates the basic syntax for the annotation and archiving of a file that contains the output of an earlier calculation into the Geodise data management system. The file can be located at a later date by querying the metadata used to annotate the file. The results returned by a query include the details of the file in addition to any user-defined metadata. The file can be retrieved from the archive using a file ID that has been associated to the file.

The Geodise data management system allows the engineer to incorporate data management activities transparently into engineering applications. By making this process straightforward it is easy for the engineer to develop a well maintained and accessible record of the EDSO process that may be shared with other members of the virtual organization.

13.3.3   Knowledge Support

It is assumed that users of the Geodise PSE will *not* be expert in one, or more, of the components that they desire to use. To enable users to exploit the full potential of all of the tools that are available to them it is necessary to provide an integrated support system.

When a user is faced with a sophisticated component which is unfamiliar, the developer of the PSE can make this component accessible in two ways. First, by hiding unnecessary complexity from the user. There are situations where it is appropriate for the user to treat a component as a *black box*. However, it is also likely that the developer will wish to expose advanced functionality

```
% Create metadata for the file
metadata.executable = 'myexecutable';
metadata.host = host;
metadata.standard.comment = 'This data was generated as an
example for "Grid computing: Software environments and tools"'

% Archive the file
fileID = gd_archive('results.txt', metadata);

...

% Query the archive
qresults = gd_query('executable = myexecutable');

% Retrieve the file from the archive
gd_retrieve(fileID, 'results2.txt');
```

FIGURE 13.5. The archive, query, and retrieval of a file using the Geodise database toolbox.

to the engineer. In scripting languages, there are a variety of ways in which a function can be overloaded to provide alternative interfaces to a component.

Second, the engineer can be guided to make sensible choices when selecting or configuring an unfamiliar component. This can be done by augmenting the user's knowledge and leading them through the decision making process. The Geodise system seeks to support the engineer to select and configure components when composing EDSO workflows [31].

The basis for this approach is the semantically consistent annotation of work—flow components. Using a common vocabulary of domain-specific terms that are specified by an ontology, it is possible to describe the available Matlab functions. Suitable components can then be recommended to the engineer by using context sensitive rules that have been constructed by an expert in the domain. Suitably constructed rule bases may also be beneficial in the configuration of components.

The relationships described by the ontology could be leveraged to compare and manipulate user-defined EDSO workflows. For example, by using case-based reasoning the design advisor could search the archive for existing exemplars of EDSO workflows that are relevant to the user's problem.

This knowledge functionality is provided through a service-based architecture [31]. These services can be regarded as another type of Grid resource that the engineer may wish to access. Client functionality to knowledge services can therefore be added to the user interface where guidance is most required. For example a toolbox of Matlab functions has been developed which provide advice about the selection and configuration of frequently used components of EDSO workflows.

The application of this technology may also enhance the search functionality of the data management system. Relationships between items may be inferred where semantically consistent annotation which references an ontology has been applied to items in the archive. In future versions of the system it could be possible for the engineer to query the archive to retrieve a collection of items based upon a conceptual relationship, e.g., a collection of geometries representing assorted aircraft components.

13.4   Application

Song et al. [4] demonstrate the application of the Geodise toolboxes in the optimization of a two-dimensional airfoil design. In this example a Matlab script was used to coordinate the evaluation of the lift/drag ratio of an airfoil design controlled by two design variables. To calculate the lift/drag ratio several commercial software packages were invoked in sequence.

The airfoil design was initially described by a parameterized CAD geometry. To calculate the airfoil geometry corresponding to any given set of design variables the geometry was rendered using the ProEngineer CAD software. To perform this calculation the Condor workload management system [27] was used to locate Windows machines with ProEngineer installed, and to execute the job.

The Gambit package was then used to generate a computational mesh from the geometry output by ProEngineer. This computational mesh was input to the Fluent CFD solver to determine the performance of the airfoil under cruise conditions. Both Gambit and Fluent were invoked on a computational cluster exposed as a Globus resource [26]. Following the CFD analysis the output from Fluent was returned to the local machine and postprocessed to calculate the lift/drag ratio for that design.

This workflow was encapsulated as a Matlab function which choreographed the submission of compute jobs, transfer of files, and the postprocessing required for the evaluation of a candidate design. This function was also responsible for the annotation and archiving of the files output by the various software packages. These files were associated into datagroups in the Geodise file archive to facilitate reuse at a later date.

The user-defined function was then invoked automatically by design search algorithms to search the parameter space. Song et al. [4] describe the exploration of the model by using a twenty-point Design of Experiments study calculated upon the Grid. This study was followed by the subsequent search of an approximate RSM model, and the validation of the best point.

This example demonstrates that the scripting of components may allow engineers to automate the exploitation of a heterogeneous collection of Grid resources during EDSO, where the engineer has access to appropriate resources this technique can be scaled up to tackle greater numbers of design variables and higher fidelity models.

The scripting approach described here is generic. The Geodise toolboxes have also been adopted to tackle optimization problems in a range of other disciplines, including earth science [32], and computational electromagnetics [29].

13.5   Conclusions

The Geodise PSE represents the product of a number of architectural decisions motivated by the design principles outlined in this document, and by the problem domain of EDSO. To develop a PSE that the engineer is able and willing to use, we believe that it is important to meet both the requirements and expectations of the engineer.

The programming model that we have used is designed to facilitate the coordination of heterogeneous collections of resources into complex, multilayered, work flows. To achieve this we have adopted a high-level scripting language which is suitably expressive to describe both the engineer's problem and the EDSO process.

The tools developed for the Geodise system demonstrate that a PSE can achieve the goal of transparent access to Grid resources. This is essential to provide the ease of use that must precede the adoption of Grid technologies by professional engineers. This transparency is achieved, in part, by integration into existing technical computing environments familiar to engineers. Whilst this approach allows the use of Grid resources to be incorporated into existing engineering practices, it also allows us to offer new functionality, such as data management, which may represent a departure from current ways of working.

The large effort required to develop a PSE means that attention to the flexibility and the potential for reuse of the toolset can maximize the return upon the investment in development. The tools that comprise the Geodise system are designed to be used independently, delivering the maximum flexibility to the user, whilst reducing tie-in into the system. New components can be incorporated to the system with relatively little effort, meaning that the PSE can be adapted to meet the engineer's peculiar requirements.

The Geodise project seeks to facilitate Grid-enabled design search and optimization. The incorporation of access to distributed Grid resources into engineering practices has the potential to reduce both the end-to-end development time, and the total cost of ownership of the engineering design process.

References

[1] NASA Information Power Grid, (2004) http://www.ipg.nasa.gov/
[2] Distributed Aircraft Maintenance Environment, (2004)
     http://www.cs.york.ac.uk/dame/
[3] A. Gould, S. Barker, E. Carver, D. Golby, and M. Turner, *BAEgrid: From e-Science to e-Engineering*, in Proceedings of the UK e-Science All Hands Meeting 2003, Nottingham, EPSRC (2003), pp. 467–474
[4] W. Song, A.J. Keane, and S.J. Cox, *CFD-based Shape Optimization with Grid-enabled Design Search Toolkits*, in Proceedings of the UK e-Science All Hands Meeting 2003, Nottingham, EPSRC (2003), pp. 619–626
[5] G. Fox, D. Gannon, and M. Thomas, A Summary of Grid Computing Environments, *Concurrency and Computation: Practice and Experience* 14, 1035–1044 (2002)
[6] E. Gallopoulos, E. Houstis, and J.R. Rice, Computer as Thinker/Doer: Problem-solving Environments for Computational Science, *IEEE Computational Science & Engineering* 1, 11–21 (1994)
[7] M.H. Eres, G.E. Pound, Z. Jiao, J.L. Wason, F. Xu, A.J. Keane, and S.J. Cox, Implementation and utilization of a Grid-enabled Problem-solving Environment in Matlab, *Future Generation Computer Systems* (2004) (in press)
[8] A.J. Keane, Wing Optimization Using Design of Experiment, Response Surface, and Data Fusion Methods, *Journal of Aircraft* 40, 741–750 (2003)
[9] A.J. Keane, The Design of a Satellite Boom with Enhanced Vibration Performance Using Genetic Algorithm Techniques, *J. Acoust. Soc. Am.* 99, 2599 (1996)
[10] M. Molinari, K.S. Thomas, and S.J. Cox, Electromagnetic Design Search and Optimization of Photonic Bandgap Devices on Distributed Computational Resources, in Proceedings of the Fifth International Conference on Computation in Electromagnetics (2004), pp. 103–104
[11] J.R. Rice and R.F. Boisvert, From Scientific Software Libraries to Problem Solving Environments, *IEEE Computational Science & Engineering* 3, 44–53 (1996)
[12] Bramley, R., Char, B., Gannon, D., Hewett, T.T., Johnson, and C., Rice, J.R., Workshop on Scientific Knowledge, Information and Computing, in *Enabling Technologies for Computational Science: Frameworks, Middleware and Environments* (Kulwer, Boston, 2000), pp. 19–32

[13] T.T. Hewett and J.L. DePaul, Toward a Human-centered Scientific-problem Solving Environment, in *Enabling Technologies for Computational Science: Frameworks, Middleware and Environments* (Kulwer, Boston, 2000), pp. 79–90

[14] S. Agrawal, J. Dongarra, K. Seymour, and S. Vadhiyar, NetSolve: Past, Present, and Future; A Look at a Grid Enabled Server, in *Grid Computing: Making the Global Infrastructure a Reality* (Wiley, Chichester, UK, 2003), pp. 615–624

[15] Commodity Grid Kits, (2004) http://www.globus.org/cog/

[16] G. von Laszewski, I. Foster, J. Gawor, and P. Lane, Java Commodity Grid kit, *Concurrency and Computation: Practice and Experience* 13, 643–662 (2001)

[17] M. Parashar, G. von Laszewski, S. Verma, J. Gawor, K. Keahey, and N. Rehn, A CORBA Commodity Grid Kit, *Concurrency and Computation: Practice and Experience* 14, 1057–1074 (2002)

[18] I. Foster, C. Kesselman, S. Tuecke, The Anatomy of the Grid: Enabling Scalable Virtual Organizations, *International Journal of Supercomputer Applications* 15, 200–222 (2001)

[19] V. Mann and M. Parashar, DISCOVER: A Computational Collaboratory for Interactive Grid Applications, in *Grid Computing: Making the Global Infrastructure a Reality* (Wiley, Chichester, UK, 2003), pp. 729–746

[20] Access Grid, (2004) http://www.accessgrid.org/

[21] C. Lee and D. Talia, Grid Programming Models: Current Tools, Issues and Directions, in *Grid Computing: Making the Global Infrastructure a Reality* (Wiley, Chichester, UK, 2003), pp. 555–575

[22] D.W. Barron, *The World of Scripting Languages* (Wiley, Chichester, UK, 2000)

[23] D.M. Beazley and P.S. Lomdahl, *Building Flexible Large-scale Scientific Computing Applications with Scripting Languages*, in Proceedings of the Eighth SIAM Conference on Parallel Processing for Scientific Computing, Minneapolis, Minnesota, SIAM (1997)

[24] Matlab 6.5., (2004) http://www.mathworks.com/

[25] Jython 2.1., (2004) http://www.jython.org/

[26] The Globus Alliance, (2004) http://www.globus.org/

[27] The Condor Project, (2004) http://www.cs.wisc.edu/condor/

[28] National Grid Service, (2004) http://www.ngs.ac.uk/

[29] Z. Jiao, J. Wason, M. Molinari, S. Johnston, and S. Cox, *Integrating Data Management into Engineering Applications*, in Proceedings of the UK e-Science All Hands Meeting 2003, Nottingham, EPSRC (2003), pp. 687–694

[30] M. Molinari, *XML Toolbox for Matlab v2.0*, (2003) http://www.geodise.org/toolboxes/generic/xml_toolbox.htm

[31] L. Chen, N.R. Shadbolt, C. Goble, F. Tao, S.J. Cox, C. Puleston, and P. Smart, *Towards a Knowledge-based Approach to Semantic Service Composition*, in The SemanticWeb—ISWC 2003, vol. 2870, Lecture Notes in Computer Science (Springer, 2003), pp. 319–334

[32] A.R. Price, G. Xue, A. Yool, D.J. Lunt, T.M. Lenton, J.L. Wason, G.E. Pound, and S.J. Cox, *Tuning Genie Earth System Model Components Using a Grid-enabled Data Management System*, in Proceedings of the UK e-Science All Hands Meeting 2004, Nottingham, EPSRC (2004), pp. 593–694

Chapter 14

Toward the Utilization of Grid Computing in Electronic Learning

14.1 Introduction

Electronic learning ("e-learning") has been a topic of increasing interest in recent years [1], mainly due to the fact that increased scheduling flexibility as well as tool support can now be combined with attractive learning material, and be offered at a widely affordable level both with respect to technical prerequisites and pricing. It has helped in making many learning situations a better experience due to the inclusion and provision of high-quality multimedia learning material that can be kept up-to-date on a continuous basis. At the same time, learning content can be made available even in remote places and without the need to travel to the site where content is being delivered. As a result, many e-learning platforms and systems have been developed and commercialized; these are based on client–server, peer-to-peer, or, more recently, on Web service architectures [47], with a major drawback being their limitations in scalability, availability, and distribution of computing power as well as storage capabilities. Thus, e-learning is currently deployed mostly in areas where high requirements in any of these aspects are not mission critical, which excludes its exploitation, for example, in most natural sciences or medical areas. This chapter tries to open a new door for electronic learning, by outlining the introduction of *grid computing* in the context of e-learning. In particular, it is shown what advantages a utilization of grid computing has to offer and, which applications could benefit from it. Moreover, an architecture for an *e-learning grid* is outlined, and the notion of a *grid learning object* is introduced as a first step toward the realization of this novel concept.

As a typical example where current e-learning systems reach their limits, consider a medical school where anatomy students examine the human body and prepare for practical exercises. Up to now, it is vastly impossible to compute, say, photo-realistic visualizations of a complex body model in real time and display the computation results on a remote screen. With the advanced functionality of an e-learning grid, students could be provided with the possibility to grab, deform, and even cut model elements (e.g., organs) with the click of a mouse. As before, the e-learning system could support the learner by giving advice on how to cut or give feedback for the actions, but beyond that virtual reality at local machines would become possible and improve the understanding of the subject considerably.

E-learning platforms are nowadays in wide use in primary, secondary, and even tertiary education, and they have found wide acceptance in applications where learning *on demand* is replacing the traditional approach of learning *in advance*. These systems can be used in a classroom, for group education, or for individual learning sessions. The most important feature of an e-learning system is its ability to present multimedia content in an interactive fashion that is typically embedded in a host of supporting functions (more on this in the next section). However, compute-intensive applications as the one just mentioned from the medical domain still lack electronic support, and the challenge that we foresee for the near future is to close this gap through an appropriate exploitation of grid computing.

The organization of the chapter is as follows: In Section 14.2, we collect several fundamentals that are considered prerequisites for our work; these stem from the areas of e-learning as well as grid computing. In Section 14.3, we begin to combine the two, and we outline an architecture that shows at some level of detail how a learning management system can be interfaced with grid middleware in such a way that an "e-learning grid" capable of handling new types of learning content results; the main ingredients upon which activities inside this grid are based is the *grid learning object*, a notion that will also be introduced. In Section 14.4, we indicate how an implementation of a grid application for some photo-realistic e-learning visualization could be obtained, thereby discussing the feasibility of our approach. Finally, we summarize our work and draw some conclusions in Section 14.5.

We mention that this chapter is an extended version of [38] and is based on [37], in which further details and explanations can be found.

14.2 Fundamentals

In this section, we introduce the fundamentals relevant to our work, which fall into two categories: e-learning and grid computing. We consider each area in turn.

14.2.1 E-learning Basics

E-learning has in recent years undergone consolidation with respect to several fundamental notions. Indeed, a general agreement seems to exist regarding roles played by people in a learning environment as well as regarding the core functionality of modern e-learning platforms; we refer the reader to [1] for a detailed account. The main players in these systems are the *learners* and the *authors*; others include trainers and administrators. Authors (which may be teachers or instructional designers) create content, which is stored under the control of a *learning management system* (LMS) and typically in a database [45]. Existing content can be updated, and it can also be exchanged with other systems. A learning management system as shown in Fig. 14.1 is under the control of an administrator, and it interacts with a run-time environment which is addressed by learners, who in turn may be coached by a trainer. Importantly, these three components of an e-learning system can be logically and physically distributed, i.e., installed on distinct machines, and provided by different vendors or content suppliers.

E-learning systems often do not address just a special kind of learner, but may rather be implemented in such a way that a customization of features and appearance to a particular learner's needs is supported. Learners vary significantly in their prerequisites, their abilities, their goals for approaching a learning system, their pace of learning, their way of learning, and the time (and money) they are able to spend on learning. Thus, the target group of learners is typically very heterogeneous; a system is ideally able to provide and present content for all (or at least several of) these groups, in order to be suitable, e.g., for a student who wants to learn about database

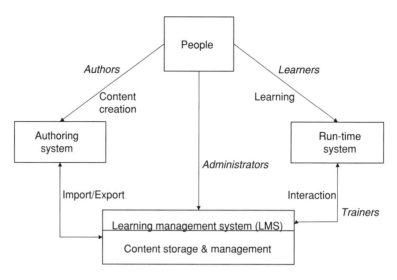

FIGURE 14.1. Generic View of a Learning Management System.

concepts or for a company employee who wants to become familiar with company-internal processes and their execution. To fulfill the needs of a flexible system as sketched, a learning platform has to meet a number of requirements, including the integration of a variety of materials, the potential deviation from predetermined sequences of actions [12], personalization and adaptation, and the verifiability of work and accomplishments [46].

Content consumed by learners and created by authors is commonly handled, stored, and exchanged in units of *learning objects* (LOs). Basically, LOs are units of study, exercise, practice, or assessment that can be consumed in a single session, and they represent reusable granules that can be authored independently of the delivery medium and be accessed dynamically, e.g., over the Web [45]. In order to make a distribution of LOs between different LMS feasible and ensure plug-and-play compatibility of content, various standards have been proposed, like IMS by the Global Learning Consortium [28], Learning Object Metadata (LOM) [29] by IEEE, or the Sharable Content Object Reference Model (SCORM) [41] by ADL. For example, the XML-based IMS Content Packaging Specification (which is also part of SCORM) specifies metadata which describes how learning resources (consisting of files) should be aggregated, along with possible course organizations. There are also more restrictive approaches for the design of LOs [5] which impose a more rigid structure. In general, however, learning objects can technically be stored in a database and are typically broken down into a collection of attributes [45]. In a similar way, other information relevant to a learning system (e.g., learner personal data, learner profiles, course maps, LO sequencing or presentation information, general user data, etc.) can be mapped to common database structures. This does not only render interoperability feasible, but also allows for process or even workflow support inside an e-learning system. Indeed, as has been shown, for example, in [46] e-learning consists of a multiplicity of complex activities such as content authoring or learner tracking and administration which interact with resources (including people such as learners and authors), with one another (some activities trigger others), and with the outside world (such as existing software systems) in a predefined way. If these activities are modeled as processes or work flows that operate on and manipulate learner and learning objects, and if they are then attributed to and associated with the various components of a learning platform, a work flow management system can in principle be employed to control these activities. Thus, it becomes possible, for example, to track the work and performance of a learner automatically, or to deliver content or process feedback. This idea can be taken to higher levels as well; for example, one can think of a college degree program that is fully supervised by an electronic system.

If a process view or even workflow management is accepted as fundamental modeling and enactment paradigm, it is a logical next step to turn this kind of learning, at least for certain situations and learner groups, into a collection of *Web services* that handle content and course offerings as well as other LMS processes, as illustrated below in Fig. 14.3. We briefly introduce the Web service paradigm next.

14.2.2   Web Services

In essence, Web services [2] are independent software components that use the Internet as a communication and composition infrastructure. They abstract from the view of specific computers and provide a service-oriented view by using a standardized stack of protocols. To specify the operations supported by a Web service, the *Web Services Description Language* (WSDL) can be used [14]. The *Simple Object Access Protocol* (SOAP) is used to exchange structured data over the Web by building upon the HTTP protocol [10]. To discover new services on the Web, or to publish existing ones, the *Universal Description Discovery and Integration Protocol* (UDDI) is employed [7]. More complex Web services can be composed out of existing ones follwoing a process composition approach and using *BPEL4WS* [3].

In Fig. 14.2, the typical steps of an invocation of a Web service are shown. In a first step, suppose that a client needs to find a Web service which provides a specific functionality. This is done by contacting a UDDI registry (step 1), which returns the name of a server (actually a service provider) where an appropriate Web service is hosted (step 2). Since the client still does not know how to invoke the desired service, a WSDL description is requested which contains the name and the parameters of the operation(s) of the service (steps 3 and 4). The client is now able to invoke the service using SOAP, which essentially puts the data in an envelope and sends it over the Web by using HTTP. The service provider receives the request and executes the desired operation(s) on behalf of that client. The results are finally sent back to the client by using SOAP over HTTP again (step 6).

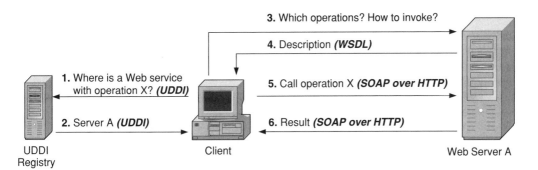

FIGURE 14.2. Invocation Steps of a Web Service.

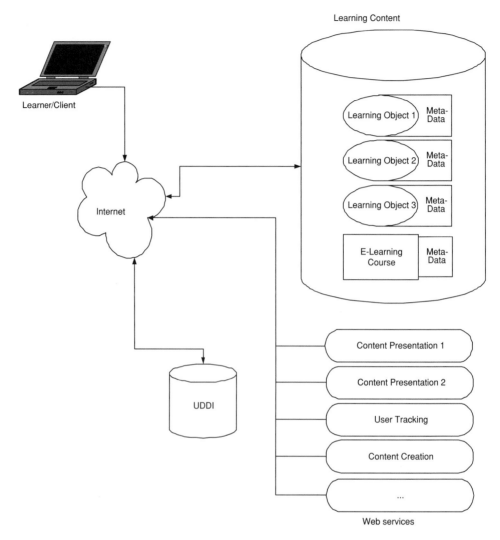

FIGURE 14.3. E-learning as a Web service.

The aforementioned view of making e-learning offerings available as Web services has recently been developed in [47]. Indeed, in an e-learning system, a variety of aspects, features, and components can be perceived as a *service* and henceforth be realized as a *Web* service, including content authoring, content configuration into classes or courses, LO management, content updating, learner registration and management, content adaptation, learner profiling and tracking, testing of acquired knowledge, tutoring, virtual classroom setups, organization of chat rooms, and the search for and presentation of content itself. Thus, the entire functionality of a learning system could be decomposed into individual activities which are modeled as processes [46] and provided as services, in such a way that the originally functionality can be reconstructed through suitable service *compositions*. In such a deviation from traditional learning platforms, all LOs, classes, and courses, which may be stored on different servers, register their offerings in a central directory with additional information on the content of the learning material. An individual LO is not stored in this directory.

A second type of Web service that is registered in the directory can be called directly by the platform to use its functionality. To this end, Fig. 14.3 shows the service subsystems that have been described in detail in [47]. Essentially the scenario centers around a UDDI repository that is capable of referring clients to content (i.e., learning objects or courses) or to external services (e.g., for tracking or other tasks). We mention that the choice of subsystems we discuss here is not exhaustive, and that various additions may be feasible. We also mention that this architecture allows for a variety of implementation choices, i.e., which part of the system is implemented in the central platform that is used by the client and what parts just call upon Web services. One of these choices is currently under development at the University of Muenster in the second author's working group; preliminary results have been described in [46–50].

14.2.3   Grid Computing

The *grid computing* paradigm [8, 17, 20] essentially intends to aggregate and unify the view on existing software and distributed, heterogeneous hardware resources like computers (with CPUs and storage) or remotely controlled instruments (e.g., electron microscopes, radio telescopes) by using uniform interfaces. In this vision, a user should be able to transparently use idle CPUs or storage on other resources in a grid, while the local autonomy is preserved. By extending the view of metacomputing [15] to a large-scale "flexible, secure, coordinated resource sharing among dynamic collections of individuals, institutions, and resources" [22], grid computing makes new applications possible, e.g., new ways of collaborative work. During the evolution of grid computing, two basic types of grids have emerged: *computational grids* which mainly focus on a better utilization of the CPU cycles of computers which do not run to capacity or run idle [19], and *data grids*, tailored to handle distributed, petabyte-sized data [4, 13, 32]. Although some problems related to the distribution of data have already been solved [6, 36], the primary motivation is to provide an integrating architecture of different systems and technologies.

An important building block for grids is the middleware which provides all grid-related services. In addition, the Internet is typically used as a communication infrastructure. In [22], a general protocol architecture for grids is proposed (See Fig. 14.4) which is also used as a conceptual framework in the rest of the chapter. As can be seen, the middleware contains five layers. The lowest *fabric layer* implements uniform interfaces for access to resources, such as computers, storage media, or instruments in a grid, guarantees interoperability, and enforces security policies. The fabric layer has to be made available locally on each resource to enable communication with the grid. The next higher *connectivity layer* defines communication and security protocols for the grid. By using cryptographic authentication algorithms a single sign-on can be implemented, so that a user has to authenticate only once in the grid and use any resources later on. The security protocols cooperate with the local security protocols of each resource and do not replace them. Next, the *resource layer* implements access to single resources and monitors their status. This functionality is required in the *collective layer*, which coordinates global interactions among collections of resources. In this layer brokers and schedulers distribute computations or data on the grid. Finally, the *application layer* contains grid applications which build upon the underlying layers of the core grid middleware. This layer can change depending on user programs, while the underlying layers always provide the same functionality. The hourglass-shaped outline of Fig. 14.4 suggests that the number of protocols and services should be minimized in

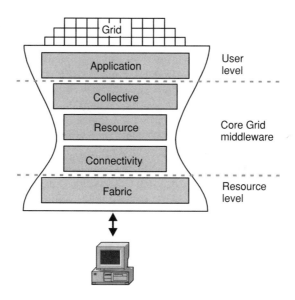

FIGURE 14.4. Layers in a Grid Middleware.

the core grid middleware in order to maximize interoperability. The wide bottom and of the hourglass implies that the fabric layer should support as many resource types as possible. Similarly, many applications should be available at the top.

Grid middleware along the lines just described has been implemented in various projects, including Globus [18], Legion [25], or Condor-G [23], to name just a few. The *Globus Toolkit* with its *Open Grid Services Architecture* (OGSA) [21] currently has the biggest influence on the development of grids. Its philosophy is to provide a bag of services and specifications which can be combined individually to form a grid middleware. The component model of Globus Version 3 is based on grid services which are actually Web services with specific extensions (e.g., interfaces) for use in grids. Grid services can be implemented in nearly any programming language and can use the Internet as an underlying communication infrastructure. This is a major advantage, since existing technology and standards can be used for grid computing, so that the complexity of implementations can be drastically reduced. The idea behind OGSA is to construct each of the grid middleware layers described above by using appropriate grid services.

Since Web services are being employed in the context of grid computing already, and since certain e-learning applications also render the use of Web services suitably, it is near at hand to consider combining the two, which will be the subject of the next section.

14.3   E-learning Grids

Complex applications which are computationally intensive and handle large data sets have been systematically ignored in the context of e-learning up to now, mainly due to technical feasibility problems and prohibitively high costs. As will be demonstrated in the remainder of this chapter, grid computing can close this gap and enable new types of e-learning applications, such as photo-realistic visualizations or complex real-time simulations. Computations and data could be distributed on a grid as soon as desktop computers of learners cannot handle them anymore. This particularly pertains to university environments where the hardware infrastructure already exists, since there are often hundreds of networked computers, ranging from PCs to supercomputers, which most of the time are not working to capacity or even run idle. We therefore propose the creation of *e-learning grids* in which grid computing functionality is integrated into e-learning systems.

As we have mentioned in the Introduction, there are many conceivable applications for *e-learning grids*. Medicine students could use photo-realistic visualizations of a complex model of the human body to prepare for practical exercises. Such visualizations, computed in real-time, could improve the understanding of the three-dimensional locations of bones, muscles, or organs. Students should be able to rotate and zoom into the model and get additional information by clicking on each element of the model. With more advanced functionality such as virtual surgery, students could be provided with the possibility to grab, deform, and cut model elements (e.g., organs) with the click of a mouse. Guided by the instructions of the e-learning system, students learn in a step-by-step manner how to successfully complete a surgery. Compared to practical exercises in the real world, such a virtual system offers several advantages, e.g., undo/redo functionality, instant feedback, standardized learning content, and availability for every student. In biology courses the ability of grids to integrate heterogenous resources could be used to integrate an electron microscope into the grid. We mention that the technical feasibility of this approach has already been demonstrated in the TeleScience project [40]. However, this project could be widely extended to integrate the controls and output of the electron microscope into a learning environment so that students can be assigned tasks or read subject-related texts while operating the microscope. In addition, the output image of the microscope could also be integrated in online tests that have a stronger emphasis on practical parts of certain subject areas. The problem of concurrent access to the microscope could be solved by assigning individual time slots for exclusive usage. Similarly, in engineering courses complex simulations, e.g., in a wind channel, can be made accessible for each student by using grids.

We next outline an architecture for *e-learning grids*. Although there is no implementation yet, we demonstrate the technical feasibility by keeping the architecture as simple as possible. The architecture gives details on a Learning Management System (LMS) as well as grid middleware, which are both based on Web services and grid services, respectively (See Fig. 14.5). In this figure, grid and Web services are depicted as rectangles containing a name as well as the most important operations. Note that grid services (with grey name fields) can easily be distinguished from Web services. The LMS interacts transparently with the grid middleware so that a learner is not aware of the grid. Furthermore, the architecture is designed in such a way that a learner will only need a Java-enabled Internet browser to use both the LMS and the grid. We explain the architecture shown in Fig. 14.5 as well as most of the operations listed in this figure in more detail in the following subsections; we begin with the upper half (Core Grid Middleware) and then turn to the lower one (LMS).

14.3.1 Core Grid Middleware

The grid middleware of an *e-learning grid* is derived from the various layers shown above in Fig. 14.4. The *fabric layer* is conceived as a Java applet, which provides uniform interfaces to all resources in the grid. For the time being, we assume for simplicity that there are only computers and no specialized instruments like electron microscopes in the grid. We will explain possible extensions later. Furthermore, locally available policy files specify usage restrictions for

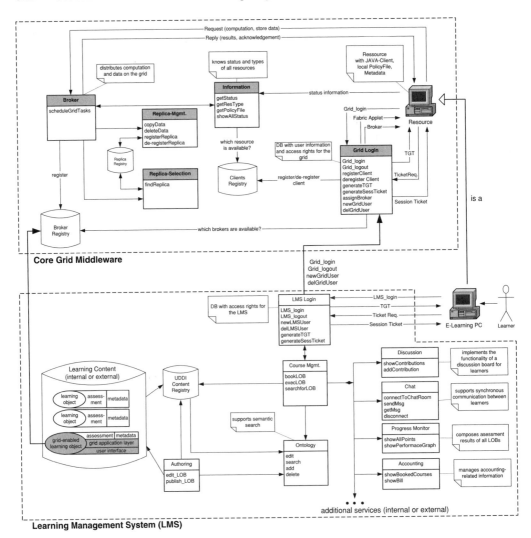

FIGURE 14.5. Architecture of an E-learning Grid.

computers in the grid (e.g., maximal CPU load, usage hours, etc.); finally, metadata describe each resource type. The fabric layer applet has to be started on each computer that participates in sharing computational capacity and storage space in the grid. This can be done while a user accesses a Web page with his or her Web browser to authenticate in the grid.

The *connectivity layer* consists of a *grid login service*. This service needs to have access to a database in which user information and access rights are stored together with a hash value of the password. The service can create new users with a newGridUser operation and delete users with corresponding delGridUser operation. When a grid user wants to enter the grid, an operation Grid_login is called, which checks the user's login name and password against the values stored in the database. If the login was successful, the computer is registered with registerClient in a Clients Registry, the latter of which contains a list of all resources currently available in the grid. Furthermore, a *broker* is assigned which can handle requests to distribute computation or data across other computers in the grid. When a client logs out, the `ClientsRegistry` is updated through a `deregisterClient` operation. The login service uses an authentication mechanism based, for example, on Kerberos v. 5 [33]. It uses a symmetric cryptographic algorithm and requires that each entity in the grid (i.e., grid service or computer) must have a specific key which must be known to the grid login service. For all computers of a grid, the hash value of the user password could be used as a key, while grid services have a key generated and registered at the login service by the respective developers. The idea of the authentication algorithm, whose details are beyond the scope of this chapter, is that a computer first requests a ticket-granting ticket (TGT). If a TGT is received, the authentication was successful and further session tickets can be requested for the communication with any other grid service. Before a computer can access the operation of a grid service, a valid session ticket must be presented, which is checked by the respective service. This procedure is executed every time an operation of a grid service is accessed, so that an additional graphical representation is omitted in Fig. 14.5. We briefly mention that there are also other approaches and libraries available to implement the single sign-on authentication. For example, the *Grid Security Infrastructure (GSI)* [24] of the Globus Toolkit uses public key encryption and X.509 certificates. To reduce the number of times for a user to enter a passphrase, the *Secure Sockets Layer (SSL)* protocol is extended by so-called proxies with limited lifetimes, which implement a delegation capability. *Shibboleth* [11], based on the *Security Assertion Markup Language (SAML)* [30], facilitates Web browser single sign on using a centralized mediator called "Where Are You From" (WAYF) service which is used to find an identity provider for a user. In principle, the exchanged SAML messages used to decide whether or not to grant access to a user at a remote location, can be seen as a counterpart to TGTs.

The *resource layer* contains an *information service* which is aware of the status and type of all resources in the grid. By accessing the clients registry it firstly determines which computers are available. It then requests from each computer some status information (e.g., CPU load, unused storage space) with a `getStatus` operation, the resource type with `getResType` and the usage restrictions with `getPolicyFile`. The list with the collected information can be accessed with `showAllStatus` and is used to schedule computations or distribute data in the collective layer.

In the *collective layer* there is a *broker*, *replica management*, and *replica selection service*. For simplicity, we assume that there is only one copy of each service. The broker implements a grid scheduling algorithm [26] and is responsible for distributing computations and data across the grid. The broker has to register in a `BrokerRegistry`, so that the grid login service and grid applications in the application layer can find it. For the distribution of data it uses the replica management and replica selection service, which implement the functionality that is typical of data grids. We assume here that the data to be replicated is read only. The replica management service can create replicas of data on computers with the operation `copyData`. When data is replicated, an entry is added to the `ReplicaRegistry` with the exact information which parts of data were replicated on which machines. When replicated data is deleted with `deleteData` the corresponding entry in the registry has to be erased with `de-registerReplica`. With the operation `findReplica` of the replica selection service existing replicas can be found when data is accessed.

All assumptions made so far can be relaxed, which leads to a loss of simplicity of the architecture. The fabric layer applet could be extended to support instruments, like electron microscopes. In this case, the information and broker service would have to be adapted since instruments cannot execute computations or store data. Furthermore, there could be more than one service of each type. For example, several grid login services could be responsible for disjoint authentication domains. Clients could look up in a `LoginRegistry` which login service is responsible for the domain they are located in. A problem arises when clients need to access resources of different authentication domains, which requires cooperation between grid login services. It is also possible to have information, broker, and replica services for each authentication domain to increase the efficiency in large grids. Similarly to the problems encountered at the login services, a cooperation between all information, broker, and replica services of each domain could be necessary.

14.3.2 Learning Management System (LMS)

An LMS generally coordinates all learning-related activities, as explained above in the context of Fig. 14.1. We assume that the entire LMS functionality including the learning contents are implemented as Web services. A learner who typically uses a PC for a learning session interacts directly only with the LMS and is not aware of a grid. The LMS offers both content which makes use of the grid as well as content that does not need grid functionality. The integration between LMS and grid will be described in the next subsection. All Web services of the LMS are accessed via Web pages, so that the learner only needs a Web browser to utilize the LMS.

In a first step the learner has to authenticate in the LMS, which is done by an *LMS login service*. This service is similar to the *grid login service*, i.e., it draws on a database with access rights and uses the same authentication mechanism for the LMS. When the learner is logged in and authenticated, he or she can access a Web page for course management, the functionality of which is implemented in a *course management service*. The learner can look for suitable courses with a `searchLOB` operation, which searches for learning objects in a `ContentRegistry`. The `bookLOB` operation is called to enroll for a course. A class can be attended by calling the `execLOB` operation.

An *ontology service* supports the semantic search for courses. It basically contains an ontology defining semantic relationships between Web services that provide learning objects. Thus, for a search term like "programming" it possible to obtain results like "C++," "Java," or "Prolog." The ontology service provides operations to add, delete, edit, or search for entries in the ontology. Next, the *authoring service* provides an environment to create, edit, and publish e-learning content in the `ContentRegistry`, so that they can be found by the LMS. In addition, entries can be added to the ontology for the semantic retrieval of content.

The Web services which provide *e-learning content* consist of three fundamental components. The first part is a learning object, which is typically a lesson (e.g., in HTML, XML, or other formats) or a course consisting of several learning objects. The assessment part defines online tests so that students or teachers can check wether a lesson is well understood and the material mastered. The last part contains metadata for search engines that describes the content in a standardized way. The functionality of the grid is used with *grid learning objects*, which also integrate a grid application layer and a user interface and will be described in the next subsection.

The LMS also comprises other services. In *discussion boards* or *chat rooms* learners can interact with instructors or other learners and ask questions. A *progress monitor* composes the assessment results from all lessons into a general overview; this can also be used to create certificates. An *accounting service* manages all processes which are related to financial aspects. It shows, for example, all booked courses or the bill that has to be paid by an individual. It should be mentioned that the functionality of the LMS can be extended by other Web services, which can either be provided internally (i.e., in a local network) or externally from other suppliers over the Web. In such a distributed environment, software agents have been proposed for retrieval of Web-service-wrapped learning objects [39]. The flexibility of Web services also allows to distribute services of the LMS on different machines in a local network or over the Web. Thus, it is expected that the LMS will be easily scalable when new content or new functionality is needed.

14.3.3   Integration of Grid Middleware and LMS

After having discussed the functionalities of grid middleware and LMS in the previous subsection, respectively, we will explain their integration next.

The *e-learning PC* is used by learners to access the LMS. At the same time, such a PC can also be used as a resource for the grid. This has been modeled by the "is a" relationship in Fig. 14.5 which also illustrates that at the same time not every resource of the grid needs to have access to the LMS.

The *LMS login service* makes it possible for the *e-learning PC* to become a resource in the grid. When the learner authenticates himself on the Web page that is connected to the login service of the LMS, the fabric layer applet of the grid can be transferred as *mobile code* and be started locally on the *e-learning PC*. This enables communication with the grid. The *LMS login service* transparently calls the `Grid_login` operation of the *grid login service* with the data and the PC of the user as parameters. This completes the authentication process of the *e-learning PC* in the grid. If a user of the LMS is not registered at the grid login service, the LMS login service could be given the authority to create new users in the grid login service, based on a trust relationship between the two services. These steps keep the login procedure of the grid completely in the background, so that the learner is not aware of it.

14.3.4   Grid Learning Objects (GLOBs)

We next propose the notion of a *grid learning objects* (GLOB) for using the grid in e-learning applications. A GLOB extends the functionality of a "traditional" learning object (in the sense of [5,45]) by adding grid functionality consisting of a specific *grid application layer* (see Fig. 14.4) and a *user interface*. The structure of a GLOB is depicted in Fig. 14.6 and is designed in such a way that it can contain both conventional e-learning content and content that uses grid functionality. Basically, a GLOB is wrapped by a Web service which makes it possible to easily integrate it into the LMS (see above). In addition, the Web service provides operations to access individual elements of the GLOB, to transform content (e.g., from XML to HTML), or to generate online tests.

The design of a GLOB is based on [5] and consists of several parts: An *overview* of the lesson, *metadata*, which is used to find GLOBs, several *reusable information objects (RIOs)*, and a *summary*. A RIO contains a *content* part with the actual content of a unit of study. The content can either be stored in a format such as XML, HTML or, as already mentioned in Section 14.2, in a database. *Practice items* can be used to generate online exercises for the learners. *Assessment items* are used to generate online tests for final exams.

An RIO may additionally contain grid functionality which is implemented as a grid service of the *grid application layer* and accessed via a *user interface*. The grid application layer implements grid applications for e-learning and uses the underlying layers of the core grid middleware. While the layers of the core grid middleware remain stable, the application layer may change

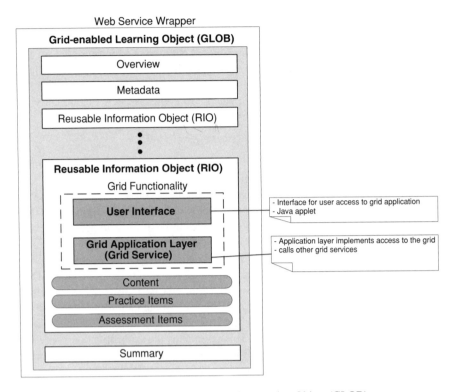

FIGURE 14.6. Structure of a Grid Learning Object (GLOB).

depending on the application. To be executed, the grid service of the application layer first has to be extracted from an RIO by using a Web service operation. It then has to be started on a computer that provides the hosting environment of the Globus Toolkit, which also supports the creation of instances of grid services. We will call such a computer a *grid application server*. During an initialization procedure of the grid service, a grid broker has to be found via the `BrokerRegistry`, so that it can be assigned tasks such as the distribution of computations or data on the grid. In addition, the grid service of the application layer is responsible for the composition of the results returned by the broker.

The *user interface* can be implemented as a Java applet that transforms user input (e.g., mouse clicks) into tasks for the grid service in the application layer (e.g., a request to recalculate a 3-D model). If the learning content is available in HTML format, the interface applet can be placed anywhere inside the content. When a user accesses such a lesson, the applet is automatically loaded onto his local *e-learning PC*. In this way no other administrative actions have to be taken, and a learner is not aware that he or she is using the grid. If the learning content is available in other formats (e.g., XML), Web service operations can be provided to transform it into HTML and embed the interface applet. Furthermore, Web service operations can be used to integrate the user interface applet into online tests generated from practice and assessment items.

The generation of GLOBs can be made easier and accessible to a broader group of people (e.g., teachers) by using software engineering tools which support the creation process and eliminate the need for programming when possible. By providing editors, content could be authored visually with a few mouse clicks for all parts of a GLOB, like overview, metadata, and RIOs. Futhermore, the practice and assessment items needed for online tests can also be edited and tested. However, the grid functionality consisting of the grid application layer and the user interface still requires programming skills. Nevertheless, readymade modules could be programmed by professional developers and made available for teaching staff, who can integrate them into the learning content. Finally, a software engineering tool for GLOBs should also provide the functionality to assemble the parts described above to a complete GLOB and embed it into a Web service, which could be generated automatically. In addition, the content registry should be updated with the data necessary to find the Web service containing the GLOB later on.

14.4 Toward an Implementation of an Application Layer for Visualization

To show the feasibility of the concepts developed in the previous section, and to illustrate the interaction between grid middleware, grid application layer, and user interface, we will now outline a possible implementation of a grid application for photo-realistic visualization that can be used for e-learning courses in medicine. To this end, we assume that learners are to be provided with an interactive component visualizing in a photo-realistic way complex models of the human body with elements like bones, muscles, or organs. By clicking with the mouse, learners should be able to rotate or zoom into the model or get explanatory information on certain elements. Furthermore, learners can suppress the rendering of different layers of the model (e.g., skin, blood vessels, muscles, etc.).

The relevant layers for an implementation of this scenario are shown in Fig. 14.7. The user interface can be implemented as a Java applet and run inside an Internet browser of a learner. The visualization component can be implemented as a grid service, run on a grid application server, and represent the grid application layer. The broker provides access to the grid, which consists of many networked resources. The user interface captures mouse clicks and movements and transforms them into commands for the visualization service (e.g., rotate model clockwise 30° around X-axis and display it again). After performing the necessary calculations, the visualization service returns an image file (e.g., in JPEG format) that can be displayed by the user interface.

The visualization service implements a computer graphics algorithm (e.g., ray tracing [16]) to render model data in a photo-realistic way. It uses the commands of the user interface, a model file and the coordinates of the upper left and lower right corners of a rendering window to compute a graphics file as output. The model data is found in a file which may contain polygon and texture descriptions or finite-element models of the human body. Before the computation of the output file begins, the area inside the rendering window is divided into several disjoint regions. For each region, an instance of the visualization service is created. This is basically a copy of the visualization service where the parameters of the rendering window are adjusted to the respective region. An instance has to calculate the color for every pixel of its region depending on parameters like view angle, texture, lighting, etc. The calculations for each pixel represent a task that is submitted to the grid broker. The broker distributes the computations on the grid and returns the results (i.e., color of a pixel) back to the instance which submitted the task. When the calculations of all regions are finished, the results are returned to the visualization service which composes them to the final result. Although this application is computationally intensive, it seems plausible that the expected network traffic will be low.

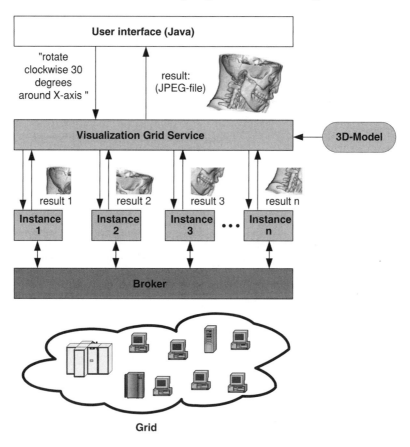

FIGURE 14.7. Layers of a Visualization Application for an E-learning Grid.

For the implementation of the visualization service, available libraries like vtk [42] or VisAd [27], which offer a wide range of graphics algorithms, could be used. In the 3-D model file different categories such as data for skin, muscles, or blood vessels need to be distinguished. To preserve interoperability, the format could be based on XML (see also X3D [31]). This would render the use of recent query languages such as XQuery [9] possible, which can be used to select only those model categories for rendering which have not been suppressed by the user. In addition, XML offers the possibility to easily add explanatory texts associated to model categories or elements. If a learner requests more information by clicking on a certain group of polygons (e.g., a bone), the user interface applet and the visualization service can identify the model element and extract the textual information from the model file by using a query. Since a model file may become huge, it could be stored on a server and identified with a unique URL. The advantage is that model data does not have to be duplicated for each instance that is created by the visualization service. Instead, the visualization service only passes the URL reference of the model file.

Finally, it should be mentioned that anatomically correct models can be obtained by using the computed tomography technique [34, 43]. The functionality of the visualization service can even be extended to support virtual surgeries, which would be in line with recent developments in the intersection of tele-medicine and Web services. To give learners to possibility to grab, deform, or cut model elements, a simulation component and physical models have to be added. These models specify the physical properties of model elements, e.g., how skin or organs can be deformed when touched, permissible positions, etc. More details for the implementation of virtual surgeries can be found in [34] as well as in [35].

14.5   Conclusions

In this chapter, we have argued that e-learning and learning management systems on the one hand and grid computing on the other, which have been considered and developed separately in the past, can fruitfully be brought together, in particular for applications or learning scenarios where either high computational power is needed or the tool sets on which learning should be done are too expensive to be given out to each and every learner. Beyond making a case for its feasibility and more importantly, we have outlined in detail an architecture for an e-learning grid which integrates core grid middleware and LMS functionality appropriately. Finally, we have indicated how an e-learning grid could be realized on the basis of suitably designed grid learning objects.

Clearly, what has been described in this chapter is intended mainly as an attempt to draw up a research agenda for an exploitation of grid computing in e-learning, and many details remain to be filled in. Yet it appears feasible to pursue the area, as there is considerable hope for being able to extend the achievements of electronic learning beyond the limits of individual computers. Future issues to be studied include, for example, transactional guarantees for service executions [44] over a grid such as atomicity, or recovery protocols that help restore an operational state after a grid failure (a problem not to be neglected, as learned from the northeastern US power grid failure during the fall of 2003).

References

[1] H.H. Adelsberger, B. Collis, J.M. Pawlowski (eds.), *Handbook on Information Technologies for Education and Training* (Springer-Verlag, Berlin, 2002)

[2] G. Alonso, F. Casati, H. Kuno, and V. Machiraju, *Web Services—Concepts, Architectures and Applications* (Springer-Verlag, Berlin, 2004)

[3] T. Andrews, F. Curbera, H. Dholakia, et al., *"Specification: Business Process Execution Language for Web Services Version 1.1,"* IBM developerWorks, 05 May 2003, http://www.ibm.com/developerworks/library/ws-bpel/

[4] D.C. Arnold, S.S. Vadhiyar, and J. Dongarra, "On the Convergence of Computational and Data Grids," *Parallel Processing Letters* 11, 187-202 (2001)

[5] Barrit, C. *"CISCO Systems Reusable Learning Object Strategy—Designing Information and Learning Objects Through Concept, Fact Procedure, Process, and Principle Templates,"* Version 4.0. White Paper, CISCO Systems, Inc., November 2001

[6] M. Beck, and T. Moore, "The Internet2 Distributed Storage Infrastructure Project: An Architecture For Internet Content Channels. *Computer Networking and ISDN Systems* 30(22-23), 2141–2148 (1998)

[7] T. Bellwood, L. Clément, D. Ehnebuske, et al., *"UDDI Version 3.0,"* UDDI Spec Technical Committee Specification, 19 July 2002, http://uddi.org/pubs/uddi-v3.00-published-20020719.htm

[8] F. Berman, G. Fox, and T. Hey, (eds.), *Grid Computing: Making the Global Infrastructure a Reality* (Wiley, New York, 2003)

[9] S. Boag, D. Chamberlin, M.F. Fernandez, D. Florescu, J. Robie, J. Siméon, (eds.), *"XQuery 1.0: An XML Query Language,"* W3C Working Draft 23 July 2004, http://www.w3.org/TR/2004/WD-xquery-20040723/

[10] D. Box, D. Ehnebuske, G. Kakivaya, et al., *"Simple Object Access Protocol (SOAP) 1.1,"* W3C Note 08 May 2000
http://www.w3.org/TR/2000/NOTE-SOAP-20000508

[11] S. Cantor (ed.), *"Shibboleth Architecure Protocols and Profiles,"* Working Draft 02, 22 September 2004, Available at http://shibboleth.internet2.edu/

[12] F. Casati, U. Dayal (eds.), "Special Issue on Web Services," *IEEE Bulletin of the Technical Committee on Data Engineering* 25(4), (2002)

[13] A. Chervenak, I. Foster, C. Kesselman, C. Salisbury, and S. Tuecke. "The Data Grid: Towards an Architecture for the Distributed Management and Analysis of Large Scientific Datasets," *J. Network and Computer Applications* 23, 187–200 (2001)

[14] E. Christensen, F. Curbera, G. Meredith, and S. Weerawarana. *"Web Services Description Language (WSDL) 1.1,"* W3C Note 15 March 2001, http://www.w3.org/TR/2001/NOTE-wsdl-20010315

[15] D. De Roure, M.A. Baker, N.R. Jennings, and N.R. Shadbolt, "The Evolution of the Grid," in *Grid Computing: Making the Global Infrastructure a Reality* (Wiley, New york, 2003), pp. 65–100

[16] J.D. Foley, A. van Dam, S.K. Feiner, J.F. Hughes, *Computer Graphics. Principles and Practice*, 2nd ed. (Addison-Wesley, Reading, MA, 1995)

[17] I. Foster, and C. Kesselman, *The Grid: Blueprint for a New Computing Infrastructure* (Morgan-Kaufmann, San Francisco, CA, 1998)

[18] I. Foster, and C. Kesselman. "The Globus Toolkit," in *The Grid: Blueprint for a New Computing Infrastructure* (Morgan-Kaufmann San Francisco, CA, 1998), pp. 259–278.

[19] I. Foster, and C. Kesselman. "Computational Grids," in *The Grid: Blueprint for a New Computing Infrastructure* (Morgan-Kaufmann San Francisco, CA, 1998), pp. 15–51

[20] I. Foster, and C. Kesselman, *The Grid 2: Blueprint for a New Computing Infrastructure*, 2nd edn, (Morgan-Kaufmann, San Francisco, CA, 2004)

[21] I. Foster, C. Kesselman, J. Nick, and S. Tuecke. *"The Physiology of the Grid: Open Grid Services Architecture for Distrubuted Systems Integration,"* Proc. 4th Global Grid Forum (GGF4) Workshop 2002, http://www.globus.org/research/papers/ogsa.pdf

[22] I. Foster, C. Kesselman, and S. Tuecke. "The Anatomy of the Grid: Enabling Scalable Virtual Organizations," *Int. J. of Supercomputer Applications and High Performance Computing* 15(3), 200-222. (2001)

[23] J. Frey, T. Tannenbaum, I. Foster, M. Livny, and S. Tuecke. *"Condor-G: A Computation Management Agent for Multiinstitutional Grids,"* Proc. 10th IEEE Int. Symp. on High Performance Distributed Computing, San Francisco, CA, 2001, (pp. 55–67)

[24] Globus Grid Security Infrastructure, *GSI: Key Concepts*, Available at http://www-unix.globus.org/toolkit/docs/3.2/gsi/key/index.html October 2004

[25] A.S. Grimshaw and W.A. Wulf. "The Legion Vision of a Worldwide Virtual Computer," *Communications of the ACM* 40(1), 39–45, (1997)

[26] V. Hamscher, U. Schwiegelshohn, A. Streit, and R. Yahyapour. "Evaluation of Job-scheduling Strategies for Grid Computing," in *GRID 2000*, LNCS 1971, ed. by *R. Buyya and M. Baker* (Springer-Verlag, Berlin, 2000) pp. 191–202.

[27] W. Hibbard, "Building 3-D User Interface Components Using a Visualization Library," *IEEE Computer Graphics* 36(1), 4–7 (2002)

[28] IMS Global Learning Consortium, Inc, *"IMS Content Packaging Best Practice Guide,"* Version 1.1.3., 2003

[29] IEEE Computer Society, *IEEE Standard for Learning Object Metadata*, IEEE Std P1484.12.1TM-2002, September 6 2002, Available at http://standards.ieee.org/

[30] E. Maler et al, *"Assertions and Protocols for the OASIS Security Assertion Markup Language (SAML)"*, OASIS, September 2003. Document ID oasis-sstc-saml-core-1.1. http://www.oasis-open.org/committees/security/

[31] *Information technology—Computer graphics and image processing—Extensible 3D (X3D), ISO/IEC 19775:200x*, Edition 1, Stage 40.20, January 6, 2003
http://www.web3d.org/technicalinfo/specifications/ISO_IEC_19775/index.html

[32] A. Jagatheesan and A. Rajasekar, *"Data Grid Management Systems,"* Proc. ACM SIGMOD Int. Conf. on Management of Data, San Diego, CA, 2003, (p. 683)

[33] J. Kohl and B.C. Neuman, *"The Kerberos Network Authentication Service (Version 5),"* Internet Engineering Task Force, Request for Comments RFC-1510, 1993

[34] K. Montgomery, Bruyns, C., S. Wildermuth, *"A Virtual Environment for Simulated Rat Dissection: A Case Study of Visualization for Astronaut Training,"* 12th IEEE Visualization Conference, San Diego, CA, 2001 (pp. 509–512).

[35] K. Montgomery, Heinrichs, L., Bruyns, C., et al., *"Surgical Simulator for Hysteroscopy: A Case Study of Visualization in Surgical Training,"* 12th IEEE Visualization Conference, San Diego, CA, 2001 (pp. 449-452)

[36] R. Moore, C. Baru, R. Marciano, A. Rajasekar, and M. Wan, *"Data intensive computing," The Grid: Blueprint for a New Computing Infrastructure* (Morgan-Kaufmann, San Francisco, CA, 1998) pp. 105–129

[37] V. Pankratius, *E-Learning Grids: Exploitation of Grid Computing in Electronic Learning*, Master Thesis, Dept. of Information Systems, University of Muenster, Germany, 2003

[38] V. Pankratius and G. Vossen, *"Towards E-Learning Grids: Using Grid Computing in Electronic Learning,"* Proc. IEEE International Workshop on Knowledge Grid and Grid Intelligence, Techn. Rep. No. 2003-02, Dept. of Mathematics and Computing Science, Saint Mary's University, Halifax, Nova Scotia, Canada, 2003 (pp. 4–15)

[39] V. Pankratius, O. Sandel, W. Stucky, *"Retrieving Content with Agents in Web Service E-Learning Systems,"* Symposium on Professional Practice in AI, IFIP WG12.5, First IFIP Conference on Artificial Intelligence Applications and Innovations (AIAI), Toulouse, France, August 2004

[40] S. Peltier, *Alpha Project: "Telescience for Advanced Tomography Applications,"* National Center for Microscopy and Imaging Research, UC San Diego 2003, https://gridport.npaci.edu/Telescience/general_telescience.pdf

[41] Sharable Content Object Reference Model (SCORM), Available at http://www.adlnet.org

[42] W. Schroeder, K. Martin, and B. Lorensen, The Visualization Toolkit. An Object-oriented Approach To 3-D Graphics, 3rd ed. (Kitware Inc., New York, 2003).

[43] N. Suzuki and A. Hattori, "Qantitative Visualization of Human Structure Using Segmented Volume Data Obtained by MRI," *IEEE Journal of Visualization* 3(3), 209 (2000)

[44] K. Vidyasankar and G. Vossen, *A Multi-level Model for Web Service Composition, Proc.* 3rd IEEE International Conference on Web Services (ICWS) 2004, San Diego, USA (pp. 462–469)

[45] G. Vossen and P. Jaeschke, *"Towards a Uniform and Flexible Data Model for Learning Objects,"* Proc. 30th Annual Conf. of the Int. Bus. School Computing Assoc. (IBSCA), Savannah, Georgia, 2002 (pp. 99–129).

[46] G. Vossen, P. Jaeschke, A. Oberweis, A, *"Flexible Workflow Management as a Central E-Learning Support Paradigm,"* Proc. 1st European Conference on E-Learning (ECEL), Uxbridge, UK, 2002 (pp. 253–267)

[47] G. Vossen and P. Westerkamp, *"E-Learning as a Web Service (Extended Abstract),"* Proc. 7th Int. Conf. on Database Engineering and Applications (IDEAS), Hong Kong, China, 2003 (IEEE) pp. 242–249

[48] G. Vossen and P. Westerkamp, *"Distributed Storage and Dynamic Exchange of Learning Objects," Proc.* 2nd European Conference on E-Learning (ECEL), Glasgow, UK, 2003 (pp. 469–478)

[49] G. Vossen and P. Westerkamp, *"UDDI for E-learning: A Repository for Distributed Learning Objects,"* Proc. 2nd IASTED International Conference on Information and Knowledge Sharing (IKS), Scottsdale, Arizona, USA, 2003 (pp. 101–106)

[50] G. Vossen and P. Westerkamp, *"Intelligent Content Discovery Within E-learning Web Services,"* Proc. 1st International Conference on Knowledge Management (ICKM), Singapore, 2004.

Conclusion

Chapters in this book cover the theme of software engineering for Grid computing. This theme has been explored from a number of different perspectives, such as specialist Problem Solving Environments (PSEs) to enable application scientists make better use of existing Grid infrastructure, to the specification of specialist abstractions to enable computer scientists design software particularly aimed to run over Grid infrastructure.

A significant number of chapters in this book cover the theme of PSEs, which also serves as an indication of the importance of these environments with the Grid computing community. The use of PSEs, and an analysis of their use, are necessary to enable a better understanding of how current Grid computing systems are being utilized by computational scientists and other domain specialists. Research effort in PSEs has matured over recent years, with an emerging interest in Grid Portal technologies (Chapter 6). Although work in PSEs predates Grid computing developments, research in PSEs provides an important bridge between application sciences and Grid computing infrastructure. A key challenge remains the ability to hide details about the underlying computational (compute and data) infrastructure from end users, thereby allowing, as is often stated, the end users to concentrate on their science rather than details about configuring parallel machines or computational clusters. Often a portal acts as a single point of interaction for an application scientist, and may range in complexity from providing application-specific visualization of results, to a more complex graphical interface that also allows the current state of computational resources to be determined. Mechanisms to standardize on portal technologies is a useful step to allow portals to be shared across different application domains (or by scientists undertaking different research within the same domain).

Perhaps the aim of software engineering techniques is also similar from a computer science perspective. Essentially, to provide abstractions for software development and deployment that are best suited to a particular use. The abstraction (whether a process model (Chapter 1) or an event model (Chapter 2)) should allow for a logical representation of key requirements of Grid computing use, thereby identifying how existing capabilities (in Grid middleware, for instance) may be made use of (to support such an abstraction), or identify limitations with current capability that needs to be addressed in future systems. Abstractions may also provide the basis for comparing Grid computing systems with other systems (such as parallel systems or mobile systems), identifying their commonalities and differences. Such a comparison is particularly useful to allow new research areas to be defined that combine features in Grid computing with these other systems.

We hope this book provides useful reading for future Grid software engineers, interested in the software process, the development of specialist tools, or for the deployment of applications over Grid computing infrastructure.

Index